WALTER REUTHER

Labor's Rugged Individualist

WALTER REUTHER

LABOR'S RUGGED INDIVIDUALIST

by Jean Gould and Lorena Hickok

ILLUSTRATED WITH PHOTOGRAPHS

DODD, MEAD & COMPANY · NEW YORK

To The Families of
May and Walter Reuther

ISBN: 0-396-06409-4
Library of Congress Catalog Card Number: 71-39225
Printed in the United States of America
by The Cornwall Press, Inc., Cornwall, N.Y.

Acknowledgments

The completion of Lorena Hickok's manuscript could not have been accomplished without cooperation from a number of sources. I am deeply indebted to members of both Walter and May Reuther's families and family connections, including my own, for the facet of Reuther's life usually not known to the general public, —that of a familial figure and ardent conservationist, as well as the dynamic labor leader. I wish to thank Walter's brother, Victor Reuther, for spending some time in talking with me about their early years in the union, also recounting anecdotes that occurred during the 1960s in Europe, and for arranging a private showing of a television tape, "Detroit Report," produced by *The New York Times* for presentation over NET on April 6, 1970, scarcely a month before Reuther's death. Lisa Reuther (Mrs. Gregory) Gesinski, the Reuthers' younger daughter, was most cooperative, as were May Reuther's brother, Leo Wolf, and his wife, Dr. Eleanor P. Wolf, sociologist at Wayne State University, with whom I stayed while doing research in the Labor Archives at that university. They generously furnished facts about the early years of Walter and May Reuther, took me with them to see the Reuthers' home in Rochester, Michigan, and also gave me permission to use a valued family photo in this book, as did Lisa. Many thanks are due Dr. Philip Mason, Director of the Labor Archives, and his able staff at the University, both for their assistance while I was in Detroit, and for sending me copies of the UAW Convention *Proceedings* I requested for consultation after my return to New York. In this connection, I owe a particular debt of gratitude to Frank Winn, Public Relations man of the UAW for years, and later Special Assistant to Walter Reuther, a post he held at the time of the latter's death. Frank, who had worked with Lorena Hickok on the manuscript, was most generous and kind in going over it with me, and in arranging interviews with UAW executives, Vice-Presidents Douglas Fraser and Kenneth Bannon; Dave Miller, Head of the UAW Retiree Center, and others.

I am also most grateful to Mr. and Mrs. Hugh Alexander, both of the UAW organizing staff during the late 1940s and 1950s, who gave me firsthand knowledge of the organizational work in the union, and of Walter in relation to his staff, as well as anecdotes of Richard Gosser's Region 2-B in Ohio and Leonard Woodcock's Region 1-A in Michigan, plus various organizing problems in the midwest and the east. Hugh Alexander also furnished details on the process of tool-and-die-making, and his wife, Dorothy (M.) Alexander, provided facts about the Women's Educational Conferences and women's role in organizing. Mr. and Mrs. George Gould were greatly helpful in giving me access to tapes of a speech Reuther made before the Toledo Bar Association in 1957, and an interview in 1963. George Gould, President of the Bar Association in 1950 and Chairman of the Constitutional Rights Committee in 1957, also furnished background material of the Gosser trial ante-dating the Congressional investigations, and, in connection with it, an unusual photo of Reuther for inclusion in this book. His wife, Elizabeth Gould, supplied details of Reuther's craftsmanship in woodworking, and the part it played in his recovery from his arm injuries. A debt of gratitude is due Dr. Edwin Daily, Mr. James Brindle, and Mr. Martin Cohen—the last two now president and vice-president of Health Insurance Plan—who furnished a detailed background of the Community Health Association set up in Detroit under Reuther's initiative. Both Mr. Brindle and Mr. Cohen were formerly on the Social Security consultative unit of the UAW staff at union headquarters in Detroit.

Thanks go to Tom DeLorenzo and Bernard Bailey of the UAW's Region 9-A office in New York City for furnishing pertinent pamphlet and UAW publication materials, also for cooperation in setting up the arrangements for the above-mentioned showing of the TV film tape, "Detroit Report"; and to Mr. Clifton Daniel, Associate Editor of *The New York Times,* who served as moderator on the program, and commented in a telephone interview on his impressions of Reuther drawn from the making of the film and other occasions. To Mr. Edward H. Dodd, Jr. and the Putney School in Vermont for photos and factual material concerning Walter Reuther's address at the graduation exercises of his daughter Linda and other events in connection with the school and the Reuthers, including Lisa's graduation. To Adelaide Schulkind Frank, former social worker and Executive Director of the League for Mutual Aid, who receives a bow for much background material of the labor movement in the 1920s and 1930s, the Brookwood Labor College, and the prominent figures of the early years of the civil rights movement in America. To writer Jean Beach of Saginaw, Michigan, for recollection of Walter Reuther's effect on students in his appearances before college audiences as well as his relationship to local leaders in the Michigan area. To May Sweet, wife of former UAW education staff writer Sam Sweet, for her recollections of the role of volunteer entertainers in struck plants during the "sit-downs." To critic Allen Hughes of *The New York Times* Music Department, who assisted in the research of name-data, and with his wife, Nina Hughes, supplied information on the Meadowbrook Music Festival and Meadowbrook Theater respectively, concerning the cultural center which the Reuthers helped to establish near Detroit. To Joseph P. Lash, author of *Eleanor and Franklin,* who recalled the Reuthers last visit to Hyde Park, knew Lorena Hickok from his close friendship with Mrs. Roosevelt, and gave me some key information regarding the genesis of this biography.

Foreword

A word of explanation is due the reader concerning my role in this biography of the late Walter Reuther. I met Lorena Hickok at Eleanor Roosevelt's "Val-Kill Cottage" in 1959, when I was there doing research at Hyde Park Library for my book on FDR's conquest of polio. "Hick" was already suffering with the rheumatic trouble which took her life, and she had some difficulty getting around. She was looking for a new publisher just then, and I steered her to mine. She had not done much traveling for some time, whereas "Mrs. R." had recently returned from a world tour (1958), besides leading a highly active life in various fields. The details of Campobello had escaped Eleanor's memory in several instances; but Hick, who had been on the island many times with the family, was able to supply the facts I needed, and also was instrumental in arranging an interview with Jimmy Roosevelt in Washington for me. And similarly, my recommendation of Dodd, Mead worked out well for her; at that time, she had been working on a book about her close friendship with Mrs. Roosevelt, dating from before the White House years and including their travels together directly after the President's death, a kind of memoir entitled *Reluctant First Lady*, which came out in 1962.

I had previously published a biography of Sidney Hillman, and as a result had been connected with the labor movement in an editorial and rewrite capacity, assisting the national education department of the Amalgamated Clothing Workers with the biennial Convention Report and various pamphlet materials. Members of my family were also in the labor field, on the organizing staff of the United Automobile Workers. Walter Reuther was a family connection of mine through his wife, May Wolf Reuther. In view of this background, therefore, my publishers asked me if I would be interested in completing Lorena Hickok's manuscript. I was, but because of other commitments, could not begin working on it right away; and before interviews could be arranged, the fatal airplane accident which took the Reuthers' lives occurred. I did have interviews with Victor Reuther and executives of the United Auto Workers Union in Detroit, as well as access to the Labor Archives in Wayne State University, where I did most of my research. The early years of Reuther's life are based on interviews that Lorena Hickok had with Walter, May, and Victor; and later with Roy Reuther, who died a few months before she did.

Hick and I did not collaborate on this book, as I did not know she was working on a biography of Reuther until after her death. In many instances the material dealing with the history of organized labor in mass industry and of the sit-down strikes in the auto industry had to be revised; but I hope that in the main I have fulfilled the expectations of the original concept as she saw it.

IN MEMORIAM

WALTER REUTHER will go down in labor history as an innovator. He probably had more "firsts" to his credit than any labor leader since Samuel Gompers or his Socialist counterpart, Eugene V. Debs, and, more contemporaneously, Sidney Hillman and John L. Lewis. If Reuther did not always succeed, it was not for lack of inspiration or effort, fountains which seemed to be overflowing within him. One of his favorite books was Walt Whitman's *Leaves of Grass,* which he knew well and read frequently. Like Walt Whitman, he "heard America singing" beneath the dissonance, and sought to bring some measure of harmony to the warring factions of the free enterprise system. If he made mistakes, it was part of his human quality; he is to be remembered equally as a labor statesman and a vibrant human being, who brought dignity and higher social standing to mass industry workers.

MAY WOLF REUTHER had already espoused the causes to which her husband dedicated his life even before she met and married him. Although she retired from an active post, she never really left the labor movement. Further, she had her own particular interest: the education of children, especially disadvantaged children of pre-school age in urban areas. Quietly she fostered and gave firm support to programs that dealt with developing the potential of the growing generation of her time. Never making a lot of noise about all she did, May Reuther was the soft-pedal to Walter's high-pitched dynamism, but part of it, the perfect complement. Like him, and with him, she was "always there" when needed, even in death.

LORENA HICKOK was a very young reporter for the Associated Press in 1920, covering the campaign tour made by Franklin D. Roosevelt as vice-presidential candidate with James Cox. FDR was much impressed with her ability, and she later became a member of his staff, as well as a close friend of the family. Her relationship to Eleanor Roosevelt was rare, even "unique" among newspaperwomen connected with the White House. She shared, along with "Tommy,"—Malvina Thompson, Mrs. Roosevelt's private secretary—and a few other staff people about whom the First Lady cared, the Christmas customs reserved for them: a stocking filled with odds and ends to open in the morning; a celebration beforehand, and a call on Christmas day. In fact, Hick's intimacy with Mrs. Roosevelt kept her from being as objective as she felt she should be in her press releases, so in the late 1930s, she resigned from the AP to take a job on Harry Hopkins' staff investigating poverty areas. It was then that she saw the abject conditions of Appalachia, the hopelessness caused by the deserted coal mines in West Virginia, even worse than in the days when Val Reuther had been so concerned about the people who worked in the mines there. She realized the goal Walter Reuther was striving for in his theme that poverty anywhere affects the whole of society; and when she left the newspaper field entirely to write biography, he was one of the first subjects she chose, though the work was not begun until 1963.

Illness prevented Lorena Hickok from completing the Reuther story before it was even half-way told, but she strove valiantly during the last few months of her life, training herself "to work over an aching back as professional singers train themselves to sing over a heavy chest cold," she wrote in her last letter to her editor, Allen T. Klots, Jr. A newspaperwoman in the tradition of "Front Page Story," forthright, determined, "Hick" died like a "pro," practically at her typewriter, in May, 1968.

Contents

Illustrations

I

Redheaded Kid
from Wheeling

Run along, Bud. We don't hire kids here."

The voice was gruff, the expression on the face of the guard outside the entrance to the Ford motor plant both antagonistic and bored. The young man facing him was nineteen years old, but he looked younger, not over sixteen. He was rather small, but sturdy, with red hair, brown eyes, and an infectious grin. He was not smiling at the moment, however, for he was there on serious business.

His name was Walter Philip Reuther, and he was applying for a job as an expert tool- and diemaker, one of the highest-paid jobs in an automobile plant. Having left high school when he was fifteen, he had served a four-year apprenticeship with the Wheeling Steel Corporation, in Wheeling, West Virginia, where he was born and grew up. A four-year apprenticeship met the requirements of a tool- and diemaker, whether he was in his teens, twenties, or thirties; but to become an expert, one who could qualify as a "die leader" with anywhere from half a dozen to thirty or forty men under his supervision, usually required from fifteen to twenty-five years of experience. Young Reuther had heard that "Ford's" was looking for die leaders, and he was confident that he could qualify.

He had been in Detroit about six weeks, having hitchhiked his way from Wheeling. His chances of getting a job when he ar-

1

rived were anything but promising. It was February, 1927, supposedly the height of the "boom," but many of the automobile plants, comprising the only big industry in the area, were closed. At every plant employment office there were long lines of men desperately looking for work. Walter, however, knew his trade, and he had enormous self-confidence, as well as a strong, healthy body and a sanguine outlook on life which never left him. Joining the crowd of men outside one of the plants at five o'clock in the morning and waiting there for hours, perhaps all day, without being admitted did not discourage him. He kept doggedly at it until he had finally landed a job as a tool- and diemaker in the Briggs body plant, at seventy cents an hour, working on the night shift from 5:30 p.m. until 7:00 a.m., with half an hour off for lunch, a thirteen-hour day.

The main reason so many of the plants were shut down was that they were getting ready to bring out new models. Before a new-model car is brought out, the plant must go through a retooling process: New dies, or patterns, for the bodies and engines of the new models, and new tools to make them must be produced. While a plant was closed for retooling, the thousands of men who worked on the assembly line were laid off, sometimes for many weeks, and not one of them had any assurance of getting his job back when it reopened. Workmen were hired or fired at the pleasure of the foremen, a practice that led to frequent kickbacks, with the worker handing over to the foreman part of his pay each week.

The Briggs plant manufactured automobile bodies. This meant that the tool- and diemaker worked mostly on very large dies. Walter preferred working on smaller, more refined dies and tools; for instance, he could make a stamping machine to cut holes in paper-thin sheets of metal. The holes must not vary more than one sixteen-thousandth of an inch. He was also anxious to get a better job at better pay.

At that time Henry Ford had ceased to manufacture his original Model T, the famous Tin Lizzie of World War One days, and the first mass-produced car ever made. Before then, automobiles had been turned out one by one, largely by hand. Ford's assembly line, something brand new in the industry, was able to produce a car that almost anyone could afford to buy. Adopted by other companies, it brought down the prices of cars generally and was a major contribution in making the auto industry the giant it is today.

In 1927, Ford was about to come out with his Model A. This meant that the plant must be equipped throughout with new tools and dies for everything from bodies, fenders and hoods down to carburetors, as Walter well knew. And so, although he had never been a die leader, he had decided to apply for the job. Following his thirteen-hour all-night shifts at Briggs, he had eaten a hurried breakfast at his boarding house before showing up at the gate to the employment office of the Ford plant in Highland Park, a suburb of Detroit. Here he encountered the guard, a tall, powerfully built man in civilian clothes.

"What do *you* want?" the man asked derisively.

"I understand Ford is looking for die leaders, and I want to apply," Walter answered evenly.

"You a die leader?" the man snorted. "We don't hire kids here. Get on your way."

But Walter Reuther was not so easily dismissed. "I don't deny I'm just a kid," he acknowledged, "but I'm an experienced tool- and diemaker, and I want to be interviewed for one of those jobs."

"We don't hire kids here," the man repeated.

"Are you a die leader?" Walter inquired politely.

"No," the man said.

"Can you make tools and dies?" Walter persisted.

"Of course not."

"Well, I can," Walter said quietly, "and I'm good enough at it to be a die leader." His logical mind proceeded, "Since you are not a tool- and diemaker, how can you tell by looking at me whether I am or not? I'd like an interview with someone who knows enough to find out if I can fill the job."

"I know you're just a kid," the man growled. "I know for sure you don't have that much experience."

Walter stared back at him undaunted. "You're not going to deny me the right to be interviewed," he said. "I want a man who is competent to turn me down if I don't have the skill."

"Look," the man told him, "if I let you in there, I might lose my job. They'd think I was crazy to send in a kid like you. They'd probably fire me for it."

Walter looked at him with that disarming grin and observed, "It seems as though you have one problem, and I have another. I don't want to make trouble for you, but I want a person who can really tell whether I'm a die leader or not. If I get turned down I want him to turn me down, not you."

For three hours the man and the boy paced up and down in front of the plant entrance, silent at times as Walter tried to think up new arguments. "You might as well let me in there," he repeated over and over, "for I don't intend to leave until you do."

The guard was weakening. He couldn't help liking this kid. The young redhead, while he obviously had a great deal of confidence in himself, was not cocky or smart-alecky. He had good manners and was well spoken. It was impossible not to admire his determination.

"OK," the guard finally conceded, "I can't get rid of you. I have no choice, but if I lose my job for this, you'll be to blame."

"I don't think you'll lose your job," Walter said, and he politely thanked the man for directing him to the employment manager.

"Where the hell did you come from?" the employment manager demanded as he looked up from his desk. "Who let you in and what do you want?"

"I understand you're hiring tool- and diemakers," Walter replied with dignity, drawing himself up to his full five feet eight inches. "I'm an expert tool- and diemaker, and I am applying for a job."

The employment manager frowned with annoyance. "Listen," he said, "I haven't got time to fool around. We're looking for die *leaders.* Even if you have served a full apprenticeship and are a tool- and diemaker, you can't possibly be a die leader. That takes more years than you have lived. I don't know how you got in, but get out."

Walter sighed. He was growing hungry, and he was tired after having worked the thirteen-hour night shift at Briggs without any sleep. "It took me three hours to get in here," he said patiently. "I don't want to go over it again, but I guess I have to. Are you a tool- and diemaker?"

"No," the employment manager said. "But I do know you have to have years of experience to be one. How old are you, anyhow?"

"I am nineteen," Walter replied.

"Well, you don't look it and I don't believe you," the employment manager said flatly.

Walter repeated the arguments he had given the guard at the gate. "I'll admit I look like a kid, but how can you tell what training and skill I have just by looking at me? If I can see somebody who is qualified to judge my skill and experience, I'll be satisfied. But until I see that man, I'll not leave this place unless you throw me out bodily."

The employment manager shook his head. "I've never been up against a proposition like this before; I don't know what to do with you."

"Who is the man who interviews applicants for jobs as die leaders?" Walter asked.

"Mr. George Gardner, the master mechanic," the man across the desk replied. "He is a very important official, with thousands of men under him."

"Why not let me talk with him?" Walter asked earnestly. "It would only take a few minutes for him to find out how much I really know. If he isn't satisfied, I'll go away. But I don't think it's fair not to give me at least that much of a chance."

The employment manager wearily reached for the phone. "Somebody will probably break my neck for this," he groaned.

Walter was seated where he could look down a long, wide corridor, and presently he saw approaching from the other end a distinguished-looking man with white hair. "I was so impressed," he recalled years later, "that I thought maybe it was Henry Ford himself."

The man was Mr. Gardner. He entered the room carrying a roll of blueprints under his arm. "Where is the applicant?" he inquired, perplexed.

"Here he is," the employment manager said sheepishly.

Mr. Gardner stared at Walter for a moment in utter disbelief, then turned to the employment manager. "You must be joking!" he snapped.

Quietly, politely, and with great dignity young Reuther explained why he was there. He ended, "All I ask is that you give me a chance to show you what I know. If you are not satisfied, I'll leave. But if you think I know my business, why not give me a break?"

Mr. Gardner unrolled one of the sheets and spread it on the table. In those days, applicants were shown, in addition to blueprints, a picture or drawing of the kind of tool desired, and they had to be able to give the exact specifications for making it, down to the smallest fraction, just by examining the pictures—side view, front view, and so on. This was called "reading blueprints." Without the proper training and practical experience, it would have been impossible for a tool- and diemaker to pass, by such primitive methods, the crucial test of his knowledge of the fundamentals in making tools. Walter Reuther demonstrated that he did know how to handle the job. He was able to come up with accurate specifications for all the pictures of prospective tools Mr. Gardner unrolled before him.

The master mechanic, now thoroughly interested, proceeded to ask the young man some involved and highly technical questions. Without hesitation Walter answered them all. It was obvious that he had served his apprenticeship well, but Mr. Gardner appeared doubtful about his experience. He was "so young."

"Well, why not give me a try?" Walter persisted. "If you are satisfied that I can do the work, I get a job. If you are not, I'll leave and not bother you anymore."

Mr. Gardner looked thoughtful. Finally he said, "All right, I'll make you a sporting proposition. We'll hire you for two days on the bench, paying you whatever we think you're worth. If at the end of two days we're satisfied, you get the job."

"You've got yourself an agreement, sir," young Reuther answered, his boyish grin lighting up his face. "When do I report?"

"At seven o'clock tomorrow morning."

It was now midafternoon. Walter hurried back to his boardinghouse, changed his clothes, and had a quick dinner. That night he reported to the Briggs plant at five o'clock, half an hour early, and as soon as his foreman showed up, he told him that he was leaving.

"Why?" the foreman asked.

"Because I've found a daytime job. I'd like to get off the night shift, for one thing."

The foreman, whom Walter remembered as "a very decent sort, whom we all liked," looked sympathetic. "I can't say I blame you," he said. "But you realize that you'll have to get tool clearance from Knox before you can leave."

In large auto plants, a tool- and diemaker, although he owns his tools, is not permitted to take them out of the factory without a pass. Knox was the night superintendent, "a tough character" more feared than respected by the men under him. When Walter informed him about the new job and asked for tool clearance, Knox demanded his reason for quitting; then he offered to have Walter transferred to the day shift.

But Reuther shook his head. "The new job pays better, too."

"All right," Knox shot back at him. "I'll give you a five-cent-an-hour wage increase."

Again Walter shook his head. "I'd like my tool clearance, if you please. I have to report on my new job at seven o'clock tomorrow morning."

It was hard to tell whether the night superintendent felt that young Reuther was too skillful a worker to lose, or whether he was just being ornery, but he refused to give the necessary tool clearance until 5 A.M. Then he finally said gruffly, "Oh, take your damned tool kit and get out!"

Walter had two hours to go back to his boarding house, clean up, have breakfast, and make it out to the Ford plant—no time even for a brief nap. He was so afraid he'd be late that he took a taxi all the way out to Highland Park, an unheard-of extravagance on his part.

At the Ford plant, young Reuther found himself in a situation that at first filled him with awe. Never before had he worked in a place so large. Here he was in an enormous plant where there were between four and five thousand skilled mechanics, most of them old enough to be his father. Fighting down his qualms, he went to work on his assignments. He was well aware that every move he made was being watched. One slight mistake, and he might lose this hard-won opportunity.

"That was the longest, hardest day I've ever spent in my whole life," he recalled when he was in his fifties. "There I was, after forty-eight hours without any sleep, so groggy that at times I could hardly keep my eyes open. And I knew that Mr. Gardner and several of the other topflight men in the department were watching me."

Somehow he got through the day. When quitting time came he was so tired that he could hardly remember what he had been doing. He staggered back to his boardinghouse, went to bed without any dinner, and slept the night through. The next day, naturally, was easier. Now he was fully alert; he knew what he was doing every minute. At quitting time, Mr. Gardner and several other important officials who had been checking his work for two days came over to him.

"We've been watching you, and you have surprised all of us," Mr. Gardner said. "The job is yours, and we'll be glad to have you with us. Your rate will be a dollar and five cents an hour."

When Walter had left the Wheeling Steel Corporation six weeks earlier, he had been receiving forty-three cents an hour. His wages were now more than doubled, almost tripled. So ended Walter Reuther's initial negotiations with management, his first bargaining session, but by no means his last. Had he followed the standard Horatio Alger tradition, after that beginning, the redheaded kid from Wheeling should have ended up as president of the company.

But although Walter Philip Reuther never became president of the Ford Motor Company, he did become president of the union that included not only all of the Ford workers, but the workers of the entire automotive industry; he also became one of the most powerful international labor leaders in the world, certainly the most imaginative among them, and, at times, a highly controversial figure on the American scene. And some of the toughest battles he ever fought were with the Ford Motor Company.

II

Reuther Family Album

IT was not entirely by chance that the redheaded kid from Wheeling, who looked, as he used to say later, as if he had "just fallen off a green apple tree," could argue his way into the job at Ford. To understand Walter Reuther and his brothers, two of whom, Roy and Victor, became closely associated with him in the labor movement, one should know something of the family history—their "Grossvater," Jacob Reuther; and, more particularly, their "Vater," Valentine Reuther, who was known throughout labor circles in the Ohio River Valley by 1903, before his children were born.

Arriving in this country from Germany in 1892, at the age of eleven, "Val" Reuther had imprinted on his mind the words spoken by his father as their ship sailed past the Statue of Liberty: "A man should always fight for freedom and brotherhood." This was the core of the socialistic philosophy in which Jacob Reuther passionately believed and which he passed along to his sons and grandsons. In the old country, he had been a stern-minded member of the Christian Socialist party that grew out of the protest against Prussian oppression in 1848. A devout but independent Lutheran who ran a small dairy farm near the village of Edigheim in Southern Germany, he had practiced what he preached by taking issue with the church for not interfering on behalf of the local factory workers. When Edigheim's sole wealthy manufac-

9

turer threatened, on election eve, to fire his employees if they did not vote for him, Jacob Reuther, outraged, decided to bring his family to America, the land of freedom and opportunity. Moreover, one of the basic principles of Christian Socialism was pacifism, and since at the time the draft was nonexistent—indeed, decried as undemocratic—in the United States, the Reuther family joined thousands of other Germans who came here to escape compulsory military service.

Settling on a small dairy farm in southern Illinois, Jacob Reuther proceeded to follow his own brand of religious socialism. Young Valentine was sent to the German Lutheran parochial school, principally because he knew no English and his father thought he would make little progress in an American public school. And although the family attended church every Sunday, Jacob, who looked like an Old Testament prophet with his long white beard and stern countenance, continued to deliver his jeremiads concerning the lack of social consciousness in official Lutheran doctrine. He felt strongly that the Church placed too much emphasis on heavenly rewards and not enough on earthly benefits for those who toiled for long hours at back-breaking labor hours in order to survive and all too often were crushed under the harsh economic conditions that existed. Following in the reformist footsteps of Luther himself, Jacob Reuther wrote fiery treatises outlining his own theology of a practical Christianity in which the Church took the lead in correcting the ills of society. But instead of nailing his ninety-five sermons to the doors when he saw that his ideas had little effect on the pastor, he left the portals of the church bare and read his lengthy papers aloud at home, conducting services for his family and any like-minded neighbors who wished to attend, thus eventually acquiring his own flock among the farmers and the few factory workers of nearby Effingham. When his grandsons, particularly Walter, read the yellowed documents written in flowing German script many years later, they were much impressed with the advanced ideas of Grossvater Reuther. And it was mainly because of his heritage that more than one minister later suggested to Walter that he could have been a clergyman.

Valentine Reuther could not help being influenced by his early indoctrination. As it turned out, his attendance at the Lutheran school was sketchy and sporadic, since he had to help with the farming in the busy spring and fall seasons. A bright boy with an alert mind, he was eager to learn and soon was picking up English words from the farmhands at haying time. And although he had to wait until he was a grown man with a family of his own before he could perfect his knowledge of the language through correspondence courses, he eventually spoke fluent and flawless English. With an eye for all that went on around him, he observed the divergent ways of life in the new country, and he was especially excited about the ritual dances of the Indians, the remnants of a tribe that still camped on the banks of the Wabash River in the 1890's.

Just before the turn of the century, Valentine Reuther, active and feeling the restrictions of farm life, headed east for the growing industrial town of Wheeling in West Virginia, where there was a large German population. He had no trouble obtaining a job in a steel mill, at wages of $1.40 for a twelve-hour day. But before he could learn much about the production of steel, a depression forced the mill to close down, and he was out of a job. He soon found another, as a driver of a delivery dray for the Schmulbach Brewing Company, at ten cents a day more; but the workday could be as long as seventeen hours when the weather was bad. He had been quick to realize shortly after his arrival in Wheeling that labor already had a firm foothold in the area as a result of the Ohio Valley Trades and Labor Assembly that had been formed as early as 1885. Now he set about organizing the brewery workers on a plant-wide basis, and served as their negotiator for better working conditions. Not that he was able to win much for them, but the people welcomed a spokesman and in a few years "Val" Reuther was a well-known figure in labor circles.

There was little time for recreation, but occasionally he stopped in for a foaming stein at the beer hall not far from the brewery, where an attractive, red-haired girl served customers at the free lunch counter. Her name, he learned, was Anna Stocker, and she, like Val, was a German immigrant and a Lutheran. She was also a person of strong convictions and high spirits. She had run away from her home near Stuttgart when her widowed mother, who had a brood of twelve children to care for and needed Anna's help, refused to allow her to marry a village lad she loved. Making the ocean voyage by herself at the age of seventeen, she had joined her brother, a steelworker in Wheeling, and found a job for herself. Val admired her spirit—as well as her red hair and shining peasant face, fresh as an apple blossom—and when he learned that she belonged to the Beethoven Singing Society, he promptly became a member.

Between the choral numbers their romance flourished. Since Anna knew little English, they spoke German together, and it became apparent that she shared Val's ideas of social justice. In 1903, after a year of courtship, they were married. They took a small flat in the working-class district of downtown Wheeling, where Anna, who had left her job, scrubbed and scrimped to keep the little place spotless and make ends meet on Val's meager salary. She sewed Gold Medal flour sacks together for bedsheets and rendered suet to make soap, saving pennies wherever possible in the hope that they could have their own home by the time children came. She rose at four in the morning to get breakfast for her husband before he reported at the brewery for work at four-thirty, and kept busy with housework and cooking all day long. She baked her own bread and rolls, and on holidays or special occasions, German pastries; her *Kaffeekuchen* and *Apfelkuchen* were perennial family favorites.

Yet Anna Reuther was no mere German hausfrau whose outlook was limited to the traditional three "K's"—*Kinder, Kirche, Kuche;* alive to the times, she took interest in more than children, church, and kitchen. She was with Val all the way in his union activities: unlike many women in her position, she did not complain when he had to be away from town on union business, more often than not paying his own expenses. She understood and encouraged his concern for the welfare of all workingmen—not just those in the brewery union—and when, in 1904, he was elected president of the Ohio Valley Trades and Labor Assembly at the age of twenty-three, the youngest man ever to hold that office, she was proud of him, proud that he was the spokesman for forty-two labor unions.

Twice during that year he went to Charleston, the state capital, to lobby for labor legislation to provide safety and improved working conditions, particularly for the miners, whose miserable plight tore at his heart and outraged his sense of decency toward his fellowmen. He led and lost a fight against accepting construction of a town library from Andrew Carnegie because he held the steel magnate responsible for the deaths of seven striking workers and the wounding of twenty more in the armed battle between strikers and Pinkerton detectives that occurred during the Homestead strike in Pennsylvania.

The mine owners' use of forced child labor aroused Val's greatest indignation. Coal mining is still a hazardous occupation, but at that time those who worked in the pits did so at daily peril. There were no safety devices to protect the men against the masses of falling rock or coal or other disasters brought on by the dynamiting. Mines were not mechanized, and the coal was hauled out on carts drawn by mules. Someone had to lead the mules, and many mine operators found children—boys eleven or twelve years old—cheap labor for this purpose. If a boy's father objected, the foreman would threaten to fire him, so the boy was forced to go into the mines. Laws prohibiting child labor did not exist.

An experienced adult miner would know how to handle himself when disaster occurred; he would try to be as calm and quiet as possible to conserve his strength and the limited supply of oxygen while waiting for the rescuers to reach him. Children, however, bewildered and frightened, would panic; often, as they stumbled blindly about, they were caught under the masses of debris and crushed to death. As the number of such tragic deaths increased, Val Reuther, along with many other concerned citizens in and out of the labor movement, protested, and in 1904 he appeared before a committee of the State Legislature which had under consideration a bill to prohibit employment of boys under eighteen in the mines. Earnestly and eloquently, Val pleaded for the bill, but the lobby organized by the powerful mine owners was too strong. He got nowhere. Yet he did not stop trying. He investigated various mining areas himself.

One morning around four o'clock he was in a town in the southern part of the state when he saw a boy about twelve years old leading a mule into a mine. A few minutes later he heard and felt an ominous rumble underground, which brought the miners who were not working and the terrified families of the men and boys known to be down in the shafts running to the entrance. Immediately the desperate rescue work began, while the wives and children stood about sobbing and praying. Presently a small mangled body was carried out. It was the child Val had seen alive a few moments earlier. With tears streaming down his own face, he watched the mother clasp her boy in her arms and press her lips against his as if she hoped her kisses would bring him back to life.

At that moment Val Reuther made a vow. "I swore to the heavens," he used to say in later years, "that I would fight that greedy system of child exploitation as long as I had a breath of life left in me."

Back to the Legislature he went. It was 1905, the year his first child, Theodore, was born. Using strong terms, he told the legislators, "You all read in the papers about such things happening in the mines. I now ask you to examine your own consciences. Who is the guilty party? Every one of you who has voted against that bill year after year. I tell you the blood of that boy whose body I saw them carry out of the mine is on your hands."

Moving though his plea must have been, he did not win that year. Twice again he went back to appear at the legislative committee before the bill was finally adopted. Val Reuther was in the midst of a struggle to ameliorate the unspeakable living conditions of the miners when his second son, Walter Philip, came into the world—significantly on the eve of Labor Day, September 1, 1907. Throughout his childhood Walter repeatedly heard his father tell the story about the little boy who was killed in the mine. The impact on a vibrant, imaginative youngster was inevitable and lasting. Walter Reuther grew up keenly aware of the needs and problems of the workingman. It was part of his inheritance from his father and grandfather.

The first decade or so of the twentieth century saw the upsurge of labor's self-assertion against the evils of industrialism through early attempts at organized action. During this period all of the Reuther boys were born, with Roy coming two years after Walter. It was a time when Eugene Victor Debs, Socialist leader and head of the rebellious railway workers, was writing to Charles Ervin, editor and publisher of the Socialist New York daily *Call*, "We are not wanting these days for material to convert into propaganda. Capitalism is cracking and leaking in 10,000 places." Debs had run for president twice on the Socialist ticket, and although he had lost both times by a wide margin, he maintained his leadership of the party with a loyal and devoted following. Val Reuther, a party member and an ardent admirer of Debs, named his youngest son, who came along two years after Roy, Victor, in honor of the inspiring, redoubtable Debs.

Before they were knee-high the Reuther boys "learned the philosophy of trade unionism . . . the struggles, the hopes and aspirations of working people every day." An outgoing man, Val Reuther always gave his family a full account of union activities and grievances against management. He expected the boys to pay attention. Once, when Victor thoughtlessly came home with the comic section from a Hearst newspaper, his father was furious. Victor had heard him say often enough that labor was boycotting Hearst publications! "Dad gave me a whipping I really felt," Victor recalled. Although Val was understanding, he brought up his sons to honor their father and mother and he demanded respect and obedience. Neither parent was unduly stern, however, and there was an atmosphere of genuine family affection in the Reuther household.

Where labor was concerned, however, Val Reuther could be hot-tempered and fiery in its defense, as he was one Sunday morning in the Zion Lutheran Church, which the family attended regularly. It was the day before Labor Day, and the new minister took the occasion to deliver a sermon against trade unions. In the middle of it, Val Reuther suddenly rose up and took issue with him in no uncertain terms. Victor, sitting beside his father in their pew, looked up at him astonished, expecting the wrath of the clergyman, or of the Lord himself, to descend on them all at any moment. But no such calamity occurred. All the Reuther boys were much impressed with their father's command of the situation, and with the attention paid to his outspoken words by the new pastor and the entire congregation. Having had his say, he turned calmly and marched up the aisle to the doors, quitting the

ch once and for all. Out of respect for Anna, he had no objec-
to her attendance or the boys' Sunday school training, which
he considered important; but he himself never went back.

While the boys were very young the family lived in a rented
house in downtown Wheeling, near the Ohio River, which was
crowded with water traffic, always exciting to a small boy. But
Walter and his brothers spent most of their boyhood in a house
which their father built on a hillside in a less congested part of
the city, at 3640 Wetzel Street in South Wheeling. A simple six-
room frame building, it had an unusual feature. At Anna's suggestion, influenced by modern plumbing just then being introduced,
the outhouse was attached to the back porch instead of being by
itself at some distance away in the backyard. This was considered
a real convenience, especially in the winter, although Val drew
the line at putting in an extra door so it could be entered from
the house. By the time Anna convinced him to do so, she had to
give up one of her kitchen cupboards. The boys were proud of
their father's ingenuity and in general pleased with the new
house, particularly since there was a vacant lot next door, fine for
baseball.

A few years after they moved, the Reuthers had their fifth
child and only daughter, Christine, called Chris by everyone, just
as Theodore, the oldest, was always called Ted. After the boys
started school, they addressed their father as Dad almost as often
as the German *Vater;* but their mother was always called *Mütterchen,* "little Mother," even long after they were all grown.

"My mother and father," Walter said more than once, "were
wonderful human beings. We had all the economic difficulties,
all the problems that many American families had in those days,
but Mother and Father raised the family around a simple basic
philosophy. My father always tried to make us understand that
our lives were going to be successes or failures not according to
material values, whether we were rich or poor, but whether we
had contributed to making the world a better place to live in."

Theirs was a busy household. Val Reuther's job as a delivery
driver meant long, hard hours. His day began at 4 A.M., when he
would be up and on his way down to the stable to hitch up his
team. The dray was huge, heavy and cumbersome, with big,

iron-rimmed wooden wheels. Carrying a towering load of kegs of beer, it was drawn by four enormous work horses, hitched two by two, tandem style. Huge and powerful as they were, they were docile and easy to handle.

The Reuther boys remembered their father always coming home late, tired, and hungry, to eat the substantial hot meal their mother had ready for him. Winter nights he would be later, because before he could come home he must groom, water, and feed his horses and bed them down for the night. During the winter, part of the grooming meant washing all the ice, snow, and mud out of the thick, tangled fetlocks. If they were not cleaned and dried, the horses' feet would become sore and infected. In the winter the driver's job was also more difficult because the roads around Wheeling had steep grades and many sharp curves. Should the heavily loaded dray start slipping on the ice going down one of those mountain roads, it would crash into the horses and injure or kill them. It took all the strength a powerfully built man could muster to hold the hand brake. The driver rode out in the open, with no protective covering and frost-bitten hands and feet were a common occurrence. Often Val was so stiff with cold he would have to be lifted down from the wagon and warmed up himself before he could tend his team.

In spite of the hardships, Val considered himself lucky to have a steady job. But when Walter was about nine years old—several years before the Volstead Act—West Virginia voted in Prohibition. The Schmulbach Brewery had to close down, and Val was out of work. Because of his union activities, Val Reuther was blacklisted in the other industries around Wheeling, which had no unions. Someone suggested that he and Anna start a home restaurant for workingmen, which he did with some reluctance, investing in the undertaking part of his small savings. One night a customer asked for a bottle of ginger beer, and Val opened the old-fashioned ice box, where soft drinks were kept cold on a big cake of ice. As he held the bottle in his hand it exploded from the abrupt change in temperature, and fragments of glass flew into his right eye, cutting it severely. He was rushed to the hospital, but would not allow them to give him any anesthetic to remove the splinters, fearing that the doctor would take out his eye while he was under the ether. With the help of a swig of whiskey he endured the pain while three men held him down. A short time later, the eye had to be removed anyhow and, to make matters worse, an infection developed in the other eye. Val Reuther had become nearly blind.

Those were hard times indeed, but the Reuthers possessed a ruggedness of their own to match adversity. For two years Anna Reuther kept her family together and somehow managed to clothe and feed four growing boys with big appetites.

"She was a wonderful manager," Walter recalled. "We had only a little money left out of our savings, but she stretched it out. We had a garden, and she did a lot of canning. And we kids helped all we could. Ted had some kind of an after-school job. Roy and I had paper routes, big ones. And I remember that I worked in a bakery shop weekends." He especially remembered the distasteful task of cleaning out the huge doughmixer on Saturday mornings. The caked dough was like cement, and he soon decided he would never want to be a baker. "In those days even a nine-year-old kid did not have to have working papers to get a job," Walter added.

A place that had much more appeal for him was the nearby glass factory. Walter loved to watch the glassblowers as they created beautiful crimson bowls or multicolored lampshades out of molten glass. As their were no safety rules then, he would walk through the factory on stilts. Almost every schoolboy at the period had a pair of homemade stilts on which he learned to walk with great speed, feeling ten feet tall, and the Reuther boys entered into the craze with zest. Once Walter, on a dare, narrowly escaped injury when he leaped from the top of a boxcar on his stilts into a mound of clay. In the glassworks he hung around every day, having learned to step carefully from station to station as he followed the fascinating procedure. First, skilled artisans created designs in steel molds—intricate lacey patterns or sometimes scenes—which were used as models by the glassblowers, who worked the boiling liquid in six different stages. The molten glass was blown through a tube, forming a large bubble at the end. Young boys were hired to twirl the tube around in the air while the bubble cooled enough so that the blower could mold it into the desired shape. Sometimes the glass was placed on a large asbestos paddle, and "carry boys" took it from one craftsman to another. Walter was a carry boy for a time. One day a boy near him who was twirling a tube let it slip from his hands, and fragments of the thin crust of glass that would form on the outside struck Walter in the face, leaving a deep cut about half an inch below his right eye. The eye was saved, but throughout his life the scar remained.

His father, alarmed at how close Walter had come to suffering the same fate as he, made him promise never again to be a carry boy. Walter kept his word, but he still hung around the workbenches of the designers, realizing intuitively that this was the basic and most creative part of the glassworkers craft. Seeing his constant interest, the men finally made a place for him on the bench, giving him a piece of steel, a hammer, and a chisel, and let him try his skill. Some of them gave him hints for carrying out his ideas, and this experience, according to his own testimony, later led him to become a tool- and diemaker. At the time, his greatest ambition was to be a designer in a glass factory, but the men themselves warned him that machines were already turning out molds in many places at a much faster rate. And soon afterward, the handicraft gave way to technology; the glass factory closed down.

Eventually Val Reuther regained his sight in his remaining eye, and it was then that he enrolled in correspondence courses. The boys would see their father with books and pencil and paper, poring over his lessons every evening, and he had probably been at it while they were at school and work during the day. A quick, avid student, Val Reuther knew the value of books; they were one of the few luxuries he permitted himself. Besides Goethe and Schiller on his small shelf of books, he treasured volumes by Thomas Henry Huxley and Robert Ingersoll. His socialism, in fact, savored as much of Robert Ingersoll as of Debs. Now he gained a knowledge of history and economics, as well as acquiring a remarkable facility in the use of English.

After regaining his sight, Val became a salesman for one of the large insurance companies. Since he was widely known and well liked, especially among labor groups throughout the area, he was able to start earning a living again. When the United States became involved in the First World War, unexpected difficulties arose from the anti-German feeling that swept the country, no matter how loyal to democracy families like the Reuthers were. A can of red paint was thrown across their porch, probably by wartime patriots who knew of Val's socialist leanings. His hero, Eugene Victor Debs, after a widely publicized trial under the Sedition Act of 1916, was convicted for speaking against American entry into the war and sentenced to jail in Moundsville, West Virginia. Val had known Debs personally during the presidential campaign of 1912, when, as a candidate for Congress on the Socialist ticket, he had been one of a select group aboard Debs's "Red Special" train, and he was much disturbed by the fact that the leader he revered was behind federal prison bars for speaking his mind in a country that was supposed to have free speech. His deep feeling for Debs led him to make the journey to Moundsville on visitors' day, taking Walter and Victor, Debs's namesake, with him to give them a close view of the man whose magnetic personality attracted people from all walks of life to his side. The encounter was an unforgettable event for both boys. In recalling his impression, Victor said, "I remember the terrible feeling when I saw those enormous iron bars. . . . And then I met this kindly man. . . ." Debs, who could arouse listeners to action with his fiery speeches, was also known for his modesty and gentleness, which won him many hearts outside the labor movement. It was once said of Debs that he went through the country on a railroad of love, and Val Reuther was one of his devoted passengers. As he left the prison with his two sons, the tears were streaming down his cheeks. Neither of the boys had ever seen their father weep before, and they never forgot this experience.

It was because of Debs that Val had run for Congress on the Socialist ticket. He was offered the nomination by the Republican party, and probably would have been elected if he had accepted. But he was convinced that Eugene Debs's ideas on government and the general economy were the best for the greatest number of people. His interest in politics, however, was by no means confined to his own party. Talking to the members of his union, he used to say, "If the men and women in West Virginia who have to work for a living would go to the polls and vote for the right kind of men to represent them in the Legislature, many, many children who were killed in the mines would be here today. Examine the records, and vote for the men who have proved they have your interest at heart. Don't just vote for your candidate because he happens to belong to your party. Vote for the best man, whatever his party!" It was a principle he himself always followed.

As a union leader, he had been flexible in dealing with both labor and management. At the time his blindness forced him to leave the labor movement, he had an unbroken record of settling contract disputes and new agreements without resorting to strikes. Late in his life, in answer to a reporter's inquiry, he explained, "I always won by politeness. There is an art in negotiating. . . ." His son Walter, taking his cue from his father, ultimately carried that art to a high degree of proficiency.

When Walter and his brothers were well into their teens, their parents sold the house in Wheeling and bought a large old colonial farmhouse with several acres of land outside the city. Val and his wife were still living in that house when they were in their eighties.

"Ted and I were both working," Walter later recalled, "and we sent money home to help pay for the house. But Dad later paid back to us every cent of it. That was like him."

Valentine Reuther was in his eighties when he went back to his homeland on his first visit. He had been away for seventy-one years, and had not spoken German for any concentrated period since he was a young man. During that visit he addressed several meetings in West Berlin; and for more than an hour, without manuscript or notes, he spoke to crowds of people in flawless German. The ovations he received were loud and prolonged.

Such was the father of the man who would become one of America's foremost labor leaders.

III

Four Young Reuthers

WALTER REUTHER and his three brothers were brought up strictly, and discipline was administered by both parents, firmly but not harshly. None of the boys in later life could remember ever having been punished severely. They also had less time to play and fewer distractions than children today have. There was, of course, no television. Radio was in its infancy. Even record players—called phonographs in the early 1900's—were beyond the means of families of workingmen, and records were limited and more expensive than they are now. Occasionally the boys would see a movie, the old silent films.

From the time of Val's accident, when Walter was nine years old, he always had some kind of weekend and after-school job. The same was true of his brothers. School activities outside of study were limited mostly to athletics. The principal business of going to school was to learn, and parents had great respect for teachers. Woe unto the boy who came home with a poor report card.

Conditioned as they were by their love and respect for their parents and by the hard times the family had to go through while they were still very young, the Reuther boys apparently accepted without question or protest the rules laid down by their mother and father.

"We were a very close-knit family," Walter reminisced when

he was past fifty, with a daughter of his own in college. "I think it was a family relationship that grew out of adversity. During the two years while my father was blind, my mother held us together, largely, as I look back on it now, by sheer faith in God." In a family with the affection the Reuthers had for each other, the children and their parents shared their social life more than most families do today.

At some time after he regained his eyesight Val Reuther bought a Model T Ford. It had no top, and his wife would be wearing a linen duster and a veil to hold her hat and hair in place when they set out for a ride on a summer Sunday afternoon. The Model T was a small car, and there were five children to be packed in along with their father and mother.

The rides were never very long, for the Model T had vagaries all its own. For one thing, they had to be sure the gas tank was always full. It was located right in front of the windshield and had what was known as gravity feed. In other words, the gasoline had to run down into the motor. There was no fuel pump, as on later models. If they started up one of the steep mountain roads around Wheeling with the gas tank less than half full, they would find themselves backing downhill because the motor was not getting any fuel.

Tires were not so good either, and the Reuthers rarely went on a ride without having at least one blowout. Then the car had to be jacked up and the tire pried and pulled off the wheel, a hard, sweaty job, even though the tires were not much bigger than bicycle tires. The inner tube then had to be removed from the casing, the hole patched with some kind of adhesive tape, and the tube worked back into the casing. Then the casing had to be tucked carefully back inside the rim on the wheel. The operation ended with the boys taking turns pumping up the tire with a bicycle pump.

"But we had fun just the same," Roy Reuther said in telling the story. "We'd drive down to Wheeling Park, turn around and come back. They certainly weren't long drives, probably five or six miles. But it was a family outing that we all enjoyed. Later we had an old 1919 Maxwell, like the famous Maxwell Jack Benny used to kid about on his radio program. Remember?"

Sunday in the Reuther family was also devoted to serious matters. Until Val broke away from it, the whole family went to church every Sunday, and the children attended Sunday school. In their Zion Lutheran Church, a child was given a gold-plated button as a reward for one year's perfect attendance record at Sunday school. Thereafter for each perfect year he would receive a gold-plated bar to be hung below the button. Each of the four Reuther boys accumulated seven bars.

Although their father never returned to church, he was interested in hearing about the sermons—quite possibly to make sure his children were not receiving doctrine with which he disagreed —and when they and their mother came home, he would question them all as they sat around the table after Sunday dinner. Since it was the largest meal of the week and usually the only one at which they had both meat and dessert, they were in the habit of lingering at table. *Vater* would ask the boys what the subject of the sermon had been and how the minister had dealt with it. Then they would discuss the question to discover the merits or demerits of his precepts. Out of this grew the "Reuther debating society," as Walter once called it. On Sunday afternoons, usually in the winter, they would assemble in the boys' big bedroom on the top floor. With their father as moderator and judge, the young Reuthers would debate on all the lively questions of the day: women's suffrage, freedom for the Philippines, the League of Nations, Prohibition, child labor, compulsory military training, naval preparedness, organized labor, and so on.

Walter always remembered with special relish one debate on capital punishment. "I argued against it with great conviction," he related, "for I was against it personally."

Frequently they would find themselves taking opposite sides of a question as a debating exercise. Ted and Roy were usually teamed up against Walter and Victor. They had to do their own research on topics their father had assigned, and this meant several trips to the public library during the week. While the debate was in progress, their father sat at a desk across the room with pencil and paper, keeping track of "points" and timing their speeches with an alarm clock. At the end he would announce the winners, basing his decision on the thoroughness with which they had done their research, their mental alertness and logic in rebuttal, and their delivery. It was the best possible training for any boy who would become an important figure in American public life.

Sometimes their voices rose to such a pitch that their little sister Christine, hearing the shouts from above, began to cry because she thought her brothers were fighting. *Mütterchen* would have to comfort her, telling her the boys were only playing a game.

In this way, Walter Reuther began to acquire his great skill as a debater and public speaker. "I had to learn to think on my feet and talk fast," he would say, reminiscing with a grin. To him it was great sport, a rousing battle of wits. In fact, with the possible exception of Victor who, probably because he was the youngest, found the assignments and preparation something of a chore in the beginning, all the Reuther boys thought these debates were fun. Walter and Roy especially found the challenge stimulating. All the boys had lively minds, but Walter seemed to be on the qui vive all the time. Often in church he could hardly sit still, and his mother called him "wiggle-britches." Outgoing like his father, he was winsome and genial most of the time, but he frequently displayed the redhead's temperament—hot-headed and stubborn when he was crossed in something he had decided to do. He possessed the unique combination of a trigger-sharp mind and lithe body, plus wonderfully skillful hands. And though he was imaginative, as the young are inclined to be, he was not an idle or passive dreamer, but an extremely active one.

Part of his energy found an outlet in sports, in which Val Reuther encouraged his sons, joining them in play as well as serious pursuits whenever he could find the time. Now and then he bought various pieces of athletic equipment—a set of bars on which the boys could chin themselves but which could also be used for high-jumping and pole-vaulting; a basketball; baseballs and bats; a punching bag and boxing gloves. The punching bag was set up in the basement right under the kitchen, and occasionally the boys' mother, driven to distraction by the thumping noises, would open the door and call down to them to stop it.

Walter and his brothers took pride in their athletic prowess.

He and Roy spent any spare time they had at the *Turnverein,* the
German gymnasium, and both boys were ace basketball players
in the Luther League of the Zion Church. Walter was about an
inch shorter than Roy, but he had such tremendous elasticity in
his leg muscles that he inevitably played center on the teams they
joined, for he was an excellent shot. Roy also went in for track.
He thought of becoming an athletic instructor, but their father
convinced him that it was a "frivolous calling." In the summertime, when the boys turned to baseball, Walter pitched and
played shortstop on their YMCA team. One season their team was
winner of the tri-state junior championship. Walter was also a
very good swimmer, and he won several trophies. Proud of their
achievements, they borrowed their mother's bread board one
summer afternoon and, standing it up on a kitchen chair in the
yard, they mounted the medals, ribbons, and Walter's swimming
trophy across the center and placed a big Wheeling pennant
above it and other ribbons at the sides. Then, standing behind the
chair in their basketball shirts, with "Zion" stamped on the front,
they posed, chests out and hands behind their backs, while their
mother snapped their photo. Like Val, Anna Reuther believed in
athletics as the best kind of recreation and encouraged their sons
in the various sports they chose.

As soon as each boy was old enough, their mother saw to it
that he went to the YMCA and learned to swim. This was important because the Ohio River provided an irresistible lure to the
youngsters in Wheeling. It was by no means the safest body of
water in the world for young swimmers, for it was always filled
with traffic including large passenger boats and freighters, stern-
wheelers, propelled by huge paddle wheels attached to their
sterns.

Almost every day in the summertime the Reuthers, along with
most of the other kids in Wheeling, would go down to the bank
of the Ohio, undress in the bushes, get into their bathings suits,
and plunge into the river, dodging traffic as they swam back and
forth from shore to shore.

"Our mother," Roy Reuther said, "knew, of course, that we
went swimming in the river, but she had done everything she
could to make sure that we knew how to swim. But the stunt

which gave us our biggest thrill she never knew about—at least we didn't tell her. A favorite sport was swimming behind one of those big stern-wheelers, getting just as close as we dared. Any kid who wasn't close enough so that the spray thrown up by the paddles washed over him was considered chicken. It was dangerous, of course, because those churning wheels caused a terrific undertow. But if our mother ever knew about it, she did not mention it."

Lively, imaginative young Walter was the experimental type. When he was in his middle fifties, he still laughed over one of his boyhood escapades that might have proved disastrous.

"I think it was during the time while our father was blind," he said. "I was nine or ten and rather small and light for my age. At county fairs and carnivals men would jump with parachutes from captive balloons. I thought it was very exciting and wanted to try it myself. Our mother bought a great big black cotton umbrella, large enough so that the whole family could get under it. So one day I borrowed the new umbrella, climbed up on a water tower near our home, opened the umbrella, and took off. The tank was thirty-five or forty feet above the ground. The umbrella sustained my weight about two thirds of the way down, and then—disaster! It turned inside out, and the umbrella and I landed on the ground with a terrific thump. Believe it or not, I was not badly hurt—no broken bones or sprains, just a few bruises here and there. But the umbrella was a complete wreck.

"When I arrived home, my mother was, of course, annoyed and gave me a good scolding, although I do not recall that she punished me, except in a very unique kind of way. She was determined to salvage something from the wreck. Although the frame was completely ruined, she managed to make me a shirt out of the heavy material that had covered it. For a long time my brothers and the other kids we knew used to tease me about the 'umbrella shirt.'" But Walter would come back with, "I bet you haven't got a shirt that sheds water!"

The Reuther boys always had jobs, but their father was particular about the kind of jobs at which they worked. Walter and Roy both had large paper routes. Their father would not permit them to deliver afternoon papers. Instead, they had morning paper routes. This meant that they had to get up at 3 or 4 A.M., go down to the newspaper plants, pick up their papers, and have them on the doorsteps before breakfast.

"His idea," Roy explained, "was to keep us from getting mixed up with gangs of tough young fellows who used to hang around street corners at dusk. At the hour when we started out they were still in bed."

It was Walter who added an anecdote connected with their paper routes.

"We would go down to the stable of the American Express Company at three or four in the morning," he said, "and hitch a ride on one of the express wagons headed downtown. This saved us a long hike. We did not have bikes, and anyway we had so many papers to deliver that a bike would not have been much help on those hilly streets. I think Roy had a little wagon, but I carried mine.

"One morning the express wagon stopped on the way downtown, and a long wooden box was placed aboard. Roy and I settled ourselves comfortably on the box. But presently the driver said casually over his shoulder,

" 'Do you kids know what's in that box?'

" 'Why, no,' we told him. 'What's in it?'

" 'Oh, just a corpse,' he informed us.

"Roy and I both jumped about a foot and rode the rest of the way downtown standing up."

Victor, the youngest, had for nearly a year the most unique job of all—a job that would have been thoroughly distasteful to the average boy.

"I was ten years old," he said, "when our mother [with the baby Chris] went back to Germany to visit her people. All my brothers had jobs of one sort or another. So I was made chief cook and bottle washer for the family. I cooked the meals, took care of the garden, and kept the house clean. Later on, while I was working my way through college, the experience proved very valuable."

There were many times when the Reuther larder contained very little to cook, especially during Val's blindness, and many a meal consisted of boiled potatoes, with an occasional can of tuna fish. *Mütterchen* knew how to stretch food out for several meals, and taught the children never to leave a scrap on their plates, quoting a German couplet equivalent to the succinct English "Waste not, want not." When she made cherry pancakes as a special treat, she left the pits in, to keep the boys from gobbling them down and asking for more right away. But no matter how little they had to eat, both the Reuthers put the biblical story of the loaves and the fishes into practice. "Mother and Father always took in every tramp that came along and sat them down at our table," Walter recalled. "Dad would always say to us, 'I want you to remember that as long as you have something to eat, you have to share it with others who haven't.'" This was the applied Christianity that Val had been taught by his father and which he now passed along to his sons.

Their mother's faith in God, while also practical, was expressed in spiritual manifestations. It was at her insistence that grace was said before every meal; and at night, even in the wintertime, the whole family huddled around the kitchen stove in their nightclothes to speak their final daily prayers, after which the boys would dash upstairs to their cold bedroom. Between hard work and play, none of them had time or thought for getting into trouble. When he was fifty-five years old, Walter remarked about the home life of the Reuthers: "If I could change the family I grew up in, I wouldn't—not one bit."

IV

From Apprentice
to Skilled Workman

WALTER REUTHER was not quite sixteen when he left high
school at the end of his second year and became an apprentice
tool- and diemaker with the Wheeling Steel Corporation.

Val Reuther wanted to give each of his four boys every possible educational advantage. But he could not then foresee a time
when he would be in a financial position to send them to college.
He also firmly believed that every boy should learn a trade that
would enable him to earn a living, no matter what other vocation
or profession he might choose. Val had great respect for a skilled
workman. Guilds, made up of many of the finest craftsmen Western civilization ever produced, had their beginning in his native
Germany. For a man to make things with his hands was part of
his heritage.

He had never had an opportunity to learn a trade himself, his
period of employment in a steel company having ended after a
few months, when the plant closed down.

"I might have done better by you," he told his sons, "if I had
become a skilled craftsman. This is an advantage I want you to
have."

Ted, the oldest, was the only one of the four boys who seemed
destined ever to hold a white-collar job. Ted had already left high
school, had taken a brief course in bookkeeping at a so-called
business college, and had gone to work in the accounting depart-

ment of the Wheeling Steel Corporation, where he spent his
entire working life, eventually rising to the position of comptroller.
Walter, it was decided, would be a mechanic, Roy an electrician,
and Victor, probably, a plumber.

Walter and Roy obediently accepted their father's plans and
learned the trades he thought suitable for them. However, by the
time Victor was graduated from Wheeling High School—the only
Reuther boy to go through high school in four consecutive years
—the family was more prosperous, and Victor was sent to the
University of West Virginia for one year, Ted and Walter helping
to pay his way.

Walter did not mind leaving high school. Academic subjects
had no appeal for him at that time. He did like to make things
with his hands, and the one subject in which he was really
interested and had high grades was shop.

"We had a very good teacher," he recalled. "He was also one
of the finest men I ever knew. We liked each other, and because
I really enjoyed working in the school machine shop, he took a
special interest in me. During my last year in high school he'd
taught me enough so that I acted as a kind of assistant to him.
Sometimes he would even let me take over and teach the class."

When Ted came home from the office one day toward the end
of Walter's sophomore year with the news that there was an
opening at Wheeling Steel in the training department for apprentice tool- and diemakers, it seemed to Walter too good an opportunity to pass up, since such vacancies usually occurred only once
every four years—the length of an apprenticeship. There was an
immediate family conference on the matter; both parents had
hoped that Walter would finish high school, if possible, but times
were still hard for the Reuthers, and the few dollars Walter
would earn as an apprentice might help to keep Roy and Victor
in school. The Reuthers deliberated together in the old-world
tradition of the family circle; and while there was probably a
certain amount of sibling rivalry among the four boys, it was
definitely exceeded by the strong spirit of teamwork that grew
out of the close family relationship.

Moreover, Walter pointed out, the instruction he had already
received from his teacher in shop, which was considerably beyond

that given to most high school students, would put him months ahead of the average beginning apprentice in making tools and dies. He was eager to start working. So it was decided that he should try for the job at Wheeling Steel.

Like all apprentices, he started in as a handyman, doing all the dirty work around the place. One of these was oiling the pulleys that operated the machines, in the course of which he was spattered with oil and grease from head to foot and came home looking like a coal miner.

He endured this greasy labor cheerfully for about a year, concentrating on his recreational life outside the factory, particularly basketball, where he perfected his technique at jumping center; short as he was, he made more baskets than many taller players. The try-out period at Wheeling Steel finally ended, and he was moved up to the tool-and-die department, where he began to learn the skilled trade for which he had left high school. Like the cutters of the clothing industry, tool- and diemakers are the aristocrats of the automotive industry, and to learn this exacting skill the worker must start at the very beginning.

"They would bring us a beat-up piece of metal," Walter explained long afterward, "and say, 'You've got to make this.' We would have to make all the drawings, design the part, make the dies, and finally fashion the piece of machinery that had to be replaced." He had to learn the various processes of grinding, drilling, cutting, and buffing as well as improve the knowledge of mechanical drawing that he had received in school, and acquire a certain familiarity with higher mathematics in order to shape the dies. It was exacting, precise work, requiring such a high degree of accuracy that in many cases the measurements could not vary more than several thousandths of an inch.

The finished casting, made of hard, heavy steel, with razor-sharp edges for cutting, would stamp out the body, gears, fenders, and other automotive parts in lighter steel. As a beginning apprentice, Walter received eleven cents an hour, most of which went into the family budget, and he "worked his tail off." But he was learning a skilled trade, one which would lead to a larger pay envelope in one of the auto factories; even then he sensed that the manufacture of cars was to become the giant of American industry.

During his second year at Wheeling Steel, a rush order to move a four-hundred-pound steel die from a press came in unexpectedly. Under pressure from the foreman, the men worked so fast that they didn't stop to think about taking proper safety precautions. Walter and three others gripped the greasy die with their hands and tried with a great heave to lift it out of the press. Too late they realized that the underside was heavily oiled, and, just as they had it almost out, their hands started to slip! In that instant they all knew they were losing control, that the die was going to crash. The only thing Walter could think of was that if he let go, one of his fellow workers would be killed. In relating the accident he observed, "Even then . . . probably as a result of my training at home, I had this tremendous concern for my fellowman . . . this feeling that he was my responsibility. . . ." So, without considering his own fate, he hung on to his side of the die, and when it fell, the tremendous crash was in his direction. The razor edge of the steel slashed through the tip of his shoe as if it had been tissue paper, slicing the big toe of his right foot clear through the bone, completely severing it.

With blood pouring from his foot, he was picked up by his co-workers and placed on the emergency stretcher to be rushed to the hospital. But as they hoisted the stretcher he yelled out, "Bring me my toe! I won't go to the hospital without my toe!" The first thought that flashed through his mind was that the accident would mean the end of his basketball career. He had always been proud of jumping center, even though he was the shortest player on the team, and all he could think of was that he wouldn't be able to jump high enough anymore, with only one big toe. His voice was so frantically urgent that his fellow workers complied, and the toe was placed beside him on the stretcher. At the hospital, the doctor tried to convince him that the only thing to do was to sew up the wound, but Walter cried out, "I want that toe sewed back on!" No matter that the blood vessels, bones, and tissues had been completely severed; he insisted—without mentioning basketball—that the doctor try to reinstate his toe. All he would say was, "You don't know how important it is to me to have two big toes!"

At last the doctor gave in, and prepared to give his crazy, hotheaded young patient an anesthetic; but, like his father, Walter refused to be put to sleep, fearing that he would be tricked if he were under the ether; he wanted to make sure the doctor did not just stitch up the wound. Although it took three attendants to hold him down, he withstood the pain and watched the physician's fumbling stabs at the hopeless task of trying to reconnect the nerves and blood vessels. Just as in the case of Val's eyes, Walter's toe, which became infected, had to be removed a few days later.

In those days, there was no workman's compensation to provide income for those who suffered from accidents on the job, nor were there mandatory safety rules. Some of the first benefits Walter was to strive for in his union leadership, they were undoubtedly influenced by this experience. He stayed at home until his foot had healed enough to bear his weight, and when he started to walk, returning to work as soon as possible, he was determined not to be a cripple. Difficult as it was, he forced himself to walk upright, without a limp. He also vowed he would play basketball again, and in the end he did, though he was "slowed down a bit for a time." And to the end of his life, Walter Reuther was reminded of the accident each time he bought a new pair of shoes: until they were broken in, he felt excruciating pain with every step. His mother and tenderhearted sister thought he was being too hard on himself when he started to walk again, but his stoicism stood him in good stead in years to come, when the trials of physical pain were to be even greater. With typical Reuther objectivity, he summed up the accident philosophically: "I was lucky. If the die had crashed a few inches farther back, it would have taken off my whole foot."

He continued on the job, but had not quite finished his four-year apprenticeship when he left the Wheeling Steel Corporation. He had worked his way up to the maximum trainee pay, forty-three cents an hour, which meant that he had already reached the point of top skill, and yet he could not earn any more until he had put in the required number of years. Moreover, during the busy season, employees of Wheeling Steel had to work seven days a week, whether they wanted to or not. Walter, having been brought up with a profound respect for the Sabbath, regarded the Sunday work as immoral, but since there was no union in the plant, the men were wholly at the mercy of the management, without right to present grievances. Being a Reuther, and the most outspoken of the boys, Walter discussed the problem openly with the workers, although he was only an apprentice and most of them were older and more experienced than he.

"Look," he pointed out, "we're supposed to be free men, not slaves, and no free man should be made to work on Sunday against his conscience."

There is a story, purely legendary, that he proceeded to lead a protest against Sunday and holiday work, and was summarily fired when the company discovered he was the instigator. But the truth is that, though the men agreed with him, they did not care to jeopardize their jobs; and he was growing restless within the confines of Wheeling. He knew intuitively that if he "was to reach out, he would have to have more elbow room," as he put it. Rumors were coming through that in Detroit, the mecca of automobile workers, where higher wages were paid than anywhere else in the automotive industry, there were good jobs to be found for skilled workmen even though plants were retooling and thousands of assembly-line employees had been laid off. There were also big plants in nearby Flint, Michigan. In addition, manufacturers like Ford were beginning to farm out to specialized companies the production of parts, such as wheels, spark plugs, carburetors.

Walter was confident that he knew enough to hold down any job in tool- and diemaking. Following a family conference around the table while finishing up *Mütterchen's Apfelkuchen,* one night, shortly after the new year, 1927, he and a co-worker, Leo J. Hoars, had hitchhiked to Detroit. Walter had found room and board with a Southern Baptist family who had been lured to Detroit a few years before by the higher wages. Though they predicted he would have trouble in getting a job just then, he had let neither them nor standing in line during the cold weather discourage him and he had been hired by Briggs Body Manu-

1927!

facturing Co. at seventy-five cents an hour for a back-breaking thirteen-hour shift. Then he had had the temerity to apply for the job of die leader at Ford, arguing his way into being hired on ability, even though he had not quite completed his four years of apprenticeship. So here he was at nineteen, working for $1.05 an hour, higher wages than his father or older brother Ted had ever earned.

As his income increased, he sent more money home each week, continuing the plan he had started with his first paycheck. He had figured out exactly how much he needed to live on and mailed the rest to the family. His father had purchased the big old farmhouse outside Wheeling, and mortgage payments had to be met. Val had written back that they appreciated the check but it wasn't necessary for him to send it. Walter had ignored him, and kept right on sending the money. There was also Victor's future to be considered. He was close to the end of his high school years, and after a summer job of digging ditches showed no interest in becoming a plumber. Rather, he thought he might like to be a lawyer. Val called this "a highbrow profession," trying to discourage him, but Victor persisted, and Walter backed him up. Roy was already serving his apprenticeship as an electrician, but Ted and Walter were able to help their youngest brother and they did.

Walter at that point had not really decided what he wanted to do. He toyed with various ideas. He was greatly interested in aviation for a while—1927 was the year Charles Lindbergh flew the Atlantic—and he thought he might become an aeronautical engineer. He even started a flying club among his co-workers at Ford. Little by little, they built a glider, but before it was finished, they pooled their money to buy a "Jennie," a biplane of World War One, to pull their glider. All amateurs, they flew by means of "eyeball navigation," using the tracks of the Michigan Central Railroad as a guide. As might be expected, they frequently had to make emergency landings, a disastrous one resulting in the death of a young club member in the Jenny at the time. The tragedy "broke our spirits," Walter related. Neither he nor the others had the heart to complete the glider, and the club disbanded shortly afterward.

But whatever he did, unless he were willing to make a life career out of tool- and diemaking, he knew he must have more education. So in the autumn of 1927 he went back to school in Detroit, enrolling in Fordson High, from which he was graduated two years later. He had to adopt a grueling schedule. Getting himself transferred to the second shift at the plant, he worked from three fifteen in the afternoon until midnight, went straight home, washed up, and ate. Between one and four A.M., he studied; then he grabbed three or four hours sleep and was up in time to make his first class. School lasted until it was time to report for work; often he barely made it.

Anyone less resilient than Walter Reuther would have been bogged down by such a routine, but his youthful energy seemed boundless. Before he resumed his high school education, he had joined the Central YMCA to get rid of some of that excess vigor in the gym and swimming pool. He had been given a long questionnaire to fill out, which included one puzzler: "What is your life's ambition?" He pondered the matter, and after some "meditation and consideration" had put down two answers: "Labor leader or chicken farmer." Long afterward, when he was a famous labor leader, he liked to begin a speech with the incident and add, grinning, "And do you know, the General Motors Corporation has been trying to persuade me for the last twenty years that I would have made a damn good chicken farmer!" On weekends and any spare time he had, he exercised at the "Y," and before many months he was playing basketball again. True to his vow, he taught himself to jump center with as much bounce as he had before he lost his toe. He also organized the Highland Park Basketball Team at Ford and jumped center with such agility that they won a championship.

Walter brought the same infectious enthusiasm to any project that occupied his attention. He was older than most of the students in high school, but he found a few boys of his own age, among them Merlin Bishop, a former coal miner who was now a crane operator at Ford's River Rouge plant, to which Walter had been transferred. Together they decided to form a club of older boys who were working for high school diplomas while holding down a job, and the first question that came up con-

cerned officers. Merlin wondered who would be president, but
Walter already knew the answer: "I wouldn't be part of any
organization I couldn't be president of," he said laughing, but
determined all the same. And so he was president as a matter
of course; Merlin was secretary-treasurer. It was the beginning
of a long relationship in the cause of social justice that in a few
years would be channeled into organizing the auto workers and
the labor movement in general. At the suggestion of their English
teacher, the boys chose the name the 4-C Club, an urban corollary
to the 4-H Clubs, with the C's signifying, citizenship, comrade-
ship, cooperation, and confidence. The object of the club was to
give poor teen-agers a hand in getting an education, because
Walter had sensed when he started attending classes that "there
were a lot of kids . . . who, when they ran into obstacles, got
discouraged and quit." Since he himself had left school primarily
because funds were low, he knew how difficult it was to keep on.
The club members raised money in various ways: They rented
old reels and showed movies in the auditorium for a small
admission fee; they sold pop and candy bars at football and
basketball games. All the receipts went into a college-loan fund
for students who wanted to go on to higher education.

Such a worthy cause was bound to receive applause from
the Board of Education and city officials. The boys found themselves sponsored by the Detroit Chamber of Commerce, composed
of men who in years to come would roll their eyes in horror at
the mere mention of Walter Reuther. He and Merlin Bishop
appeared before the Kiwanis Club, Rotary, and other civic groups
to explain the goals of the 4-C Club. With his insatiable curiosity
and quick, bright mind, Walter proved to be a brilliant student
once he applied himself. As he never took up smoking or drinking,
mostly he seemed to be a model young man. At work, too, he
won the approval of his immediate bosses by proving even more
skillful than he had indicated by his blueprint reading. He advanced rapidly and worked on the most delicate precision jobs
with consistent accuracy. The foreman who hired him was so
impressed with his ability that he invited Walter to dinner in
his home, and his wife also was quite taken with the young
visitor. The couple, who had no children, urged him to visit

them often; and one night they suggested that Walter come to live at their house; he would be like the son they never had.

Surprised and deeply touched, Walter hardly knew what to say. He was well aware that this kind offer would mean security and advancement in the company, an opportunity that most young fellows would have seized and many would have envied. The latter was the most troubling factor in making his decision: he had been conditioned all his life to see things from the point of view of the worker, and he knew well what the auto worker's plight was in those days. Yet he did not want to hurt the couple who had been so generous. As diplomatically and gently as he could, he explained to them that he was afraid it would somehow change his relationship with his boss on the job; he might be getting something he wasn't earning; or even if he wasn't, his fellow workers might *think* he was, and he didn't want them to get a false impression. He had no desire for favors to which he wasn't entitled, and felt the whole situation would be awkward. His would-be benefactors were disappointed, but they understood his dilemma and respected his considerate refusal.

Although he had put "labor leader" above "chicken farmer" (to a great extent pure whimsey on his part), Walter was still not sure what he wanted for his life's ambition when he received his high school diploma at the age of twenty-two. Shortly after his twenty-first birthday, his father had returned his weekly check with the succinct line, "I won't take any more money from you." This was Val Reuther's way of recognizing that his son had come of age. On Walter's next visit to Wheeling—he was in the habit of going home whenever he could, for the big holidays and his vacation—his mother suggested that he open a savings account with the money he had been sending home, and he took her advice. But as he listened to the talk around the plant, he decided to make some small investments. He bought a few shares of Kelvinator stock and persuaded his brother Ted to go in with him on making the down payment on a lot in Dearborn. Otherwise he continued to live frugally, even when his wages went up, and put part of his paycheck into his savings account each week. By the time he finished high school, he, like Victor, thought he might become a lawyer.

Victor meanwhile had spent one year at the University of West Virginia. Morgantown, where the university is located, is in the coal mining area, near some of the most notorious "company towns" of that period. The youngest Reuther made a point of seeing Scotts Run, where the miners and their families lived in miserable shacks, beaten black with coal dust, along a street down either side of which ran a ditch filled with yellow, sluggish water. That filthy water was used for everything; the people had no other supply. They washed their clothes, bathed, cooked, and drank out of those stagnant streams. The few doctors in the area could not figure out why there were no typhoid epidemics. Company physicians were apt to dismiss the situation with a shrug. Apparently the people had built up an immunity to the disease over years of such conditions. Inspecting many of those dilapidated, rat-infested hovels, Victor became thoroughly familiar with the unspeakable situation in which the miners were forced to work and live. As his father years before, he was outraged and determined that if he became a lawyer he would find some legal means of preventing the mine operators from perpetrating these crimes against their employees.

During the summer vacation, after he had completed his year at the university, he and Walter got together on a family visit in Wheeling.

"Why don't you come up to Detroit?" Walter asked him when they had exchanged news and stories. "They have a city college there, and it probably won't cost the two of us any more than you have to pay at West Virginia." He was referring to Detroit City College, which eventually became Wayne State University. "We'll enter together and study law."

Victor welcomed the idea and went back to Detroit with Walter at the end of his vacation, though the family was loath to have them both leave at once. In such a closely knit familial relationship the partings were always a wrench, especially for their little sister. At the time of Walter's first trip back for the Christmas holiday in 1927, she had cried so piteously, begging him to stay, that he had told Mütterchen to "keep Chris in the kitchen or someplace" on his next visit until after he had gone. Roy, who found things much more lively at home when all the boys were there together, just like old times, decided to join his brothers on completing his apprenticeship as an electrician.

Soon after they reached Detroit, Walter set out to find a place where they could live more cheaply than in the boardinghouse. With a few members of the 4-C Club, including Merlin Bishop and his younger brother Melvin, he and Victor moved into a basement apartment. Melvin Bishop was to become also a sturdy pioneer in the labor movement and a close friend of Walter, though they were to part in a bitter quarrel more than two decades later. Five young men—six when Roy came—shared a space just big enough for three, but they were not there much, since they were all going to college and, with the exception of Victor, working. For the second time in his life Victor, who, without training, could not get a job as an auto worker, became "chief cook and bottle washer." The marketing was taken over by a student from India, who was a much better bargainer than Victor. He suggested in late summer that they go to the country to buy fresh fruit and vegetables from the farmers for canning, to be used during the winter when farm produce was scarcer and more expensive. Walter had bought an old secondhand Ford, and they made several trips, returning with a load of string beans, peas, carrots, onions, corn, tomatoes and, toward fall, peaches, pears, and bright red Jonathan apples.

"We decided," Victor recalled later, "to put the stuff up in one-gallon jars. A whole gallon may seem like a lot, but there were six hungry young men to be fed.

"We went to a secondhand store down in a poor section of the city. The proprietor had literally hundreds of dusty glass one-gallon jars sitting around. We asked the price, and I was all for buying them, but my young friend from India shook his head. I don't remember what the price was, but anyway he showed no further interest in the one-gallon jars. Instead, he asked the proprietor how many five-gallon jars he had.

" 'How many do you want?' the proprietor asked.

" 'Oh, fifty or sixty,' my friend told him.

"The proprietor, looking very unhappy, shook his head. He had only about half a dozen five-gallon jars.

" 'But could you use the one-gallon jars?' he asked, hopefully.

'I've got lots of those, as you see, and I might make you a price
on them.'

"After some haggling, my Indian friend decided the price was
low enough, and we walked out of the store with fifty one-gallon
glass jars, for which we had paid about half the price originally
charged."

In telling the story, Victor Reuther would wind up with a
grin and this statement: "That was my first lesson in collective
bargaining." He did the canning and preserving, skills he had
acquired when he kept house for the family at the age of ten
during his mother's visit to her homeland. "I canned everything
in sight," he said; "made soup and preserves, and I did all right.
I don't recall that any of it spoiled, and it lasted us all winter."

In the fall of 1929, Walter and Victor registered at Detroit City
College, intending to study law, as they had planned.

"We spent a good deal of our spare time, which wasn't much,"
Victor said, "sitting in court rooms, listening to lawyers plead their
cases. During a recess we would go out into the corridor, and
sometimes we would hear the lawyers joking about how they had
'put this one over' on the jury."

To the serious-minded young Reuthers the prospect of spending their lives in the legal profession grew less attractive. Lawyers
struck them as being cynical and somewhat frivolous. Their
father had been a dedicated union man. Walter's experience in
Wheeling when he had tried to rouse the workers against the
seven-day work week; the veiled response he got from assembly-
line workers here in Detroit; and Victor's observation of the
miserable existence of the coal miner in Morgantown naturally
influenced their thinking and activities. None of the auto plants
had or would tolerate unions, but that didn't stop the redheaded
tool- and diemaker from discussing the subject around the Rouge.
He even had some deaf-mute workers teach him their sign
language so he could communicate with them. It did not take
either of the Reuthers long to decide on switching their majors
from pre-law courses to sociology and economics so that they
might have "more socially useful careers," in Walter's words. He
had a real passion for knowledge in these fields, and true to
form, took on a full load of thirteen to seventeen credit hours a

semester. This meant that he had to continue getting along on three or four hours sleep a night, but he seemed to thrive on it, and even took on outside activities. He was always full of what in the vernacular of the factory worker was called "piss 'n' vinegar." Earnest though he was about his purpose in life, his laugh was ready and robust, teasingly triumphant when he had won a victory, whether in basketball or—later—in contract negotiations. And if his temper burst forth unexpectedly with firecracker sparks it burned out just as quickly, as reason and control took over. At work he was well liked by both men and bosses, the latter not yet aware of his union or any other "radical" leanings. He was a die leader now, with as many as forty men under his supervision at times, disproving the theory that a man needed twenty-five years of experience to hold down the position. Ability was all that was needed, and of that Walter Reuther had an abundance.

V

From College Student
to Campus Rebel

BOTH of the Reuther boys were exceptional students, not only because they had quick, bright minds, but because they were already more knowledgeable in their chosen field than most sociology and economics majors. The future Wayne State University was then in its infancy, a striving municipal college temporarily housed in old Central High School. Faculty and student body were small, allowing individual attention and interchange of ideas between the two, so it was not long before Walter and Victor were well known to their teachers and college administrators.

The Dean of Men, who taught sociology, took great interest in them, especially Walter, who, with a good job that paid the top rates of the period, had shown that he knew the value of education by returning to high school and then coming on to college after receiving his diploma. The Dean was interested also in the way the young Reuthers coordinated their assignments. Their minds seemed to synchronize as perfectly meshed gears; in class, one of them might start a sentence and the other finish it up. Because of Walter's tight schedule, the brothers were given permission to submit one paper instead of two on an assigned subject. Frequently Walter would start a theme with one eye on the clock, and then, grabbing his coat, say to his younger brother, "You finish it up, Vic; I have to go to work!"

The boys often stayed after class to talk with the Dean, and he spoke of relating their academic studies to life. The disastrous stock-market crash of 1929 had brought on the historic depression of the thirties, which was deepening month by month. Busy as he was, Walter started a new organization, The Social Service Club, with himself as president, Victor as vice-president, and Merlin Bishop as the third-ranking officer. Ostensibly formed as a correlative to social studies, it was allied with the League for Industrial Democracy, a campus arm of the Socialist party* and soon became the outlet for action on the crucial issues of the hour. Walter had been attending some of the meetings of the Workmen's Circle, a Socialist Labor group, and when he heard that Norman Thomas, who had succeeded Debs as the perennial presidential nominee of the party, was going to speak at the Circle as well as other places in the area, he invited him to give a talk on campus, under the auspices of the Social Service Club. This was probably about the time Thomas was making appearances advocating socialism as a solution to the depression. The democratic free-enterprise system seemed to have failed with government officials apparently paralyzed, which brought on a rash of nationwide, frank discussions for a basic change of government. In Toledo, soon to be the scene of a bloody battle in the automotive industry, notably the strike at Auto-Lite, the college itself sponsored a series of Open Forums to figure a way out. One of these was a debate between Norman Thomas and Scott Nearing, a well-known political science writer and professor, on the relative merits of socialism and communism. The debate ended in a draw, with heated pros and cons on both sides from the audience during the discussion period that followed.**

Thomas was of course a pacifist; and as there was a rumor that the ROTC program on campus was to be made compulsory,

* Originally the Intercollegiate Society of Socialists, founded in 1905 by Upton Sinclair, Jack London, and Clarence Darrow; Walter Lippmann and Ralph Bunche were early members, spreading Socialist philosophy among students.

** Nearing was later fired from the college for advancing Marxian theory in his classes. Claiming false indictment, he retired to his property in Vermont, where he developed the making of maple-sugar products, writing a book on the benefits of turning to the soil, a volume that had a sudden popularity in the late sixties, when a new generation of dissidents, the hippies, discovered it, creating a demand for a new edition.

he was the logical choice as the first speaker presented by the
Social Service Club. When the rumor became a definite proposal,
the Reuther brothers, in the best tradition of their grandfather,
threw their own energies and the full weight of their club membership into the opposition, making the students realize the
threat to democracy in any sort of compulsory military training,
reserve officers or otherwise. At one rally, Walter gave the opening arguments against ROTC, except on a purely voluntary
basis, and Victor wound up with the closing speech. Their efforts
were rewarded by the defeat of the proposal.

Another campus issue which became a *cause célèbre* was the
controversial matter of a swimming pool. The building in which
classes were held had an inadequate gym, equipped with few
athletic facilities, and there was no swimming pool. The students
were eager to have one, and the administration cast around for
some way to solve the need. Finally they announced that an
arrangement had been made with Webster Hall, a large resi-
dential hotel nearby, for the use of the hotel swimming pool by
students in the mornings, when patrons rarely swam. The students were overjoyed, of course; but their jubilation was soon
chilled when they learned that the agreement had a clause barring
Negro students. Walter and the Social Service Club were immediately up in arms. They had wanted a pool, he said, but not
at that price! With the others, he began organizing his first picket
line: they had posters and placards made up, denouncing both
City College and Webster Hall; then, calling a rally, they threw
a cordon of college students around the hotel, keeping regular
picketing hours without a letup.

The demonstration drew city-wide attention. News reporters
got hold of the story, and the papers played it up with photos
and editorials criticizing the administration of the municipal
institution that would have permitted racial discrimination in a
commodity for students if the more socially minded among them
had not protested. The contract was quickly canceled. The students lost their pool privileges, a keen disappointment to all; but
Walter Reuther had savored his initial taste of victory in a picket-
line contest over a principle basic to his whole being. Doubtless
there were many students who wished he had kept his mouth

shut, but where the question of human rights was concerned he could no more keep quiet than he could prevent himself from plunging into the thick of any battle for social justice.

This was the second time he had stood up against racial prejudice since coming to Detroit. Before then, though he knew the problem existed, he had never come face to face with it; certainly there was no such feeling in the Reuther family circle. The "whole business" wasn't real to him until he ran headlong into stubborn resistance to his theory of applied Christianity from the Southern Baptist family he had roomed with on his arrival. Detroit had been teeming with racial tension from the time Henry Ford had offered his historic five-dollar-a-day paycheck to unskilled workers back in 1914, opening the floodgates of full employment—or so they thought—to thousands of poor people from the South. Black and white came pouring in: hill billies from Tennessee and Kentucky were thrown together with Negroes not only from the same states but also from farther south. The mixture was dynamite, which in few years, and again more than three decades later (in 1968) was to explode in some of the bloodiest race riots of both eras. But to the unsuspecting Walter Reuther in 1927, it seemed incredible that a family who were devout Christians like his Baptist boardinghouse keepers, and who were very good to him, could harbor such antagonistic loathing toward "their brother who is black," as he told them one Sunday after they had repeatedly asked him to go to church with them and he refused again. Were they merely Sunday-Christians? he wondered. But they in turn wondered at his attitude; with a prejudice ingrained for generations, they simply could not or would not understand it. Finally, when they asked him once more to go to church with them, he made them a proposition: he would go if they could answer one question for him. They would be glad to, they said. But when the question came— Did they think Negroes, who had followed the Scriptures and led a true Christian life, would go to the same Heaven as they? the man and his wife both answered indignantly, "Of course not!"

Walter, with an angelic smile, had told them, "Now, you see why I can't go to church with you."

The Southerners still shook their heads, but they did not ask him again. However, the incident had marked the beginning of a concern for minority groups and racial equality that was to last throughout his life.

At the moment, after the success of their tryout, Walter and Victor rallied their club members to reinforce the picket line at the Briggs body plant. Roy had found a job there as an electrician, and was working under the same sweatshop conditions Walter had experienced, until a young firebrand named Emil Mazey had decided the moment had come to strike against the unfair practices. It was Walter's first contact with a staunch standard-bearer of labor unions, one who would be his lifelong associate and one of the top-ranking officers in the UAW.

The lively if crowded household of active, working, studying roommates was, for all its frugality and cramped quarters, not without a certain *Gemütlichkeit*. On weekends when they were all there, the Reuther brothers, carrying on their father's custom, might get up a Sunday afternoon debate on some topical subject; or they would sing some of the old German folksongs he had taught them. Occasionally, on Saturday night, after they had finished studying at about eleven o'clock, they would go out on "whore-ology tours," an extra curricula course on their own. They didn't have to go far for research: plenty of girls were on the streets and once they were sure that the boys' questions were simply a matter of academic interest and did not come from detectives in civilian clothes, they gave detailed, often graphic replies about their profession. It was most enlightening, Merlin Bishop recalled. At home on weekends, Victor's bubbling pots of soup, stew or preserves frequently gave off a delicious fragrance, and there was a lot of good-natured joshing but rarely any real bickering among the boys. They were all too busy, preoccupied with studies and the problems of the depression.

By the summer of 1932, business had slowed down almost to a standstill. As one company after another was forced to retrench or close doors altogether, the number of unemployed kept rising: four million during the winter of 1930–31; eight million by the summer of 1931; twelve million in the winter of 1932; fifteen million before the summer was over. Lines of shabby, hungry men and women waited for hours for a cup of weak coffee and a doughnut, or a little watery soup and a piece of bread. Often the queue would extend all the way around a city block.

Detroit was one of the worst hit of the big cities. There, as in many industrial areas, the resources of local and state governments were running out, and even the Salvation Army had difficulty in fulfilling its traditional role of feeding the hungry. From the windows of their basement apartment, the boys would see the feet of poor people passing by, some having nothing but burlap sacks wrapped around as makeshift shoes; often the footsteps would stop at the nearest garbage cans, which were raided regularly by the hungry.

Walter Reuther himself was not affected. As a die leader in the employ of the Ford Motor Company, he was making more money than he ever had before, $1.45 an hour. Henry Ford, in spite of the depression, had abandoned his Model A, and was planning to go into production with a much more powerful, up-to-date car, the V-8. All his plants were shut down for retooling, and with the exception of the tool- and diemakers, his 250,000 employees were out of work. Nobody knew when they would get their jobs back. National elections were coming up in November, with Franklin D. Roosevelt running against a weary and perplexed Herbert Hoover, who could only reaffirm his forlorn hope that prosperity was just around the corner. Another candidate was Norman Thomas, Socialist, who was not given a ghost of a chance. Many American intellectuals had great respect for Thomas personally, but probably did not plan to vote for him because they did not believe he could win.

Walter supported Norman Thomas, and the Reuther brothers, Merlin Bishop, and a few others plotted an extensive campaign throughout the state in defiance of all obstacles. The worst hurdle was right near home, in ultraconservative Dearborn, where it was considered heresy to back a Socialist. Public meetings were forbidden, and a petition to hold a rally was denied. Refusal was like waving a red flag to Walter Reuther once his mind was set on an idea; this time it evoked another, brilliant, scheme. The lot he and Ted had bought was only a few blocks from the factory, and he knew from the little prelaw study he had had that a man commands full rights on his own property. Building a two-by-four wood platform over the rumble seat of his old Ford coupe, he drove it onto the vacant lot belonging to him, and with megaphone in hand clambered up and began making a speech for Norman Thomas. The idle unemployed were everywhere that year; soon a large crowd gathered to hear about the candidate and his proposed sweeping changes in the economy. Police came to investigate the crowd, and as Walter had expected, tried to stop him. "This is private property, bud," one of them called. "Get out of here!"

Walter's face lit up in his wickedly triumphant grin. "I know it's private property, officer," he said. "I happen to own it." He had come prepared and flashed the deed in the cop's face.

Confounded in their authority, the police were stumped; but only for a few minutes. After a hurried conference, they returned with stakes, which were pounded in the four corners of the lot as markers for roping it off. Walter could make a speech on his own property within the law, but his listeners would have to stay within the lines of the lot. Naturally the space couldn't hold much of a crowd, and the people soon dispersed.

Undaunted, young Reuther planned to carry the campaign into rural areas and northern Michigan. He and Merlin Bishop were to take Merlin's secondhand seven-passenger Buick brougham—converted into a two-passenger sleeping car by the ingenious campaigners—and cover the fruitbelt and farmlands, with stops in such towns as Muskegon, Lansing, Port Huron, Bay City, Grand Rapids, and as far north as Traverse City. Victor and another recruit continued the campaign trail from there on through the Upper Peninsula, into the mining region around Newberry, Michigan. Roy Reuther, although as dedicated as his brothers to Socialist philosophy and their father's theory of applied Christianity, was the most reserved of the Reuther sons; he had little liking for public speaking and throughout his long career in the labor movement rarely made appearances in person or on radio and television. He preferred to make his contribution to society in a behind-the-scenes role.

Walter, on the other hand, was a born speaker. Besides the eloquence he had inherited from his father, he had other personality traits that helped to captivate an audience: humor; a fiery delivery that did not rely on old-fashioned oratory and evangelism but rather on reason and logic; and a special faculty for getting close to people. Now, he and Merlin toured the state on weekends or during any spare time they had, driving along with a huge eight-foot poster reading "Vote for Norman Thomas—Repeal Unemployment" fastened on the top of the car and a homemade platform attached to the rear bumper, plus plenty of paper ammunition in the form of pamphlets and lists of old Socialists from Debs's final campaign in 1920. Walter was hailed with new hope as Comrade Reuther by those who saw in him a red-haired version of their beloved Gene; who chuckled over his words of biting wit in ridicule of the hapless Hoover. For his part, Walter was having the time of his life. He had a warm feeling for people and enjoyed hearing their reactions to his ideas. He would spend hours talking with some chicken farmer about economics, until Merlin would have to remind him of the territory to be covered in two days' time.

During his vacation that year, Walter campaigned for Thomas in his home town, and with his brothers' help he organized a big rally for the Socialist candidate in the West Virginia area. On his return to Detroit, he of course carried his campaigning into the Ford plant, presenting Thomas' "sweeping changes" and the plan to repeal unemployment with particular emphasis. His fellow workers, the few who had jobs and the thousands who milled around outside the employment office, liked to hear "the young redhead" talk. He spoke with such conviction, and what he said seemed to make sense. But on election day, as he later acknowledged, "almost to a man, they voted for Franklin D. Roosevelt."

And so, incidentally, did his father! Val Reuther, staunch admirer of Debs as he had been, continued to examine the records of the candidates and "vote for the best man, whatever his party." He had been following Roosevelt's record as governor of New York, when in the darkening months from 1930 to 1932, FDR was one of the few who had taken measures to bring his state out of the depression.

As Walter talked to his fellow workers in the Ford plants for Norman Thomas' political platform, he also had continued quietly advocating a union in the auto industry; but until now, he had not received much response. Ford had not cut the pay of its work force the way most firms had. Walter as die leader had not been affected at all. But after the election, when business in general slacked off even further, the pay cuts began.

One day the foreman lined up the men just before the lunch hour and announced a five-cent pay cut. Whatever the workers felt, they made no verbal protest; but then, right after lunch, a second five-cent-an-hour pay cut was announced! The men were furious. Management would have done better, Walter thought, to cut them ten cents all at once. The deaf mutes, who until now had shown little interest in unionism, didn't even bother trying their sign language, but handed Walter a note on which was scribbled, "Let's start the revolution now."

A few weeks after the election, while he was still one of the highest-paid mechanics in the Ford Motor Company, with forty men under his supervision, Walter found the fatal pink slip in his pay envelope: he was fired for "incompetence!" His organizing efforts had probably been disclosed by company spies, who were distributed through Ford factories to ferret out and report any attempts at unionizing the workers. He was also blacklisted, which meant that he could not get a job in the auto industry anywhere in the United States. "In fact," he used to boast, "I think I may have enjoyed the distinction of being number one on the blacklist!"

He was actually relieved, even elated, at being let out of his job. For several months he and Victor, at the instigation of their sociology professor, had been planning a laboratory course of their own, studying working conditions in other parts of the world. Walter's dismissal meant that their chance to broaden their horizons was at hand. He went home that night feeling he had been liberated. "I've been fired," he told Vic. "Now I'm free and nothing stands in our way. We can go on that trip."

Their dean, whom they had to notify, was delighted to hear they were going and confessed that he had wanted to join their side in some of their campus battles, but had had to stand by because of administration policy. Walter had guessed that the Social Service Club had proved a gadfly instead of a boon to the college faculty. "We were certainly a big load off that professor's mind," he said afterward, chuckling.

In the meantime Henry Ford, who would fire one of his highest-paid and presumably most valuable die leaders because he suspected him of being a "Communist organizer," did not hesitate to enter into business deals with the Russian Communists if those deals might show a profit. Ford had sold a complete set of the tools and dies for his Model A to the Soviet Union. Russians came streaming into Detroit to study American industrial techniques in the department Ford had set up for them in one of his plants, as part of the agreement.

Joseph Stalin had just begun a five-year plan to industrialize his vast domain, and Russian representatives were recruiting foreign engineers and skilled workmen. American engineers and men with the training and background of Walter Reuther were to help build the big power dams, like the one at Stalingrad, and to teach the Russians how to manufacture automobiles, trucks, and tractors.

Naturally it occurred to Walter that here was his chance to earn his way while taking the professor's advice to see the world. He applied to the Amtorg Trading Company, the business branch of the Soviet government, as an experienced die leader, and was immediately offered a job. There would be a place for both him and Victor in an automobile plant near Gorki, he was assured. But they would have to get to the Soviet border on their own. So the Reuther brothers decided to head for Russia, although they had to wait a short time until Victor was twenty-one. Before he came of age he could not get a passport without his parents' approval, and he and Walter had doubts about that.

Walter had saved some eight hundred dollars. Early in January, 1933, he went to the bank and withdrew the money, since he and Victor were preparing to leave on their journey. A day or two later there was a run on the bank and it was forced to close its doors—one of the first of a long list of banks that suffered the same fate during the next two months.

"Walter used to say he felt guilty," Victor recalled, "as if drawing out his eight hundred dollars had started the run on that bank!"

VI

Travelers in Nazi Germany

ONE cold morning in January, 1933, Walter and Victor Reuther were awakened before dawn by their brother Roy, who had come to say good-bye, as he was leaving for strike duty. The workers at Briggs were still out, since the company refused to recognize their union. Roy was cooking in a makeshift kitchen for the men on the picket line. He had to be out there early, for a mug of steaming hot coffee, however weak and tasteless, was a godsend to a man about to take his place at dawn in the slow procession moving doggedly back and forth, back and forth, for hours in front of the plant gate. Although he probably would have preferred accompanying his brothers, Roy was steadfast in his support of the strike and felt he should stay with it till the end. In February, while Walter and Victor were on shipboard, Detroit police smashed the picket line, inflicting a wound that scarred Roy for life when he was shoved against a spike in an iron fence.

As soon as it was light, Walter and Victor drove out of Detroit in Walter's "old beat-up Ford," heading for Wheeling to see their parents before setting out on their adventure, which, though they did not know it then, would last nearly three years and take them around the world. They thought they had better break the news gradually at home, but as it turned out, Val and Anna Reuther raised no serious objection. They were not terribly happy about the prospect of a lengthy separation, Victor thought, but of course they had no idea quite how long it would be, or where the boys were going to be working, or when. However, Walter felt that both parents understood the need for young people to reach out and do the things they wanted to do. Their father definitely approved their plan to get a practical background to tie in with the recent academic training in economics and sociology, and which they could apply in their future careers, and their mother took comfort in the fact that her sons would be visiting her home town and would meet some of her relatives. As to the prospective jobs in Russia, all the Reuthers were interested in discovering whether the Socialist theory would work when put into practice; and all shared a certain excitement at watching a relatively backward country move into modern industrialism. Almost every night during their farewell visit, Walter took Victor to his old teacher's machine shop at Wheeling High for a short refresher course, so the younger brother would at least know the rudiments in auto mechanics as an instructor in Russia.

After saying good-bye to the family, Walter and Victor boarded a bus for New York, having no definite plans beyond eventually arriving in Russia and reporting for work. Their passport visas to enter the Soviet Union had not yet come, but that was not unusual, for in 1933 the United States had no diplomatic relations with the USSR. The young Reuthers would go to Germany first, and they hoped to see something of the rest of Europe before entering Russia. They carried with them letters from their parents to their German relatives, and from some of their college professors to colleagues in Europe. The night before they sailed from New York they had dinner with a group of professors and writers, all liberals and friends of their professors at the college in Detroit —a glamorous experience for two young men who put such high value on learning and intellectual achievement.

Whatever misgivings Anna and Val Reuther may have had about the trip were allayed to some extent by the fact that their sons would be able to send back news of the German relatives. Conditions in Germany, from the scanty reports that filtered out, were unsettled and ominous, and an obscure, psychotic Austrian house painter was rapidly rising to power. Old President von Hindenburg had been forced by popular clamor to appoint Adolf

Hitler Chancellor of the German Republic, the Reich. After her defeat in World War One and the subsequent downfall of the Weimar Republic, a weak, short-lived attempt at democracy, Germany had suffered serious inflation and greater unemployment than the Reuthers had just left in the United States. For several years the country had been in a terrible economic depression, and in their desperate search for a leader, the German people apparently did not care who he was or what he did, so long as he did *something*.

The Reuthers arrived in Hamburg on February 24, 1933, after an eight-day crossing, in steerage. They had to make the trip as cheaply as possible, for Walter's savings could not last forever, and they had already spent some of it on equipment. "Before we left Detroit," Victor recalled, "we went to some secondhand stores where automechanics hocked their tools when they were out of work. Walter bought a lot of tools and instruments, some very delicate and expensive. And we also outfitted ourselves with heavy clothing which we thought we'd need—and certainly did."

The brothers' first contact in Hamburg, a wealthy businessman to whom they had a letter of introduction from one of their professors, unfortunately turned out to be among the many who had been converted to Nazism. He was, in fact, a recently appointed party proselyte, who was trying to promote Hitler's regime of hatred and brutality, not only among native Germans but those of German background in other countries. He welcomed Walter and Victor as two most likely prospects, not realizing that he was dealing with two "radical" trade unionists, one of them a dynamic, fiery-tempered torchbearer for the brotherhood of man. At the mention of Hitler's vow to "hang a Jew from every lamppost," the Reuther wrath came down on the prominent industrialist's head with lightning velocity. Walter hurled a volley of invectives, abetted by Victor's variations, against the man for embracing such doctrine or expecting them to be so gullible as to fall for it. Without giving him a chance to recover from surprise and retaliate, they slammed out of the house, still steaming.

Luckily, they had another letter to a Hamburg citizen, this one from a fellow worker of Walter at the Rouge plant, whose uncle lived in the German seaport town. An unemployed dock worker, he was happy to receive greetings from his nephew in Detroit, and invited the travelers to stay with him. Here the atmosphere was openly antagonistic toward the *Führer,* and at night they could hear the gunfire of the storm troopers, who rode up and down the streets taking shots at the anti-Hitler placards in workers' windows. The two Reuthers had been there about three days when one night shocking news came from Berlin. The Reichstag—the German House of Parliament—was burning. Excited voices over the radio shouted that a large area of the city was lighted up as flames roared up the broad stairways, spread through the historic old palace, and shot up to the roof. Fires had apparently started simultaneously in several parts of the building. Obviously they had been set deliberately; nothing could save it.

Walter and Victor took the next train to Berlin, and they were among the first visitors to be shown through the charred, still smoking ruins by young Nazi guides, who assured them that the fires had been started by Communists. This was hard to believe, especially coming from Hitler's handpicked corps of henchmen. From the beginning the Reuthers were disgusted and dismayed by the conduct of the storm troopers, who swaggered through the streets, pushing people off the sidewalks, or racing in their cars, shooting into peoples' homes at random, as they had in Hamburg. They wore brown shirts, and when they met, each would stiffly raise his right arm, shouting, *"Heil Hitler!"* At first, Walter and Victor thought this was funny, and mimicked the salute in private, but it did not amuse them long.

In May of that year, a mob of German students dragged some twenty thousand volumes out of the library of the University of Berlin and burned them in a huge bonfire on a street called Unter den Linden, with the smiling approval of Dr. Joseph Goebbels, Hitler's Minister of Propaganda. Into the flames went many priceless books, the work of some of the finest writers, philosophers, poets, and scientists Germany had produced. Many of the authors were Jews, but not all of them. Some were foreigners—Jack London, H. G. Wells, Havelock Ellis, André Gide, Émile Zola, and even so dangerous a character as Helen Keller! The Reuthers were in England at that time, but they heard about it; and there were other book burnings in university towns all over Germany, some of which they witnessed with horrified, incredulous eyes. Having been brought up with respect, even reverence, for books, their father's greatest treasures, they could not understand how the people of Germany could even countenance, let alone bring to power, a mentally warped politico who sponsored such vandalism and wanton waste of intellectual wealth.

Not all Germans were for Hitler, of course. On the train going to Berlin they had been in the same compartment with a worried trade-union officer, who was shot the next day by the Nazis, and two young workers, who showed much interest in the American labor movement. One of them, a small, wiry fellow by the name of Emil Gross, kept asking questions about conditions in Detroit factories, trade-union organizing among auto workers, and such. When they all left the train, he gave the brothers his address, which was not far from the station, and invited them to stay at his house while they were in Berlin. After their tour of the Reichstag ruins they looked him up, and discovered that his house was headquarters for a group of anti-Nazi students and workers, who were glad to have the like-minded young Americans with them.

Walter and Victor stayed with them about ten days, and during most of the nights left their clothes on so that if they were raided by storm troopers—as they expected to be any moment— they could all make a fast getaway. At least once the Americans saved their friends, when they were holding a secret meeting of German students and some "brownshirts" burst in. Walter and Victor called out loudly in English: "We're foreigners, students. You can't touch us." The storm troopers left without dragging anybody off. But the trick would not always work, and on another night they all slid down a rope from the window of a student's room just as the Nazis broke in the front door.

Emil Gross—whose nickname was *der Kleine* ("the little fellow"), probably because his body belied his surname, which means "large" in English—was the leader of the embryo resistance, and his courage and stamina lent strength and guidance to all of them. The Reuthers grew very fond of Emil during their stay, but decided it was time for them to head south to see their relatives. Later, they heard that two nights after they left, the storm troopers had not only raided the resistance headquarters, but wrecked the house, killing all the students except one or two who managed to escape. Shocked and worried though they were, Walter and Victor both agreed that if two people got out safely, *der Kleine* must be one of them; and sure enough, he turned up as they were leaving for Dresden! His plan was to join them in their journey, he told the overjoyed Reuthers, and then, at the southern border, cross into Switzerland, where he could take refuge for a time. The three traveled together from Dresden to Nuremberg and on down to Stuttgart, not far from Scharnhausen, where *Mütterchen's* relatives, still living in her native village, were eagerly waiting for her sons. They bade good-bye and Godspeed to Emil; and the next they heard from the intrepid little worker, he had left Switzerland for Amsterdam, Holland, where he set up another reesistance movement, called the New Beginning.

The Reuthers could not help admiring Emil's stubborn opposition, which, from all that they had seen, was more than justified. Besides their own experiences in Berlin, they had learned on a brief stop at Edigheim, their grandfather's old village, that a cousin had been arrested by the Gestapo and spirited away, no one knew where. There was worse to come. For the rest of their lives the Reuther brothers would never forget the scenes that took place in the once peaceful village where their mother was born. At the outset, a squad of storm troopers marched through the streets, stopping at certain houses, which they entered, dragging men out and beating them almost to death. When the brothers asked who the victims were, they were told that these were union leaders, most of them from small locals. Since trade unions had in a way started in Germany, with the medieval guilds, the brown-shirted bullies had no trouble finding union leaders to maul. The next day they built a bonfire of all the union flags in the village square, shouting that they would build the Third Reich on the ashes. As one union member reached out to rescue his flag from the flames, he was clubbed and beaten in front of everyone. A Lutheran pastor looked on with a pained expression, helpless to stop the brutality. Important union officials, the Reuthers learned, were apt to be taken away in the middle of the night, destination unknown. Long after the Reuthers left Germany, the outside world learned about the concentration camps, where many of those men died. Presently unions were abolished, along with all political parties save Hitler's own.

Except for one uncle, who was vice-mayor of the village—and with whom his American nephews had "some pretty rough arguments"—Walter and Victor were glad to learn that their relatives were anti-Nazi. They were especially pleased by two lively girl cousins whose father belonged to the typographers' union, and who didn't hesitate to speak their minds.

One evening they invited the girls to go to a movie house in Stuttgart; a Nazi propaganda film was playing, and Walter was curious to see if there was anything in it to make the party more appealing to the populace. He could find very little, except that the absurd yet menacing face of Adolf Hitler shouting irrationally seemed to have a diabolical magnetism for the audience, sending them into mass hysteria. And at the end, as a huge reverse swastika flashed on the screen and the band struck up, the people rose in a body, right arms stiffly stretched forward, palms down, to sing the "Horst Wessel Song." Walter was determined not to salute that twisted emblem and all it stood for, or sing the frenzied song. He stayed in his seat, and Victor and the girls stuck with him. At first the patrons around them nudged them to stand, with stage-whisper curses; but when they wouldn't budge, shouts of "They're Communists! Throw them out!" resounded above the singing and people began to shove them. Walter and Victor shouted back in English, "We're Americans—tourists!" waving their passports. But the overwrought crowd paid no attention; and the brothers, suddenly realizing the danger of the situation, stood up, taking the girls by the arms and "got them the hell out of there fast," as Victor put it, amid further scuffling and pushing. None of them was seriously harmed in the hair-raising but somehow exhilarating experience of defying the new dictator. In a quieter moment they realized, however, that even at that early date, before the "referendum" took place, the German people had no choice except to conform completely or pay the price.

Before leaving Scharnhausen, the boys bought bicycles in Stuttgart; pedaling was a cheaper way to travel than by train, and they both had strong, muscular legs. Their visas for Russia were supposed to come to Berlin, through an American friend, John

Rushton, who had worked with Walter at the Rouge and had preceded them to Gorki by several months. So Walter and Victor rode back up through Germany in easy stages, only to learn, when they checked at the office of the Amtorg Trading Company, that the papers had not arrived and the clerks could give them no indication how long it would take. This was their chance to make the "social engineering" tour of western Europe they had outlined to the family in Wheeling. Their plan was to go through factories, mines, and mills, exchanging ideas with trade unionists, Socialists, and economists in as many countries as they could manage to investigate. And in the next nine months or so they visited several countries besides traveling all over Germany and Austria. They went to Belgium, Holland, Switzerland, France, Italy (where Victor caused their second clash with totalitarian rule when he tried to get a snapshot of *il Duce* during a parade in Rome, bringing cries of *"Basta!"* and threatening fists from fierce guards), and to England, Scotland, and Wales; they went everywhere.

They carried bedrolls, and usually bedded down in open fields, preferably on a haymow if they could find one. One night in France, exhausted after a long day's pedaling, they spread their tarpaulins over what appeared to be a stock of straw, but in the morning they found they had been sleeping on a mound of manure! They "ate off the land," Victor said, "spending very little for food." Sometimes, for a few cents, they would buy vegetables from the farmers, and maybe a bit of meat or fruit, or an egg or two, or some cheese. "And sometimes," Victor added, "I'll admit we snitched our food out of the fields." They were traveling during the spring and summer months, cooking outdoors.

From time to time they returned to Berlin, to see if the visas had come, but the answer was always "Not yet"; and though they were annoyed because it took so long, they used the delay to good advantage by extending their "social engineering tour," in the course of which they were drawn into performing an unexpected serivce to the forces of freedom. As they presented their letters of introduction to the German colleagues of their professors in Detroit, the Reuthers learned that many of the German university professors and students were opposed to Hitler. Even then they were secretly organizing inside Germany the movement that William L. Shirer, in *The Rise and Fall of the Third Reich,* described as "a small and feeble" underground against Hitler. Through some of these people, as well as Emil Gross, whom they saw in Amsterdam when they toured Holland, the two young Americans soon became active in the movement. From Emil they heard that small underground headquarters had been set up in Switzerland and the British Isles by people who had managed to escape. Since the Reuthers, as Americans, could cross the borders without difficulty, their contribution to the underground consisted chiefly in transporting messages back and forth between those still in Germany and those who had escaped.

As there were a number of British automobile plants Walter and Victor wanted to inspect, they made several trips to England, taking their bicycles aboard the little channel steamer at Cherbourg. After sightseeing in London, making contacts here and there, they headed for rural and industrial areas. Roads in England were rough, often covered with loose, untarred gravel. They had very little to eat, for funds were running low, but somehow they kept going. They were shown through the Ford, Austin, and Morris auto plants, went down into the coal mines near Manchester, and saw textile mills in North Wales and Scotland.

Not wanting to neglect the cultural aspect, they made a trip to Shakespeare's home, Stratford-on-Avon. When they were seeking shelter from the wind by riding close behind a truck on a gravelly road near that town, Walter had to turn sharply as the truck made a sudden swerve. His front tire blew, and he was thrown into the road, getting a nasty gash all along his arm from the stones. A passing car took him to the nearest hospital, where his arm was treated and put in a sling. The two brothers continued on their tour, but for three weeks Walter was severely hampered, and Victor had to hold the handlebars for him as he got on or off the bicycle. More than once they thought of turning back, but as usual, determination won out over adversity. Besides, they had a mission to deliver messages for the German underground.

It was a risky business that required acting ability, patience, and secrecy. They would leave London and travel to some small town in the Ruhr, Germany's most important steel-producing area. Going to a designated bookshop, they would ask for a certain rare volume. If the bookseller would say he didn't have it, nor expect to get it in, Walter, who was usually the spokesman, would feign surprise. "Why, we were told we could find it here! Do you know of any other shop that might carry it?" The man would give them the name of another book store, and they would begin the act all over. Sometimes they had to contact as many as eight names before reaching the right person; and in the finale of each mission, the moment of exchange was a unique and thrilling climax, involving a singular and mutual emotion. In Walter's words, "It was amazing the instantaneous bond that seemed to spring up between us, what we felt for him and he for us . . . as if we had known each other all our lives and been the closest of friends. Yet we had never seen each other before—and probably never would again. It was one of the strangest sensations of my life. It resulted, I suppose, from the fact that we were both engaged in a desperate business, with our lives at stake if we were caught, and this gave both of us a feeling of solidarity—it made you feel in that moment that the man you had made contact with and were talking to was the closest human being in the whole world to you."

Although he and Victor completed many such missions—always with the same extraordinary effect—they were never detected by the Gestapo. When they were in Russia, they heard that *der Kleine*, rash enough to go back to Germany, had been arrested and carried off, undoubtedly to a concentration camp. They could learn no details, and no further news came from him directly, so they feared the worst. The Reuthers remembered him through the years and used to talk about him sometimes. Then, one day in 1958, when Victor was in his office in Washington, where he was Director of the International Affairs Department of the UAW, he received a call from someone in the State Department asking if he would see an important German publisher. He said of course he would; and who should walk into the office but *der Kleine!* Victor could hardly believe his eyes, and in telling the incredible epilogue, he related, "I called Walter in Detroit, and at first he thought I was kidding him. We took the next plane out there, and you can imagine what an evening the three of us had, talking over old times and hearing all the things that had happened to

Emil." Gross had somehow survived the concentration camp; and following World War Two had become a publisher of trade-union journals in West Germany.

Spring and summer and the early autumn came and went. The boys had run out of funds, so their father cashed in a small life insurance policy and sent them the money. Finally, in late November, they received their visas—with help from John Rushton at the Molotov plant—and, shipping their bicycles ahead, they took the train across Poland into Russia.

VII

"The Workers' Paradise"

It was thirty degrees below zero that night in December, 1933, when Walter and Victor Reuther arrived in the town of Gorki, 250 miles northeast of Moscow, where jobs awaited them in the sprawling automobile plant Henry Ford had built for Joseph Stalin.

The Reuthers still had on the knickers and jackets they had worn while bicycling through western Europe. Assuming that they would need immediately the tools Walter had bought in Detroit and had had shipped to the Russian border, they had left their heavy winter clothes and their bicycles to be sent on to them in Gorki. The tools were heavy and cumbersome. Some they had packed in suitcases, the rest they carried in knapsacks on their backs.

So cold and stiff, after their long trip in a crowded, practically unheated train, that they felt as though their legs might break as they gingerly bent their knees, they managed somehow to squeeze themselves aboard a broken-down old trolley car, packed in so tightly that they could not even find room to set down their heavy suitcases. Some of the Russians clung to the roof, others, to the sides. As the car swayed and lurched over rough tracks, they were continually shoved and jostled by their fellow passengers. Since they spoke no Russian, they were not even certain that they were headed for their destination. They had repeated the name "Molotov" over and over, and some of the Russians had pointed at the trolley car. Apparently they had grown accustomed to directing foreigners to the plant.

The boys came to the end of the line at the edge of the town, and off in the distance, far out in the night, they saw the shadowy outlines of the big plant. They still had a mile and a half to go— on foot. Stretching and readjusting the packs on their backs, they picked up their suitcases and started out. It was so cold that the air seemed to freeze their lungs every time they took a deep breath.

When they finally arrived, they looked up John Rushton in the *Amerikanski pasholik,* or American village. In his chilly cubicle in a barracks they were gratefully gulping down hot tea when someone noticed that one of the pockets in Walter's jacket had been neatly slit open and the contents removed.

"This," Walter used to say years later, with a grin, "was my introduction to the workers' paradise!"

Fortunately the few precious American dollars he had left were in a money belt strapped around his waist under his clothing, and his passport was in an inside pocket, less accessible. The papers that had been taken were letters, of value only to Walter.

"It was probably done by kids," their host explained. "There are gangs of them roving about all over the place. Orphans, mostly, homeless and hungry. What they were really after was your foreign money. American dollars will bring a lot of rubles on the black market."

Early the following morning, Walter and Victor moved into their quarters, an icy little cell eight feet long and seven feet wide. When their bicycles arrived, they had to hang them from the ceiling. They were shown a one-burner electric stove which they would share with the family of an Italian skilled workman who had fled from Mussolini.

When the Reuthers went over to the plant, they found that it was entirely unheated, except for one small heat-treat department, where they tempered metals. Here they went to warm up every little while, as their hands would get stiff in the below-zero temperature of the workbench, even though they wore heavy gloves, part of their winter clothing, which soon arrived. They wore flannel-lined shoes and sheepskin coats.

Foreign engineers and skilled workmen had put up the building, built and installed an electric plant, put in the wiring, set up the old Ford basic machinery, and had left. Only about forty foreigners, mostly tool- and diemakers from the United States and western Europe, remained. It would be their job to teach hundreds of peasants—most of whom had never even seen any equipment more complicated than a pitchfork or a wheelbarrow—how to make tools and dies for a Russian version of the Model A Ford.

Walter, with his superior skill and his obvious ability to get along well with the workmen, became a foreman. Under his general supervision were several hundred untrained peasants and a "brigade" of sixteen *udarnik* (shock-troop) workers that received special training as tool- and diemakers. Until he learned to speak Russian, he could communicate with them only through an interpreter and by showing them with his own hands what they were supposed to do. Victor had picked up enough knowledge of tool- and diemaking and assembly lines so that he was a valuable assistant. Surrounded by people who speak a foreign language, one masters that language rather quickly, and the Reuthers did. They were the youngest foreign employees, and, on a three-shift basis, worked eight hours a day, six days a week.

Teaching illiterate, untrained peasants how to make tools and dies was slow work—painfully slow. So much precision was required. Walter recalled that they worked several months before they produced a single usable die. They would often have to make fifteen or twenty before they turned out a perfect one. Part of this delay was due to the administrative inefficiency of Soviet bureaucracy: the blueprints would not come through in time for his department to produce their monthly quota of dies; and half the time no "part prints" at all. Also, safety rules were lacking. In a letter of complaint to the Moscow *Daily News*, Walter pointed out these flaws, and made certain suggestions which would correct them and ensure better production. His letter brought action, and reforms were made, increasing production. By the time Walter and Victor left, eighteen months later, the Russians were making only five or six dies a month. But, slow and awkward though they were, they managed to produce a crude copy of the Model A.

"Those first cars," Victor remembered, "looked a little like a Model A, although they were built higher, up off the ground, more like the old Model T. This was necessary, for a car that hugged the ground could never have made it over the terrible Russian roads. In that entire area there was only half a mile of paved road, approaching the plant.

"The doors didn't fit well, and some of the functional parts that require very special skill on the part of the tool- and diemaker did not work as they should. The paint job was bad, but to the Russians the appearance of the car was unimportant, so long as it could be driven. And, with all its imperfections, they were slowly turning out cars that could be driven—after a fashion."

They were, of course, by no means the first automobiles ever manufactured in Russia. In Moscow, there was a big automobile plant which, back in the Czarist days, before World War One, had turned out beautifully made—and very expensive cars. And there was still in Russia a nucleus of highly skilled engineers and well-trained mechanics, although many had been shot as counterrevolutionaries. But good as they were, they were unfamiliar with American mass-production methods, the assembly line, the tools and dies that were essential in its operation. It was the American assembly line, turning out inexpensive automobiles with amazing rapidity, that Stalin wanted and needed to industrialize speedily this vast country, with its unlimited resources and its millions of illiterate, untrained peasants. Many Russian engineers and skilled mechanics—Communist party members, who could be trusted—were sent to the United States to study American assembly-line production at firsthand.

From the beginning, the Reuthers were impressed by the patience of the workers, their earnest desire to learn, their eagerness to take advantage of the promises held out to them by their Communist bosses. Nobody had ever promised them anything before. Now, far off in the distance, there was held up a bright, shimmering dream of a beautiful life, in which they all could share—if they worked hard enough for it.

For the present, of course, they were little better off than they had been under the czars. Food was very scarce, clothing almost unattainable.

Practically every ounce of steel that went into those cars had to be imported from the West—from Sweden, Germany, England, the United States. The Russians had some steel mills, but many of them were old and obsolete, and even the big new mills in the Moscow and Leningrad areas and the Ukraine were not all equipped to turn out the kind of rolled steel used in the making of the body of an assembly-line automobile. Since the ruble was worthless outside the Soviet Union, the Russians had to ship any goods they had in exchange for foreign currency with which to buy that costly steel. So the peasants, who had always been poor anyway, had to tighten their belts even more patiently, their eyes fixed on that far-off dream.

They started laboriously learning how to build those first crude assembly-line cars that were a source of wonder and pride to them. Although none of them could own one, they found themselves in possession of some articles they had never expected to have. Real leather shoes, for instance. Most of the workers came from small villages and farms. All their lives they had gone barefooted in the summertime, had wrapped their feet and legs in burlap and straw during the long, cold winters. Working in the plant, they had to have shoes, for the floor was littered with sharp-edged scraps of steel which would cut their feet. So they were issued shoes, the money to pay for them being taken out of their meager earnings.

Victor Reuther recalled seeing them approaching the plant, over that half-mile strip of pavement, in their bare feet or wearing their clumsy, shabby winter footwear, carrying those precious shoes. Not until they reached the plant entrance would they sit down on the curb, carefully wipe their feet, and put on their shoes.

"I was puzzled, and asked them why they did it," he said. "They looked surprised and shocked. What? Wear out those beautiful leather shoes walking through the mud or on that hard pavement? Unthinkable!"

The peasants' idea of the wonderful future ahead was given to them mostly by alert, well-trained young Communists, sent out from Moscow to indoctrinate them, to exhort them to work harder, to make bigger sacrifices. Comparatively few of the workmen were actually taken into the party—the Communist party in Russia has always been the party of the elite. The idea was to hold out promises to the peasants that would make them docile, willing to make sacrifices—and work.

"Of course, everything was run by the Communists," Walter recalled. "The management was Communist. They had a union in the plant, to which everybody belonged. But it didn't mean anything—it was just a propaganda device. For it, too, was run by the Communists and had no bargaining power. The Communist management, the Communist-dominated union, and the Commnuist party in the plant, to which some of the men belonged, were referred to as the Triangle.

"On top of that, we were overrun by Communist inspectors from Moscow, who had no knowledge whatever of what they were inspecting. They were a nuisance, for when we finally did get started, they kept fouling up my assembly line."

As part of that bright future ahead, all the peasant were supposed to learn how to read and write. Almost to a man, they were illiterate—they had never had any chance to be anything but illiterate. The young Communists from Moscow were very much in earnest about this, and the peasants were slow, but willing, pupils.

Education for the children was compulsory, and the system was spreading rapidly throughout European Russia and her Asiatic "republics." In the early 1930's, however, the education, beyond reading and writing, was confined almost entirely to work with tools—shop. And the government was turning out thousands of hastily and not very well trained "technicians." Not much could be expected of an educational system in a land where there was practically no paper, where the most precious possession a child could own was a common lead pencil. But the young Communists from Moscow were diligent and earnest.

That the workers acquire culture was also part of the system. Speakers came from Moscow and solemnly addressed the workers about culture. They must have culture.

"The men were puzzled," Victor recalled. "Culture? What was culture? And what to do about it?

"One department in the plant met the situation by sending to Moscow for a lot of artificial palm trees. These were set up in the huge factory lunchroom, the *stalovaya*, where we all ate our main, noonday meal. I've never seen anything funnier than Russian waitresses—barefooted, of course—dodging around among those artificial palm trees serving bowls of cabbage soup or *kasha* (cereal), and big hunks of black bread! Even the workmen, anxious as they were to carry out instructions from Moscow, thought it was funny. So, they finally moved them out of the stalovaya and set them up alongside one of the assembly lines, where they looked even funnier. I think I have a snapshot of that somewhere.

"Well, a great rivalry sprang up between departments as to who could produce the most culture. Someone got the idea of metal spoons. Never in their lives had those men eaten with knives and forks, let alone metal spoons. We all ate our food—whatever we had, usually cabbage soup—out of big old wooden spoons. It used to bother us foreigners, for it is impossible to get an old wooden spoon really clean and sanitary.

"So, Walter made up a little die and fashioned, out of scraps of steel from automobile fenders, some metal spoons. They really weren't very good spoons. They had a burr around the edges, which Walter didn't have the tools to take off. If you didn't watch out, you'd cut your lip! But the cabbage soup tasted better out of them. At least you knew they were clean."

The day the metal spoons were introduced was the occasion for a big celebration in the Molotov plant at Gorki.

"We had a brass band," Victor recalled, "speakers from Moscow, and everybody made a big thing out of it. This was no laughing matter. Here was culture—the genuine article. The reaction of the workers may be judged by what happened that night. The following morning not a single one of those metal spoons could be found in that entire plant! The men had taken them home with them!"

The spoons, of course, belonged to the plant. None of the workmen were allowed to own anything—not even a rather crudely made metal spoon. The Triangle held a solemn meeting and found a solution. Each of the peasants had to have a pass, with his picture on it, to get into the plant. From that day on, each workman had to surrender his pass on entering the plant. He would get it back when he left only if he returned a metal spoon.

Thus did culture come to "the workers' paradise."

But even as the Russian peasants went earnestly about their work, struggling to acquire skills that would have been difficult for men with backgrounds far above anything they or their ancestors had ever known, completely docile, asking no questions, things occurred that to the Reuthers and to the other foreigners were disturbing—things they could not accept.

At four o'clock one morning, they heard the secret police break down the door of their Italian neighbor. Without a word of explanation or reassurance to his wife and children, he was dragged away. The Reuthers, who had opened their door to see what was going on, knew they had better not ask any questions, or make any protest. "He was a fine workman, and we had grown to like him very much," Victor recalled. "Later we were told that he was a Communist, but a Trotsky Communist. Trotsky, of course, had broken with Stalin and had had to flee the country for his life. The next day we heard that our Italian friend had been 'liquidated'—shot, and no one could even sympathize with his family for fear of coming under suspicion of being a 'Trotskyite.'"

There were also the young Austrians, whose fate was much the same. They had fled their country to get away from Dolfuss, the Austrian chancellor who became a quasi dictator. The young Austrians were Social Democrats, and eagerly they had crossed the border into "the new Russia—the promised land."

At first, they were treated as heroes, taken about from city to city, wined and dined, until, Victor said, "The Russian Communists had squeezed every drop of propaganda they could get out of them." After that, for most of the Austrians there was only disappointment and frustration.

Some of them were sent to work in the plant at Gorki. But since they had little training or skill, they had to start at the bottom like the Russian peasants, at very low pay. (Rates were based on a worker's skill and productivity. Some months Walter made as much as 400 rubles a month, while Victor earned 250, and an assembly-line apprentice, about 90 rubles per month.)

Life in Russia, now that they were no longer on display as heroes, was disillusioning to the Austrians. They had lived much better, much more comfortably, in their homeland. The food here was unpalatable. Always, day after day, that watery cabbage soup, or a bowl of coarse brown kasha.

"We hardly ever saw any meat," Victor said. "Months might go by without even a scrap. Occasionally we'd see a little butter, but we always turned it over to the children of other foreigners."

It was rare for foreigners to eat in the common dining room with the workmen, as the Reuthers did daily at lunchtime. But since their chief interest was in people—how they lived, how they worked, their hopes and aspirations—Walter and Victor shared the physical deprivations of the peasant workers to a greater degree than most foreign engineers and technicians, some of whom lived fairly comfortably in colonies, like the Commune Ruthenberg. Here there was an international cafeteria, where the brothers usually took their evening meal; at least a little variety was provided, since the different nationalities took turns cooking their traditional dishes. One night the Poles might provide the menu; another night, the Italians; Victor probably contributed some of the German recipes he had learned from *Mütterchen*, and so on. The foreigners bought and prepared their own food; and as such, the Reuthers were permitted to buy, from the scanty supplies in the stores, little luxuries, occasionally an egg or two, sometimes some withered fruit, all priced way out of sight for the Russians or the unlucky Austrians.

For the self-exiled Austrians, the tasteless, scanty food, their dreary cold living quarters, the long gray days that seemed to stretch ahead of them endlessly, were bad enough. But the thing that disturbed them more was the constant, strict, severe discipline administered by the Communists.

Presently they began to express their discontent. They were troublesome, hard to handle. And so they disappeared, a few at a time, without any explanation from the secret police who took them away. Their families would appear in the dining room with their eyes red from weeping, but no one spoke of the vacant chair at their table, which came to be a dreaded symbol of dictatorship, to the Americans particularly. "We learned later," Victor said,

"that many of them had been sent to Siberia and liquidated.
A very small number became dedicated Communists, trusted
enough so that they were sent abroad as spies or infiltrators. We
were told that some were taken into the Red Army and sent to
fight in Spain, but we never really knew. All those who had been
sent to the Gorki plant disappeared."

The Russian peasants in the plant were subjected to the same
severe discipline, but that was the way they had always lived
under the czars. Brutality? That was simply a part of life. Their
forefathers, and fathers in many cases, had been serfs, slaves.
They were still existing under rules that must be obeyed—if they
wanted to go on living. But there were differences: beautiful
leather shoes, even though the money to pay for them was held
out of the workers' pay. And the satisfaction of seeing those crude,
ugly automobiles they had helped to make coming slowly off the
assembly line. Then, too, there was the "Red Corner" social center, where a foreman might play a few bars on a balalaika, and
some of the workers would dance a *kazatska* or sing ballads during
the lunch hour. Finally, there was a shop library in the Red
Corner, with books for the benefit of people who had never been
allowed to learn to read! (No matter if the pages contained mostly
Communist propaganda.)

And always, far off on the horizon, that beautiful dream of a
life in which they would eventually have a share. No longer were
they half-slaves, whose masters had less consideration for them
than they had for their fine horses. Their new masters even called
them "comrades!"

To the Reuthers, after the long, hard winter, the spring and
summer of 1934 seemed like a relaxed vacation period even when
they were working and they joined the "volunteer labor program"
to plant and cultivate several acres of vegetable garden for the
general consumption. Since industrialization drew farm labor
away from cultivating the land, the resultant food shortage
prompted the state to enlist factory workers to till and seed the
soil during their "spare time." Walter and Victor helped to put in
beets, carrots, tomatoes, even corn, though it was hard to grow
and used mostly for cattle in Russia. They took part in leveling

the ground and planting trees and flowers in a "social city" next to the Molotov works. The brothers lived near the Oka River, where they found a fine beach and superb swimming in cold, clear waters. Men and women swam nude together, and though the Reuthers were rather startled at first, they soon got used to it. They joined in departmental picnics, went for moonlight walks with young *marushkas*, or sped up and down the river in motorboats run by Model A engines turned out by the plant.

And in late July, both Walter and Victor, along with other foreign *udarniks* who had helped to increase production, were awarded a twenty-two day excursion trip down the Volga to the Caspian Sea and back, actually a governmental grant in lieu of pay increases. They were shown a mining area, the Donbas basin, and given a tour of southern cities like Yalta, Batum, and Baku.

In October, the Commune Ruthenberg held a joyful harvest festival, in spite of "blistered hands, stiff backs, and aching muscles, all free gifts of the day's potato-digging *subotnik*," as Walter phrased it with a sly dig at the government in a long descriptive letter he sent to the Moscow *Daily News*. But, he went on to relate, "All were forgotten in the swing and rhythm of the songs and dances," and in the gay, cooperative spirit of the occasion and the benefits derived from the fresh vegetables they had enjoyed all summer, plus the final harvest of 2½ tons of potatoes, over 500 head of cabbage, and about 50 pumpkins. His letter was featured in the *Daily News* as proof of the success of the great Soviet Socialist system. And indeed, he and his younger brother no doubt genuinely enjoyed the occasion; they were young, healthy, and ready to add their high spirits to those of their fellow workers. And if his letters were usually peppered with complaints of inefficiency, coupled with suggestions for remedying the cause of it, Walter was only too glad to send in a glowing report for a change.

As part of his tremendous response to life in general, Walter could enter into a joyous demonstration as wholeheartedly as he did in an organized protest. He had great capacity for fun, a facet of his personality that has not been properly delinated by writers thus far. During his stay in Gorki, working at the Molotov plant, he was always brimming with curiosity, taking it all in—the good, the bad, the irritating. But the "hero of production," as he had been proclaimed, had many private reservations about the benefits of the "classless society" and the "rule of the proletariat."

VIII

Social Engineering

ALTHOUGH they shared the same unattractive living conditions and were fully aware of the hard, repressive discipline administered by the party officials in charge, the outlook of Walter and Victor was entirely different from that of the unhappy Austrians.

The Reuthers had not come to the Soviet Union to live. They never had any intention of remaining permanently. They had come to watch and study for a time a most fascinating experiment, an attempt to industrialize with incredible speed a vast hinterland, using for the most part labor that had never handled any but the most primitive tools. They took advantage of every opportunity they had to examine it as part of their "three-year course in social engineering."

Always they traveled during their vacation periods. They did not lack funds, for, according to Russian standards, they were well paid for their work in the Gorki automobile plant. Since they were paid in rubles, which were worthless outside the USSR, they spent their earnings freely on travel. When their jobs at Gorki ended, they had several thousand rubles, which they proceeded to spend on probably the most extended trip any foreigners had been permitted to take over Stalin's empire, which covers more than one seventh of the earth's land area.

For four months they traveled, from spring until early autumn in 1935, sometimes by train, sometimes by boat, sometimes on their bicycles, and sometimes on foot. Great power dams, steel mills, and huge plants designed to produce all kinds of heavy machinery were under construction in European Russia, near the Soviet Union's western borders. These had been started under the supervision of American engineers and skilled workmen from Europe and the United States during Stalin's first Five-Year Plan, which ended in 1933, about the time the Reuthers arrived. They were largely completed, or nearly so, and it was not difficult to gain permission to visit them.

But by 1935 the gigantic industrialization plan was moving steadily and rapidly toward the east. The Russians, using skills they had acquired from the Westerners, were carrying their program beyond the Ural Mountains into Asia, even into the far reaches of Siberia. These eastern enterprises—the great sprawling factories, the towering smokestacks, the experiments in the use of metal and chemicals, the efforts to irrigate the desert in that immense area—were usually closed to foreigners, and only a few people outside the Russian knew they existed.

The Reuthers, however, had made what the Communists considered an outstanding contribution in the development of the automobile plant at Gorki, and were given letters of introduction. Doors were opened to them that would have remained closed to most foreigners.

They started by riverboat on a trip of their own down the Volga to Stalingrad. Colorful and fascinating was a voyage on a Russian riverboat in 1935. They passed ancient towns and cities whose new smokestacks belched out clouds of black smoke over domes and towers that looked half Mongolian, half Byzantine. Reaching Stalingrad, they inspected its big, modern steel mill, its enormous tractor plant, and its great dam, capable of producing nearly two million kilowatts of power.

From Stalingrad they proceeded into the Ukraine, once wheat country, "the bread basket of Russia." They were still raising wheat and other food crops in the Ukraine—or trying to raise them. But without much success. For in the Ukraine, as in parts of the Caucasus and Crimea, Stalin, determined to increase productivity by the use of big, heavy farm machinery, had run into stubborn opposition on the part of most of the farmers. Talking with the commissar, who knew a little English, the Reuthers learned that the peasants had been for centuries raising crops on a small piece of land, using the most primitive methods and equipment. It was impossible to employ modern tractors, combines, and other huge machinery on very small farms. So they were combined into big collective farms, where the farmers worked as laborers under the direction of Communist bosses from Moscow, using machinery with which they were unfamiliar, and were unable to collect any money for their crops, which had to be turned over to the government. This was too much for the farmers—probably from the beginning of time the most independent of all men. Thousands of them had revolted in the 1920's and had been shipped off to Siberia, presumably to be shot. Ironically, other Russians sharing their fate included some three thousand Cossacks, the ferocious fighters and noted horsemen who before the revolution had many times relentlessly ridden down crowds of peasants and workers who had tried to protest against the cruelty of the czars.

The Communist bosses had been obliged to replace the exiled farmers with whatever labor was available—much of it from the cities. These new hands knew nothing about farming, resented having been forced to leave their homes, and were slow and apathetic. Yet with all the unrest, the Reuthers passed through many neat little villages, with double rows of new whitewashed cottages, where the worker-farmers lived. New schools had been built for their children. There were parks and playgrounds. But little food was produced. Even in Stalin's time, restrictions had to be lifted so that, as an incentive, the farmers were permitted to sell a little of their produce at a small profit.

Nor were all the Russian peasant factory workers as contented as those the Reuthers had known at the Gorki plant apparently were. Thousands of them were restless; they had been moving about from job to job, looking for better pay, more comfortable homes. In 1933 the Communists had issued a new passport system, under which a worker had to go where he was told to go, stay there, and take whatever job he was told to take. Thousands of families were compelled to move out of the cities to find homes and work in small communities. Undoubtedly the city workers were homesick, but they were still no worse off than they had been before.

In Moscow, which Walter and Victor visited more than once, the first time witnessing a May Day parade, standing within a stone's throw of Stalin, the bright, clean store windows were filled with merchandise—but there was very little on the shelves inside. The Reuthers were reminded of the bread lines back home as they saw residents of Moscow waiting two or three abreast for endless hours in the street outside a store. But these people, unlike the hungry unemployed in Detroit, had money, which they hoped to spend if they managed to get inside. More often than not the store would have to close its doors before they all made it, because everything had been sold. And they would have to come back the next day. Prices were sky-high. Sometimes it would take a man three years to save enough money to buy an overcoat. Except for cabbage and black bread, there was little food in Moscow, as everywhere else. Sugar was rationed—allowing eight hundred grams a month per person (about one and three-quarter pounds). Hardly ever was there any meat or butter for sale, and seldom any fruit. There simply was not enough of anything. Paper was so scarce that every scrap was precious, and there was never enough for the schools. Whatever paper there was available was used mostly for printing Communist propaganda books and leaflets, displayed in stacks on street corners and in the parks.

Obviously priority was given to the children in the distribution of the scanty supplies of food and clothing that were available. Everywhere the Reuthers went, even out in the remote cities and villages in central Asia, the children looked well fed, healthy, and neat, although their clothing was more often than not worn and shabby. Well-mannered children they were, solemnly curious about these strangers from the West. They were apparently receiving good medical care, although doctors in Russia in the middle 1930's were few in number. Later, physicians would be turned out by the thousands, mostly women, and sent where they were needed. No doctor in the USSR was permitted to engage in private practice. All were employed by the state.

The Ukraine, when the Reuthers arrived, had ceased to be devoted predominantly to agriculture. In every city there were new plants, turning out tractors, combines, trucks, parts of machines to be shipped over the new railroads that were being laid, always toward the east. In the northern Ukraine, on the Dnieper River, the second-largest hydroelectrical power dam in the world had been completed in 1932 by three thousand Russian workers under the supervision of American engineers, a plant capable of developing 750,000 horsepower, enough to serve an area of seventy-thousand square miles.

Down into the Crimea they journeyed to the ancient city of Sevastopol, on the Black Sea, then north and southeast to the Caucasus. On foot they hiked along the Georgian military highway and proceeded from Ordzhonikidze and Tiflis down through the oil fields to the big oil center at Baku, on the Caspian Sea. Traveling frequently by slow, badly equipped Russian trains they passed through Tashkent and the fabled city of Samarkand, which was conquered by Alexander the Great more than two thousand years before. At the time they reached the southern border of central Asia, that area was off limits and no other foreigners had been permitted to visit it. The Reuthers slept in goatskin tents with the natives, communicating with them in spirit if not in words.

Fascinating experiments were going on in some of those enormous plants that had been completed or were nearing completion in the general area into which they were traveling. To the north of their route, 150 miles south of Moscow, the Russians had built an entirely new city, called Bobriki. It was surrounded by deposits of fireclay, gypsum, phosphates, very good iron ore, and high-grade quartz sand for making glass. And in the Kazakhstan Mountains, in central Asia, the Russians had discovered a plant called tausaghyz, which is found nowhere else in the world and is richer in rubber content than any other plant except the tropical rubber tree. Even then the Russians were beginning to turn out a very good synthetic rubber.

Tashkent and Samarkand are on the southern edge of the great Asiatic desert, which the Russians were trying to fertilize. Cotton was being raised around Tashkent and Samarkand. And everywhere factories were going up, miles and miles of steel rails being laid, and thousands of miles of straight highways built, needed for the five-ton trucks used to transport the synthetic rubber. One of the major problems confronting Stalin as he began his second Five-Year Plan had been the lack of transportation facilities between European Russia and the industrial empire he was building beyond the Urals. Building of highways was given top priority, and railroad lines were to be increased by nineteen thousand miles of tracks.

Tashkent and Samarkand and the surrounding country are in Moslem territory, which presented a problem to the atheistic Communists. While they relentlessly eliminated the Moslem leaders—as well as the large feudal landowners—the Russians eased the situation somewhat by encouraging the people to pursue their ancient cultures, their music, for instance. In every town, there were theaters, with plays being performed in the native language. But the alert, carefully trained young Communists from Moscow were everywhere, attempting to indoctrinate the people. The Reuthers discovered that the health and literacy programs were by no means confined to European Russia.

Here it was possible for the Reuthers to have more contacts with the Russians than they would have been able to have elsewhere. In Samarkand they met a Russian woman teacher who had been there for two years. She told them about her efforts to emancipate the Moslem women, among them a harrowing story of women's rebellion.

One night thousands of them gathered in the old Mosque square. A big bonfire was built, and she urged the women to tear off the hideous horsehair veils, which they were obliged to wear in accordance with ancient Moslem tradition, and toss them into the flames. Many of the women did so. But that night nearly all of them were murdered, either by their husbands or by other infuriated Moslem men. However, a beginning had been made, and by 1960 foreign visitors saw no horsehair veils in Samarkand. Slowly but steadily the Westernization of Samarkand, which was a great city centuries before Moscow was built, was proceeding. The Russians did preserve much of the beautiful ancient architecture, for the "old city" still stands, next to the "modern."

The Reuthers decided in Tashkent that they would travel to

China, and go home from there, but first they had to return to Moscow to have their passports processed. They made the trip on dilapidated old trains. Sometimes there would be a new locomotive, but it would frequently break down, causing delays.

Back in Moscow, the brothers prepared for another long trip, on the Trans-Siberian Railway, all the way to the Chinese border. They still had enough rubles to pay their fare to Harbin, in the Chinese province of Manchuria. But in American money they had only about $150, which their father had sent to them after cashing in another small insurance policy.

On a late summer day in 1935 they boarded a train which by Russian standards in the 1930's, was good; but the trip took ten days and eleven nights, and since the Reuthers traveled at the cheapest rate, they had no berths, but slept on wooden benches in a small, crowded compartment.

"Believe me," Victor recalled years later, rubbing his back, "a wooden bench gets awfully hard in eleven nights!"

There were no dining-car facilities, but the train made frequent stops, and at each stop they would dash out to the nearest market to buy whatever they could—"perhaps a shriveled-up apple, maybe an egg or two." Hot water for tea was always available in the stations. And they had taken with them some chocolate and cheese, which, as foreigners, they were able to buy in Moscow, and several large loaves of the inevitable black bread.

They shared their compartment with three English passengers —a young physician and an Oxford student en route to China to visit their parents, who were missionaries, and a retired lieutenant colonel in the British Army, who told them he was an aluminum manufacturer in Shanghai. His name was Lt. Col. Hayley Bell.

Victor remembered him as "the very image of a British Army officer in the movies—C. Aubrey Smith—tall, lean, truly majestic in his appearance, with that broad English 'a' in his speech." He had fought in the Boer war, he told them.

During the endless hours, as the train moved slowly across Siberia, which looked flat and treeless, with here and there dreary little towns, there was plenty of time for conversation. And when Colonel Bell discovered that the Reuthers had worked for eighteen months in a Russian automobile plant and had traveled extensively—even out into central Asia—he was obviously fascinated. He asked so many questions, expressing interest in all sorts of details, that the Reuthers were somewhat surprised and wondered why. Yet, with nothing else to do but talk, they discussed their experiences with him for hours, answering his questions as fully as they could.

When the train finally reached the border, they were surrounded by Japanese officers, who informed them that Manchuria had been taken over by their government, was no longer a part of China, and was now called "Manchukuo." Their passports read "China."

"Oh, that doesn't matter," the Japanese officer in command assured them. "Just take your pen, cross out 'China,' and write in 'Manchukuo.'"

Whereupon Colonel Bell drew himself up in all his British majesty and exclaimed, "Good heavens, man, I can't issue myself a passport!"

And he warned the Reuthers that, if they followed the Japanese officer's suggestion, they would be falsifying their American passports. The brothers decided to follow his lead. While the argument continued, a train was waiting at the border to take them to Harbin, whence they would continue down into China. With dismay, they watched it pull away. There would not be another train for three days!

When the train returned three days later, Colonel Bell remained obdurate until it became obvious that it, too, was about to depart, leaving them behind again. Then he savagely scratched out the word "China" on his passport, wrote in "Manchukuo," and without a word—the Reuthers hot on his heels—stalked across the street to the telegraph office and wired the British consul in Harbin: "I have just recognized the state of Manchukuo. Now the other sixty million British may feel free to follow." The Reuthers, having altered their passports as the Japanese directed, also wired the American consul in Harbin. They boarded the train and proceeded to Harbin and Mukden, where Colonel Bell would embark on a boat down to Shanghai. The Reuthers were headed for Peking.

At Mukden they all had several hours' wait, and the colonel

suggested that they take a ricksha ride around the city; he would direct the runners to points of interest. Walter and Victor were horrified; it was against their principles to be toted around by other human beings. "Not on your life," Walter protested. The colonel shrugged and accused the young Americans of allowing their idealism to stand in the way of cheep coolie labor. "You may as well take advantage of it," he said.

"That's British imperialism!" Walter flung at him.

Colonel Bell only laughed, and jumped into the nearest jinricksha, waving good-bye to them as the coolie, with a happy grin, picked up the shafts of the man-powered carriage and trotted off. Toward dusk, the Reuthers were returning to the station, hot and tired from their tour of the city on foot, Hayley Bell, cool and comfortable in his ricksha, passed by, calling out to them, "Behold British imperialism!" And he doffed his pith-helmet. All three shouted with laughter, and the Reuthers called back to him a fond farewell. It was the last they saw of the courtly colonel, who took the boat to Shanghai, while they continued by train to Peking. All the way down to the Chinese border, they were constantly checked by Japanese agents, who boarded the train at every stop to question the Reuthers, stamping the boys' passports again and again. It was puzzling.

At Peking, they found about twenty ricksha boys lined up, hoping to pick up passengers who needed rides to the hotels. Walter and Victor had been discussing the ethical problem posed by their British friend's surprisingly callous attitude toward this cheap coolie labor: Was it ever justifiable for a person who practiced applied Christianity to let himself be carried around by a poorer brother? Their money was running low already, and they were still a long way from home; but the ricksha boys looked at them so beseechingly, and they were so in need of the few cents' fare, as the Reuthers well knew, that it was impossible to keep on saying no. One of the letters of introduction they had been given was directed to a professor at the university some thirteen miles out of town; the best way to get there would be by ricksha; so they finally gave in and hired a double. The two little coolies were delighted, but the Reuther boys felt guilty about their "man-power" transportation. After a few miles, Walter had a brilliant idea: He and Victor would pull the ricksha a while, letting the coolies ride for once in their lives.

Victor agreed it was a great solution. They called a halt, got out, and tried to make the astonished runners understand that they were to get in. Walter said, "They thought we were nuts! But we managed to shove them inside; then Vic and I picked up the shafts and started down the road at a fairly fast clip for quite a way." Or so it seemed. But before long they realized they were not moving very fast and were out of breath; after all, they were not "pros," like the coolies. Their unwilling passengers were probably feeling as guilty as they, for they soon persuaded the Reuthers to get back in and ride the rest of the way.

For part of their journey to reach the China coast, the travelers had booked passage on a Yangtze River boat, not aware that a recent rampage of the Yellow River had ruined the rice crop and inflicted widespread famine. The 1935 flood was one of the worst in Chinese history. Each time the steamer docked at a river town, parades of children, beating on tin cans and begging for food, would dog the footsteps of foreigners. At Hankow, famine-crazed men who knew there was rice aboard the steamer leaped on deck from the dock, only to be clubbed to death by burly Sikh sailors, who threw the bodies overboard into the yellow water, a nightmarish scene to the young Reuthers.

Farther downstream, a fleet of Chinese junks carrying flood refugees obstructed the steamer's course, causing it to jam into one of them, which carried about forty Chinese, men, women and children, all of whom were thrown into the water, to the Reuthers' horror. Walter later related to a *New York Times* forum: "They all drowned before our eyes." Neither the captain nor his crew made a move to save them. When Walter and Victor protested hotly, the captain laughed at them. "You don't understand China," he said. To the brothers' insistence that it was wrong to let forty people die without lifting a finger to save them, he replied calmly, with quiet significance, "Six million people will starve in China this year because the crops have been destroyed." To this the young Americans had no answer, but it was such scenes as they had just witnessed that reinforced their concern for humanity, and impelled Walter Reuther as a powerful labor leader to serve on panels like *The New York Times* Forum on World Food Supply.

After reaching Shanghai, Walter and Victor boarded another boat and sailed across the East China Sea to Japan. They bought bicycles, which were very cheap in Japan, and set out to see the country. No agents had checked on them in China, but here it began once more. Whenever they stopped at an inn, three cups of tea were set out, the third cup for the Japanese officer who was following them! And again their passports were stamped and restamped. They knew they were being tailed, but they couldn't understand why, and not until years later did they find out. Shortly after World War Two, Victor was sent to London on some labor project by the government. He decided to look up their old friend, the colonel, only to discover that he had died during the war, and that on the day of his death, Winston Churchill had stood up in the House of Commons and eulogized him, saying that if the British government had paid more attention to the reports and advice of Hayley Bell, the war in the Pacific would have taken a much more favorable turn than it did.

"So—the man was a top British agent!" Victor said in recounting the end of the mystery. "Walter and I were too inexperienced to realize it, but the Japanese knew! And that was why they were so suspicious of us." He also learned some years later that the British actress Hayley Mills is a granddaughter of Colonel Hayley Bell, whose daughter had married the distinguished actor John Mills.

As their tour of Japan ended, the Reuthers found themselves completely out of money, and were living on raw fish and seaweed. In desperation, they appealed to the American embassy, which directed them to the steamship lines, where they presently found jobs on the U.S. Dollar Line steamer *President Harding*, sailing for San Francisco.

"We got signed on suddenly," said Victor, "and we didn't have time to sell our bikes. So we just rolled them down the gangplank, where a group of coolies, loading coal on the dock, made a mad scramble for them."

To get their jobs, they had to join the maritime union, which they willingly did. Walter was put to work as a "grease monkey" in the engine room, while Victor became a deck hand, mopping and polishing brass. Several days out, they crossed the international date line.

"What day is this?" Walter asked the following morning.

"Wednesday," Victor replied.

"And what day was yesterday?"

"Wednesday."

They looked up the chief engineer and explained that they thought they were entitled to a day's pay for that extra Wednesday.

He shook his head and told them they would gain a day on the return trip.

"But we'll not be on the return trip," Walter protested.

"Well, you worked that extra day for the Lord," they were told. "No extra pay."

Since there was nothing they could do about it, the Reuthers argued no more, until one morning they looked out their portholes and saw waving palm trees and pretty girls carrying leis and they realized that the ship had docked in Hawaii.

Again they sought out the chief engineer and asked for shore leave.

"Impossible," he said. "We'll be here only one day. No shore leaves for any of the crew."

Walter pointed out that this might be the only chance they would ever have to see Hawaii.

"Sorry," the chief engineer said, "but if I let you two go ashore, it would raise hell with the rest of the crew. Nothing doing."

Walter looked thoughtful, then grinned.

"Remember that extra Wednesday we worked for the Lord?" he asked. "Well, I talked it over with the Lord last night and He said it would be all right if we spent that day seeing Hawaii!"

Laughing, the chief engineer gave them a shove down the gangplank, and the Reuthers saw Hawaii.

At last the ship docked in San Francisco, the Reuthers were paid off, telegraphed their parents, and with their sea pay, bought bus tickets to Wheeling, West Virginia.

Some thirty years later, Walter and Victor Reuther summed up their three-year course in social engineering in this way.

"It gave us a chance to see at first hand the way people in far-away countries work and live, and to understand that despite language barriers and cultural differences, people everywhere long and strive for the same basic human goals—the chance to have a job with some degree of security, some greater opportunity for their children than they themselves enjoyed. And, of course, they hope to have all of this in an atmosphere of freedom.

"We returned to the United States with a far greater understanding and appreciation of the importance of a great democratic heritage such as we have in our country, but with the realization that the security of that heritage could not depend only on the words of the Declaration of Independence and the Constitution—that it could be made secure only by strong, living democratic institutions. We felt that we could make a contribution in that direction by helping American workers to build strong and democratic unions. That was why we went into the labor movement."

IX

Labor Pains

WHEN Walter Reuther returned to Detroit near the close of 1935, American big industry—giant complexes, including steel and automobiles—was like a volcano filled with boiling lava that was threatening to blow off the cap.

Already fissures were appearing in management's outer crust as millions of workmen, walled up inside, wholly at the mercy of their employers, fought down their fears and anxieties, began organizing and joining forbidden labor unions, and desperately looked for leaders.

Their decision to get together and fight back at the bosses was born of frustration and deep, bitter resentment. There was frustration because the New Deal, which had seemed to promise so much in legalizing labor's right to organize had apparently overlooked their plight, concerned as it was with getting business, both big and little, rolling again after the great depression. There was resentment at the foreman who could hire them or fire them at his pleasure; at the "stretch-out" system—the speedup on the assembly lines, which left a man worn out at forty, to be cast aside; at twelve-hour shifts and low pay. Inarticulate in most cases, but very real, was the resentment at being treated as nameless robots, the callous affront to their dignity as human beings. In the mass-production industries, labor did not consist of people, with rent to pay, doctors' bills, grocery bills, with hopes and aspirations for their children. It was simply a commodity. If one small bit wore out, it could be cast aside and a fresh unit inserted, without slowing down production.

Strikes among unorganized workmen started breaking out in a rash all over the country in 1933 and continued until the middle thirties, when the big battles began in automobiles and steel. Some of those early strikes were fairly large and surprisingly successful. Apparently management, unaware of the growing unrest, was caught off guard and stunned. But most of the strikes were small—some lasted only a few hours—and ineffectual. For the majority of the new unions were weak, had no funds, were without skilled leadership. And there was always the threat of a man losing his job if he joined a forbidden union.

Some form of unionism had existed in this country for more than a century, beginning with the shoemakers' revolt in 1815. The American Federation of Labor, started in 1886, by Samuel Gompers, the cigarmaker, consisted almost entirely of "craft unions," in which one man in a factory, on a construction project, or in a print shop, would belong to one union, covering the men performing his particular job, while another man in the same shop, but with a different job, would belong to another union. On the whole, management had found craft unions, divided as they were, more of a nuisance than a threat.

In the early 1930's the millions of unorganized workers, desperate, realizing that a union was essential if they were to raise their standard of living, naturally turned to the American Federation of Labor for leadership and help, since, in spite of serious flaws like "jurisdictional strikes" and internal struggles, the Federation was firmly established. They received little recognition, let alone help or badly needed leadership from the officers of the craft union, who were content to maintain the gains of the past. Under Samuel Gompers, one of the giants in labor history, the AFL had made a definite contribution to the organization of labor in the United States, but since his death in 1924, it had not moved with the times or the economic changes in the country. As old Sam Gompers lay dying in his home in San Antonio, Texas, he had whispered to his trusted lieutenants, gathered at his bedside, "Keep the faith."

To his successor, William Green, a former coal miner, his words apparently meant, "Preserve the status quo." Lacking the imagination and sharp perceptiveness of Gompers, Green seemed to feel that everything ran along smoothly enough on the whole, so why change? Opening the gates to millions of angry, deprived workers in tightly controlled mass industry could only mean trouble. A few industry-wide unions had existed within the AFL, such as the brewers', to which Val Reuther had belonged when the boys were small. And notably there were the coal miners, led by the able, truculent John L. Lewis, with his bushy eyebrows and a taste for Shakespeare, who was already becoming a legend in the labor world.

By the early 1930's it had become apparent to Lewis, if not to the majority of the other leaders in the AFL, of which he was vice-president, that in an industry built on mass production, the time-honored craft system simply would not work. Here hundreds of men would be working on an assembly line, each performing with lightning rapidity one single operation. Hundreds of craft unions in that setup? Ridiculous. In other big plants, such as those producing tools and dies, one skilled workman might handle several highly technical tasks, which could place him under the jurisdiction of four or five craft unions.

As Lewis saw it, there could be only one solution. Every man in the plant should belong to one union, as all men in a coal mine belonged to the United Mine Workers. Only with one big union, covering millions of men in each mass-production industry—a strong union, with able leadership and ample funds—did labor, in his opinion, have a chance.

Lewis tried to put over his idea at the 1934 convention of the AFL, but got nowhere. At the next convention, however, in October, 1935, in Atlantic City, Lewis advanced like a general, with carefully planned strategy and a group of respected and experienced labor leaders at his side. The idea of the effectiveness of a one-union setup had begun to catch on with some success. David Dubinsky had tried it in the ladies' garment industry. As head of the International Ladies' Garment Workers, he had become one of the most powerful labor leaders in the country. Workers in the men's clothing industry eagerly flocked into the

Amalgamated Clothing Workers, led by Sidney Hillman. Nobody had to tell Dubinsky and Hillman that John L. Lewis' plan would work. They knew.

The new unions received little encouragement or practical assistance. William Green and the national heads of the AFL craft unions seemed to want only to keep their organization neat, tidy, as well controlled as it had been in the past. The auto workers referred to Green as "Sitting Bill."

The fight between the forces of Bill Green and John L. Lewis at the AFL convention in 1935 was prolonged and violent. At one point Lewis and Bill Hutcheson, ultraconservative national head of the carpenters' union, got into a fist fight on the floor of the convention. Hutcheson emerged with a bloody nose, while Lewis smoothed his rumpled hair, straightened his tie—and smiled.

Despite his eloquence, his skillful maneuvering, and the devoted efforts of his associates, Lewis did not win. The convention voted down his proposal that the AFL welcome the millions of unorganized into the fold. As Lewis put it, he was compelled to watch the American labor movement "broken on the rock of utter futility," unless he could devise some new plan, outside the AFL.

The day after the convention adjourned, Lewis held a meeting with eight other labor leaders in an Atlantic City hotel. They were: Dubinsky and Hillman; John Brophy of the United Mine Workers; Tom Kennedy, lieutenant governor of Pennsylvania, and Philip Murray, also of the United Mine Workers; Charles Howard of the typographers; Max Zaritsky of the hat workers; and Tom McMahon, who had been working against difficult and dangerous odds to organize the textile workers in the South.

Out of that meeting came the Committee for Industrial Organization—the CIO. John L. Lewis had lost the battle, but not the war. His CIO was destined to become the most militant and effective labor organization in the country. Without its early leadership and help, millions of workmen in automobiles, steel, and other mass-production industries probably would have been delayed for years in building the unions they so badly wanted and needed. On November 23, 1935, Lewis wrote to Bill Green, whom he addressed as "Dear Sir and Brother," a letter resigning as vice-president of the AFL.

Although he was well aware of the situation in the automobile industry, Lewis in the beginning concentrated his efforts on steel. It was a difficult assignment, for the steel workers were much more intimidated by management than the automobile workers.

From the start, enthusiasm for organizing unions had been greater in the automobile factories than it had been in the steel mills. The auto workers set up small, local unions loosely attached to the AFL, although there was no united organization until several years later. In 1933, there were at least four "federal local unions," as they were designated by the AFL: the Associated Automobile Workers' Association, the Mechanics Educational Society of America, the Automobile Industrial Workers' Association, and the Auto Workers' Union. In 1934, the AFL called together representatives of these federal local unions, and, after an address by President William Green, they formed a sort of conference of such local unions in the automobile industry. In 1935, the parent body issued them a charter as an international union, but they had no autonomy. It was commonly known as a "probationary charter" by the membership, since their officers and executive board members were appointed by the AFL.

The appointed leaders proved inept at handling the abuses of layoffs and pay cuts perpetrated by Ford and other big companies against the workers under the deceptive "merit clause" of the National Recovery Administration (NRA) code for the automobile industry. Disgusted by the timidity and bungling of ineffectual leadership, the newly chartered international union in another year held a convention in South Bend, Indiana, elected their own officers and board members, and became an autonomous international union affiliated to the AFL.

However, when Walter Reuther returned to Detroit in the winter of 1935, men were dropping out of the union in droves from fear of losing their jobs. Total membership had fallen to about 20,000. Those who remained were dedicated unionists, spurred by passion and faith to help their fellow workers, who were growing desperate. Unrest was rampant; one could feel it in the air. It did not take Walter long to grasp what he once called "the sense of little people marching" in spite of the heavy yoke they had to bear. The hard core of union workers burned for action. They had found a hymn in the old IWW anthem "Solidarity Forever," singing the lines with militant zeal:

When the union's inspiration through the worker's blood shall run,
There can be no greater power anywhere beneath the sun . . .

These words, sung to the tune of "The Battle Hymn of the Republic," sounded a battle cry in young Walter Reuther's soul; and, like his father and grandfather before him, he was eager to enlist in the cause of labor.

X

West Side Local 174

THE welcome Walter Reuther received from management on his return to Detroit after his three-year trip around the world was as cold and bleak as the raw winter weather. For the red-headed young man from Wheeling who had distinguished himself by becoming, in an incredibly short time, one of the highest-paid mechanics in the Ford Motor Company, there was no job anywhere in the automobile industry.

Automobile manufacturing at the end of 1935 was slowed down. Many of the big plants were closed, for retooling. Victor, now qualified to work on the assembly line, looked around, then took a job with the American Friends Service Committee, lecturing across the country on his experiences in Europe, especially those in Germany, and the alarming trend toward another world war. The Quakers, as always, were trying to promote peace.

But while Victor could not get work on an assembly line, most of which were not moving, there should have been plenty of jobs available to Walter in his former capacity as die leader. He was just the sort of expert for whom employers were looking, but since Ford had fired him for union and political activity, every employer in the industry knew it, as he immediately found out when he began to make the rounds of the employment offices.

Twice during the months that followed he tried to get in by using a semiassumed name, "Walter Philips," his second name being Philip. Once he barely got a foot inside the door. The second time he lasted a month and had just received a raise when "Harry Bennett's men" caught up with him.

Harry Bennett's men were a large private army under the direct control of a former pugilist, Harry Bennett, who was for years closer to Henry Ford than anyone else in the company. A man in Walter Reuther's position was under constant surveillance by Bennett's "servicemen," as they were called.

Walter's first attempt at getting a job was with the Murray Body Company, one of the largest so-called "independent" body manufacturers in the industry. Actually, the company was independent in name only, since it sold most of its output to Ford. Every new employee had to be cleared with Bennett, as Walter discovered. In later years he would tell the story:

"Murray was just starting a major program for a new model; that necessitated hiring a lot of tool- and diemakers. They were advertising for them. I applied for a job as Walter Philips, was interviewed, and hired. But I still had to pass a physical examination before I could report for work. By the time they were through interviewing me and hiring me, the company doctor, who gave the physicals, had gone to lunch. The employment manager said the doctor would be back about one o'clock and told me to wait for him. If I passed my physical, I could report for work the next morning.

"I was sitting in the employment manager's office reading a Detroit newspaper when out of nowhere, four big, strong-arm guys from Harry Bennett's private army, apparently on the lookout for me, came swaggering in and, without any warning, picked me up and threw me out into the street. And that ended it—no job.

"Some years later, our union got a contract with the Murray Body Company. While we were waiting for some typing to be done so that we could sign the contract, I was chatting with the vice-president of the company and asked him if he would mind doing a bit of reminiscing. He said no, and I told him about the incident. He smiled and said he remembered it well, and that it had always been a source of embarrassment to him, because he knew exactly how badly they had behaved in those days. But they were helpless. Nobody on the blacklist could be hired, no matter how much they may have needed the skill you had. No matter what I did, they'd catch up with me."

Several months later, during the summer of 1936, Walter landed another job, with the Frederick Coleman Tool-and-Die Company, on the west side of Detroit. It was a smaller company than Murray, a little more obscure. This time, "Walter Philips" lasted thirty days.

"The job I was working on was a rather intricate die," he recalled. "It was what we call a perforating die. It consisted of about a hundred little punches. The punches had to punch holes in a very thin sheet of metal; each little hole had to match exactly a corresponding little hole in a sheet of steel underneath. The holes had to be punched at what we call a very close tolerance. In other words, they had to be exactly the same size, to match the holes underneath. I think the tolerance had to be within three or four tenths of a thousandth of an inch. If it varied more than that, it wouldn't work properly."

That particular type of job, requiring the greatest exactitude, was the kind Walter liked best. The big, heavy tools and dies like those used in the making of a fender never interested him so much. He finally finished the die, placed it in the punching press, and the chief inspector came over to watch him test it.

"The way to find out if it will cut the thin metal properly," Walter explained, "is to put a piece of newspaper in where the thin metal is supposed to go. If it will cut the newspaper, it will cut the metal, for the newspaper is thin and soft and even harder to cut."

The chief inspector watched as Walter dropped the die, with its little punches, down on the newspaper. The die was raised, and the chief inspector and Walter examined the newspaper carefully. Each hole was cut cleanly, sharply, and accurately.

"Young man," the inspector said, "this is an excellent job you've done. It's one of the best jobs we've turned out in this plant in a long time. You ought to feel proud of it."

"Well, I'm very pleased to know you think it's such a good job," Walter replied, with his boyish grin. "But wouldn't it mean more if you told the foreman about it?"

"I'm quite willing to do that," replied the inspector.

Walter went over and brought the foreman, whom the men called "High Ball John" because he was always trying to get more work out of them.

High Ball John also carefully examined the piece of newspaper, and he too complimented the redhead.

"If I've done such a good job, and I've been here thirty days," Walter said quickly, "don't you think it's time I got a raise?"

"I'll talk it over with the Old Man tonight." The foreman nodded. The Old Man was Frederick Coleman, owner of the plant.

As Walter punched the time clock at seven o'clock the next morning, High Ball John came over to him.

"Well, last night after you went home," he said, "I had a chance to talk to the Old Man, and he agreed to give you a ten-cents-an-hour increase." Walter thanked him and went to work.

"That happened about seven o'clock," Walter said with a reminiscent smile. "At nine-thirty that same morning I was fired."

In the office where he went to get his papers, Walter found High Ball John and some of the management officials.

"Why am I being fired?" he asked.

"You are being discharged for incompetence," he was told.

"That's very strange," Walter remarked, "At seven o'clock this morning I was given a raise for doing a very good job. At nine-thirty I'm being fired for being incompetent. My skills must have deteriorated with amazing rapidity in two hours and a half." The foreman had no comeback for him, so Walter continued, "You know why I'm being discharged. You've caught up with me. I'm being discharged for trying to organize a union in this plant. And I plead guilty. Before I leave, I'm going to finish the job, or you'll have to throw me out bodily. I'm not going to leave."

Apparently the management at the Coleman Tool-and-Die Company did not use the strong-arm methods of Harry Bennett's men. He was not manhandled or thrown out, but spent the rest of the day in the plant, trying to persuade the workmen to accept union cards. When he left, he was satisfied that he had made some progress.

"It was slow work," he recalled. "Trying to get a man to join a

union, you were always up against the fact that it would possibly
cost him his job. And if he became active in the union, he'd be
placed on the blacklist. He had his family to think about. So, no
matter how much he wanted to join, he would simply shake his
head. But frequently he'd tell me his troubles. You see, the ground
swell was there, and I knew it. I could sense their frustration,
their resentment at the way management was treating them. It
was only a matter of time before it would break out. All they
needed was someone to give them encouragement, support,
leadership."

His brothers, Victor and Roy, experienced the same feeling as
they went about their jobs. Victor sensed it as he spoke to groups
of workingmen in the various cities he visited while lecturing on
international affairs for the American Friends. Roy, who had kept
his brothers informed of the changes in the labor picture while
they were away, had urged them to come back from Japan (instead of going on to India as they had thought of doing) because
the trade-union movement among auto workers in Detroit and
elsewhere was taking forward strides.

While working as an electrician after the strike at Briggs was
over and his injury had healed, Roy, like his brothers, had decided
to acquire more education, and had taken courses at Wayne University. By the time they returned, he had a teaching fellowship
at Brookwood Labor College, a unique experimental school at
Katonah, New York. Housed in a handsome country estate do-
nated by a distinguished Quaker family called Fincke, Brookwood
was a training center for prospective union leaders, some fifty
miles up the Hudson from New York City. It was financed by a
group of well-to-do liberals and the labor unions that had formed
the CIO; devoted to practical courses like parliamentary law,
public speaking and economics, the college was undeniably so-
cialist-pacifist in outlook. Walter and Victor, after the reunion
with their parents in Wheeling, had visited Roy, who gave them
a briefing on the situation in Detroit; and both had addressed the
student body, who were eager to hear a first-hand account of the
"experiment" in Russia, and the effect of Hitler on western
Europe. Victor, much impressed with the labor college, went
there when his first tour for the Quakers was completed, to do

some research and writing. And Roy went on from there to take a summer course in Adult Education at the University of Wisconsin. He became Director of Adult Education for the Board of Education in Flint, Michigan, financed by federal funds, before returning to the labor movement. By the summer of 1936 all three Reuthers were active union organizers.

Walter, however, was bursting to get into action right away and soon did, in Detroit, where he decided to settle. From all Roy had told them, the time was ripe for a major organizing drive among mass-production workers. The Wagner Labor Relations Act, with its Section 7-A clause, giving labor the right to organize, had been enacted. Employers were supposed to permit workers to vote in secret ballot on the question of having a union shop with the organization of their choice. But management ignored the law by carrying it into court, which meant it must go all the way to the Supreme Court before the constitutionality could be established, involving months of delay. The National Labor Relations Board, set up to see that its provisions were carried out, often was forced to report to President Roosevelt that it was unable to fulfill its duties. There were a number of unions in Detroit, each confined to its own plant, most of them small and weak. Still Walter Reuther went doggedly ahead, talking to automobile workers, trying to get them to join a union. He had no money, except for a meager pittance as recreation director of WPA; and received no salary. He did not even get streetcar fare for his organizing expenses.

Presently, however, he did receive support—strong, capable, heart-warming support—from an entirely unexpected source. Late in the afternoon of a cold January day, Walter found he had enough pennies for a streetcar ride. As he climbed aboard, he saw an attractive young woman whom he had met, once, before he started on his trip around the world, at a meeting of the Workmen's Circle, a Socialist labor group.

May Wolf, small, slender, with sapphire-blue eyes and wavy auburn hair, several shades darker than Walter's sandy red, confessed later that she had forgotten that first meeting—a mere handshake and a how-do-you-do. But Walter had not forgotten, and he quickly made his way through the aisle and settled himself in a vacant seat beside her.

"I was teaching those days," May said, "physical education in a public school. I had a long, hard day, and I was tired. So tired that, although I wasn't interested at first, I just let him go on talking."

But May Wolf also was involved in the labor movement, so deeply involved that, after teaching all day, she spent most of her evenings helping to organize a teachers' union, of which she was a charter member. Talking was Walter's specialty, and before long, May Wolf found herself spending evenings attending labor meetings with him.

It was well that talking was one of Walter's strong points, and that his subject was close to his listener's heart. For May Wolf, both beautiful and intelligent, had many suitors, among them an important city official, who kept the living room in the La Salle Street apartment of her parents full of flowers. But May's parents began to wonder when she kept seeing that redheaded labor organizer night after night. At first they took little notice beyond the fact that he seemed to be a nice young man whom they had seen and heard at the Workmen's Circle (and besides, May was always going to union meetings of one sort or another). But when their meetings became a nightly occurrence, after the streetcar encounter in early January, her mother and father could not help wondering.

An inkling that May was really interested in Walter came when she asked Eleanor Paperno, her brother Leo's fiancée, with studied casualness, "Did you hear Walter Reuther speak at the Workmen's Circle or at the League for Industrial Democracy last week?" And when the answer was Yes, she inquired, "What did you think of it?"

"His content was good," answered Eleanor, whose judgment was apt to be considered and critical—and whose mother taught English in Detroit high schools—"but his grammar was dreadful!"

"It was?" May seemed surprised. "How do you mean?"

"Well, he said things like 'he don't,' and he used the subjective personal pronoun when he should have used the objective; that sort of mistake grates on my ears."

May burst out laughing. Here was the English teacher's daughter voicing her opinion, all right! And although it eventually became a family joke, Walter himself was most distressed by the criticism when May mentioned it to him that evening. He worried for fear others, a different audience, perhaps would feel as Eleanor did. Perhaps he should have completed his college education, for future appearances. . . . But the need to organize the people in mass production was so urgent! And certainly his present audience—many of them foreign born—composed of auto workers, socialists, and other liberals concerned with economic and social problems, would have no fault to find with the mechanics of his word structure. In fact, one of his assets as an up-and-coming labor leader—and later as a powerful union president—was that Walter Reuther spoke the language of the workingman in clear, lucid, decisive sentences. In his talks on "Russia's Economic Policy Today" before campus chapters of the League for Industrial Democracy, there may have been others who were as critical as Eleanor, but for the most part, and certainly among workers, his listeners were more interested in content than in the fine points of grammar. Nevertheless, he was concerned about the matter for some time.

When May announced in March, after a whirlwind courtship of two months, that she and Walter were going to be married, her parents were astonished and not a little agitated. Though Walter was a vigorous young man with a winning smile and a promising career as a labor leader, he was at the time a penniless, struggling organizer. Not that the money mattered—everyone was poor in the thirties—but their daughter could have had her "pick," and was pursued by an important gentleman who would have given her immediate economic security. Moreover, Walter was of a different religious faith from the Wolf family—the most serious hurdle he had to overcome; but since neither he nor May allowed the matter to make one bit of difference in their feeling for each other or their intention to marry, and since both were strong-minded, independent young people, the Wolfs could hardly oppose it. And as soon as they came to know him well, May's parents forgot their objections. Her mother, especially, loved Walter from then on as she loved her own sons.

The young couple decided on a civil ceremony. They were married at the city hall on Friday, March 13, 1936, and left immediately afterward for Mt. Clemens, where Walter had to address a labor rally—a characteristic honeymoon for the future labor leader and his bride. "If I had not been interested in the labor movement," May said with a smile, "we never would have married!"

For some months they shared the La Salle Street apartment with May's parents. They had little money; May turned over most of her sixty-dollars-a-week salary to the labor movement, and she had neither the time nor the energy for housework. In addition to teaching all day and helping Walter evenings, she squeezed in a night course in typing and shorthand at one of the high schools, so that she could serve as her husband's secretary. They were rarely at home for meals, usually grabbing a sandwich and a cup of coffee wherever they happened to be. "I was so thin the mattress hurt my hips," May said. And Walter added that they hardly slept at all.

There was the question of union offices that could be used as headquarters of the West Side local to which Walter belonged. Composed of only thirteen members, it was practically without funds. One day he was riding in a car with Dave Miller, a Scotsman who had served his apprenticeship in the labor movement in Glasgow as chairman of the Streetcar Men's Union, where he had attended the 1912 Wales convention, presided over by an assistant of Ernest Bevin, that later became famous for the "cradle-to-the-grave" welfare plan. Dave, dour but kindly, a staunch unionist who never lost his faith (or his Scotch burr), had grave doubts that they would ever find an office, but as they drove past the corner of Thirty-fifth Street and Michigan Avenue, Walter grabbed his arm on the wheel, shouting, "Stop the car, Dave! I saw a sign on that store-front building; maybe we can afford some space in there." He was out of the car like a shot, and came back in a few minutes, frowning slightly. "We can get a cubbyhole up there"—he pointed to the second floor—"and more space in the basement, but the guy wants ten dollars deposit, and I haven't got it."

Dave reached down into his pocket and came up with the

deficit Walter needed to make the deposit. Later the local was able to borrow a little money for rental of the small second-floor offices and the basement, which they fixed up with an old second-hand mimeograph machine as the Publicity Department. Here, under Frank Winn, a progressive young journalism graduate from the University of Texas, who proved to be a most capable publicity director, handbills were written on a rented typewriter, and turned out literally by hand on the old mimeograph machine.

In the spring of 1936, a UAW convention was held in South Bend, Indiana, from April 27 to May 2. The newly chartered union was determined to elect its own officers and executive board, and Walter Reuther was equally determined to participate in the proceedings. A local had to have at least fifteen members to be entitled to a delegate, but his local (of thirteen) got around that by asking each of the members to chip in every month for two members who hadn't joined yet. They then received a bona fide charter, and a call to the convention, with a credential for one delegate. At that time, auto workers were afraid to come to meetings regularly because of company reprisals for any union activity. Reuther himself gave a graphic, amusing account of the preparations for, and his part in, the convention.

"Only seven of our members showed up at the meeting we called to elect our delegate. Since I was the most active member, I was chosen by acclamation. So I stood up before this 'great mass of organized workers'—six members in addition to myself—and solemnly thanked them for their confidence in me. Next, one of the brothers made a motion that since Brother Reuther was unemployed and was devoting all his time to the union without pay, he should be given whatever money there was in the treasury to finance his trip.

"Our financial secretary was a sister, and she thought we were getting a bit reckless. So she modified the motion to read that, upon his return, Brother Reuther was to return to the treasury any money that was left over. The motion passed. The sister opened her handbag and handed me five dollars. That was all the money we had!

"Well, I hitchhiked my way to South Bend, and five of the brothers went along as observers. They, too, were unemployed.

I checked in at the cheapest hotel I could find. It had running water and inside plumbing, but that was about all. I asked the clerk for the biggest double bed they had. He coldly informed me that all their double beds were standard size. So I rented a room with a double bed—standard size. What the clerk didn't know was that, while I was the only one paying rent, five other men shared the room with me. We put the mattress on the floor and three of us slept on that, and three, on the box spring. We had very little money—we lived on hamburgers, and not many of them."

At the convention's opening session, the eligibility of "Delegate No. 86, Walter Reuther of Detroit, Michigan," was angrily challenged by several members of the East Side local on the grounds that he had falsely given the name of a plant that was supposed to have employed him. A squabble ensued, during which one delegate declared hotly, "Brother Reuther has never been employed in the Ternstedt plant since this organization was established!" *

After further wrangling he was seated anyway, largely because of the testimony of a worker from the women's division, Sister Tombar of Local 147, who stated that he *had* worked at Ternstedt *under an assumed name* during December, 1935 and January, 1936. The Hearing Committee then found that Brother Reuther was eligible for membership in the UAW, and as a result would be eligible for a seat at the convention.

Delegate Reuther (86) made his voice heard early in the proceedings, on the second day, at the Tuesday morning session. His opening words—"Brother Woods has talked about economy. It seems his big mistake was that he tried to judge the future by the past. *What we have tried to do is judge the future by its possibilities*" †—represent a key to his whole outlook, a key to his ultimate goals, even at this early date. He went on to say that economy was not the main issue; that the main issue was "whether or not we are going to leave this convention unified . . . into *an effective instrument with which we can organize auto workers.*" ** He sug-

---

* Reuther later admitted that he had not worked at Ternstedt, but that its selection (rather than the Coleman plant) had been "tactical," since it was in the district of the local (No. 86) he was representing; Ternstedt was merely his "assignment," he argued.
** Italics mine.

gested salaries of only $3,000 instead of $5,000 a year; and cited the Amalgamated Clothing Workers, which had built up a membership of a hundred thousand and whose president, Sidney Hillman, received only $7,500 a year. "Let us start low," Walter said, "instead of creating big, fat salaries right away, and see if they merit a raise to five thousand dollars." His point was that they could do a much better job of organizing with five men throughout the field than with three men (at $5,000). "Five men would make it possible to weld this union into a powerful organization, a powerful international union," he finished forcefully. He also advocated an eight-dollar-a-day limit on expenses, a reflection of his own frugality from his family's early training.

His second opinion, voiced that same morning, also mirrored his father's influence: he spoke in condemnation of Hearst newspapers, and moved to boycott them because of a headline in the morning paper which read: "40,000 auto workers oust Dillon, leave AFL," completely misleading those who did not bother to read the article. "While we are here to unify and solidify our ranks *within the AFL*, the enemies of organized labor in America are at work," Walter said angrily. He moved that a committee be appointed to draft a resolution condemning such misrepresentation, and that a boycott be initiated. The motion was seconded, and he further suggested that the *reporter not* be condemned, since his story was accurate; but that the headline, written in Chicago, was deliberately misleading. He added that they should work on the reporter to join the Newspaper Guild! The next day, the convention heard the report of the committee, with the telegram sent to Hearst and the Chicago AFL; the Hearst paper came out with another story and another headline—"Auto Workers Allegiance to AFL is Held"—in the afternoon edition. Telegrams came from John L. Lewis and Heywood Broun, the latter congratulating the UAW on its forthright stand against Hearst. Walter, with his sense of showmanship, timing, and drama, rose to point out the *power* of the UAW *acting in unity*, accenting those words to drive home their importance.

An interesting address at this convention was given by Dr. I. W. Ruskin on "Occupational Diseases," starting with "Machinists' Boils," from oil and grease infection on the skin; "boilermakers'

deafness" from noise; and "occupational hernias," much of which
was due to lack of medical aid when the accidents occurred. He
also discussed "speed-up neurosis," which, the doctor said, was
dramatically illustrated by Charlie Chaplin's fine picture *Modern
Times.* He then cited Leon Henderson's Labor Board report of
1934, condemning the speed-up system and factory conditions.
Richard Frankensteen, already prominent in union activity, rose
to give a graphic description of 315 cases of acute lead poisoning
in the UAW membership, all the facts of which cannot have failed
to take effect on Reuther the freshman delegate whose prime
goals were to become medical care of workers, and safety and
health regulations in the factory. The main business of the convention came the following day as the delegates elected their own
officers and executive board after Francis Dillon, the AFL "pro-
bation-period" president, had withdrawn. Homer Martin was a
former preacher who had worked in an auto plant for a time and
become so imbued with unionism that he preached its theories
and goals with a fiery zeal, stirring the workers to such a pitch
that they were moved to join the ranks. He was elected president,
largely on the strength of his oratory. Wyndham Mortimer, a wily
veteran of many campaigns, was vice-president; and George
Addes, who had made a name for himself by his two-fisted,
shrewd handling of a strike at Autolite plants in Toledo, was secretary-treasurer. And the spunky redhead from Detroit succeeded
in being elected to the Executive Board by a wide margin, getting
more votes than anyone else—30—a figure challenged by Roy
Speth, of the same group that challenged his seating, as not being
democratic. Walter was on his feet at once. "All this talk about it
being undemocratic is sheer nonsense when a man can get thirty
votes out of a possible thirty-eight," he exploded, and that ended
the controversy.

The closing address was by Norman Thomas as guest speaker
on the "Forces Against Labor in the United States." William
Green, president of the AFL, then turned over the $25,000 in the
AFL treasury to the UAW and declared the auto workers an
affiliate but autonomous union. A final piece of business, usually
not noted, was the decision to organize plants in Flint, Michigan.
In telling the story of that 1936 convention in South Bend, Walter

summed it up succinctly when he said, "We had faith—faith in an idea. . . . We were deeply convinced that free American workers could be brought together into voluntary association, that they could build a strong, industrial union and through that union speak a language that would be listened to by the great corporations. On that 1936 convention we staked our hopes and our futures."

As soon as he returned from the convention, he called the officers of the West Side locals—five others besides his—and persuaded all six locals to merge into one, so that together they could do an effective job of organizing. The other leaders accepted his idea, and he was elected president of the new organization. After the merger they had seventy-eight members, and they called their new union West Side Local 174, the number assigned to it by the International Union. And Brother Walter Reuther carried a membership card in West Side Local 174 (by which name it is still known) till the end of his life.

XI

First Big Break

ALTHOUGH the situation in Detroit had not changed visibly by the late summer of 1936, when Brother Walter Reuther thumbed his way home from the first UAW convention, more and wider cracks had begun to appear in the hard, tough crust inside which management had always held its employees under tight-fisted control. The breaks showed in other cities, in other industries—notably in rubber.

Early in the year, John L. Lewis and his CIO had won their first important victory with a successful strike at the Goodyear Tire & Rubber Company of Akron. CIO's greatest strength lay in John L. Lewis' 500,000 United Mine Workers, which had 300,000 members even in the depths of the depression. During the summer of 1936, Lewis concentrated his attention on the U. S. Steel Corporation—Big Steel.

There was one obvious reason why Lewis should be interested in Big Steel. Thousands of his coal miners worked in so-called "captive mines," owned by Big Steel. Since no labor unions were permitted anywhere in Big Steel, these men, along with the thousands of steel workers, were unorganized. He wanted those "captive miners" in his union, and he believed that great masses of steel workers could be drawn together into an extremely powerful industry-wide CIO union.

Lewis, with Philip Murray, his intelligent, mild-mannered lieutenant, set up the Steel Workers' Organizing Committee—the SWOC. In April, 1937, Big Steel yielded. Within a month, fifty-nine of its affiliates had joined. The SWOC took in 113,700 members in 1936. By the end of 1937 it had 510,000.

But Lewis had not forgotten the automobile industry, still unorganized with the exception of a few local unions and its infant UAW. In the late summer of 1936, he sent a check for $100,000 to Detroit. Considering the size of the organizing job to be accomplished, it was hardly more than a token contribution, but the money was welcome as a start. It would be up to the UAW to organize by themselves for the most part. But in the end this fact gave them an independence within the CIO which the Steel Workers' and most other CIO unions did not enjoy.

Hanging about the plant gates as the workmen checked in and out, young Reuther had become more and more convinced that their resentment would before very long overcome their fear of being fired. Always Walter Reuther had that kind of intuition a man must have if he is to become a leader. So he persistently continued to try to hand out union cards to automobile workers, who backed away, shaking their heads. He would keep talking, man to man.

"What's the use," he would argue, "of trying to keep a job that won't support your family? You know that there will be a long layoff every year, while they're retooling. And there's no certainty that you'll get your job back when they begin hiring again. So you polish apples for the foreman. No self-respecting American citizen should have to curry favor that way to hold his job. And you know what the stretch-out system does. It will happen to you too, if it goes on. You'll be an old man at forty, wrung out, thrown aside, with kids to raise and get through school."

And even if they were scared of management, the men listened with interest, a gleam of hope in their eyes.

So convinced was Walter Reuther that the break would be coming soon that he persuaded Victor to give up his job with the American Friends and return to Detroit. He wanted Victor around when things began to happen. As soon as he heard that the Kelsey-Hayes plant, where a number of Local 174 members were already employed, was taking on more men, he thought of Vic.

He knew that *he* couldn't get in, not only because of the blacklist, but because, as president of the local, he had tried to speak for the workers there and had been told bluntly by the company that he did not represent their workers; and they would not give him a hearing. He called his brother long-distance and outlined to him the explosive situation in Detroit. "They're hiring at Kelsey-Hayes, so if you're interested, come out right away," he finished.

Victor was attending a Quaker conference in Philadelphia—with his bride of a few weeks, Sophie, who came from the labor movement in the mill towns of New England, a bright girl who had received a scholarship to Brookwood. Victor had been doing some lecturing in foreign affairs at the college, and had soon fallen in love with this quick-minded, bright-eyed listener. Their courtship in the idyllic setting was as rapid and as filled with "shop talk" as Walter and May's had been. Like his brother, and many dedicated people in the labor movement (including Sidney and Bessie Hillman, two decades earlier), Victor was on a labor leader's honeymoon; but at Walter's call, he left immediately for Detroit, telling Sophie he would send for her as soon as he found a job and a place to live.

The next afternoon he "hired on" as a punch-press operator at the Kelsey-Hayes plant, which manufactured wheels, brake drums, and brake shoes, principally for Ford. Since he had never worked in an automobile plant in the United States, he had no record of union activity against him and was not on the blacklist; but from the day he punched the time clock, Victor deliberately placed his job in jeopardy by circulating among the men, trying to draw them into the union.

John L. Lewis' $100,000 made it possible for the UAW to hire some organizers, and Roy became the first Reuther to go on the union payroll; his participation in the auto strike of 1933 gave him priority over his brothers. He was hired to organize the automobile workers in Flint, where he was still head of the WPA adult education program, a post he now relinquished. Walter called on his former roommate, Merlin Bishop, who joined the ranks inside the Kelsey-Hayes plant, along with several other early unionists, among them George C. Edwards, a Harvard graduate vitally interested in labor problems (now a justice of the

Federal Court of Appeals in Detroit). The largest single organization of auto workers was the Automobile Industrial Workers'
Association, which had merged with the UAW right after the
South Bend convention. It was headed by Dick Frankensteen, a
beefy former football guard, who loved a good fight. With the
CIO support, Frankensteen became chief organizer in Detroit and
received a salary. Membership in the local unions began to increase.

The strength of Frankensteen's organization was demonstrated
soon after it joined the UAW. Chrysler had tried to meet the
growing unrest earlier by instituting an employee's representation
plan which the rank and file referred to as a "company union,"
but which the UAW welcomed as better than nothing, since it
included a seniority procedure in hiring. At the beginning of the
new-model production season in September of 1936, however,
management did not recall some of the more active union leaders
in accordance with their seniority. Rebellion broke out in the
Chrysler-Dodge plant, and the local union threatened to strike.
After considerable excitement Chrysler finally yielded to the extent of rehiring those who had been passed over. Although the
agreement did not amount to much more and the company did
not relax its opposition to the UAW as bargaining agent, the rein-
statement of the men whose seniority rights had been ignored was
a tremendous victory for the union organization. Small raises in
pay were also granted, along with some changes in working conditions.

As the weeks passed through the autumn and early winter,
Walter Reuther, still unpaid by the union, and jobless except for
his part-time post as recreation director for the WPA, concentrated his attention on the Kelsey-Hayes Wheel Company, where
Victor was employed. Victor, aided principally by George C.
Edwards and Merlin Bishop, who was the educational director
of the UAW, although Kelsey-Hayes didn't know it—all three persuasive young men—continued quietly to lead their fellow workers, one or two at a time, into the union.

One reason for Walter's interest in Kelsey-Hayes was that the
plant was on the west side of Detroit, in an area covered by his

Local 174. But he had another reason, which could be applied to other efforts to organize the industry, as he explained:

"In an integrated industry, where production flows from one plant to another, if you pinched off production in one or two outside plants that supplied parts for the assembly line, you could exert maximum leverage upon the bargaining process with a big manufacturer, like Ford, without having a broad, general strike. If Kelsey-Hayes, which supplied wheels for the Model A, went on strike, the Ford assembly line would inevitably slow down and eventually stop. At least that was the way it looked to me."

By early December, Victor and his fellow union organizers were convinced that there was enough interest among the five thousand Kelsey-Hayes employees to warrant a strike so they set about seeking a collective decision among the workers. There had been a recent speedup in the stretch-out system which the workers were finding intolerable. Kelsey-Hayes employed women, and one day one of them, a big Polish girl, fainted on the job from exhaustion. This gave the Reuthers and their fellow strategists an idea. They held a meeting at Walter's home. The girl was present, and she agreed to faint again—only this time it would be a fake faint. A date and an hour were fixed. Two union men were told how to pull the switches that would stop the assembly line. At that moment, several of the men were to yell, "Strike!"

The appointed day and hour arrived, the girl "fainted," and the plan worked as effectively as its originators had hoped it would. Victor jumped up on a big packing crate and began making a speech, urging the workers to join the union, then and there. As the machines stopped, workers came crowding in from all over the plant, to see what was happening. A worried personnel manager hurried in and began pulling at Victor's trouser legs.

"Get them to go back to work," the personnel man ordered, as Victor looked down at him smiling.

"Walter Reuther's the only one who can do that," he said.

"Who's he?" the personnel manager demanded. "Where can I reach him?"

Victor gave him the telephone number at Local 174 headquarters, where Walter was waiting for the call.

"I'll try to get them back," Walter promised, "but I'll have to get into the plant to do it."

A company car was sent for him. Walter climbed up on the packing crate and continued where Victor had stopped, pointing out to practically the entire working force of Kelsey-Hayes the advantages of joining a union. The personnel manager frantically grabbed him by the leg.

"Get 'em back to work!" he pleaded.

Walter shook his head. "Can't do a thing until they join up," he answered.

In the meantime, the workers were crowding about Victor, reaching for membership cards and hurriedly signing them. Caught completely off guard, bewildered and desperate, the plant management hastily met with a committee of the workmen. It agreed to negotiate with a union shop committee, and the men went back to work. An early date was set for negotiation talks, but when it arrived, representatives of management failed to show up.

"As president of 174, I was there with the shop committee," Walter recalled. "We sat waiting from ten in the morning until three in the afternoon, but nobody came near us. Of course we knew what had happened; Ford, as the company's largest customer, had ordered the meeting called off. So we left, and there was a strike.

"That was a strike that didn't need to happen and it wouldn't have happened if it had not been for Bennett and Ford. It wasn't a long strike—only about ten days. Ford must have needed those wheels pretty badly. Kelsey-Hayes was released from the squeeze, we negotiated, and signed a contract."

Negotiating a labor contract those days was apt to be somewhat slow and awkward, according to Victor.

"The trouble was that neither side had had any experience. Neither management nor labor knew how to conduct negotiations or draw up a contract. But under the contract we finally signed, we achieved a seventy-five cent an hour minimum wage for *all* employees: my pay was raised from thirty-four cents an hour to seventy-five, and the pay of a woman who worked next to me was raised from twenty-seven to seventy-five cents an hour. We insisted on equal pay for equal work with the seventy-five-cent minimum. Also, no one lost his job for joining the union and going on strike. And the stretch-out was slowed down."

The UAW had won its first strike—the first important strike in the automobile industry, following sitdown strikes earlier that fall at the Midland Steel Plant on the east side of Detroit, and at the Bendix Plant in South Bend, Indiana. All three of them were instrumental in effecting the organization gains to come.

Before that victory, Walter had spent endless unrewarding hours outside the gates of the automobile plants, attempting to persuade workmen to sign union membership cards. Now the men began to come to him, crowding into the shabby little headquarters of Local 174.

"Our union dues were a dollar a month," May Reuther recalled. "Usually the hand that reached out over the shoulders of the crowd around my desk would be holding a crumpled dollar bill. But sometimes the applicant would hold out fifty cents or a quarter, saying earnestly, 'Look, lady, I know this ain't enough, but I'll pay the rest next week. I want one of those cards right away.'"

By the end of the year, less than six months after it had been organized, the membership of West Side Local 174 had jumped from 178 to more than 2,000. Walter and Victor had been acting as unpaid union organizers, and May was given a salary of $15 a week, most of which she turned back into the union treasury.

"Undoubtedly the lowest-paid secretary in Detroit," her husband would say proudly.

XII

"Sit-down!"

ENCOURAGED by the signal gains made at Chrysler-Dodge, by Walter Reuther's amazing victory at Kelsey-Hayes, the spirit of "Solidarity Forever" surged forward in a wave of spontaneous strikes. In telling of the sudden rush to join the union in those early days, Reuther related, "A guy we never heard of would call up and say, 'We shut down such-and-such a plant. Send us over some coffee and doughnuts.' So we'd send over the stuff. Later on, we'd organize central kitchens and mobile feeding units. Our organizing committee was in session continuously."

Toward the end of 1936, the leadership of the UAW began to consider the possibilities of organizing one of the Big Three —General Motors, controlled by the Duponts and the house of Morgan, an empire extending all over the country and employing 250,000 workers. The move had to be approached with careful planning, though events were occurring so rapidly that there was little time for lengthy deliberation. John L. Lewis and Philip Murray were still concentrating their efforts in organizing the steel workers, as the CIO had set the steel industry as its prime target for mass organization, and believed that the first real breakthrough would come there. After sending the initial financial contribution to the UAW, the CIO let the auto workers' union shift for itself for the most part; occasionally men like John Brophy and Allan Haywood came to help out in specific situa-

tions, and at some point during the 1936–1937 period, Adolph
Germer was sent in as CIO regional director. While Lewis and
the CIO leadership did nothing to discourage the UAW from
making as much progress as it could, it is likely that they never
fully comprehended what was actually happening in the industry,
or did not fully believe the fast-moving events of the previous
months. Millions of American workers, restless under the complete domination of the employers, were ready for a strike, but
if the GM strike failed, what would happen to their newly
awakened interest in unions? The UAW leadership realized that
a strike at GM was inevitable, but they hoped it would not begin
until after the first of the year, for two very good reasons. They
didn't think the union would be prepared for it before then, and
they hoped to wait until Frank Murphy, the new governor, whom
labor had supported, would be installed in office. Another factor
to be considered was the most feasible starting point.

Flint, Michigan, was the heart of the GM empire because plants
there manufactured some of the most vital parts and components
of its highly popular and profitable models, Chevrolet and Buick;
a Fisher body plant was also located there, one of the main
sources of turret tops, without which GM could not turn out any
complete cars. It was logical that the battle should begin in Flint.
Roy Reuther, Robert Travis, and others who were leading the
struggle inside the plants became increasingly aware in late fall
and December of 1936 that if the strategy was to succeed at all,
they had to take drastic action. Gamble or not, the time was
ripe. The strike that was called on December 30, 1936, became
one of the biggest the nation had ever seen, eventually involving,
directly or indirectly, some 250,000 workers.

Flint was practically a company town, seemingly impregnable
to any onslaught by organized labor. Almost all the families were
dependent of GM for their livelihood: in a one-industry town
like Flint, the merchants, laundries, restaurants, gas stations—the
employers and their employees—exist on the money spent by
those who work in the plants. GM virtually owned Flint. The
courts, city officials, and police were in large measure under its
control. To maintain its power, GM, instead of organizing a private army on its own payroll, as Ford had done, hired the Pinker-

ton Detective Agency, long experienced in strikebreaking. It was said that GM paid to Pinkertons almost twice as much as the salary of its president, Alfred P. Sloan, who was drawing $375,000 a year. In addition, and working with Pinkertons, GM had an inside force of people in the plant that were used as spies, willing or unwilling. It was extremely difficult for the head of a family to resist the orders or threats of a foreman on whom his job depended. The system made the task of a union organizer in a GM plant truly hazardous.

"You never knew," said Roy Reuther, "whether the man working next to you was a loyal union member, as he professed to be, or a company spy." He and Robert Travis, who took over the organizing drive in Flint after Wyndham Mortimer was forced to leave town because of plant espionage, knew that the spies and Pinkertons watched everything and made regular detailed reports to the company. Spies attended union meetings—it was later learned that one of them had even been a delegate to the 1936 UAW founding convention in South Bend. The day after a meeting, one or two men, most trusted and valuable to the union, would be fired. The spies checked on a worker's life outside the plant, his friends, the bars he visited, even his reading habits. They were everywhere, keeping the UAW in such a state of distrust that little or nothing could be accomplished.

But even in Flint, Roy Reuther and Travis, noting an increasing resentment among the workers, began steadily building the loyalty of rank-and-file union members, and slowly built up the strength of the Flint locals. They had to work carefully, never certain that the plans to move against GM were not being revealed to management. Small groups were selected to carry out plans; no member knew who the other members were, or what assignments they had been given to prepare for the showdown with GM.

As tensions increased and unrest rose, the workers themselves took over the situation. They started calling wildcat strikes on their own. The fall of 1936 was marked by a spate of sporadic work stoppages in the Chevrolet and Fisher body plants and a long walkout in Atlanta. The Flint stoppages were quickly settled, and the workers, encouraged by minor victories, grew bolder and more impatient. On December 18, William Knudsen, after rejecting a union demand, held out a dim ray of hope by stating that GM did not want to discourage union organization; that he felt "collective bargaining is here to stay," but that it should take place "before a shutdown rather than after." UAW president Homer Martin, supported by George Addes, rushed to request a conference with the GM executive vice-president to discuss the speedup, job security, discrimination, and the abuse of piece-work rates. Knudsen, in granting the audience, called it "a personal interview," and merely agreed that GM would see union representatives on a plant-by-plant basis, hardly more than telling an employee to "take matters up with the plant manager" to settle grievances. Martin naïvely reported that the meeting was "completely amicable," but he was soon enlightened by Lewis and UAW officers that such a procedure would mean slow death to the union, since the overall GM policy was set at the top, and individual plant managers had no choice but to carry it out. Such negotiations could hardly be called collective bargaining; they would be dragged out endlessly, the sides unequally matched, the unions singly unable to cope with a giant corporation. A stalemate took place.

Then, on December 28, the struggle that was to become labor history began. Aggravated by a long string of unsettled grievances, nearly one thousand workers at the Fisher Body plant in Cleveland, which turned out turret tops, halted production by sitting down at their jobs. The next day, Flint's Fisher Body plant No. 2 followed suit after the management fired five union spokesmen for requesting collective bargaining. And the next night, December 30, 1936, workers in the more important Fisher Body plant No. 1 noticed that the vital dies were being loaded on freight cars for shipment. Consulting excitedly with Bob Travis, they realized that if these dies were shipped, GM would be able to set up production in a location where unions were extremely weak; the Flint workers would have to halt the shipment to save their jobs. To a man, the night shift of more than a thousand men voted to sit down and stay until the dispute was settled. By New Year's Eve, both Flint plants were occupied by sit-downers in a festive mood, and they made up a ditty to the tune of "The Martins and the Coys" to celebrate the crucial battle that was to last more than six weeks, spreading shop by shop across the country. And with it, the term "sit-down strike" skyrocketed into national fame.

Throughout the strike, and for months thereafter, those words would appear in bold type on front pages of the newspapers, while citizens who were not involved would argue endlessly whether a workman had the right to strike simply by sitting down at his machine, doing nothing, refusing to budge. He was, after all, trespassing on private property. The idea did not originate with the General Motors strikers. The sit-down strike had begun in Europe. It was first used in the United States in 1933 at a meat-packing plant in Minnesota, where it was successful. It had been used with increasing frequency, mostly in small factories. Usually the sitters won, because the employers would find no means of getting the strikers out without damage to their property.

A sit-down was comparatively easy to organize. It could be— and in many cases was—staged by the men in the plant, without outside help. At a given signal, one or more of the workers would shout, "Sit down!" Switches would be pulled, the machines would stop; executives, foremen, and anyone else who cared to leave would be escorted out, gates would be locked, and the workers would remain inside, impervious to threats or pleas from their baffled employers. GM executives were definitely alarmed by the daring takeover of the Fisher plants. In both, the initial activists were joined by scores of unionists who until now had been less bold, and several hundred stayed inside overnight. Soon more than six thousand workers were idled, since the strike-free Chevrolet assembly plant could not turn out cars with its supply of car bodies cut off by the sit-downs; the technique worked much the same as it had in the Kelsey-Hayes strike, but on a larger scale. In Cleveland, where Wyndham Mortimer was leading the sit-down that started on the twenty-eighth, the strike was so firm that UAW officials decided it was no longer necessary to continue the sit-down. The UAW members, who had planned a New Year's Eve party inside, marched out wearing paper hats and blowing tin horns made from metal scraps. They vowed to set up a picket line so strong that GM could "never run the plant," and the pledge was carried out.

John L. Lewis in Washington was astonished by the rapid turn of events, and at first tried to prevent the sit-downs from spreading, since he was still concentrating on Big Steel, but he saw quickly that it would be impossible to check the mounting strike fever of the infant auto workers' union. He recognized that their battle against the GM giants would have to be completely won or completely lost, and rallied by throwing thorough resources from the CIO behind it. President Roosevelt in the White House, while sympathetic to labor, was nettled by the whole situation, taking the stand of a bemused but benign neutral. Conferring with Secretary of Labor Frances Perkins, he revealed his quizzical reactions to her. "Well, it's illegal, but what law are they breaking?" she quoted him as questioning. "The law of trespass, and that's about the only law that could be invoked. . . . But shooting it out and killing a lot of people because they have violated the law of trespass . . . I just don't see that as the answer. . . . Why can't these fellows in General Motors meet with the committee of workers? Talk it all out. They would get a settlement. It wouldn't be so terrible."

GM was not in the mood to accept Miss Perkins' recommendation to "talk it all out." Corporation executives shrieked to the high heavens that the sit-down strikers were breaking the law and predicted that company property would be ruined, estimating that the occupied plants with their equipment were worth more than $50 million. Actually, the strikers did almost no damage, and, except for a buoyant New Year's Eve celebration, when liquor (sent in from outside) flowed freely, a strict discipline was maintained. The union banned alcohol and smoking in the interest of safety; the plants were kept clean, and the equipment was protected. Food was sent in from outside—bread, big buckets of coffee and, as often as possible, more substantial fare prepared in makeshift kitchens set up by fellow strikers outside; strikers ate it in the plant cafeterias, which were kept spotless. All this meant little to General Motors officials, who, on January 4, 1937, rejected all union demands, started a back-to-work movement, and asked for federal action to oust the strikers. It rushed into a state court, and obtained an injunction from Circuit Judge Edward D. Black, of Flint, ordering the sit-downers to leave the plants and refrain from picketing.

When the sheriff, with a hundred Flint policemen and sixty GM guards, arrived to enforce the order, he was met with derision from the five hundred union stalwarts staying inside. He retreated amid boos and catcalls from the strikers, who had helped vote him into office and in some cases were his neighbors. However, GM guards regained control of the plant gates during the distraction; and if the injunction had been allowed to stand, it could have broken the strike. But the CIO general counsel, Lee Pressman, acting on labor's charge that GM owned Flint—courts, city officials, police, press, and radio—looked into the list of GM stockholders, and was overjoyed to find that Judge Black held 3,365 shares, then valued at $219,000. The exposure of the unlawful conflict of interest, plus UAW demands to impeach the judge, voided the injunction, and brought unsavory publicity to GM.

Exhilarated at winning the first round, the UAW Executive Board, including the high-spirited Walter Reuther, met in Flint the next day to create a Board of Strategy, which authorized strikes against every GM factory in the country. Delegates from fifty locals demanded a thirty-hour week. A CIO organizer declared the union had one hundred thousand members. Nearly a thousand of them formed a motorcade of 150 cars past the Fisher plants, honking their horns to encourage the sit-downers inside.

The upsurge of victory spirit proved premature, for GM was not deterred by the failure of its first legal offensive. The company supported the formation of the "Flint Alliance," headed by George Boysen, a former Buick paymaster who had become the owner of a small spark-plug plant. A well-paid New York public-relations man was brought in, who started a high-pressure campaign to support GM's "back-to-work" movement and downgrade union strength among nonstriking workers. He received the support of many who had not belonged to the UAW when the strike began and were anxious to return to work at any price. He also got full cooperation from the city manager, police officials, and antiunion citizens. By uniting the two forces, Boysen and the public relations man accused UAW officials of communism, blasting the strike as the work of "outside agitators," and calling on all loyal Flint citizens to rise up and drive the interlopers out of town. The immediate effect seemed ominous: the Alliance claimed fifteen thousand members signed up in the first day of operation from its headquarters in the heart of the city.

The UAW, sensing that its very life might be at stake, quickly launched a counterattack. Roy Reuther spoke over a public-address system to nonstriking Chevrolet workers as they were changing shifts, strongly denouncing the Flint Alliance as a "company union" financed by General Motors. In the midst of his speech, someone started a minor riot by ripping off the loud-speakers. Eight men were injured before police quieted the disorder and he could continue. He urged a march on the Flint jail to demand release of two UAW loyalists arrested earlier. "We'll show these police they're not dealing with children! If they want trouble they'll find ten thousand men marching on Flint!" His fighting words brought police with tear guns to disperse the crowd and set up roadblocks to halt the legions of union ranks from all over the Midwest. From Cleveland, Toledo, and Akron they poured into the strike-besieged city, ready to join the battle.

Walter showed his own strength in Detroit the next day by calling a sit-down at the Cadillac plant there, halting production and idling another 4,800 GM workers. Then he and Victor Reuther led a powerful delegation from Detroit's West Side locals, joining the reinforcements headed for Flint, their sound truck in the van. The Boysen Alliance retaliated the influx by trumpeting the signatures of eleven thousand more Chevrolet employees who allegedly denounced the strike, claiming contentment with the status quo. The strike took on the aspect of a civil war, with battle lines stiffening.

Within the plants, the union continued to maintain strict discipline. There were separate men's and women's "dormitories," with beds made of car cushions, some labeled "Hotel Astor" or "Hotel Sloan," a slur at Alfred P. Sloan, GM president. A UAW "chief of police" inspected for cleanliness, and directed daily showers for all in factory washrooms. Fire drills were scheduled regularly, along with practice at hurling metal pipes or car hinges toward a substitute target in case the opposing forces decided to invade the factory. As usual, the exuberance of the beginning of the strike soon wore off, and the strikers grew restive unless they had something to do, cut off as they were from the outside world, from their families and friends. Merlin Bishop, who had been appointed the UAW's first national education director, helped them to pass the time by "turning the plants into a labor college," and taught classes in parliamentary law, public speaking, labor history, and history of the auto industry. The study took the strikers' minds off being isolated, and at the same time gave them a better perspective on the long-range goals of the union.

Recreation also played an important part as a morale builder. In Detroit a labor-entertainment center sprang up, composed largely of volunteers, all interested or connected with the labor movement. There were a theater group, a dance group, and various musicians who offered to serve as entertainers in struck factories. Revues on the order of the famous "Pins and Needles" of the garment workers' struggle in New York were hastily put together and sent to plants in Detroit, Flint, and towns like Anderson, Indiana. May Sweet, then recently engaged to Sam Sweet, education director of a large East Side local, related her experience in the Cadillac plant where Walter had called the sit-down (which lasted ten days and ten nights). A stenographer in a Detroit office, she played the mandolin in a musical unit, and on one occasion when they played for the strikers they did not get out before the gates were locked, so she had to spend the night in the factory. In the morning she was late for work, but she had to plead illness as her excuse. "If I had told my boss the real reason I'd have been fired," she said. "Most business-men were not sympathetic to sit-downers."

The drama group sent productions of labor plays to Flint to entertain the strikers; even the New Theater League and the Union Dramatics Club of New York City dispatched companies to perform dramas of social significance, forerunners of "audience participation" plays, on the bare "boards" of a factory floor. If no other diversion, the strikers soon had a popular sit-down song to sing, with lyrics by a union lawyer:

When the speedup comes, just twiddle your thumbs.
Sit down! Sit down!
And; When the boss won't talk, don't take a walk.
Sit down! Sit down!

General Motors was now feeling the pinch. The big Chevrolet assembly line slowed down almost to a halt, as did Cadillac and LaSalle in Detroit. The output of both Pontiac and Oldsmobile was sharply cut. In essence, the whole giant corporation was in a squeeze, losing millions of dollars because of fewer than a thousand workers entrenched in two key factories. It was inevitable that GM should try a strong-arm tactic. On January 11, management shut off the heat at Fisher 2; and a few hours later Flint police, surrounding the entrance, announced that no further food supplies would be permitted to pass into the plant. A ladder placed against a window by pickets in an attempt to smuggle in a single shipment was torn down at once. Groups of cold, hungry sit-downers huddled together inside, shivering as dinnertime came, wondering what to do. Shortly before 7:00 P.M., Victor Reuther appeared on one of the UAW sound trucks, making his regular evening round to play "Solidarity Forever," and give his daily report on the so-called "negotiations" that were supposedly going on but getting nowhere. He had hardly pulled up when the truck was surrounded by picket captains shouting, "They're trying to freeze our guys and starve them out!"

Victor, grabbing the microphone, pleaded with police to let food go through; but the police turned a deaf ear on his appeals. He then shouted a stern order to "take the gates" and moments later a band of fighting unionists rushed the gates from both sides, swept the police away, and carried coffee, bread, and other food into the plant. The police, briefly conquered, returned two hours later, fifty strong, armed with clubs, and at 9:00 P.M. charged the pickets guarding the entrance. After scattering most of them, the police shattered a pane of the locked doors, poked in a tear-gas gun, and fired it. The sit-downers inside fell back, and police rushing to the windows, blasted them with buckshot through the glass. The battle was launched. Momentarily halted by tear gas, the strikers rushed to the roof of the plant to let loose a

terrific barrage on the police below, who were not attacking
pickets. The hours of target practice stood them in good stead as
they hurled two-pound car hinges from makeshift catapults—
stretching inner tubes between crisscross ironpipes—down upon
the heads of attacking police. Heavy bolts and nuts were also used
for ammunition, while below, the pickets fought hand to hand
with clubs, knives, soda-pop bottles, anything. The battle raged
for three hours. Victor Reuther, Dave Miller (who had come
from ten days and nights in the Cadillac plant), Bill Carney (on
loan from the United Rubber workers), and other strike captains
took turns at the sound-truck microphone, roaring encouraging
orders to the embattled union army. When the police tried to tear
down the sound apparatus to silence them, a flank of husky
unionists beat them back. Sheriff Thomas Wolcott, summoned to
the battle zone, had his car overturned by pickets within minutes
of his arrival. Its glaring headlights at a crazy angle, it lit up the
scene of chaos—broken glass, rocks, door hinges—in the factory
yards. Still the battle continued.

At midnight, the police gathered for one more assault, but the
strikers now turned a powerful GM fire hose they had managed
to hook up square onto the attackers. The powerful spray of icy
water knocked them back, while a fresh barrage from the roof
rained on their heads; and they turned at last, ran fifty yards to
a bridge near the plant gate; then, running another fifty yards
across it, disappeared into the night. Dave Miller laughed in telling the tale. "You never saw cops run so fast. We called it the
Battle of the Running Bulls!" At dawn, a triumphant chorus of
"Solidarity Forever" rang out from the plant, in spite of the havoc.
Fourteen of the strikers had been shot and wounded by police
bullets; dozens more were injured, cut, or beaten. A bloody battle, but fortunately the use of force was not repeated. GM executives, embarrassed by the whole situation, offered a lame apology,
stating that the corporation "had never intended to" shut off the
heat and would not turn off any facilities again. Governor Frank
Murphy, however, read a warning into the pitched battle, and
decided to send twelve hundred national guardsmen into Flint
purely to maintain order, not to evict the sit-downers or break
the strike; he also decreed that food be permitted to pass through

the gates. Murphy was in a touchy predicament: he had been elected largely by labor's support, and indeed, was sympathetic to their demands for a better living. Yet it was his duty as governor to protect property rights under the law, and the sit-downers were violating that law. He finally took a middle course by keeping the national guardsmen on the scene (using an abandoned schoolhouse as barracks) and brought pressure on General Motors to start serious negotiations with union representatives.

The day after the battle, Walter Reuther staged another sit-down strike in Detroit, at the Fleetwood Division of Fisher Body, as a "sympathy gesture" for the Flint strikers. This pushed the number of idled GM workers up to 112,000. General Motors, more outdistanced in production every day by its competitors, tried at first to whip up an antistrike, back-to-work frenzy through the Flint Alliance; but then appeared to yield to Murphy's pressure and agreed to meet with the UAW, provided the strikers would leave the plants first; they promised not to operate the factories for fifteen days. The UAW did not trust GM, but, also under pressure from Murphy, gave in, a truce was announced at 3:00 A.M. on January 15. Bargaining was to begin three days later, when the plants were emptied. Walter and Dick Frankensteen led 650 strikers out of Fleetwood and Cadillac in Detroit, with flying banners and union bands, into the waiting arms of wives and children. Beaming, Walter led the chorus of voices in a parody of an old World War One ballad:

> The boss is shaking at the knees,
> He's shaking in his BVD's.
> Hinky, dinky, parley voo!

Sit-downers in Indiana also left the plants: and in Flint, the townspeople rushed to stores and restaurants again, even before the struck factories were emptied. But just as the sit-downers there were about to leave, a United Press reporter, Bill Lawrence, discovered and exposed an exchange of messages between Knudsen and the Flint Alliance that indicated Knudsen was planning to meet with Boysen's antistrike forces. Although Knudsen tried to deny it, the union felt they had been double-crossed, and, instead of being emptied, Fisher plants 1 and 2 remained occupied, while the union called for reinforcements. GM called for another injunction, this time from a Judge Gadola, who did not own GM stock; he ordered an evacuation by 3:00 P.M. on February 3, a sweeping command that dashed UAW hopes for settlement.

On the night of January 27, strike leaders met gloomily in their Flint headquarters. Robert Travis pointed out that the morale inside the plants was weakening after the month-long siege and the sudden fade-out of the prospective victory. They would have to pull some decisive, dramatic stroke to hearten the strikers and break GM's resistance. Obviously, the new target would have to be Chevy plant No. 4, where the assembly line was still operating at a slowed rate. Another plant, Chevy 9, a ball-bearing factory, was still going, but No. 4 was the most desirable target.

Roy Reuther reached across his desk, drew a sheet of cardboard from the folds of a freshly laundered shirt, and with a blue pencil started to sketch a diagram. "What we need," he said quietly, "is a diversionary action." He drew two squares, one marked Chevy 4, the other Chevy 9, some distance apart. He then drew lines away from Chevy 4, the objective, toward Chevy 9. The plan was simple. Word would be leaked out to company spies that a sit-down would be started on January 29 at Chevy 9. "They will rush everybody to Chevy 9, to stop us there," he explained. "They won't be paying much attention to our real objective, Chevy 4. There will be a fight at Chevy 9, naturally, and we'll lose. But if we can hold out thirty or forty minutes there, it will give us time to take over Chevy 4, which will have been left practically unprotected."

On the appointed day, hundreds of Pinkerton men, GM security forces, and nonunion workers gathered in and around Chevy 9, as Roy had predicted. At a given signal, several men inside yelled, "Sit-down!" Then, for about forty minutes, the strikers valiantly fought company police, who hurled tear gas inside. Outside, a UAW Women's Emergency Brigade, decked out in bright-red berets, took long poles to poke in plant windows so the men could get air. A sound truck with a microphone, protected by several hundred strikers who had come from out of town as before, was set up to lend reality to the scene. The battle raged inside and out. Meanwhile, at Chevy 4, a handful of GM guards were taken by surprise before they could call for help by a group of union "Commandos," rushed there from union headquarters. One of the leaders was Walter Reuther, who had been called in secretly from Detroit to assist in carrying out the scheme.

He took charge the moment they had control, directing the building of a strong barricade against the factory doors. "I drove those guys—we had to work fast," he said afterward. "And we did: It took them three days to tear down what we had built up in a few hours." Word had been sent to Chevy 9, where the disturbance stopped as if someone had turned off a sound track. A shout of victory had gone up as soon as they learned Chevy 4 was in the hands of the strikers. For years, Roy Reuther kept that piece of cardboard on which he had drawn his battle plan. Those outside Chevy 9 went in a body to Chevy 4 and took up pickets posts outside. The Women's Emergency Brigade locked arms and defied police: "Nobody can get in except our men." It was one of the most spectacular maneuvers of the labor wars of the 1930's, and its stunning success put the workers into a state of exultation that was matched in intensity only by the outrage and fury of the management.

GM demanded action, and even Governor Murphy, feeling duped by the deceptive tactics, for once went against union interests, ordering the National Guard to surround Chevy 4 and threatening to drive the strikers out if necessary. Finally he ruled that only Chevrolet workers could stay, so Walter and Roy Reuther had to get out, and the sit-downers were left without leadership. The Guard posted howitzers and machine guns at strategic points, while an army of union sympathizers kept coming from all over. By truck, by battered car, on foot, they came carrying signs bearing slogans; men with their wives and daughters poured into Flint from Lansing, Toledo, Akron ("shock troops" of rubber workers), Pontiac, and of course Detroit. Walter led a phalanx five hundred strong from the West Side locals. Just before taking off, he and the other UAW Executive Board members had decided to appeal to John L. Lewis for help, and CIO attorney Lee Pressman agreed to call him.

As the zero hour on February 3, 1937, drew near, the men in the struck plants, armed only with makeshift weapons, sent a

telegram to Governor Murphy, informing him they had decided
to stay on in the face of certain death for many at the hands of
the militia. They warned him that the use of "murderous weapons
would mean a bloodbath," and that he would be held responsible
for their deaths. John L. Lewis, who had received the call from
Pressman at 3:00 A.M., arrived at the eleventh hour, and used
all his histrionic ability to dissuade Murphy from ordering the
troops to fire. If they did fire, Lewis thundered, "Mine will be
the first breast those bullets will strike!" He vowed to join the
men in the barricaded factories. His words, plus the presence
of a citizen-workers army which, carrying the American flag,
circled the factory lawns, proved effective psychological warfare. Murphy really wanted a peaceful settlement; instead of
issuing the dread order, he prevailed on Knudsen to meet with
Lewis. The deadline passed without gunfire. At the White House,
President Roosevelt, after a hasty conference with CIO leader
Sidney Hillman, phoned Lewis to propose a temporary settlement whereby GM would recognize the UAW for one month.
Lewis insisted on at least six months, so talks were stalled.

Tensions in Flint remained high as negotiation attempts see-
sawed back and forth. The mayor pleaded with both sides to
stop walking the streets "armed with sundry pieces of wood and
missiles." At one point, GM again shut off the heat in occupied
plants, but after a warning that the sitters would burn oily rags
to keep warm, the company relented. Finally, on February 11,
the end came. Under the single-page contract signed by GM,
the union received the big prize it demanded: recognition of the
UAW as the sole collective bargaining agent for its members in
General Motors. The firm would comply with the National Labor
Relations law, men would be permitted to join the union, none
of the strikers would be fired; they could wear union buttons
in the plant, and discuss union affairs or recruit new members
during lunch hour; injunction and contempt-of-court proceedings
against sit-downers in both Flint and Cleveland were to be
dropped. A five-cents-an-hour wage increase was granted. But
the gain that set the weary sit-downers to cheering, shouting
"Solidarity Forever" as they marched out of the plants and down

the main street of Flint, was the fact that they now had a bona
fide union. Workers everywhere rushed to join.

In Walter Reuther's office headquarters of West Side Local
174, there was happy bedlam. For days and nights May Reuther
sat at her desk signing up new members, too elated to realize
how tired she was. More bushel baskets had to be brought in to
file the cards. "We had almost no equipment those days," she
said laughing, "but we found a way to file the cards somehow!"

Walter, as elated as she, declined to take credit for himself
or the other leaders. "What we were going through," he said
later, "was a great social and economic revolution. Tens of thousands of workers who had never belonged to a union, who had
never had any of the privileges of collective bargaining, suddenly
stood up and wanted to be counted. We didn't organize them.
We merely facilitated their coming together." By early summer,
West Side Local 174, which had started ten months previously
with seventy-eight, had leaped to a membership of thirty thousand in more than forty plants. While he was still relatively
unknown to the public, Brother Walter Philip Reuther, not yet
thirty years old, was being regarded with interest by other labor
leaders of considerably higher rank. Who was this redheaded
upstart, anyway?

XIII

Battle of the Overpass

THE triumph in Flint led to a doubling of the overall membership in the UAW—from 100,000 to 200,000—and brought a fresh wave of sit-downs flooding through the auto industry. The crest was reached in March, 1937, when 192,642 workers sat down at their jobs. At least 60,000 of these were in Chrysler plants, the second of the Big Three to capitulate, although the corporation held out for several weeks before yielding to UAW demands for a union shop. Studebaker and Cadillac followed in the foaming wake. Walter Reuther, with his awareness of mass mood, his sense of timing and intuitive talent for strategy, realized that this rushing tide of events must be "taken at the flood" if the course of a workingman's life was to be permanently altered for the better. Now was the time to strike an undisputed giant of the industry, the Ford Motor Company.

Henry Ford's edict a month earlier, that his company would never sign with the UAW or any other union, only served as a spark plug to the young labor leader's determination, and, as usual, his imagination soared—literally—to produce a unique "stunt" as a campaign starter: He and Victor hired a small plane, wired it for sound with UAW loudspeakers under each wing, and, while the pilot navigated "by the seat of his pants" across the city to circle over the huge River Rouge factory of Ford, they spoke into hand microphones to broadcast union propaganda just as the shift of thousands of workers was changing. Unfortunately, the air was murky with the moisture of a gray April day; and, although the pilot flew as low and as slowly as he dared, their words were lost down the wind and fog. But the men looking up got the message: Here was union leadership with enough guts and imagination to flaunt organized labor from the skies in the faces of company guards, spies, and goons on the ground. The press had given advance notice of the bizarre UAW device, thereby drawing attention to Reuther himself as well as the UAW. He had released the story of the flight and of a proposed rally the union was to hold, boasting that the membership inside the plant was already a thousand strong, a slight exaggeration, but it made the papers, including *The New York Times*. He was shrewd enough to know that the UAW organizer who could prove to be responsible for signing up Ford would stand a good chance for the UAW presidency, especially if Homer Martin continued his shilly-shallying, as he gave good indication of doing.

Walter, as president of West Side Local 174, was within his jurisdictional territory (geographically) in organizing the Ford workers. He had cleared his participation in this largest drive of the union with Richard Frankensteen, head of organizing for the entire Detroit area, and he was not discouraged by the fact that the air stunt had failed to go over as successfully as he and Victor had hoped. The main thing was that they had been noticed by the press, by thousands of workers. . . .

And by Bennett's boys, somebody reminded him. By now Bennett had built up his army of ex-convicts, thugs, and musclemen to number three thousand. They tried to keep the workers in subjection by terroristic methods, so that, out of fear of losing their jobs, they trembled at the thought of joining a union even if they wanted to become affiliated. Among Bennett's handpicked henchmen were "Legs" Laman, rumrunner, kidnapper, and squealer, who after six years in prison was paroled in the custody of Ford—through Bennett; Angelo Caruso, leader of the Detroit Down-River gang; Sam Cuva, who had been given life imprisonment for murdering his mother-in-law. Under the guise of "rehabilitating these unfortunate men," Bennett was in fact reactivating them in crime. His first question in employing a new recruit was "Can you shoot?"

Walter knew this as well as anyone in the labor movement, but he went right ahead, planning his campaign, undaunted by the threat of Bennett's bully boys or the ineffectiveness of the airplane stunt, which had been merely an opening gambit.

By May 26, 1937, the newspapers had become well aware of the nature of Harry Bennett's "Service Department," although the Detroit public, save for the Ford employees, had not. When the press heard * that Dick Frankensteen, a former football star, and Walter Reuther, president of a West Side local with thirty thousand automobile workers on its rolls, were going out to distribute union leaflets at the River Rouge plant, it assumed that there would be trouble. Every paper in Detroit, some papers from other cities, and all the press associations sent reporters and photographers to the scene.

Reuther and Frankensteen arrived about an hour before the end of the day shift, when thousands of the eighty thousand workmen employed at the plant would come streaming out of the gates on their way home. They drove to the plant, accompanied by two more union men, a clergyman, and a representative of Senator La Follette's Civil Liberties Committee, who were to act as observers, and three or four women carrying leaflets.

The plans had been carefully worked out. Frankensteen had in his pocket a permit, issued at Dearborn city hall, by some clerk who seemingly did not quite realize what he was doing. Reuther and Frankensteen carried no leaflets. The leaflets were to be handed out by women, many of whom were following aboard streetcars. Everybody, including the leaders, had been instructed not to start any argument if they were ordered to leave, simply to walk quietly away. They were unarmed.

The encounter took place on an overpass that had been built to enable the Ford workers to enter and leave the plant, as the shifts changed, without crowding the highway and slowing down traffic. There was some dispute as to who owned the overpass. Since it led to the plant gate, the company claimed ownership,

* From advance notices sent out by WPR, and the publicity department of West Side Local 174.

but Reuther and the other union leaders insisted that it had been
built by the State Highway Department and was therefore public
property.

As he mounted the two flights of iron steps leading up to it,
Walter Reuther noted that the overpass appeared to be more
heavily populated than was usual. There was a large group of
reporters and photographers, many of whom he knew, but loiter-
ing along the railing were men he did not recognize. They might
have been curious onlookers—he did not know.

Reuther and Frankensteen stopped in the middle of the overpass and were immediately surrounded by reporters and photographers. The two labor leaders were standing with their backs to
the plant gate, so they did not see something that started the
cameras clicking. For out through the gate marched what must
have been the most evil-looking aggregation of men ever seen in
Dearborn, Michigan. The trained eyes of reporters detected
bulges under the jackets of some of the men, indicating that they
were wearing shoulder gun holsters. Several wore dark glasses as
a disguise of sorts. Scowling and moving with menacing deliberation, they advanced toward the group in the center of the overpass.

Reuther and Frankensteen did not see them, but some of the
newspapermen did, and, as they leaped for safety, they shouted
warnings. But they were too late.

"Hey, you!" growled one of the toughs.

Walter turned around, smiling.

"You're on company property—get the hell off this bridge!"

Reuther and Frankensteen immediately started for the stairs.
Again they had their backs toward the advancing thugs. Before
they had taken two steps, they were surrounded. As the others in
their group watched in horror, their jackets were pulled up over
their heads, blinding them and pinning down their arms. A dozen
powerful sluggers were all over them, beating them savagely.

In testimony before the National Labor Relations Board some
weeks later, Walter Reuther described the treatment he received:

"Seven times they raised me off the concrete and slammed me
down on it. They pinned my arms and shot short jabs to my face.
I was punched and kicked and dragged by my feet to the stair-

way. I grabbed the railing, but they wrenched me loose. I was thrown down the first flight of steps. They picked me up, slammed me down on the platform and kicked me down the second flight. Down on the ground, they beat me and kicked me some more. . . ."

In later reminiscences, Reuther said he was actually dragged down the steps by his feet.

"My back hit the edge of every one of those iron steps," he said. "I still cannot understand why it was not broken."

"Get them goddamn cameras!" someone yelled. "Smash 'em!" Out of the dozens of cameramen on the bridge, only a few escaped with their plates intact, and cameras undamaged.

The reporters were attacked, too—cursed, shoved around, knocked down. Several returned to their offices that evening with black eyes and other facial bruises.

As Walter Reuther landed on the cinders beside the streetcar tracks, bleeding and groggy, a streetcar stopped nearby, and some women began to file off—all carrying bundles of leaflets. Reuther's assailants turned their attention to the women, tearing the leaflets from their arms. Those who tried to resist were knocked down. A Dearborn mounted policeman rode up as they had one of the women on the ground, kicking her in the stomach. Someone said later that his expression was almost pleading as he said,

"Stop it! You'll kill her!"

Lying on the cinders, Walter saw a car coming down the highway. The driver slowed down and beckoned.

"Dazed as I was, my whole body hurting, I managed to scramble onto the running board. That's how I got away."

The driver was one of the photographers who had managed to flee with his camera and plates intact—Arnold Freeman of the Detroit *Times*.

While Bennett's servicemen seemed to center most of their attention on Reuther, Frankensteen fared even worse, probably because he, a former football guard, tried harder to defend himself. Reuther, only five feet eight inches tall and rather slightly built, apparently relaxed after his vain attempt to grab the railing, and let them have their way. A man relaxed can take much more punishment than one who tightens his muscles and tries to fight back. But even a strongly anti-Reuther writer years later described the mauling he had received as "a cruel beating."

The fighting went on for some time after Reuther escaped, spreading out to the other plant gates and into the nearby streets. A union man walking along a street two blocks away was so viciously manhandled that he spent months in the hospital with a broken back.

A fact that Bennett had failed to take into consideration was that, if a newspaper man is physically mistreated while on an assignment, the press reacts somewhat as police react when a cop is killed. Detroit would not soon forget what it saw and read in the newspapers the following day.

The photographer who had been able to save all his plates had a complete photographic review of the beatings, beginning with the advance of Bennett's servicemen through the gate to the ruffians climbing all over Reuther and Frankensteen, to their starting to drag Walter down the steps by his feet. In sequence they resembled a motion picture. Some of the other photographers had come out with a few undamaged plates.

The reporters omitted none of the details in the stories they angrily pounded out on their typewriters. No mercy was shown toward anyone in the Ford management. Mr. Ford, with his vast industrial empire, might still be considered by outsiders Detroit's leading citizen, but never again would the people of Detroit have complete confidence in his "essential kindness." Unable to stop the papers from publishing those stories and pictures, the Ford publicity department was destined to spend months trying to repair the damage, to no avail. Henry Ford himself made a few attempts to "explain," but they were inept and futile.

Harry Bennett at first denied that any of his men had been engaged in the brawl. The toughs who attacked Reuther were "just loyal Ford employees trying to protect company property." He told one reporter that most of the ex-convicts in his Service Department were "physical wrecks." Nobody believed him. He apparently considered it inexpedient to try to defend them as he once did to a magazine writer:

"They're a lot of tough bastards, but every goddamn one of 'em is a gentleman."

Bennett's boys were still not finished with Walter Reuther. Their second attack was staged with an attempt at secrecy in Reuther's home. It occurred not quite a year after the beating on the overpass—April 9, 1938. Victor Reuther's wife, Sophie, was celebrating her birthday, and Walter and May were giving a small party for her in their apartment—with the three brothers, their wives, and a few close friends present. They had ordered some chop suey sent in for a late supper.

The doorbell rang, and Walter answered it, reaching into his pocket for money to pay for the order. But when he opened the door, he was confronted not by a delivery boy with an order of chop suey, but by two burly hoodlums—one pointing a revolver, the other carrying a blackjack.

They shoved Walter aside and slammed the door behind them. The man with the gun herded the startled guests, including Roy and Victor, to one side of the room and kept them covered. The man with the blackjack started after Walter.

"Come on," he growled. "We want you."

With the agility of a monkey, Walter leaped into a corner, grabbed a lamp and threw it at him, momentarily distracting him. Sophie pounced on a jar of pickles, heaving it at the intruder right after the lamp. Then Walter slid to the floor with his back planted firmly against the wall.

May recalled, "He began kicking out with both feet, edging along the floor with his back against the wall. The man tried to grab his feet, but Walter was too quick for him. Against those flying feet, the thug couldn't get hold of him. Finally Walter kicked the club out of his hand, and Roy grabbed it."

This attracted the attention of the man with the gun for a split second, and one of the guests, Al King, slipped out into the kitchen, opened a window and jumped out, landing two floors below on soft ground, miraculously unhurt.

"Aw, let's plug him now!" the gunman snarled.

But the man who had escaped was shouting, and the sound of runing feet outside could be heard in the apartment.

"We'd better get the hell out of here!" one of the pair said hastily. And they ran out.

The police found no trace of them, but a few days later a man called offering their names for five thousand dollars, if Walter would meet him in a dirty, run-down saloon in a tough part of the city. Walter insisted on going, but he did not go alone. Since he did not drink, Walter's acquaintance with saloons was very slight indeed, and he was accompanied by several of the West Side Local's huskiest members.

The union put up the money, he was given the names, and two men were arrested and brought to trial. They were identified as Bennett's boys, admitted everything, but insisted that Walter had hired them to stage the attempted kidnapping for publicity purposes. They managed to convince the jury and were acquitted.

Some three years later, Henry Ford, after remarking sententiously, in an unguarded moment, to a reporter, "If you can't lick 'em, join 'em," was about to sign his first contract with UAW. Someone telephoned the union headquarters and identified himself as one of the pair. He could not reach Walter, but talked to Victor Reuther. He suggested that he and his partner, Mr. Bennett, and Walter have "a friendly little dinner" together. Mr. Bennett had decided that he had better do some fence mending.

The Reuthers were not given to profanity, but it was said that the language that came from the other end of the telephone would have put a hard-boiled dock worker to shame.

The caller evidently could not believe his ears. The surprise in his voice sounded almost genuine as he said: "I was just hired to do a job. . . . You guys didn't take that *personally*, did you?"

XIV

Strife and Confusion

THE mauling he had received on the overpass from Harry Bennett's men quickly made Walter Reuther one of the most widely known figures in the labor movement.

The public stared with horror and sympathy at photographs of his bruised face in newspapers and magazines all over the country. When subsequent pictures showed him to be a very attractive young man, sympathy turned to liking. He always looked as though he had just had a shower and a shave, and had put on a clean white shirt. When he appeared as a witness at hearings before the National Labor Relations Board some weeks after the attack, his battered face had healed, but to millions of workingmen, growing more restive in the iron grip of their bosses, he had become a symbol of martyrdom.

They thought of him as a new type of labor leader, youthful, dynamic, attractive. He had his rivals, but he was in the top tank of UAW leadership from the time of the 1936 convention. Like Local 174, other UAW locals, too, had grown with remarkable speed in less than a year. Walter had organized and led the first important strike in the automobile industry, ending in victory as the Kelsey-Hayes Wheel Corporation signed a contract with his union. In the triumph of the nationwide sit-down strike against General Motors, with all the excitement and publicity, the Kelsey-Hayes strike had been overshadowed, but it would always be remembered as a milestone in labor's advance.

As president of Local 174, Walter received no salary. His wife had by now given up her $60-a-week teaching job, although she was still hired by Local 174 as his secretary for $15 a week, and was still turning most of it back into the treasury. Some months earlier, Roy and Victor had been taken on by UAW as paid organizers, but not until the late summer of 1937 was Walter hired as an organizer, the last of the Reuthers to go on the union payroll. His salary was $25 a week, plus streetcar fare. The twenty-nine-year-old redhead still had a long way to go.

Even that early, however, Walter Reuther had begun to exhibit in his character and personality certain traits that won him fervent admirers—and fervent enemies. The enemies would by no means be confined to big industrialists and die-hard right-wing politicians, but would include some even more hostile and implacable opposition within the labor movement itself.

His admirers supported him because he had a down-to-earth, intuitive understanding of the average man, a passionate belief in man's rights and dignity as a human being, an abiding faith in the innate good sense and capability of man. However, the extreme left wing of the UAW, those who still believed in "the Soviet experiment," opposed his strong support of democracy as the most effective means of bringing beneficial changes to labor. Homer Martin regarded Walter's obvious ability, his popularity with the rank and file, as a threat to himself as president, a post for which Martin was proving poorly equipped. Inept and shallow, Martin was the opposite of Reuther, who, as he advanced in the labor movement, would be forever coming up with new ideas that management regarded as "crackpot" and which dismayed his elders, who feared those ideas might upset the balance of power and so lose the gains labor had already made.

Walter could talk—and did. Somebody once said, "If you ask Walter the time of day, he'll tell you how the watch is made." A few of his friends thought he sometimes talked too much; but in the years after he became president his speeches at union conventions held the delegates' interest from start to finish; they followed his words with close attention, although the speeches were often an hour or more long. They did not get restless or noisy or leave the hall as they often did when others talked, because his convention addresses were concerned mostly with issues of vital interest to UAW members. The people who heard him speak frequently, such as reporters or staff members, may have become bored at times, or said to themselves with a smile, "Oh, yes, this is No. 4, or No. 6," since they were so familiar with his pet theories; but even they would listen; for Reuther had that special quality of "audience pull" so necessary to a public figure, particularly a labor leader. One of the international representatives (who was among those able to identify his topics by number) remarked recently, "When Walter spoke you could have heard a pin drop." By some lights an "intellectual," he nevertheless spoke the language of the men, and they listened, and understood his words.

Brother Reuther could also be pithy, probing, and persuasive at the bargaining table. He was frequently called in to conduct negotiations with management from the beginning, and was probably a better negotiator than any of the UAW officers at that time, though none of the would have admitted it. His physical energy and stamina were almost incredible. Given two hours' sleep on a couch in a union office after an all-night bargaining session, he would arrive at the next meeting as fresh, neat, and alert as though he had had twelve hours' rest, a faculty which never left him despite a number of endurance trials, like the brutal beating at the overpass.

Above all, Walter was singularly lacking in self-interest. As president of a local with thirty thousand members, for many months he received no salary. Later, when he passed up one opportunity for salary advancement after another, even some of his staunchest admirers were unable to accept his attitude as sincere. There would always lurk in the backs of their minds the suspicion that he was merely holding out for a bigger prize.

Walter Reuther was inclined to have a single-track mind. During the middle 1930's the single track was the building of an industrial union powerful enough to obtain and protect the rights of the workingman. With hope and a flash of courage aroused by the successful termination of the General Motors strike, great masses of American workers in the early spring of 1937 rushed headlong into the labor movement.

At the time, he thought of it as the beginning of a revolution.

Not a violent overthrow of the government, as had happened in
Russia, nor destruction of the economic system, with its profit
motive, but changes made to meet those wrought by the growth
of giant, mechanized industrial complexes. All through his career,
Walter Reuther firmly believed in the free-enterprise economic
system. He had observed communism at first hand in Russia, and
though he respected the Russian Communist leaders for the tremendous advance they had made in the industrialization of an
illiterate peasant population, he had observed that those achievements had been accomplished at the expense of the peasants
themselves, who were deprived of all freedom and given only the
most meager necessities of life. Such a system would be unwork-
able in the United States. The free-enterprise system could
operate for the good of all if management could be persuaded to
make some adjustments, to face up to the fact that it could not go
on forever drawing off an excessive share of the profits while
neglecting to see that its potential customers, the working men and
women, earned enough to buy the products they worked to make.
He was still trying to persuade management to accept that point
of view thirty years later.

In that spring of 1937, a tidal wave of sit-down strikes swept
over the country. They hit not only the big plants with assembly
lines, but also hotels, department stores, five-and-dime stores,
laundries, beauty shops, barber shops, and undertakers. In Chicago, the wet nurses struck, demanding more money for the milk
they fed to other women's babies. Some labor leaders, holding a
meeting high in a Detroit hotel, were trapped there when the
elevator operators struck without warning.

For a time the sit-downs were amazingly effective. Employers
did not know how to cope with them. Neither they nor the rebellious employees had experience in negotiating in working out a
contract. Excited calls would come into Walter Reuther's office.
A voice on the line might shout exultantly:

"We've taken over the store, locked the doors, and have the
keys! What do we do next?"

After a brief period—triumphant for the sitters, puzzling and
dismaying for the employers—the wave of sit-downs receded rapidly, and, with one or two exceptions, sit-downs were not used

again in authorized automobile strikes. They had served their purpose as vehicles for recognition of the union as collective bargaining agent, the main goal to begin with, which most of them attained; and because of that they had a lasting effect in producing and developing higher wages, better working conditions, and a more powerful labor movement. The fact that membership had increased by several million during the short period in the last half of the decade of the thirties was ample proof of the effectiveness of sit-downs, but there was no more need for them, even before they were declared unconstitutional by the U. S. Supreme Court in the last days of the thirties.

In the days directly following the success of the sit-downs, however, unexpected snags arose within the organized plants for a number of reasons, involving both management and labor. The corporations that had signed contracts with the UAW felt that they had done all that was required of them and refused to grant any further concessions to solve the day-to-day problems that inevitably arise in a factory and which cannot possibly be foreseen in contracts. The corporations insisted that unless there was a specific clause in the contract covering a given situation, they did not have to accede to the demands of the shop stewards presenting the grievances of workers. Much depends on the intelligence and ability of the shop stewards, of course, and in 1937, few had the experience to handle the burrs and bugs of everyday situations popping up in a plant. Many of the stewards had been the leaders of the sit-downs, who naturally wanted to perpetuate their prestige as militant chiefs, a leaning which made them hotheaded negotiators, ill suited to the spirit of compromise so necessary to successful negotiations.

Their impatience may have been due to the fact that workers in general tended to take the initiative, often on the offensive. The long pent-up emotions set free by sit-downs could not just disappear as soon as the men returned to their jobs. Now, with the security of a union contract safeguarding their position, they felt they could at last talk back to foremen. And the foremen in turn, resenting the loss of their former powers, resisted dealing with shop stewards whenever they could, reluctant to realize that they could no longer fire men at their own whims, run departments unchecked by the rank and file (and scarcely by upper echelons), or control the workers by handing out favors here and there.

Their restricted role was a bitter pill that the foremen had to swallow for the first six months of 1937; but in May, after the CIO was defeated by the Little Steel interests led by Tom Girdler, the automobile magnates, hoping to get rid of the union, began chopping away at the stewards' powers by delaying tactics, putting off meetings with the grievance committee, or ignoring complaints altogether. Since an industrial union depends on the steward system for the negotiation of plant grievances, which enables it to exert power consistently, the failure of corporations to recognize the stewards' rights can ultimately cause the union to disintegrate. For the next three years, the corporations would try to side-step the stewards, angering the workers, which led to dozens of wild-cat strikes, some of them no more than work stoppages of five minutes—a disruptive method of procedure, but the only weapon that individual unions could use to wring some small concession from management. Maybe the issue at stake was no more than cleaner washrooms, the lunch-hour schedule, or a cot for the first-aid room, or the need for such a room if the plant didn't have one; but management would balk at having to negotiate the matter with underlings who had been given a title and some authority, and the workers in general, having won victory in the sit-down strikes, felt cocky enough to sit down at the slightest provocation and without authorization; they were still "feeling their oats," and still felt an urgent need to uncork the anger that had been bottled up for years against a ruthless factory regime in which they had no voice.

The UAW top leadership faced a perplexing dilemma, and President Homer Martin, a miserable administrator, was hardly equipped to deal with it. Appealing to the CIO for advice, he acted on John L. Lewis' suggestion to write a leter asking General Motors for improved working conditions and exclusive bargaining rights in return for conceding the corporation the right to fire wildcat-striking workers! A labor leader who does not support his membership quickly loses its respect, and Martin's clumsy attempt to solve a complex situation by a single letter cost him face with both sides. General Motors was not inclined to grant concessions; and union members were so dismayed by the terms of the letter that a national conference of shop delegates from GM locals denounced it by a sweeping vote. Martin was forced to withdraw his ill-advised suggestion, and the day-to-day conflict continued.

Walter Reuther was deeply disturbed, if not alarmed, by Homer Martin's inept, conniving methods. His own means of convincing the corporations that they had to deal with stewards was much closer to the feelings of the rank and file. He wrote forcefully in his local's publication, the West Side *Conveyor*: "It looks very much as though General Motors does not want an agreement with the UAW. Now let's see what it would mean if the union decided to call off negotiations. The workers would then be free to demand a lot of conditions and wages that are due them, and they could sit down every time these were denied. . . . There would be a lot of strikes if there were no agreement." His thinly veiled threat that wide-scale sit-downs might be resumed if GM continued refusing to acknowledge stewards' rights showed a much more perceptive understanding of the workers' mood than Martin's misguided, wishy-washy letter.

Martin's next move was not calculated to win over the men on the assembly line, either; he tried to enlarge his own powers by limiting the autonomy of the locals. Lewis had just pledged the CIO to adhere to contracts and to discipline any locals that did not. This may have served very well for Lewis' United Mine Workers, but did little to solve the specific problems of the auto workers.

In his frenzy to establish his strength in the presidency, Martin began firing people preemptorily if they questioned his ideas. Merlin Bishop, for example, who was head of the National Education Department of the UAW, was fired four or five times within six months by Martin, every time he went out of town with one of his henchmen, who would get his ear and convince him that Bishop's ideas were "radical." Then Walter would have to undo the damage and talk him into reinstating Merlin. It was Martin's capriciousness that was the worst, the most dangerous of his

traits. Even one of his supporters commented in despair, "He always says Yes to the last man who talks to him."

Just how dangerous his irrational moves—which worried Walter Reuther, his brothers, and the other younger leaders more than
personality deficiencies—could be, came to light in his scheme to
appease the rank and file, who were clamoring for definitive action against recalcitrant employers. One day Martin told Frank
Winn to draft a telegram to the locals in Atlanta (which had been
especially insistent), calling a strike for seven o'clock the following morning.

Frank stared at him in amazement: There had been no Executive Board meeting on the matter, no plans for a strike vote. "But
how can you?" he began. "There isn't time . . ."

"Oh, I don't intend to go through with it," Martin interrupted.
"Before seven tomorrow I'll get them on the phone and tell them
that the strike is off. I'm just trying to scare GM."

Again Frank stared at him. "Are you serious?" he asked incredu-
lously.

"Of course," Martin snapped. "Now get busy and draft that
telegram."

Frank got busy, but not drafting the telegram. Instead he
called John L. Lewis in Washington, outlining Martin's prepos-
terous scheme. The CIO chief quickly squashed the maneuver,
giving Martin a severe dressing down. The next day the UAW
president fired Frank Winn.*

Soon afterward, as a further means of polarizing his power,
Martin fired a number of the most capable organizers, among
them Roy and Victor Reuther. His charge was that "an outside
organization is trying to seize control of the union."

Martin's efforts to split the Reuther strength had begun earlier,
when he tried to downgrade Victor by offering him the rural territory around Adrian, Michigan, or possibly upstate New York.
But Victor chose to remain in Detroit, at the hub of activity, and
after he was fired from the organizing staff, he headed the educa-

---

* Sick of Martin's high-handedness anyhow, Frank Winn went to Brookwood
College as visiting lecturer for a year; but late in 1938, as matters came to a
showdown, he returned to Detroit and the Reuther faction of the anti-Martin
group, which was soon to oust the erratic ex-preacher.

tion department of the West Side local, where he and Walter would be able to work closely together. He had been made organizer for Indiana directly after the Flint strike, where he and Roy had both done yeoman work, because of his courageous handling of a rally in Anderson, Indiana, the night after the settlement in Flint had been reached. Two GM plants in Anderson, Delco-Remy and Guide Lamp, were on strike, and the UAW organizers, one of whom was Sophie Reuther, were attacked and chased out of town by vigilante groups just before a big rally to clinch the campaign. Receiving an excited phone call from Sophie, Victor rushed into the breach with some of the strike committee from Flint. His purpose was to read the agreement to the Anderson strikers, explain its provisions, and lay the groundwork for an NLRB election. He was greeted by a hostile mayor, the police, and businessmen in Anderson with the same threat the other organizers had received, "to get out of town, or else." In vain he tried to explain that a settlement had been reached; but he went ahead with arrangements for the rally anyway. He was unable to hire a hall until he finally located an abandoned, rat-infested old movie theater. There was no heat in the building. Victor and a few of the strikers got hold of a dozen or so oil heaters, a dangerous device at best. They lined them up in the aisles, and the theater was a little warmer than it was out in the street when the GM workers, many accompanied by their wives and children, crowded in.

The place was packed when Victor mounted the platform, keeping a wary eye on the oil heaters. He had just about finished his speech, when suddenly the noise outside increased from the few insults and catcalls they had been hearing to a menacing roar of angry voices. A mob of "enraged citizens," mixed with police, ostensibly there to keep order, but actually urging the crowd on, threatened to break down the shaky old doors. Moments of sheer agony passed for Victor and his men as they rushed to extinguish every one of those oil stoves. As the workers and their families left the theater, a few were roughed up, but all managed to get out safely. Victor leaped into his car, and as he drove out of town, some cars followed him, the occupants shouting threats and insults. However, following the rally, there was no further serious difficulty in Anderson, and the union was recognized in the Delco-Remy and Guide Lamp plants.

Homer Martin, heady with the fantastic growth of the UAW after the successful Flint sit-downs and the fact that he was now the elected leader of an organization of 400,000 members, also felt himself assailed on all sides by the various factions and possible contenders for his post within the union. Of the latter, he seemed to fear Walter Reuther more than anyone, perhaps because Walter was flanked by his two brothers, and that may have been his reason for firing Roy and Victor as organizers. Further, he mistrusted the "radicals," and, like most demagogues, he made the mistake of lumping them all together. He was referring to the Communist party in his charge that "an outside organization" was trying to take over the union, thereby implying that the Reuthers were CP members, although he must have known better. Not that there were not Communists and Communist sympathizers of every degree in the UAW during its formative years, as well as Socialists, Democrats, and Independents. They had all worked together against a common adversary to win recognition of the UAW and the right to organize; but now that the first big battle was over, an internal struggle for power inevitably arose. The "family" of the union was fraught with fraternal wrangling and rifts in the brotherhood of workers; two prinicpal groups, roughly referred to as "pro" and "anti" Martin, were splintered into factions of varying degrees to the right and left. Martin himself, who was backed by the top officers, all in favor of his plan to centralize power, was advised by Jay Lovestone and his Stalinist-opposition sect of Communists which could hardly be called conservative, and was as "outside" as any.

The anti-Martin group, to which Walter Reuther and his brothers belonged, was composed of ardent young "radical" unionists of both Communist and Socialist political persuasion, a kind of coalition group held together by their opposition to Martin, and in which the Communist bloc was undoubtedly the strongest because it was the most cohesive. The Socialist group, much smaller and more diffuse, was led by Walter Reuther, who, although increasingly uneasy about the CP's role in the coalition,

felt that the immediate goal of the newly recognized UAW must
be to checkmate Martin and his craze to centralize power in himself. In his eyes, the greatest danger to the UAW was its president;
all those who shared his view must stick together no matter what
their individual political affiliation. For this reason, the coalition
was called the Unity caucus, while the Martin group took the
misnomer of the Progressives.

By the time the 1937 UAW convention rolled around in August,
it was difficult to tell who was on which side of what political
party and why. Walter had emphatically denied that he was or
had ever been a Communist party member at the NLRB hearings
held right after the bloody battle of the overpass, when the Ford
counsel tried, through loaded questions, to make it appear that
the Reuthers had gone to Russia not only to work at the plant
at Gorki but to learn Soviet revolutionary methods in order to
overthrow the United States government. This was indeed a "red
herring," having nothing to do with the hearing except to discredit Reuther as a dangerous character who merited the beating
he received. And in spite of the fact that the NLRB found the
Ford Motor Company guilty of "unnecessary brutality," although Walter had declared he "was not a Communist and never
had been," he was looked upon with suspicion by Martin and his
followers. In his own Unity group he was looked upon as an
uncertain quantity politically because he was impatient with all
factions, because he wanted to get on with building a strong
auto workers' union, organizing the Ford plants to expand the
union's power, but to do it by the democratic process. Among
the anti-Martin forces, Wyndham Mortimer was a much more
influential leader than Walter Reuther at this time, with George
Addes, not a CP member but more "radical" than Reuther,
second. Yet, when the Unity caucus met in Toledo, just before
the convention, to plan its strategy against Martin, it was Walter
who was sent to South Bend, where the Progressives were meeting to prepare their moves. (Others in Toledo besides Mortimer
and Ed Hall—who were both vice-presidents—were Robert Travis, of Flint fame, who had been demoted, and Emil Mazey,
who had been ousted as organizer of the Briggs plant: all prominent and capable in union affairs.) Walter went with the offer of

a "peace plan" which he had helped to draft: to "disband political parties in the union, make Frankensteen a vice-president, and reelect Mortimer and Hall." He was earnest and sincere, but the Progressives, unwilling to listen, would not hear him out. He was booed from the hall, and this was one of the few times in his career when he could not command the attention of the audience.

In this atmosphere of fraternal hostility, not to say warfare, the second UAW Convention was held in Milwaukee late in August, 1937, a noisy, bickering combat, with members stooping to personal attacks instead of discussing important issues, one caucus being more raucous than the next. Walter, distressed by the disruptive effect of such behavior, made a plea for an end to "emotionalism," a return to constructive thinking by the delegates toward a concerted and *unified* effort to organize the entire automotive industry. He proposed abolishing preconvention caucuses altogether, but the suggestion was put aside. Martin initiated a move to break up Reuther's large West Side local by altering the representation in favor of smaller locals; but his motive was so transparent that when Walter jumped up to declare the procedure "undemocratic," it was quickly voted down. Finally John L. Lewis, who had come to Milwaukee with several other CIO officers, including David Dubinsky, to invoke harmony into the proceedings of the obstreperous convention, worked out a compromise, accepted, if not enthusiastically, by both sides; the five top officers, including Mortimer and Hall, were reelected; two new vice-presidents were elected—Frankensteen and R. J. Thomas; and the Executive Board was increased from twelve to seventeen, with Martin "enjoying a majority." Further, conventions were to be called biennially (instead of annually), thus ensuring another two years in office for Martin. The last provision was a disappointment to Walter and the anti-Martin faction, since they had hoped to vote in a new president the following year. But at the moment the compromise plan was probably as good a solution as any, and the next day Walter again urged the delegates to forget their differences and act in unity to defeat their common enemy, the corporations which still opposed organized labor.

His speech fell on deaf ears, for it was extemporaneous: He had been delegated by the anti-Martin coalition to lead a credentials fight that had been put off until after election of officers. But when he stood on the podium and saw the angry faces of the challengers, with "blood in their eyes," he thought to himself, "My God, if I bring up a credentials dispute now, the blood will run in the aisles!" (The officers had already been elected anyhow; and Walter was astute enough to realize that, with the top CIO executives present, he would make a better showing as a potential UAW president if he spoke for peace and harmony rather than to force an issue which would only prolong the embattled atmosphere.) But the Martin group paid him little heed, and the last-minute switch made "his own guys sore at him," as he said ruefully afterward. He was sincere in his feeling that political factionalism should now be forgotten, and was in no sense trying to curry favor with Lewis or the other CIO executives. In fact, his independent spirit had already rubbed Lewis the wrong way and was later to arouse the "Eyebrows'" active opposition to "the redhead."

Similarly, the Communist party members—in the union and outside it—were soon to cause trouble for him (and Victor) because he turned down the chance to join the party when approached by Louis Budenz, a prominent CP leader. As mentioned earlier, the labor movement at that time looked on CP members merely as domestic "radicals" seeking a solution to the economic problems caused by the depression. Walter, with his logical mind and natural curiosity, asked some questions of Budenz concerning the autonomy of American CP members; and when he learned that he would have to submit to Soviet discipline, especially on foreign affairs, he flatly refused to join. From then on, a coolness developed between the CP members in the union and the Reuther brothers, which caused the defeat of Victor for the office of secretary-treasurer when the Michigan CIO Council was formed in 1938, and which would ultimately lead to bitter enmity. Contrarily, the members of the Socialist party in the UAW criticized Walter severely for being on too intimate terms with the CP faction. In point of fact, he was rapidly becoming a New Deal, or Social Democrat, as so many of the Socialist party members did after Roosevelt's reelection in 1936. But in the power struggle that continued to be waged within the union he would have to

veer and tack in order not to be blown off the course he intended
to pursue: the presidency of the UAW.

Homer Martin, meanwhile, with his increased majority on
the Board, was riding high on the wave of his momentary victory.
He fired organizers at the slightest show of dissidence and tried
to muzzle any local mouthpiece from voicing in print views
contrary to his own. When he sought to suspend publication of
the West Side local's *Conveyor* as being "subversive," Walter
simply ignored the order, which in itself was an indication of
Martin's blindness to the situation. Perhaps his greatest error
at this time was his failure to sense the coolness between the
Communists and Reuther. If Martin had been aware of the
possibilities, he could have approached the Reuthers as allies,
but he chose to regard them as CP sympathizers, and continued
to go on his own high-handed blundering way down the primrose
path to self-destruction as a labor leader. In June, 1938, he suspended five dissident UAW top officers, among them the three
most thoroughly entrenched with the rank and file: Addes,
Mortimer, and Frankensteen. (As recently as April, Richard
Frankensteen had been Martin's "assistant president," but now
he was switching sides—a mark of the cat-and-dog hassle, the
denunciation and maneuvering that wracked the adolescent union
with near-disastrous growing pains.)

Martin then began committing a series of unbelievable blun-
ders. In August the officers who had been suspended appealed to
the National CIO for aid in forcing Homer Martin to reinstate
them; but before Lewis could hand down a decision, the UAW
president denounced his right to interfere. "I will not turn over
the international UAW to John L. Lewis," he boasted tactlessly,
apparently not realizing that he was in no position to challenge
Lewis' authority, or that his remark would only ensure Lewis' support of the dissidents. The result was that he had to retreat with
injured dignity as a CIO committee, headed by Philip Murray
and Sidney Hillman, took away part of his power by discharging
some of his supporters and reinstating the expelled officers. Martin's next move, in an effort to recoup his loss of prestige and
power, was to enter into shady negotiations with the Ford Motor
Company. With incredible naïvete—or wily cunning—he asserted

that Henry Ford didn't know the truth about labor conditions in his own plant but that, once he learned the facts, he would negotiate with the union; and that it was better to initiate negotiations from the top, thus avoiding a costly strike.

His highfalutin hopes were dampened at Ford's refusal to meet with the UAW ex-preacher–president; but with everlasting, misguided, optimistic gall, Martin pressed for a deal with Harry Bennett (Ford's "representative"), who was, of course, only too happy to oblige. The exact nature of the arrangement was never known; but late in January of 1939, R. J. Thomas, till then a fairly loyal lieutenant of Martin, suddenly left his side, charging that meetings had taken place at which an official of the Ford Company and Martin had discussed plans to separate the UAW from the CIO. He, Thomas, had been asked to sit in on some of the secret sessions. This was the last straw for the rank and file as well as the aggravated Executive Board. Whatever the workers might feel toward one leader or another, they felt a deep loyalty to the CIO as the parent body of industrial (mass-production) workers. The mere suggestion that the UAW president was attempting to have them rejoin the old AFL (as R. J. Thomas' statement implied) was anathema to UAW membership as a whole, and foretold Martin's finish. The Executive Board voted to call for a convention immediately.

Sensing that this had been his fatal blunder, Martin, hysterically desperate, fired fifteen of the union's twenty-four Executive Board members at one fell swoop, and refused to see the bewildered, angry shop delegations that came to him for explanation. His behavior had always been theatrical: At one point during the melee that began the Milwaukee convention, he had stood up, throwing wide his arms as if on a cross, and bellowed in martyred tones, "You are crucifying me as they crucified our Lord, Jesus Christ!" Now, assuming the role of a hardened gangster, he hired bodyguards and barricaded himself behind locked doors in the hotel room he maintained in downtown Detroit. When he did finally open the door to forty members from Reuther's West Side local, he greeted them with a gun, jamming it into the ribs of the man at the head, who was onto him by now.

"Get that gun out of my belly, Homer!" he commanded. "That's a hell of a way to greet a union man."

Martin retreated, although protesting that he "meant business," slamming the door in their faces, calling out that he would see them later. The men went down to the lobby to wait. In the afternoon, Walter, who had been conferring with R. J. Thomas, arrived with two other officers.

"What's the story?" he asked the men. And when he heard what had happened, and further, that Martin had cut off elevator service to his rooms on the fourth floor, Walter merely nodded. "Come on," he said to the two with him. They took the elevator to the fifth floor and walked down one flight to Martin's rooms. The confrontation between Martin and the trio headed by Reuther came to nothing except to arrange a meeting at the union hall, which in turn amounted to a stalemate, both sides exchanging verbal—and physical—blows. The upshot of it all was that Martin, in a huff, declared he would call a convention of his own, leaving the CIO.

In March of 1939, there were two UAW conventions, hardly equal in size: Martin's followers, who held their "rump" session in Detroit, represented no more than sixty thousand members at most; and, while those delegates gave him an hour-long ovation, their number amounted to less than a fourth of the total membership. Soon Martin was to make his suicidal move as a labor leader by affiliating with the AFL, making his splinter union completely ineffective except as a tool for the employers.

The anti-Martin convention, held in Cleveland, represented the majority of the UAW locals, but faced a far greater problem in electing its leadership. Martin was gone at last, and the Communist party members had certainly helped to defeat him; but now the greatest danger to the union was that, since the CP faction was the most tightly organized, it might try to take over. Who could prevent this? Its delegates put up a slate headed by Addes and Frankensteen (now revealing the latter's motive in leaving Martin's side), both staunch and popular union leaders. Opposing the CP's strongly controlled bloc was a small group of liberals—mostly Socialists—led by Walter Reuther; and some mine-run, middle-of-the-road members, led by R. J. Thomas.

Walter had been going through an internal political struggle of his own. Although he still admired the basic share-the-wealth principle of socialism, he repudiated the Soviet-Stalinist application of it; and he could see, from his failure to gather any real voting strength for Norman Thomas in 1932 and from the ineffectiveness of the Socialist party since then as against the successful measures of the Roosevelt administration in solving the problems of the depression, that labor's best chance of achieving its goals in the United States was through the democratic process, largely through the Democratic party. In 1937 (only a few months after his physical beating at the battle of the overpass), Walter had consented to run on a Socialist-Labor ticket for City Council in Detroit—his sole venture in the political arena—and with the rest of the slate had been badly beaten at the polls.

A few months before the Cleveland convention, in the November, 1938, elections, he had felt that Socialists should back Governor Frank Murphy for reelection, since he had supported labor and not allowed the National Guard to attack workers in the decisive Flint strike; but the Socialists wanted to run their own candidate for governor. At that time, he had offered to resign formally from the Socialist party. He had really not been active since his return from Russia because he was too involved in the trade-union movement, his dominant interest in life. He and May had attended a few lectures at the Workmen's Circle by speakers whose ideas they were interested in hearing, but neither one had taken an active part in Socialist party politics for several years, nor had Victor and Sophie. His father had voted for Roosevelt from the beginning and was for the most part a New Dealer. (The Reuther brothers always remained in close touch with the family in Wheeling, and recently had brought their little sister Chris, now of college age, up to Detroit to attend their "alma mater," which had become Wayne University.* Though none of them had much income, the brothers took care of their sister's college education.)

As far as Walter's resignation from the Socialist party was con-

* Later Wayne State University, as part of the Michigan higher education system, which houses UAW history and convention proceedings in its Labor Archives division.

cerned, however, he was asked by an aid of Norman Thomas not to hand one in, as it would look to the public like an act of open hostility. Since Walter felt no hostility toward the Socialist party, but simply felt that no third party had ever been or probably ever would be successful in the United States, he agreed not to make any formal break; but by the time of the 1939 convention he had just about drifted away completely.

In the eyes of many, especially a paternalistic labor leader like John L. Lewis, who called him a "Socialist idealogue," Walter Reuther's name was still too closely associated with the Socialist party for comfort. The CIO was anxious to prevent the Communists from taking over the convention, yet Lewis had sworn that as long as he was president of the CIO, Walter Reuther would never be president of the UAW. So again Sidney Hillman and Philip Murray were sent to the convention to see that a "compromise" candidate was selected. Of the four principal contenders—Reuther, Addes, Frankensteen, and R. J. Thomas—the last was easily the most neutral, the least likely to be controversial. Walter, sensing this, went to Hillman before the balloting came up to convince him that Thomas would be most widely accepted.

Although different in temperament and separated in age by about twenty years, there were a number of similarities between Walter and Hillman. Both came of Socialist background swayed by the New Deal to democracy; both were visionaries in that they could see the social changes that must be made in order to cope with advancing technology; and both were pragmatists, flexible enough to alter plans or settle for less until more could be gained. Walter, being younger and thus stronger physically—Hillman at this time was suffering from the series of heart attacks that took his life at a relatively early age—was the more "radical" of the two; and Hillman, perhaps because of Lewis' attitude, did not quite trust him. Yet they understood each other and, in the main, respected each other. (When either Walter or Victor spoke a little Russian to Hillman, who was born in what is now Lithuania, he would smile, pleased and half amused by their efforts.) Together they worked out a deal whereby Walter pledged that his caucus would support Thomas in return for Reuther's appointment as national head of the UAW's General Motors Department, a shrewd proposition on his part. R. J. Thomas was proposed by the CIO, and accepted with little debate, as the CIO officials had bluntly warned the Communists to refrain.

Walter, reelected to the Executive Board, along with most of those Martin had suspended (except Wyndham Mortimer and Ed Hall, left out for the first time since the union's inception), found himself facing a test of his new authority a few weeks after the convention. General Motors, seizing the opportunity of the split and the resultant loss of strength in the original UAW, combined with Martin's claims for recognition of his union, gave notice that the corporation was cutting off all collective bargaining. Their edict naturally brought on a new rash of strikes as a test of union solidarity, the most important one at the Briggs body plant, which the UAW won in early summer. But GM pulled a seemingly clever tactic by asking the NLRB to hold an election to ascertain which union was authentic in representing the workers, the UAW-CIO, or Martin's rump AFL union. But Walter Reuther bested the GM scheme with a clever strategy of his own, a strategy strike, as he called it. (Martin had tried to beat him to it by calling a strike at a GM plant in Flint, but the majority of the workers ignored his picket line and kept on their jobs.) At a hot Fourth of July meeting of the Executive Board, Walter outlined his plan to his fellow Board members as they sat around the table in their shirt sleeves at union headquarters.

His years of experience as a tool- and diemaker came to the fore as he spoke. He knew full well how vital the skilled workers and engineers who designed and made tools were just now when GM was entering its plans for a new 1940 model. His strategy was twofold: first, to close down GM at the height of the retooling time, so that the new models would be delayed, thus putting GM at a grave disadvantage with Ford and other competitors; and second, to pull out only the skilled tool-and-die workers, so that the assembly line could continue as long as the 1939 models were being produced. This way, if GM issued the annual summer layoff, the production workers could collect unemployment insurance. He made it sound like a sure-fire thing, but he knew, and he could see from the faces around him, that the others knew they would be taking a risk. So he explained, choosing his words

carefully and emphasizing them: "A strike in tool and die, maintenance, and engineering is opportune now because GM has been
rushing to complete a great program on 1940 tools and dies, jigs
and fixtures. A victory for the skilled men will establish the UAW-
CIO as a bargaining agent nationally. . . ." His voice underlined
the supremacy of their industrially organized union without
mentioning the rival AFL auto workers Martin had managed to
convince. Continuing, "The watchwords of the GM workers are
solidarity and discipline—power under control," he convinced his
own followers that his way was wiser, and promised production
workers that their action would take place when the union felt
the moment had come.

Two days later, on July 6, 1939, the first group of eight hundred
key tool-and-die workers were pulled off the job in a dozen GM
plants. As Walter had foretold, GM kept its production lines going
for a few weeks, and then announced a layoff of all assembly
workers, who began to draw unemployment compensation at
once. (He had been relying on this factor, since the union's
strike funds were low.) The plan was working, easing the inner
tension of the UAW officers, but the strikes by the skilled workers
brought violence and near-riots in Cleveland, Pontiac, and Detroit, particularly the last, where the largest tool-die shop in the
country, Fisher 23, was striking. In addition, Reuther, spurred
on by the success of his strategy so far—and by GM's plaintive
cry, from President Knudsen himself, that it was not fair of the
UAW-CIO "to embarrass the corporation at a critical time"—
urged other UAW-CIO members in smaller Detroit tool-and-die
plants to boycott any work coming from General Motors. When
he received word that they did, he couldn't help crowing gleefully: "This puts GM right behind the eight ball!" Frank Winn
and his staff ran off a strike bulletin: "GM is squirming. The heat
is on and the solid ranks of the UAW-CIO will keep GM's seat
hot, or hotter, as long as needed to bring GM to decent terms."

Finally, when GM began to feel the pinch of losing out on sales
to Ford and Chrysler, the corporation grudgingly capitulated,
agreeing to begin negotiations so that NLRB elections could
determine which union represented the majority of the workers.
The "shot-gun marriage" contract, as Walter called it because

both sides were reluctant to come together on terms, wary of each other, was significant for a number of reasons. Not the least of these was that it marked the beginning of a give-and-take relationship, at first sparring, but eventually a definite rapport between Reuther and Charles E. Wilson, both rising stars on their opposing sides. Walter, symbolically, as it turned out, sat directly opposite Wilson at the negotiating table. Both were in a bitter mood, their recent struggle still rankling. Negotiations started early and went on till all hours. One night, as Reuther and his committee sat listening, Wilson outlined a fresh proposal and went on to develop a series of at least eight variations. He was still continuing at around midnight, when Walter suddenly pushed back his chair, bursting into his robust laugh; he "laughed like hell," a reporter related. Then he said, "I'm going to offer a recess until morning. I damn near took that last position of yours, Wilson, and it's not as good as the first one you offered!" The general laughter all around eased the tension, and there was nothing Wilson could do but accept the recess call for the night. At another session, Knudsen wagged a long finger at the UAW-CIO redheaded chairman, admonishing him with, "Now, see here, Reuther, we don't want any commissars in America!"

Walter's reply, which he repeated at UAW and other conventions, contained a capsule of his union and political philosophy over the years: "We don't want commissars any more than you do," he told the GM president. "But what you and other powerful leaders of American industry do about helping make democracy work for the average man will determine whether we get commissars or not." Still another sign of the mature, farsighted leader he would become was Reuther's proposal at this early date of a guaranteed annual wage for auto workers. With a fistful of federal employment-bureau figures, he proved that the industry's most skilled workers had averaged less than six months' employment a year for the past five years; he always had facts and figures to back up his points, one of the benefits of those Sunday afternoon debates in Wheeling; and those who called him a dreamer or fanatical visionary found him a practical one indeed.

In the contract that was finally reached, GM recognized the UAW-CIO as the sole bargaining agent for the tool- and diemakers in the forty-two plants the union claimed organized by them, raised the workers' minimum pay, and improved overtime provisions. In return, the union signed a no-strike agreement for the 1940 year of new model cars. Walter realized the importance of the recognition of the CIO union as the exclusive bargaining agent, but he also pointed out to his fellow unionists that an equally important GM concession was its agreement to raise wages *in more than one plant*. The outcome as a whole lifted the entire morale of the CIO auto workers and brought renewed organizing fervor, "a whole renaissance of our union," Walter called it later. Among others, the Chrysler Corporation plants were quickly brought under union contract.

In the NLRB elections which followed, the UAW-CIO carried forty-eight GM plants with more than 120,000, while Homer Martin's AFL rival gathered a measly 5,600 votes in a mere total of five plants. Martin knew he was wiped out as a labor leader, and nine days later resigned as head of the UAW-AFL, with a whimpering statement that he had always "served labor to the best of my ability." Undoubtedly his ability was not great, but even so, he remains a grotesque and sorry figure in labor history. He had no moral struggle, however, in accepting a post as a "manufacturer's agent" with the Ford Motor Company shortly afterward, and, albeit in oblivion, flourished in the golden garden of Mammon located in Dearborn, Michigan.

For Walter Reuther, although he had made great strides by the end of the 1939 conflict, a thorny path still lay ahead.

XV

Folk Hero

As they prepared to do battle with the last of the Big Three in their fight to win recognition for their union throughout the automobile industry, the United Automobile Workers faced a unique situation.

In their previous struggles with General Motors they had taken on a huge corporation, backed by the unlimited financial resources of the Duponts and the house of Morgan. Twice they had won.

In the third and last engagement they were actually confronted by one man, an American folk hero, Henry Ford, who reigned as absolute monarch over a vast industrial domain owned entirely by his family. Moreover, having started life as a poor boy, a business failure until forty, he was among the first of the "self-made" men.

Corporations like General Motors were not particularly popular with the great mass of the American people. Hence the "sitdown" strikers who occupied the company plants in 1937 enjoyed a certain amount of public sympathy and support.

Henry Ford was the genius who had invented the assembly line, bringing down the price of automobiles. He had won the admiration of workingmen all over the country when in 1914 he announced that he would pay his workmen five dollars a day, more than twice the prevailing rate in the industry. Just how well he had lived up to that promise the public did not know. The Five-Dollar Day had built up around the man a myth—the public image of a genius who generously shared his profits with his workers. His reputation had been tarnished somewhat by the beatings the ruffians under his man Bennett had given Walter Reuther, Dick Frankensteen, the women carrying union leaflets, and the newspapermen and photographers in the battle of the overpass in May, 1937. But most of the blame was attributed to Bennett, and Ford lived on, in the public mind, a folk hero. Fighting a folk hero is more difficult than fighting a big corporation.

The UAW was itself in a stronger position than it had been when it first took on GM. With the exception of Ford, the entire automobile industry—small companies as well as GM and Chrysler—was in the fold. UAW had nearly a million members; its youthful leaders had gained experience; it had the unlimited support of its parent organization, the CIO, and, most of all, the backing of the United States government. The National Labor Relations Act, which required Ford to permit his employees to form a union, had been declared constitutional by the Supreme Court.

A careful study of Ford's biography would reveal that his attitude toward his employees, harshly paternalistic, suspicious, at times ruthless, originated with the man himself, long before he had ever heard of Harry Bennett.

Ford's first difficulty with labor began in 1913. He had installed, in a spacious new plant in Highland Park, a Detroit suburb, the first moving assembly line in the automobile industry. A bare chassis would be placed at one end of a long conveyor belt, and in minutes, a finished Model T rolled off the other end. Hundreds of men lined up along the conveyor belt, the parts of the car were brought to them, and each man would perform one task, over and over again—putting in a screw here, tightening a bolt there, assembling the motor, part by part, putting on wheels, lowering the body onto the chassis, and so on. A workman's job never varied as the endless line sped by. By the end of 1913, a complete Model T rolled off that line every three minutes! The grandfather of automation had been born.

Ford himself was as awed by his invention as his competitors were dismayed. He actually deified it, calling it "the new Messiah" of the automobile industry. He continued to play with it, increasing the speed of the conveyor belt so that his workmen had to strain every nerve and muscle to keep up with it. Thus began the "speedup," which was to arouse so much resentment among the workers in the 1930's. Mr. Ford's assembly line had been adopted by the whole industry, and the faster the conveyor belt, the more cars per minute were produced, keeping the labor costs down.

Ford's one thousand workmen in the Highland Park plant did not take kindly to the "new Messiah." Drawn to the assembly line at first by curiosity, they soon became bored and restless and, as Ford increased the speed, antagonistic.

The Five-Dollar Day did not reflect Ford's attitude toward the men on his assembly lines. He expressed it himself when he remarked one day: "The assembly line is a haven for those who haven't got the brains to do anything else." Hiring rules were arbitrary: no women, no men under 22, no family men who were not supporting their dependents, no divorced men, no men who, according to Mr. Ford's conception, were "living unworthily." Included among those who "lived unworthily" were all men who smoked or took a drink, even occasionally in their homes. With so vast a labor supply at his disposal, Ford could afford to be arbitrary. Discipline was harsh. Before the plan was a week old, several hundred foreign-born workmen took a day off—without pay—to observe a Greek Orthodox Church holy day. They were all fired the following morning. A man had to work for six months as an apprentice, at $2.34 a day, before he was eligible to receive $5 a day, and herein lay the heinous loophole in Ford's "generous" wage offer. His competitors and the public apparently did not understand that, if Ford wanted to cut expenses, he could fire all his "apprentices" just before they became eligible for the Five-Dollar Day and take on more at the same rate, $2.34 a day.

The men who managed to stay on were perfectly suited to Ford's purposes. They were submissive, would take any amount of pushing without protesting, gave him no trouble. A man with a family to support, earning twice as much money as he had ever earned before, was no complainer, even though, as the speed of the assembly line went up and up, he would be so exhausted that he could barely stagger home at night.

At that time—nearly three years before he ever heard of Harry Bennett—Ford began to develop a spy system. Under the benevolent disguise of doing social work among the families, his spies would gain admission to the homes and report back on workmen who were "living unworthily." Families of Ford five-dollar-a-day employees were forbidden to take in male boarders. Ford considered it "an evil custom" and part of the pattern of "living unworthily." The head of a family caught "living unworthily" was called in for a lecture and was placed on probation, his pay cut in half. Sometimes his full pay would be restored in thirty days, sometimes it took months. If at the end of six months he had not convinced his boss that he had reformed, he would be discharged. Men on the assembly line were encouraged to spy on each other. Years later, workmen and the small portion of the public who had become aware of conditions in the Ford plants attributed them to Harry Bennett, but Bennett was actually carrying out a policy inaugurated by Henry Ford himself, only doing it more efficiently— and at huge cost. By that time, Henry Ford, neurotic and suspicious, apparently trusted no one save Bennett. His son, Edsel, was nominally president of the company, but was subjected to constant harassment by Bennett for being a suspected "liberal."

Ford met Bennett in 1916. Within a short time, Bennett, probably using Ford's spies as a nucleus, started building up his private army—by the middle thirties it numbered eight thousand, including some of the country's most notorious gangsters. At the River Rouge, there was one "serviceman" to every thirty employees; in some of Ford's western plants, it ran as high as one to every fourteen.

Ford increased his public image in 1926 when he announced that all his employees were to be given a five-day week. He was the first major employer to do so. For this he was eulogized even by the AFL. But again, there was a trick in it, which his workmen discovered when they received their first weekly pay envelopes after the plan went into effect. They contained only five days' pay.

Mr. Ford was not paying for any workless days, although he didn't tell that to the public. At the same time he again started speeding up his assembly lines, so that two months later he announced:

"We are today producing the same number of cars with the same number of men as we formerly produced within the six-day week."

He did not say that he had also cut his payroll by millions of dollars. The workmen did not protest. Discussing conditions at the plant, they had learned, was an unhealthy practice, even in their homes. The company's "social workers" were not above bribing children with candy to repeat what their fathers said about their jobs. So the fathers just worked harder and harder, faster and faster, but as they paid their grocery bills out of a pay envelope minus one day's wages, they must have been something less than enchanted with that free Saturday they were too tired to enjoy.

Ford had some forms of tyranny he exercised outside the plant. One summer every man on the assembly lines was ordered to raise a garden, on his own time. If he did not have available land, a plot was set aside for him on the Ford estate. As they fought fatigue, sweat, and mosquitoes, the men must have silently cursed him; and their resentment gave rise to a secret parody on the Lord's prayer, little known outside Ford's, surpassing his own "new Messiah" in sacrilegious assumption. Still remembered by retired workers, "The Ford's Prayer" began impiously:

"Our father which art in Dearborn, cursed be thy name," and continued in like caricature or distortion through the rest of the famous traditional lines, with a few verses added for good measure.

By the 1930's, Ford had become less concerned with whether or not his employees were "living worthily." He now had a new obsession, shared with Bennett—organized labor. With mounting fury he watched the timid, faltering steps of automobile workers to organize the industry. At first there were only a few small, weak local unions, fairly easy to stamp out. But the manufacturer was uneasy about his own employees. Bennett's men were constantly having men fired for suspected union activity. Young Walter Reuther, probably because he had been one of the company's most highly skilled tool- and diemakers when he was fired and blacklisted in 1932, was the object of special attention from Bennett's men. They tailed him day and night as he followed his discouraging routine of trudging from plant to plant, trying to get workers to join a union. When the locals that had managed to survive in other companies got together in South Bend and formed the infant UAW, Ford and Bennett took note of the fact that Reuther had been elected a member of the Executive Board. More than ever before, Reuther was a marked man. Hence the severity of the beating he received in the battle of the overpass and the subsequent attempt to kidnap him in his own home.

Ford had always frowned on conversations between his workers in his plants. It was wasting time. From the early thirties on, two Ford workers talking to each other meant only one thing to Ford and Bennett. Even though they might be discussing a subject as innocuous as baseball scores, it was assumed that they must be plotting to start a union. Talking in the plant was forbidden, and fraternization outside the plant, under the watchful eyes of Bennett's spies, could result in dismissal.

His fierce determination to keep the UAW out of his company led Ford in the 1930's to excesses in discipline far beyond anything he had ever inflicted on his workmen in the past. By 1939, as the real struggle began to get underway, the life of a Ford worker was not unlike that of a felon in a penal institution. He even had a number, as prisoners have, which appeared on a badge he wore and on his time card. Nobody ever called him by his name—he had no identity. If he worked on the assembly line, as most of them did, he would rush from the time clock to his place on the line and there he would stand for four hours, with half an hour off to gobble his lunch, followed by four more hours, on his feet, always under the eyes of his foreman or one of Bennett's men, straining every muscle to keep up. During those four-hour stretches he could not leave his place even to get a drink of water or to go to the washroom. In other companies—where working conditions had been far from ideal—there were stand-by men to relieve a workman who had to leave the line for a few minutes. Not so at Ford's.

Nobody in the Ford plants below the rank of executive was

ever permitted to sit down. A story circulated discreetly outside
the plants during that period involved a Ford executive who came
across a workman seated on a keg of nails splicing wires. The
executive kicked the keg out from under the workman and sent
him sprawling, whereupon the workman jumped up and with a
wicked right to the jaw knocked the executive down. "You're
fired," the executive gasped as he regained his feet. To which the
grining workman replied: "The hell I am! I work for the telephone
company!"

A Ford worker was not permitted to sing, whistle, or hum a tune
to relieve the monotony of his job. If caught laughing, he was in
trouble. He'd better not be caught smiling, either. He could be
fired for it. But the greatest offense of all was talking. The only
voices ever heard were those of the foremen, exhorting the men to
greater speed, threatening them with dismissal if they showed
fatigue, and the curses of Bennett's men as they dragged and
cuffed some hapless wretch to the employment office to be fired.
For years on the Ford assembly line men worked side by side, in
absolute silence, their faces as void of expression as they could
make them. It was called "Fordization of the face."

They carried it home with them at night. A newspaperman observing Ford workers just off duty on payday as they did their
weekly marketing once noted that they never spoke to each other,
that the wooden expression on their faces never changed while
they scurried about as though their very lives depended on getting those errands done without a single wasted motion. A neurotic himself, Henry Ford was making neurotics out of his workmen. Psychologists later, as stories came out at hearings before
the National Labor Relations Board, called it "job neurosis."

For years Ford workers lived in constant fear of losing their
jobs. Not only could they be discharged for the most trivial
offenses, they could be fired for "looking old." Very few men at
the age of forty could withstand the strain of the speedup—this
was true generally in the industry. A man of forty was apt to have
a family of half-grown children, with more to come. That was not
a matter of concern to his employers, particularly Henry Ford. If
he could no longer keep up the pace, he was out—through. At

Ford's, men in their thirties who began to turn gray were suspect. Many of them started dying their hair.

Ford men had also suffered physically more than the workmen in other companies did by plant shutdowns. All the other companies had a seasonal closing while the plants retooled for new models. For a quarter of a century, Ford continued to turn out the Model T, with no retooling, while his associates, including his son, Edsel, toward the end tried to persuade him to bring out a new model. "Big Bill" Knudsen—who had once worked for Ford and had been fired—had developed for GM a new low-priced car, the Chevrolet, equipped with self-starters, shock absorbers, demountable tire rims, and many other mechanical improvements which the Model T did not have, plus a much more attractive body. It cost more than the Model T, but not enough so that it was out of the price range of the average buyer. The Chevrolet ended the career of the Model T. In 1927, Ford abruptly dropped the Model T—after fifteen million sales at a gross value of $7 billion—the foundation of the vast Ford fortune. One hundred thousand Ford workmen were thrown out of jobs while Ford's designers and engineers and tool- and diemakers spent eighteen months, at a cost of $100 million, getting the Model A into production. The Model A was not a great success—it was too much like the Model T. Ford found himself at the bottom of the Big Three, unable to compete with the Chevrolet, and with Chrysler's new Plymouth. Again came a prolonged layoff, while the company tore its plants apart, designing and building the tools for the V-8, Ford's first attempt at a modern low-priced car. This shutdown came during the great depression. Unemployed Ford workers in Detroit were reduced to the practice of following milkmen on their early morning rounds through neighborhoods where families were affluent enough to order three or four quarts at a time. "We'd always leave one bottle behind," one of the men said years later, "and swipe the rest for our kids, who needed it."

In the early 1930's Henry Ford had 130,000 employees, the majority of whom worked on his assembly lines. Practically to a man they were growing more and more resentful, a resentment all the more bitter because they did not dare express it. Thousands and thousands—probably the largest percentage of them—were suffering from job neurosis, and articles were being written about nervous exhaustion among workers resulting throughout the industry from the speedup on the assembly lines. Ford's comment: "We learn of nervous exhaustion among workers who have been driven by mass production only from books in the library, but never from the men themselves." No Ford employee, in constant fear of losing his job, would have dreamed of telling any of his superiors, from his foreman up to Ford himself, that the "new Messiah" had driven him to the point of nervous exhaustion.

As his first line of defense, Ford depended on Bennett and his private army. The spies were more effective than Bennett's ruffians, since it was almost impossible to identify them. The NLRB once estimated that between 1937 and 1941, about four thousand Ford workmen had been fired for real or suspected union activity.

At the River Rouge plant, Local 600, with only a handful of members, struggled for existence as the spies pointed out the leaders. Bennett's idea was to "knock 'em off as soon as they show their heads." The leaders they knocked off were usually Communists—former party members later reported that Local 600 was dominated by Communists for years. In the 1930's hardly anybody save a Communist would have dared expose himself as a union man, since it inevitably meant his discharge.

Whether or not they realized it yet, however, Ford and Bennett were now facing a UAW far stronger, more experienced, better led and with much more substantial support, both financially and morally, than that which had won the first big sit-down strike against General Motors. CIO had given some assistance in that strike, but now it threw all its resources behind the drive against Ford. John L. Lewis sent in Michael Widman, one of his most experienced organizers, to direct operations, and rank-and-file members of CIO locals outside the automobile industry from coast to coast pledged their personal support, even to marching in the picket lines, should there be a strike.

Under CIO leadership the Ford Organizing Committee was set up, staffed by UAW vice-president Richard L. Leonard and Emil Mazey, chief assistants to Widman. Discharged Ford workmen, all too familiar with Mr. Bennett's practices, were also in important posts. The committee membership was secret, the names kept under lock and key. It held few meetings, in out-of-the-way hiding places.

The rank-and-file members of CIO locals across the country in plants outside the automobile industry were in a position to make a substantial contribution. One of UAW's most difficult problems was establishing contact with Ford employees, either as individuals or in groups. Very few Ford men would risk being seen talking to a UAW organizer, most of whom were known to Bennett's men, or wanted to be caught stuffing a proffered union leaflet into his pocket. Union meetings of Ford workers were small and secret. Any outsider would have been suspect—even if he could have found his way into a meeting.

The most obvious way to get the attention of the Ford men was by wide distribution of union leaflets—most of which, the union realized, would be thrown away unread. Still, if they blanketed the area around a plant with literature, some of it must eventually be picked up and read. Their first attempts, in May, 1937, resulted in the battle of the overpass. They tried it again in the late summer, sending one thousand men with leaflets, while Bennett's bullies, still smarting under the disastrous publicity of their attack on Reuther, looked on sullenly, but did nothing.

Bennett thought he knew how to stop the flow of leaflets. Since the city of Dearborn owed its very existence to the Ford Motor Company, Bennett had no difficulty getting an ordinance passed by the Council forbidding distribution of leaflets on Dearborn streets leading in the direction of the River Rouge during the daily periods when the plant was changing shifts, calling the area "congested." To avoid court tests of the ordinance, organizers who were arrested were briefly jailed, and released without charges; so no trials were held, but distribution of leaflets was cut down. The ban lasted until October, 1940, when it was declared unconstitutional, by one of Dearborn's two city magistrates, a woman, Lila Neuenfelt, who was backed up by the county circuit court. Within forty-eight hours, UAW was at the River Rouge gates with 35,000 handbills, and thereafter the Ford Organizing Committee distributed 50,000 copies of its newspaper, *Ford Facts*, every two weeks in the River Rouge area. While not neglecting other Ford plants around the country, the union concentrated its heaviest assaults in the Detroit area. The River Rouge, employing eighty thousand men, was the world's largest automobile plant, and Ford also had his Highland Park and Lincoln plants, with smaller payrolls.

While the company and the union were still moving cautiously, Benson Ford, Henry Ford's teenage grandson, inadvertently tipped Harry Bennett off on one of the most daring—and amusing —tricks ever inflicted on a manufacturer. The Ford Organizing Committee had a radio station, so small and weak that very few Detroiters even knew of its existence. One day Benson asked Bennett if he ever listened to "those CIO fellows" on the radio. Bennett said he couldn't—the union had no radio. "Oh, yes, they have," the boy assured him. "I listen to them all the time in my car." He then showed Bennett an extra radio selector button on the dashboard of his Ford, and out came a voice—possibly the voice of Walter Reuther—talking union propaganda. "You ought to listen to them sometime," Benson remarked. "I get a kick out of them."

Bennett's investigation revealed that a radio installer, a union man at the River Rouge, who had somehow managed to escape the ax, had been inserting in every Ford on that assembly line an extra selector button that would bring in the CIO-UAW station.

Ford cars were being driven all over Detroit with union propaganda issuing from their radios if the driver desired. Since all Ford employees were ordered to drive Ford cars, thousands of River Rouge workers, once the word had been passed around, undoubtedly listened to R. J. Thomas, Walter and Victor Reuther, and all the rest of the most persuasive union speakers as they drove to and from their jobs. For the company to call in every Ford car in the area and have that button removed obviously would have been impossible. Apparently the story never got into the newspapers. If it had, the Ford Motor Company would have been the laughingstock of the country.

XVI

The Inevitable

BY 1940, Ford and Bennett should have realized that they were confronted not only by the UAW-CIO, but by the United States government, an infinitely more powerful force. When Congress passed the National Labor Relations Act in 1935, most large employers, especially Ford, refused to take it seriously. Inevitably, they reasoned, the law would wind up in the Supreme Court, which would pass on its constitutionality. When the Supreme Court threw out the NRA in the summer of 1936, their hopes soared. In the summer of 1937, however, the Supreme Court validated the National Labor Relations Act, and it became irrevocably the law of the land. Whether they liked it or not, Ford and his chief executive, Harry Bennett, had to submit to hearings before the National Labor Relations Board (set up to carry out the provisions of the law) whenever a petition was filed by a union, an individual employee, or a group of employees seeking an election or charging unfair labor practices.

For three years following that 1937 decision, despite the adverse effect of the battle of the overpass and "the chop suey incident"—as the Reuthers all referred to the attack on Walter by the intruders at Sophie's birthday party—and in the face of Walter's successful distribution of UAW leaflets at the Rouge plant gates, Harry Bennett's brutal gang of servicemen systematically resisted the law, keeping the workers in constant terror in order to preserve Ford's "open shop" as long as possible. By 1940 the NLRB had found the Ford management guilty of unfair labor practices in nine plants. At the hearings of cases filed by the UAW, the testimony—some of it almost unbelievable, in places like Dallas—revealed that Ford had illegally dicharged 2,566 workers for union membership. The court ruled that these workers must be reinstated and be given back pay totaling two million dollars.

Probably the most damaging case against Ford involved the River Rouge plant. Hearings on the battle of the overpass occurred a few weeks after it happened. From the late summer of 1937 until 1940, the Board continued to collect evidence against the company's labor relations at the River Rouge plant, as thousands of complaints came in. Walter Reuther, of course, was one of the principal witnesses at the early hearings, but there were many more—discharged Ford employees, many of whom had been manhandled by Bennett's gang, and even some of Bennett's former servicemen, who had resigned and were willing to testify for the government.

By January 1 of 1941, the NLRB had completed its early investigation of the River Rouge plant, and when its findings had been upheld by the United States Circuit Court of Appeals, the Ford Motor Company requested the Supreme Court to review the case. This was a mistake, for the Court rejected the plea. Thereafter, every day the company refused to cooperate with the NLRB at the River Rouge plant, Henry Ford was running the risk of being cited for contempt of court. Eight days after the Supreme Court had rendered its decision, notices were posted throughout the big, sprawling plant that the company would comply with court order, and that employees could exercise their right to organize a union. Union men who had been discharged as far back as 1937 were reinstated, with several million dollars' back pay.

Immediately workers who had been fearful and ambivalent about joining a union began to sign up with UAW-CIO Local 600. Many departments of the River Rouge elected shop stewards. Grievance committees walked boldly into executive offices, where none of them had ever been before, demanding that the company start bargaining at once.

Ford began to make a few small concessions here and there.

Even Harry Bennett showed signs of unbending—a little. One morning a group of shop stewards came into his office, in the basement of the River Rouge plant, without even having asked for an appointment. They demanded to know why two dozen union leaders in their department had been suddenly fired without explanation. Bennett almost rendered them speechless by passing around cigars—on Ford property. They hesitated a moment, then lighted them. The roof did not fall in, as they half expected. "Would you boys care to have a seat?" Bennett asked them. Some of them sat down rather gingerly, but the chairs did not collapse. After hearing their complaint, Bennett called in the mill superintendent, gave him a dressing down, and ordered him to reinstate the discharged men at once. When the shop stewards had left Bennett's office, one of them said in awe, "I've been working at the Ford plant for ten years, but this is the first time anybody around here ever offered me a seat!"

All that unprecedented cordiality was only a cloak, behind which Ford and Bennett frantically cast about for some means of thwarting the union and the government. Bennett suddenly turned on the union with new fury, firing its leaders right and left. Only when the government forced it on the company would a union election be held, and when the UAW won, Bennett remarked: "We'll bargain till hell freezes over, but they won't get a goddamn thing."

Since 1937, Henry Ford had been trying out company unions, "make-believe unions," the UAW had called them. They had different names, but all were formed with one idea—to make the employees think they had a union, although it had no bargaining power and was completely dominated by management. Among them were the Liberty Legion of America, the Workers' Council for Social Justice, the Independent Automobile Workers' Association, and the Ford Brotherhood of America. Although in some cases the employees were compelled to join them, they never had anything but a paper membership. When Homer Martin in 1939, having been ousted as president of UAW, came along with his idea of setting up his AFL-UAW in the Ford plants, in opposition to CIO-UAW, Bennett and Ford welcomed him with open arms.

LEFT: Walter (left) and Roy Reuther, displaying their sports trophies won in high school years, c.1925. RIGHT: Roy Reuther rallying Chevrolet workers to join sit-downs, Flint, Michigan, 1937.

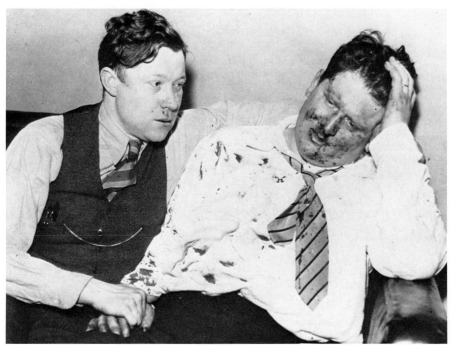

Walter Reuther comforting bloodied Richard Frankensteen after both were beaten up by Ford "goons" at Battle of the Overpass, May 26, 1937.

May and Walter Reuther (then UAW vice-president and chief union negotiator at GM) at home with daughter, Linda, age 3, December 4, 1945.

Wide World

RIGHT: Walter in his basement workshop of Appoline Street home, putting final touches on a coffee table, December 4, 1945.

Wide World

Associated Press

Walter Reuther at his first election as President, UAW-CIO, March 27, 1946, is shown here on shoulders of cheering backers after nomination.

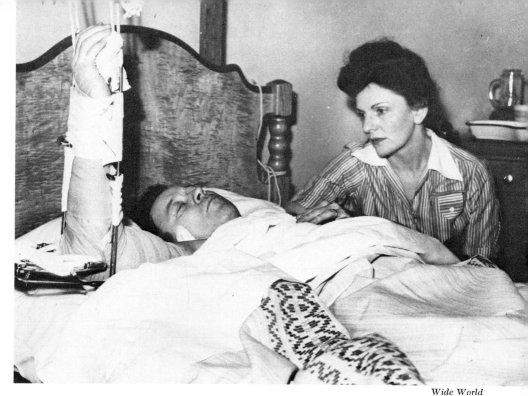

May Reuther holding vigil at Detroit Hospital after the shotgun attack on Walter's life, April 20, 1948.

Victor, Roy, and Walter Reuther (left to right) after attempt on Victor's life by a shotgun assailant, May 24, 1949.

Walter (right), Roy (left), and the oldest Reuther brother Ted, leaving Ford hospital, with (left to right) May; Victor's wife, Sophie; and Mrs. Roy Reuther, after a family visit to Victor, May 26, 1949.

BELOW LEFT: Reuther, surprised by news photographer as he emerges from a special session of the UAW Executive Board regarding Gosser scandal in Toledo, Ohio, c.1950. With him is attorney George J. Gould, President of the Toledo Bar Association, who was "waiting to take Walter home to supper." (Note square of foam rubber in Reuther's injured right hand.) Photo by Tom O'Reilly of Toledo *Blade*, courtesy Mr. Gould. RIGHT: "Walter" displaying a prize catch for the benefit of his nephews, Peter and Tommy Wolf (see inscription) c.1951. Courtesy Mr. and Mrs. Leo Wolf.

Wide World   *United Press International*

LEFT: "Let's dance" was the caption on this April 2, 1951, photo, when CIO President Philip Murray addressed the UAW convention. RIGHT: Reuther in politics, with Adlai Stevenson, just before the latter addressed a Labor Day rally in Flint, Michigan, September 3, 1952.

With President Truman in the Truman Library, 1959, when the former President played host—and the piano—for Walter Reuther.

United Press International

Walter, flanked by brothers Roy (left) and Victor (right) at ICFTU (International Confederation of Free Trade Unions) meeting in New York, 1952.

President-elect Eisenhower greets CIO leaders, November 28, 1952, just before Reuther's surprise election to the Presidency of the CIO. Ike is shaking hands with Allan Haywood, CIO Executive Vice-President, considered the favorite. Others (left to right) are Jacob Potofsky, David McDonald, and James Carey.

Happy son, Walter, with proud parents, Valentine and Anna Reuther, CIO convention, December 1952, when Reuther was elected CIO President.

Preliminary meeting of AFL and CIO leaders to plan merger of the two bodies, February 9, 1955. At center are George Meany and Walter Reuther.

Historic moment of merger: George Meany, AFL President, and Walter Reuther, CIO President, lifting a giant gavel together to open Merger Convention, New York, December 5, 1955.

LEFT: Walter Reuther in New Delhi, India, with Jawaharlal Nehru, 1956.

Walter Reuther, looking fondly at his daughter, Linda (seated, left, back to camera), as "Speaker" at the graduation exercises of her class at the Putney School, Putney, Vermont, June 10, 1960.

United Press International

Walter Reuther with leaders of Sane Nuclear Policy, Republican Alf Landon (1936 Presidential candidate), Democrat Eleanor Roosevelt, and Socialist Norman Thomas, 1960.

"Hands across the bargaining table" between UAW President Walter Reuther and Ford Vice-President in charge of Industrial Relations, John Bugas, as contract agreement is reached, September, 1958.

United Press International

The Walter Reuther family with Mrs. Roosevelt at Hyde Park, c. summer 1962. (Left to right) Lisa, May, "Mrs. R.," Walter, and Linda. (Mrs. Roosevelt died November, 1962.) Courtesy Lisa Reuther Gesinski.

With JFK: At Hyannisport, arriving for weekend just after Reuther endorsed Kennedy for President, 1960.

United Press International

United Press International

With other leaders of massive civil rights march on Washington, 1963. (Left to right) Martin Luther King, Rabbi Joachim Prinz, A. Philip Randolph, President Kennedy, Walter Reuther, Roy Wilkins (NAACP), and, visible behind Reuther, the head of Vice-President Johnson.

Walter Reuther, the oarsman, takes his colleagues (left to right) Senator Hubert Humphrey, Willy Brandt (then Mayor of West Berlin), and their host, Swedish Premier, Tage Erlander, for a row around the lake at Erlander's home in the Stockholm suburb of Harpsund, July 14, 1963, during an informal international economic conference.

United Press International

With LBJ, as President Johnson arrived at Atlantic City airport to address UAW national convention, March 23, 1964.

Walter Reuther pickets with Cesar Chavez and "grape strikers," Delano, California, December 16, 1965.

Receiving an honorary degree from Tuskegee Institute. At bottom (left) is Dr. Martin Luther King, who gave commencement address, May 31, 1965.

Wide World

Walter Reuther as he led contract talks in 1967, accompanied by Leonard Woodcock, then UAW vice-president (now president): three-year contract signed.

Wide World

With Robert Kennedy, at UAW national convention, May 8, 1968, as delegates cheer before Kennedy's address.

Conducting an informal tour of his beloved Family Education Center at Black Lake near Pellston, Michigan, a few months before his plane crashed in flight to the center, 1970.

Scene of crash, plane wreckage, near Pellston Airport, Michigan, May 10, 1970.

United Press International

At Memorial Services held in Ford Auditorium, Detroit, May 15, 1970, Senator Philip Hart eulogizes UAW President Walter Reuther and his wife, May Wolf Reuther.

Victor Reuther, his wife, and two sons, John (left) and Erick (right), pause at Walter's bier.

United Press International

Mourners among workers and family: Workers at Ford Motor Company, St. Paul, Minnesota, stand with bowed heads as the assembly line stopped for three minutes.

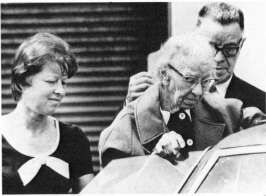

ABOVE: Mrs. Valentine Reuther, Walter's eighty-six-year-old mother, with his sister Christine (Mrs. Eugene Richey) (left) and brother Theodore (right), leaving the memorial service.

LEFT: The Reuthers' daughters, Lisa, 22, and Linda, 27, (left to right) clasping hands as they walk away from their parents' caskets after the services, May 15, 1970.

This, too, would have been a company union. The AFL-UAW failed miserably in gaining any following.

Bennett, in the meantime, continued to goad the workers to the point of no return. During March, 1941, shutdown after shutdown took place in the plants, most of which were settled on union terms, the company agreeing to meet with individual plant committees, though it still refused to sit down with national union leaders and bargain collectively. But in another sharp turn of company policy, on April 1, Ford suddenly refused to meet with any union committees, and he fired eight members of the grievance committee of Local 600 (variously employed in the rolling mill, the pressed-steel and the tire plant, and in B buildings). That was the last straw. Without a word to—or from—top leadership, the men in the Ford plants walked off their jobs, refusing to go back until the company rehired the committee men. At the rolling-mill plant, where the entire work force of six thousand had come to a halt, anger soared at the sight of 110 Dearborn policemen who were rushed to the scene. But as thousands of workers from other buildings came marching toward the rolling-mill plant, the police beat a hasty retreat. The shutdown spread from one building to the next, starting late in the afternoon until, by evening, there was an eerie stillness over the entire huge Ford complex at River Rouge. The strike, which broke out like spontaneous combustion, caught the union leaders by surprise.

They had been contemplating a called strike, but only if it was necessary in the near future. No date had been set, no directive sent out. At first the officials did not know what happened; but the news, which seemed incredible to them and to all Detroit, spread like wildfire: "Ford is shut down!" Late in the evening Walter Reuther and the other Executive Board members received a call from Mike Widman to a hasty meeting with the Ford organizing committee; and at twelve-fifteen on April 2, a strike against Ford was called officially. At the Rouge, the order was received with a rousing hurrah, and in the darkness a parade of shouting men magically formed, marching down the unlit road to the union hall half a mile away.

The extraordinary all-night meeting that took place was an unprecedented event in the labor history of America. Men talked their hearts out, all night long, airing their anger without fear or anxiety for once. They milled around, speculating on their chances of success, laughing, telling stories of incidents leading to the shutdown in their own departments; and, although the leaders kept the meeting going with some degree of formality, it was more significantly a talk-fest for the workers themselves. It was as if the tightly wound wellsprings of their very souls had suddenly been released, and as they began to unwind, they became animated, confident, eager for the action to come. They found sheer pleasure in seeing the way the union strike committee went into operation: a soup kitchen was set up, as well as a union first-aid unit; and instructions were handed out to strike squadrons. Now the experience and know-how gained in the GM and Chrysler battles were put to good use as the details of running an effective strike were worked out. The Ford workers were impressed with their new-found selves and their union.

Emil Mazey, former Briggs worker and the local's president, presided at the all-night session and called on all the prominent union leaders—CIO director Mike Widman, R. J. Thomas, George Addes, and Walter Reuther, Mazey's model in matters of leadership. Walter spoke with his usual zest and fire; for some weeks he had interpreted the growing militancy among the workers as a good sign, and he felt that Widman was an overly cautious man, frightened by these auto strikes. The men responded to Reuther's enthusiasm with their own heightened feelings, and Mazey long remembered that night as "among the most exciting in our whole experience in the labor movement. It was like seeing men who had been half dead suddenly come to life. And did they come to life! It was hard to keep things going, hard to organize, so eager were they just to mill around and talk and let some steam go. That night you really understood what the union could mean to men."

Dawn brought the decisive test. Harry Bennett had placed big ads in all the Detroit papers designed to get workers to report to their jobs "as usual." Behind his scheme was the fact that hundreds of Negroes were still inside the plant, too timid to have joined the strikers in the shutdown, terrified of both union and company officials—fearing punishment either way they went—whom Bennett intended to use as his battalion; in the next day or two he brought several hundred more Negroes up from the South to add to the ranks.

The site of the Rouge auto plant complex was the hub from which a series of converging roads led in all directions like the spokes of a wheel. Inside this circle and the high wall surrounding it, Ford servicemen were stationed at the main gates, armed and ready for action. It would have meant exposure to attack immediately if pickets had tried to approach those gates or penetrate beyond the walls. Outside, the union had devised its own clever strategy: The incoming roads were blocked by barricades of automobiles, some of them old, broken-down cars dragged there and parked at right angles across the pavement. At Eagle Pass and Wyoming Avenue, at Miller Road and Airport Drive, at Schaefer Road and Dix, the barricades prevented anyone from getting in or out of the plant without the pickets' approval. Ignorant of this, Bennett's men were waiting at the gates, prepared to smash the picket lines to let strikebreakers through; but 6 A.M. came and went, and nobody appeared for work.

After an hour's wait, an angry Bennett ordered the first assault on the pickets. In the words of the Detroit *News*, "Iron bolts and nuts flew through the air in a wholesale barrage from the factory roof, while several hundred Negroes with steel bars and knives charged out of the main gate, No. 4, of the Rouge plant in two assaults on the UAW picket lines there." Taken by surprise, the union men were injured, thirty-six so severely they had to be treated at the strike hospital, and the picket lines were disrupted. But not for long. Thousands more strikers rushed to the front, armed with baseball bats, sticks, and their sheer muscular power. Picket lines were patched up, and at 9 A.M., when Bennett's men were ordered to charge again, they were met with a barrage of blows that beat them back. The lines held; the union showed decisively, despite bloody noses and heads, that they had shut down mighty Ford, and would keep it down. Thousands of auto workers and the curious rubbernecks who drove out to see the unbelievable with their own eyes helped to keep the roads blocked for days, while the battle raged on and the Dearborn police stood idly by, watching the regular attacks on picket lines as if they were mere spectators. Their patently paid-off indiffer-

ence aroused grim anger in the strikers and their leaders. Emil
Mazey declared at a mass meeting, "If we need a labor holiday
to win this strike, we'll have one," and his thinly veiled threat of
a general strike in Detroit was understood by all.

For ten days the armed conflict continued. The Ford Company,
through Bennett, tried every trick in the book to beat the union.
Statements were issued declaring the strike to be a Communist
conspiracy. An injunction was obtained ordering pickets to clear
the roads leading to the Rouge. Bennett's servicemen did not attack the strikers on the picket line—there were too many—but
they exploited to the hilt the Negroes held captive inside. Several
times a day those who had been brought up from the Deep South,
supposedly for "jobs," were driven to the roof and into the area
between the wall and the plant, and commanded to throw pieces
of pipes, nuts, bolts, and other suitable missiles at the pickets, who
promptly hurled them back. At intervals the Negro "workers"
were forced to charge out to the gates for hand-to-hand fighting;
if they did not obey immediately, they were beaten by servicemen. As a final insult, Bennett claimed they were sit-downers,
who were damaging the property inside the plant. This, of course,
proved on investigation by federal authority to be a colossal hoax.
Next, the company tried to organize a back-to-work movement
among the three thousand Negroes who had joined the shutdown
in the beginning. Arranging a mass meeting in Detroit's black
section, Homer Martin, now claiming he was an official AFL
organizer, weaseled into the fray by urging the striking Negroes
to "march back in a body" to break the strike. Aside from the fact
that his turncoat act caused his final ruin in labor's eyes, his fool-
hardy move could easily have caused a race riot.

However, the union countered this hazard with a group of
Negro leaders, among them Walter White of the NAACP, Louis
Martin, editor of the Negro paper the *Michigan Chronicle,* and
the Reverend Horace White of the influential Plymouth Congre-
gational Church, who mobilized the sentiment in Negro neighborhoods in favor of the UAW-CIO. Their persuasions soon caused
the back-to-work movement to collapse; and even the AFL unions
in Detroit denounced Homer Martin as a strikebreaker. Now the
problem remained to get the Negroes out of the plant; more than

eight hundred were still inside, captive. Using loudspeakers, Walter White and the rest mounted a sound truck and began cruising around and around the fortress, pleading with the Negroes to come out. Union leaders, including the Reuthers, took turns at the loudspeakers trying to convince the Negroes they would not be harmed by the pickets if they came out. About a third of them did, but most stayed in, intimidated by Bennett's servicemen. The Dearborn police still did nothing. Finally, federal conciliator James Dewey went in and persuaded the remaining Negroes to leave the premises.

At this point, Michigan governor Van Wagoner proposed a settlement that was largely a compromise, but the UAW quickly accepted it; and Ford, though also reluctant, accepted "with reservations." The strike ended on April 10. The agreement was very simple: Ford consented to an NLRB election, which he had been contesting and delaying up until then (this was really the main purpose of the strike); and second, if the UAW-CIO won the election, the company would forthwith recognize the union as the sole collective bargaining agent and negotiate a collective agreement. At this preliminary peace conference, his emissaries were a knot of prizefighters and plant detectives from Bennett's Service Department!

The election was held late in May. The results were self-revealing: the UAW-CIO received 51,886 votes to 20,354 for the UAW-AFL, out of about 80,000 votes cast at the Rouge plant alone; less than 3 per cent voted for "no union" and some were undecided. It was a cause for jubilation even some twenty years later, as Walter Reuther recalled those figures. "It was certainly one of the most resounding victories any union ever won in an NLRB election," he said joyfully. Harry Bennett's view saw the election as "a great victory for the Communist party, Governor Van Wagoner, and the National Labor Relations Board." At other Ford plants, results compared very favorably with the River Rouge victory, signalling a mandate for collective bargaining negotiations.

Now the Ford Motor Company did a complete about-face. In a history-making reversal of policy, Harry Bennett, negotiating with Philip Murray, agreed to a union shop, dues check-off, grievance machinery, seniority, time and a half for overtime, premium pay for night workers, and two hours' pay for employees called in but not given work. After the contract was signed, the UAW negotiated wage increases which would give Ford employees an additional $52 million in wages within a year. Probably the most important concession on the company's part was that of granting a union shop, and while UAW leaders were more than pleased, they were also somewhat puzzled about this, until Walter Reuther and Emil Mazey figured out what lay behind the move. Harry Bennett must have planned to bore from within, his idea being that if everyone had to belong to the union, his servicemen would get in and take over the union that way. But the union negotiators immediately blocked it by insisting that all servicemen be put in uniform, so that they could be easily identified. Since they were not production workers, the union refused to admit them. (As it turned out, Bennett and his goon squad of servicemen were rendered unnecessary by the very existence of the union shop, and were soon disbanded by Ford himself.)

"The Flivver King," as he was dubbed in the title of Upton Sinclair's novel built around the life of Henry Ford, later attributed his change of heart toward unionism to the influence of his wife, Clara. At the time the UAW campaign was launched, he was so depressed at the progress of labor organizers, whom he labeled "the worst thing that ever struck the earth," that he vowed to close down the company altogether; but his wife said if he did, she would leave home. "Never underestimate the power of a woman," Ford said sagely, in one of his beatific moments. It is more likely that his intuitive business sense told him it was cheaper to work with the union than to fight it with the huge sums of money he was paying the plant detectives and spies of Harry Bennett.

For the UAW and the entire CIO, the unionization of Ford, long the most invincible and declared foe of organized labor, the defeat of this "last citadel of open shopism" was a most important milestone in labor's climb to power. Ford Local 600 was soon to become the largest in the world, and would own a $200,000 union hall. It was also to provide the setting for a serious intraunion struggle because of pro-Communist officials in control, a fight resolved by the rise of the Reuther group. For Walter, who had relinquished his claim to the directorship of the campaign for the sake of internal harmony, the present victory was a source of deep satisfaction. The open warfare that he had launched in the battle of the overpass had been won with flying colors.

XVII

The Planner: "Five Hundred Planes a Day"

If Walter Reuther did not play a prominent role in the organization of Ford or in negotiating the first contract, it was not because he did not aspire to such a role or did not have a valid claim to the directorship of the campaign. After all, he had worked for five years at Ford, "in the B building, back before the depression, when they were driving fellows in the Skilled Trades Department, not only on the production lines," as he had said when the Executive Board was discussing the directorship. Internal politics in the UAW did not end by any means when Homer Martin left. Intense rivalry for power still existed, and there was still an element of Communist influence in the union, which Walter and others were seeking to eliminate.

Among those who were serious contenders for top leadership in the union were Walter, R. J. Thomas, Dick Frankensteen, and George Addes, to name the four most conspicuous ones. Each of these leaders, and all of the various factions in the union, knew that the person or the group responsible for the successful organizing of Ford would gain an enormous political advantage. It is to their credit that, whatever their differences, they all frankly admitted this was true and that a contest to determine who would take over as director might postpone the organization of the union at Ford indefinitely. It had already been delayed too long, largely because of the fight with Martin. So they had agreed to

184

remove the prestige of organizing the last and largest giant of the industry from the International Union political arena, and had asked the CIO to appoint a director from outside the ranks of the UAW. The appointment of Widman by Lewis did remove the campaign from the internal politics of the auto workers union, and none of these four top leaders participated directly in the organizing campaign or its supervision because of this agreement among themselves, and with the CIO, beforehand.

If Roland J. Thomas had been a more dynamic labor leader, he might have seized the opportunity of his post as president to assume the directorship. But ruddy faced, paunchy Thomas, a former welder from Chrysler Corporation, as UAW's president was the same easy going, amiable, honest union man he had always been. He enjoyed nothing more than a good poker game with the boys, where he would rhythmically chew tobacco while placing his bets judiciously. It was once said that a straight flush held more meaning and pleasure for him than any automotive chart on industrial productivity. He also loved his beer, and if some rank-and-file worker invited him to stop for a drink at one of the Jefferson Avenue bars, he rarely refused. Having come from the ranks himself, he had no trouble being one of them socially, and he understood the psychology of the worker perhaps better than more intellectual leaders. In comparison with Walter Reuther, he was undoubtedly limited. Certainly he believed in unions. He had been known to risk his career defending Negro workers, and he realized to a certain extent that labor had broader social responsibilities than "wages, hours, and working conditions," but his ability to act on that principle was restricted by his meager imagination and lack of creative ideas.

It was his misfortune to become president of the UAW at a time when history was enacting a crucial drama of drastic change at home, and the role that the trade union movement had to play in such a complex situation was simply beyond Thomas' grasp. In his 1940 convention address he proclaimed, "We do not want the blood of one automobile worker to flow across the seas." A year later he was asking for "guns and butter," hoping, like many Americans, that a large-scale war could be fought without curtailing civilian commodities. But he had no idea how to spread the work force to include both butter and guns as the demand for the latter grew greater and greater. He was honest and conscientious, but during the war years he was a bewildered, inadequate leader.

Walter Reuther, on the other hand, was just the opposite. Bristling with ideas, he tackled every problem with the power of an electric dynamo, an energy that amazed both his friends and enemies, on both sides of the bargaining table. Even at this early date, others stared with unbelief at the redhead's capacity for work, for the quick transformation of his ideas into action, for his sheer endurance. His regular working day was more than twice the number of hours he sought for union members; if he took off six hours for sleeping out of the twenty-four, it was a lot for him. Even in sleep, his mind kept ticking away busily, and if it startled him awake with an idea, he kept a pad and pencil handy on a night table so he could jot down a few notes before he went back to sleep. Luckily, he had the athlete's ability to "turn off the switch" physically within a few minutes, perhaps just because of his health habits: after cramming two days work into one, he would top it off with a five-mile hike, swinging along with great strides, his strong "pouter-pigeon chest," as one biographer called it puffed out, his muscular legs moving at a pace that would leave a marathon walker far behind. Then he would follow it up with a cold shower when he got home, to "tone up" for the next day before he finally tumbled into bed. He almost never slowed down.

His wife, May, used to say that if she found him sitting still, he must be ill, and this was usually the case, although he rarely had anything more than a cold, and even that could not slacken his pace for long. Since May was his "private secretary" during these years, both of them lived a life brimming with unionism; they ate, drank, and slept it. And even if, once in a great while, they took a day off, Walter's phenomenal energy still wouldn't let him lounge around. During one summer in the late 1930's, some of May's relatives had persuaded Walter to drive up to a cabin on Spider Lake in northern Michigan for a day or two. They had just arrived when he noticed that some patches of underbrush and straggly alders obscured the view. He thought it should be cleared, so while everybody else headed for the lake, "he marched into the brush with a hatchet," his brother-in-law recalled; and, as much as he loved swimming, did not take a dip until the job was done.

Much later, some of his assistants convinced him that he should take a true vacation. Since he had never really had one and was always advocating more leisure time for people, they insisted that he should do a little firsthand "research" and discover its merits for himself. His answer was that he would get bored; but he was passionately fond of fishing, and when they told him of a lake in northern Michigan that was well stocked with trout, he finally consented to give it a try, and off he went. A few days later, a postcard came to the UAW offices with the note: "I caught five fish on Monday, seven fish on Tuesday, and six fish today, and I'm going to catch all the fish in the lake before the end of the week." The message was a standing joke for years. "That's Walter for you!" somebody said with a chuckle. And another, "Every one's the big one for Walter. Everything's for keeps. He even goes after trout with all twenty guns roaring."

In the summer of 1940, however, Walter Reuther had far too much on his mind, far too many problems facing the union and its leaders, besides several projects of his own, part personal, part arising out of the national-defense crisis, to be even remotely contemplating a vacation. For one thing, at the age of 33, and in good health, he was subject to draft induction. He was also on the Advisory Board of the defense training program in industry, and, in spite of his pacifist background and his basic belief that wars cannot be won on the battlefield, Walter at this time felt it necessary to "take up arms against the sea of troubles" engulfing Europe. Like many people, among them former pacifist poets and playwrights—most notably Robert Sherwood, soon to join Roosevelt's staff of wartime writers—the Reuthers were strong interventionists against the threat of Hitler. Walter and Victor particularly, having seen and experienced firsthand the horrors of Hitler's dictatorship and the ruthlessness of Russia's—tactics which applied to any totalitarian state in varying degrees—both felt it was a matter of expediency to prevent world inundation from the waves of military destruction by the dictators threatening Europe.

The situation across the Atlantic looked all but hopeless. Most of Europe was in the hands of Hitler. The Battle for Britain was about to begin, and the main defense of the United States was a thin line of British pilots in small, mostly obsolete planes, trying to fight off Hermann Göring's giant bombers. If England were to fall, the United States would be next on Hitler's list, and Roosevelt knew it. On May 16 of that year, 1940, he had gone on record in an address to Congress with these words: "I should like to see this nation geared up to the ability to turn out at least fifty thousand planes a year." A startling statment in those days; even among the President's admirers, the majority regarded that goal unattainable. His enemies ridiculed him, and Americans generally refused to take him seriously.

One American, however, who took him seriously was Walter Reuther. To him, the figure of 50,000 planes a year was a challenge. He could not have resisted any more than he could resist the impulse throughout his career to grab a sign and march in a picket line whenever he saw one. His quick, inventive mind immediately went to work, and he came up with a plan that suggested a figure three times greater than FDR's: "500 Planes a Day"—in other words, *150,000* planes a year—was the bold title of the ingenious proposal he submitted to the President's office through Philip Murray of the CIO on December 23, 1940. Although the catch-phrase figure, "500 planes-a-day," was probably exaggerated, the basic premise of the plan was sound: principally to put idle auto manufacturing capacity to use in the production of airplanes so desperately needed. To implement the idea, he proposed pooling the resources of manpower and machinery into a central war-plane production body which would lessen competition among companies and include labor in carrying out the provisions; in effect, labor would become an integral part of the production setup. He went so far as to suggest a nine-member board, composed of three representatives each from management, government, and labor.

Roosevelt was so favorably impressed with the constructive ingenuity of the proposal that he asked Reuther to the White House for a more detailed discussion, and greeted him with, "Ah, here's our young engineer!" The effect of the plan on the public was sensational, controversial, and instrumental in bringing Walter Reuther into prominence as a national figure. Editorial writers analyzed the plan for its merits and faults; management objected strenuously to labor's entry into the executive scene; and in the labor movement there was fear expressed over the risk labor might be taking if it worked hand in glove with management, thus relinquishing its rights as a free bargaining agent. At any rate, the widespread publicity marked the emergency of Reuther as a labor statesman, with far-reaching ideas and a sense of labor's social and economic responsibility.

The germ of the plan had been seeded on a summer morning several months before, when Walter and May were driving to the UAW offices. At the insistence of R. J. Thomas, who, with Philip Murray, felt that he was needed in the war effort at home more than in the army, Walter had appealed his Selective Service rating of 1-A, subject to immediate induction. Both union officers had feared that many of the younger leaders would be inducted because of their eligibility, and that the union would suffer in strength and status if key people throughout were to be taken away by the draft. They had asked Walter if he would be willing to use his as a test case, and he had agreed to be "a guinea pig," as he said a year later in defending his action before UAW Communist-faction members. His draft board had not granted him an occupational deferment, but had reclassified him 3-A, on the basis of May's "dependency," which he had listed since she would lose her job if he was inducted; and the board could rule on the dependency question at once, without having to wait for a decision on Reuther's "essential contribution to the defense program."

The whole question of their finances was laughable. May was still earning less than $20 a week: her salary was $1,000 a year, and Walter's only $2,500 a year, although his own West Side local felt that he, as president, and a member of the International Executive Board, should receive a higher salary. But Reuther never wanted much for himself—and his attitude was not an affectation. He seemed to take something of the ascetic's pleasure in simple living. Even in the matter of dress, though he was always fastidious, and looked more like a bright young businessman than a labor leader—he never employed a tailor in his life, but bought his suits, black or dark blue, off the rack in medium-price retail clothing stores for men. Yet, just as he had made do on very little during his boyhood, he had managed somehow to save a little more than a thousand dollars in the four and a half years that he and May had been married. They had been living with her parents, of course, but they had been contributing to the household expenses, and to be able to save anything, even on their combined salaries, was remarkable. Both he and May wanted to have a place of their own eventually, and when the Selective Service Board granted deferment they began looking around, casually, for a little house within their reach.

On this particular summer morning in 1940, however, Walter forgot all about their plans when he saw, while passing the site of a Packard aircraft-engine plant being built with government funds, that concrete footing foundations were just being poured, although the contract had been awarded for some time. He was ready to explode; it would be another eighteen months before the "damn plant" would be ready to produce the first engine. Hitler could bomb us off the earth by then! Suddenly he recalled that the Gorki plant had been tooled for civilian and military production at the same time. Detroit's factories all had idle floor space; an industry that could produce eight million cars a year had been turning out only four million since the war effort began. And so the conversion plan to produce "five hundred planes a day" in auto plants had been born.

Always a man of action, Walter outlined his "brain wave" to Sidney Hillman at the next meeting of the Advisory Board in Washington. Hillman, then associate director of the Office of Production Management, of which William Knudsen, lately of General Motors, had been appointed director, was as much a visionary, a man of expediency and direct approach, as Walter. He was enthusiastic in his prompt approval, telling the young UAW executive to go ahead with the development of a prospectus.

Back in Detroit, after the meeting, Walter enlisted Ben Blackwood, an expert tool- and diemaker from GM as his chief assistant in conducting a survey of the auto industry's basic and potential production ability. Marshaling the opinions of twenty-five of the union's top technicians in the plants, and using the Federal Trade Commission statistics, over which he poured nightly, Walter was able to cite case after case of companies operating far below capacity, of assembly lines set up but standing idle. There were thousands of feet of unused floor space in the Detroit and Cleveland areas, thousands of unemployed tool- and die-makers waiting for work. He pointed out that "both automobile and airplane motors are combustion engines, essentially the same mechanism for generating power by exploding gasoline. Both motors contain cylinders, carburetors, pistons, crankshafts, valves, spark plugs, ignition systems, etc. . . ." There was scarcely any aspect he failed to touch on, even to construction of inexpensive hangars for the welding of wings and fuselages, which could be stamped in body shops like Briggs and Fisher.

For the actual presentation in writing, Walter called upon two of the ablest talents: Edward Levinson, who had joined the UAW publicity staff in the late thirties, one of the most perceptive, witty, and knowledgeable labor newspapermen in the country*; and I. F. Stone, the brilliant, incisive, liberal analyst on current affairs, then just beginning to earn his reputation as a hypercritical but scholarly, if eccentric, journalist. It was part of Reuther's own talent to choose these two, whose stylistic touches can be seen in the printed pamphlet that was finally issued at the request of many organizations and bureaus who wanted to study it. The opening sentences, in the light of America's "Aid-to-Britain" program, were appropriate and attractive: "England's battles, it used to be said, were won on the playing fields of Eton. This plan is put forward in the belief that America's can be won on the assembly lines of Detroit." And the memorandum concluded eloquently: "The merit of our plan is that it saves time, and time is our problem. Normal methods can build all the planes we need —if we wait till 1942 and 1943 to get them. This plan is put forward in the belief that the need for planes is immediate and terrifying. Precious moments pass away as we delay."

* Edward Levinson's *Labor On the March*, first published in 1938, contains one of the most authentic accounts of the sit-down strikes; when the book was re-issued by New York University Books in 1956, Reuther wrote the introduction, paying great tribute to "Eddie" Levinson.

When all was ready, he offered R. J. Thomas, as UAW president, the task of submitting his idea to FDR, but Thomas had been wary of both the plan and its creator. He held that union men should "tend to their knitting"—not try to meddle with management or production problems. Afraid of becoming the laughingstock of the labor movement, he said bluntly, "You're not going to make a horse's ass out of me." Walter had been just as well satisfied; he had done his diplomatic duty, and was free to seek a higher level. Philip Murray, his next contact, had just become president of the CIO, due to a quixotic move on John L. Lewis' part, one that was fortuitously timed for Reuther. Lewis had failed to back FDR for the third term and stayed away from the Democratic convention in July (1940)—the first Walter had ever attended. At a pre-convention labor caucus, he and Victor had spoken up strongly for the reelection of the "man in the White House," citing the record of the New Deal, of Social Security, the defense program, etc.

After FDR's nomination, the Reuthers had then campaigned whenever they could for the President, assuming that the CIO head approved the third-term nominee. But Lewis had never declared himself, and eleven days before the election he had come out publicly in a network broadcast for Wendell Willkie, adding that he would resign from the presidency of the CIO if FDR won a third term. Labor—especially the UAW—was aghast and angered. When, in the face of the close results at the polls in November, FDR did win, Lewis followed through on his vow by returning to his mine workers union for the rest of his life, leaving the way clear for Walter P. Reuther. No one had commented on this particular circumstance, but it is likely that, with Lewis out of the International CIO picture, Reuther had decided to forge ahead as fast as he could.

Philip Murray had succeeded "John L." as president of the CIO. Murray, though reserved, was much more receptive to Walter's latest "pipe dream" for solving the world's problems, perhaps because of Hillman's approval. (It was said that when the initial proofs of the pamphlet appeared, the title read, "500 Plans a Day," a symbolic error!) Murray's reaction had been, "I don't know a damn thing about this, but if you say it makes sense, I'm agree-able." And he had shown the paper to Roosevelt.

And so it was that almost overnight, just after the Ford campaign had been launched by Widman, Walter Reuther had become a fairly well known national figure. Knudsen, of course, objected strenuously to labor's having an equal share in the setup of production, the nine-member board, and the overall attitude best summarized in the next-to-last paragraph: "Labor offers its wholehearted cooperation. All that labor asks is intelligent plan-ning, a voice in matters of policy and administration, recognition of its rights, and maintenance of its established standards." Knudsen was having trouble enough with Sidney Hillman, the elder statesman of labor, who continually handed out defense contracts or negotiated for them over the phone on his own before Knudsen learned about his activity, without having that young smart-alec "Socialist" from the UAW butting in with *his* notions. The former GM executive refused to consider the plan seriously, arguing that the pooling of resources, and such, were "socialistic devices." Reuther retorted that the real objection of the auto industrialists lay in having their plants drafted as men were having their lives drafted; and this in turn would cost them precious competitive profits. Knudsen remained adamant, and was all for pigeonholding the plan completely; but the thinking public would not allow it to drop. Widely read columnists like Dorothy Thompson, Walter Lippman, Raymond Clapper, and others demanded a hearing for Reuther's ideas, and he appeared on an open forum at the National Press Club in Washington.

He was highly elated when word came that President Roosevelt had turned over the "500 planes" treatise to the new Defense Council, and had declared that if it could be expedited, it would be a "major contribution." Walter predicted gleefully, if too previously, "In six months, we can put ten planes into the air for Hitler's one!" Just before the year ended, he was invited by the chairman of the Securities and Exchange Commission to dis-cuss his proposal with prominent figures of the New Deal at one of the famous Sunday morning breakfasts at the Cosmos Club. Such men as Leon Henderson, Paul V. McNutt, Tommy Corcoran, and Harry Dexter White listened to him explain the plan in detail, and then discussed it for several hours. White was so taken with the whole concept and its young progenitor that he arranged a meeting between Walter Reuther and Secretary of the Treasury Henry Morgenthau that same afternoon. The latter, a close friend of FDR, promised to urge the President to hold the full-scale hearing that the plan merited, although he was sharp enough to realize that its chances of being put into effect were slim. He commented frankly, "There is only one thing wrong with the program. It comes from the 'wrong' source."

Much the same sentiment had been expressed at the breakfast by a War Department labor advisor who, after conceding, "It probably can be done," demanded rhetorically, "but who the hell will pay attention to a squirt of a labor leader?" Still, Walter could not help feeling optimistic, and celebrated Christmas with his family in high spirits. Then, on New Year's Day, 1941, an AP report from Washington asserted that "defense experts . . . had concluded with reluctance that Reuther's recommendations were impractical and must be rejected." Anyone less sanguine or persistent would have given up, but not Walter. After reading their objections, he said to May, "I don't know who these 'experts' are, but they don't know what they're talking about! I'm not licked yet, not by a long shot!" And two days later, on January 3, he was back in Washington to press his case. He met with Robert Lovett, special assistant to the Secretary of War, and in two weeks, with an Air Corps plane assigned by Robert P. Patterson, Undersecretary of War, he was winging his way to large airplane factories, where he checked out some of his ideas.

Finding that the plan was undoubtedly feasible, he sought a confrontation with Knudsen, who, as head of the OPM, could have been the deciding force in bringing success. They had met at the bargaining table during the General Motors negotiations, so each knew the other's attitudes and quirks. (Walter's tenacity was evident even then, causing Knudsen to remark that he wished the labor leader would take a job selling used cars for GM. "*Used* cars?" Walter wondered. Knudsen nodded grimly. "*Used* cars," he repeated. "Anybody can sell new cars!") Now they sparred again, with Knudsen growing more adamant as Walter continued to press, proving the practicality of conversion. Knudsen's principal objection continued to be the nine-member agency in which labor would have an equal voice with management and government. "It just won't work," he declared obstinately. And he emphasized the statement in testimony before a Senate hearing committee by adding, "I'm against it," in flat refusal to continue consideration. When Reuther, with Hillman there to back him up, suggested that they all three tour an auto plant and together inspect the possibilities, Knudsen claimed that he didn't have the authority to take the labor leader into any plant. At that point, Walter lost patience. He issued an angry statement to the papers: "Mr. Knudsen and I met previously, on opposite sides of the table. I thought on this matter of national defense we might sit on the same side. I was mistaken." He was furious, but he still did not give up.

He made one more attempt before conceding that the plan had been shelved, at least temporarily. But his faith in it was not shaken, and he predicted privately that if the world situation continued to worsen, the government might still make use of the basic premise. At any rate, the proposal had placed him on the national scene as a practical genius endowed with idealism, an image he would flash upon the public time and again to heighten his dramatic rise to power. Further, it served to point up the difference between leaders like R. J. Thomas and himself, and in that sense would prove a useful tool in his immediate goal during the next few years—the presidency of the UAW. Whatever the outcome, he felt it was not yet "curtains" for the prologue that would lead to an increase in labor's potential bargaining ability by its entrance into the arena of economic planning from which industry had always excluded it.

Sometime during 1941, May and Walter finally found and moved into a little house that filled their requirements: a small, medium-priced house, big enough to accommodate a child or two, but not large enough to be a burden, financially or physically. The $7,750 white brick-and-frame, six-room bungalow, for which Walter had just the amount—$1,265—to make the down payment, was located at 20101 Appoline Street, an address that was destined to become famous within the decade. One of the first things Walter did was to fix up a workshop in the basement, just like the one his parents had always had in Wheeling; he made some kitchen cupboards for May, as Val Reuther had done for Anna. Walter had been wanting a "shop" all the time they had lived in apartments with May's family, though he certainly had no time for any extensive wood- or metalworking. He and May picked out simple maple furniture for the rooms, and May put ruffled curtains at the windows. When the inside was complete, Walter turned his attention to the outside with his usual vigor. Their lot was small, but he kept the lawn in good shape. One spring a neighbor happened to look out her window and saw a man with his back to her in the Reuthers' yard, attacking the weeds with a ferocious will. She called to her husband excitedly, "May's got a wonderful new handyman—look at him go! I must get his name." Of course the "handyman" was Walter Reuther.

Most of the time they were settling in their first real home, Walter was busy with union affairs, trying, as director of the GM department, to negotiate a new contract without having a strike— which he did, winning a pay increase—and lining up forces against the Communist element in the UAW, which he had been trying to oust as early as 1938. Specifically, his target was the group headed by George Addes who, though a tireless worker and not a Communist himself, was influenced by CP members and willing to accept the services of any who would be mass-industry organizers. A devout Roman Catholic of Syrian parentage, swarthy, with dark curly hair and smoldering dark eyes, George was a native of La Crosse, Wisconsin. He had won both fame and a loyal following as one of the top leaders of Auto-Lite Local 12 in Toledo, who in 1934 had conducted a bloody battle for organized labor to a successful conclusion. He had been secretary-treasurer of the UAW since its inception, a formidable opponent to unseat, but Walter Reuther, backed by both his brothers and his own powerful West Side local, meant to do his best.

Dick Frankensteen, his other chief adversary, had been playing a game of hopscotch in trying to win the presidency, leaping from one side to the other or planting his two feet in both areas at once, so that no one could be sure where he stood politically for any length of time. Since the 1940 convention, when the UAW had passed a resolution condemning the "brutal dictatorship" of Stalin, along with Hitler and Mussolini, without mentioning the Communist influence in the union, Dick had become friendly to the anti-Communist forces. He and his wife had visited May and Walter in the new house, and the two rivals had talked about teaming up to defeat the Communist element at the 1941 convention by replacing Addes, if possible, with Richard Leonard, an Executive Board member and Reuther ally; they had also pledged to support each other for a vice-presidency. As for the presidency, R. J. Thomas, while poised rather uncomfortably on his fence-straddling seat, clung to his incumbency so tenaciously—and would, indeed, have been a good president in ordinary circumstances—that it was hardly logical to consider removing him at this time.

The Addes-Communist-led faction, however, had been behaving in the wildest way for some time because of the nonaggression pact between Germany and Russia. Several CP-led locals had called unplanned and mismanaged strikes in newly organized plants under defense contracts. One was a seventy-day walkout at Allis-Chalmers in Wisconsin; another occurred at North American Aircraft in Englewood, California, the latter holding contracts worth $300 million for badly needed planes. Roosevelt had to call out troops to seize the plant—an unprecedented order in peacetime—before the workers resumed production. A few days after the seizure, a CP-dominated Plymouth Local 51 sent in to the Wayne County CIO Council a resolution denouncing the "imperialist war" in Europe as one that did not justify aid to Britain, when, on June 22, 1941, Hitler suddenly decided to invade the Soviet Union. The American CP members were caught completely off base; their gyrations as they wriggled and squirmed in a lightning about-face would have left a drill sergeant speechless. Local 51 nearly burned up its mimeograph machine getting out a second resolution, appealing for "aid to the victims of Nazi aggression." The UAW Communists shifted from irresponsible strike calls to stern opposition to all strikes; Sidney Hillman, once decried for his constant effort to avert defense strikes, was hailed as the workers' hero.

It was such shenanigans that made Walter and the Reuther group decide that the time had come to start a concerted move-

ment against the Stalinists in the UAW. In drafting a resolution
for the UAW convention in August, which would bar them
and fascists from union office, he wrote, "No matter how
often the Communist party line may change, we shall have no
part of a policy of appeasement either with the agents of Stalin
or Hitler." He and May traveled to the convention, held in Buffalo,
with Dick Frankensteen and his wife, driving south for a brief
tour of the Smokies on the way. It was a means of getting Walter
to take a holiday without feeling that he was shirking his responsibilities; he and Dick could cement their pact of friendly cooperation and plan the details of their convention strategy. Walter's compulsion for work was such that he could relax more
easily if he felt he was still on the job, at least partially. When they
stopped for a steak roast on a mountaintop toward dusk, he built
the fire and managed the meal. They had bought five steaks, one
apiece, with an extra one for the two men. But just as they were
ready to cook the last one, they heard a rustling in the woods—the
meat was gone, and the glittering eyes of a raccoon stared out at
the picnickers. Walter roared with laughter. "I guess he needed
it more than we do!" he chuckled, with a glance at Dick's wide
girth. The three-hundred-pound Frankensteen hardly shared his
mirth, but reluctantly agreed.

Events did not turn out as they had anticipated. The convention
opened with a bitter debate as the Reuther brothers and Frankensteen challenged the seating of the CP-led delegates who had
called the ill-advised strikes. The opposition lashed out at Walter
in particular. At one point, with a brawl threatening, R. J. Thomas
rapped for order repeatedly; he always had to bang the gavel
more than once; as one organizer said, "When R. J. rapped for
order, all pandemonium broke loose!" Finally he was able to
intone, his red cheeks puffing out, "We don't have . . . Reuther
on trial. I am not even on trial now. Let's stick to the issues."

The debate on the resolution to prevent Communists or Fascists
from holding office, introduced by Victor, brought an even greater,
more vicious attack on Walter than the first issue, hitting below
the belt by pouncing on the draft-board ruling. John Anderson,
an avowed Communist, but not an officer, began the barrage
with: "The 'Royal Family' that sponsored this resolution has in

its ranks a man that would sooner face cameras than bullets."
He went on to accuse Walter of "hiding behind the skirts of his
wife" in seeking deferment. This was foul play of the first water;
and, though many in the hall knew the true story, many more
did not. R. J. Thomas, to his credit, immediately rose to Reuther's
defense, informing the delegates that he, Thomas, had been the
one who told the board that May would lose her job if Walter
were inducted. The victim then spoke in his own defense with
his usual vehemence, revealing the fact that "Brother Thomas and
Brother Murray" had asked to use his as a test case, and he had
agreed to be a "guinea pig." With mounting indignation he finished, "I think it is damned dirty and damned unfair when people
inside of our own union, who *know* Brothers Murray and Thomas
asked for this deferment, play politics with it."

Though momentarily stopped, the opponents of the resolution,
which was offered as an amendment to the UAW constitution,
tried to counteract the Reuthers' resolution by introducing a
motion to bar Socialists as well as Communists. But their maneuver was a stupid blunder, since they did more "red-baiting" than
they accused Walter of doing, and as their motion was even less
democratic than any possible antidemocratic aspect of his, they
only proved his estimate of them had been correct. He finally
declared, after another vitriolic attack by Anderson: "Personally,
I am getting damn sick, and I think this convention is getting
damn sick, of talking about Walter Reuther. I think we came
here to do a job for the membership, but certain people will stoop
to any level in order to try a smear campaign."

The debate ended by the adoption of a strong amendment, one
that the Reuthers could support, representing a victory for them
on that score. Walter's growing power and prominence was
evidenced by the force of the attacks upon him from within the
UAW, perhaps not unmixed with jealousy at the attention he had
been receiving in Washington and around the country. During
one of the calmer sessions, he had given a full report to the convention on the fate of his "500 planes a day" proposal, taking
care to put the plan in the best, and industry in the worst, light.
"If industry had put its best foot forward and proposed the plan,"
he said, it might have been adopted, but people in Washington

were afraid to fight and push it through because they knew organized industry stood solidly against this proposition."

On other scores the Reuther group did not fare so well, largely because Dick Frankensteen left Walter and changed over to the other side at a word from Allan Haywood, representing the CIO, who told him that the parent body wanted Addes to remain in the secretary-treasurer spot, and that Dick had no need to divide the vice-presidency with Reuther—he could hold that office by himself. Without hesitation, Dick threw his votes to George Addes; and Thomas, learning that the CIO was backing Addes, felt that he, as UAW president, must go along with the endorsement. Even so, it is a measure of Reuther's rising influence that Richard Leonard, while he lost, came close to wresting the secretary-treasurership away from Addes.

Walter himself, perhaps as a result of Leonard's losing, almost missed out on being reelected to his post on the Executive Board. Tired of the constant backbiting, bickering, and resort to personal attacks, like the one on the draft ruling—which must have been as painful and irritating to May as to Walter himself—he didn't care to stay around for the vote. Although he rarely went to the movies, he suggested to May that they take in a picture playing near the convention hall. Leonard Woodcock, then a promising regional director and strong supporter of Reuther, would keep a watch on the vote. Just as they were coming out of the movie, they saw Woodcock, who had been trying to find them. He thought he had better break the bad news to them: the count, when he left the hall, showed that Reuther had been defeated. Walter shrugged his shoulders, accepting the verdict philosophically; all was fair in love and labor politics, and he could always be a tool- and diemaker. He may have been just talking, but May immediately suggested, "Why don't you go to work in the Rouge and become president of Local 600?" Obviously there was no doubt in her mind that if Walter did go back to Ford's, he would soon be president of the world's largest local.

However, when they returned to the auditorium, they discovered that an error in tabulating had made it appear that Walter was out; but when the entire count was completed, he and his allies had not only been reelected, but had added a couple of seats to the Reuther bloc on the Board. Walter grinned at May; both of them probably had been quite sure inwardly that he would not have to go back to Ford's. Walter received a $500 a year raise, bringing his salary up to $3,000 a year; with his belief in small salaries for union officers, he had not spoken for the raise, but the rest of the Executive Board felt that *their* salaries should be higher.

Whether because of his own experience in house hunting, or because he was primarily interested in workers as people, and the way they lived or were able to live on their earnings, Walter was made chairman of the UAW Housing Committee, then becoming a crucial post because of the influx of labor to fill defense jobs. Three months after the convention, on December 7, 1941, he and Edward Levinson, now writing publicity for the union, drove to New York, where Reuther was to report to the Executive Board meeting there on the plans and progress of his committee. Their car had no radio, and as they drove into town, the shouts of the "Extra" hawkers jolted them with news of the Japanese assault on Pearl Harbor. Reuther's reaction was instant and typical.

"Well, Eddie," he said, "this means we'll have to rewrite our report. Let's go and wash up and I'll see you in my room in twenty minutes." As they worked on the revision, he predicted to Eddie during a pause that the Board would have to adopt a pledge against strikes in the coming wartime emergency; and the UAW was the initiator of this drastic expedient. The wheels in his brain also began to turn toward his "conversion" plan once more; within the week, on December 13, he was speaking to the Union for Democratic Action in New York, emphasizing labor's right to recognition as a full partner along with industry in the war effort. And he came up with another version of his original idea: Ford, General Motors, and Chrysler could pool their facilities and use a single set of tools and dies for making necessary military equipment aside from planes; that way they could tool up in half the time and turn out three times as much as under the present schedule.

He was listened to with new respect, called to Washington to testify before a House Committee on production mobilization, made chairman of the union division of an industry-labor advisory committee designed to spur conversion of the auto industry, and sent by the War Department on a fact-finding tour of the plants, covering much the same ground included in his original plan. Even Knudsen at a news conference, when asked if industry could convert more quickly now than a year earlier (when Reuther first presented his idea), conceded, "Of course. There's nothing else to do. Conversion is toolmaking. Take all these machines you have and see if there isn't some way to utilize them." Indeed, at one point the Reuther plan came close to being accepted completely; for about twenty-four hours soon after Pearl Harbor, it hung in the balance; and industry was finally forced to adopt a diluted version, since the huge war production would not have been possible in an industry geared to a competitive economy.

Walter could not help crowing inwardly at the industrialists' sudden conversion to his point of view, though it angered him to think that a declaration of full-scale war was necessary to move them. Donald Nelson, chairman of a new War Production Board, who consulted Reuther on the essentials of converting idle machinery, remarked to a board member; "He's quite a fellow. . . . Three-fourths of the dollar-a-year men . . . are scared to death of that little fellow. And they ought to be scared of him—because he's smarter than they are."

The climax and denouement of the Reuther plan's dramatic history came when Charles E. Wilson, president of General Motors, challenged the young labor leader to a face-to-face debate, which took place on March 31, 1942, in the auditorium of the General Motors building. The scene brought to full fruition the training Val Reuther had given his sons in the early Sunday-afternoon debates in Wheeling. On one side sat Wilson, white-haired at fifty-one, portly, flanked by three GM top officials, on the other was Reuther, the thirty-four-year-old redhead, aided by his close advisers: his brother Victor, Ben Blackwood, and an organizer for the CIO's Designing Engineers' Union. The moderator was George V. Denny, Jr., famous as chairman of "America's Town Meeting of the Air," radio's widely popular discussion program. Questions had been posed by fifty-six newspaper and magazine writers, bringing national attention to the debate. Cross-questioning was between the two principals, "Mr. Wilson" (as Reuther made a point of addressing his opponent), and "Walter" (as the GM president familiarly referred to the fiery young labor leader). The debate, an endurance contest, lasted six hours. It began in fighting fettle, sustained most of the time, but ended on a note of harmony as the two pledged to "rise above partisan considerations," as Walter said, "and go down the line arm in arm, uniting in effort and will . . ." Wilson echoed his sentiments in less idealistic terms; but in a demonstration of his words, the two contestants from such widely divergent levels of American life [as a labor leader and a big industrialist], rose at last, grinned, and shook hands. With arms around each other's shoulders, they passed beneath a poster urging in large letters PLEASE KEEP THE BOMBS AWAY. Smiling into the news cameras, they made a joint statement: "That's our job and we'll do it."

Granted that the debate had all the elements of a publicity or propaganda stunt, it was nonetheless effective in publicizing the much-needed cooperation in the war effort; and, as the Detroit *News* said in an editorial, the debate, while it was a draw, was actually (on the grounds of their final agreement and handshake) "a victory for both contestants, and for America."

Certainly Walter Reuther had won a place in the limelight of both the labor movement and the nation.

XVIII

In War and Peace

$\mathbb{F}$ROM the moment FDR made a formal declaration of war, Walter Reuther exhibited "the atomic spirit of action," as *Fortune* magazine called it, that he had shown in his conversion plan. During the four years of the war, that spirit kept him "just churning and spinning off ideas," according to his own description, and he admitted that "some of them made a lot of sense and some of them didn't go very far." The point was that his energy and inventiveness never seemed to lag. He was in Washington almost as often as in Detroit, and May had to get used to being without him frequently, which proved to be a preparation for later years when, during negotiations, she would not see much of him for weeks. In 1942, about a year after they moved into their house on Appoline Street, she resigned as his secretary to await the birth of their first child, a daughter born August 25, whom they named Linda Mae.

Walter's official post was as a member of the Labor-Management Policy Committee of the War Manpower Commission; but unofficially he served as a key adviser to Sidney Hillman and Undersecretary of War Robert P. Patterson on production problems of the metalworking industries. He often consulted with the President and Mrs. Roosevelt, and with the Secretary of the Interior, Harold Ickes, or Abe Fortas, the Undersecretary.

Walter's friendship with the Roosevelts, particularly Mrs. Roosevelt, began at this time. Eleanor Roosevelt had the gift of being a good listener, especially when she felt the person talking to her had something to say; and she, even more than the President, realized that young Reuther had a good deal to say. His talk made sense to her partly because he was ready to follow it up with action and proved correct more often than not.

In Detroit, Walter's fellow officers in the UAW were becoming increasingly doubtful about his outside activity, and were probably envious of the attention he was receiving in the nation's capital. After all, he was not president of the union, but an Executive Board member and head of the General Motors department. As the latter, he should be "tending to his knittin'," as Thomas said, and let FDR handle the overall fabric of capacity wartime production. Certainly the war posed plenty of problems right in Detroit for the auto workers' union and its leaders. Perhaps the chief question concerned wage demands and the weapon of the strike. Should the union devote all its energies to the war effort, running the risk of losing some of the gains won in hard-fought strikes? Or should the union come first and the war effort second? It was a dilemma never really resolved to the satisfaction of all concerned. Though a solution of sorts was accepted, the argument that began with the declaration of war was still going on when peace was proclaimed.

Initially, Walter Reuther tried to negotiate a new contract with General Motors that would preserve the double time pay for Sunday work, but the corporation balked on the grounds that plants were on a seven-day work-week schedule during the war. Walter, always the innovator, took the unprecedented step of inviting Charles E. Wilson to speak at a meeting in February, 1942, with UAW local leaders from ninety GM plants. The men were impressed by the presence of a corporation head, but not by his reasoning. Reuther had skillfully cited figures, showing that GM profits per employee had gone up from $983 to $1,366 during the year's time, so the union leaders argued that GM could easily afford to continue to pay double time on Sunday, war work or no. When Wilson commented that their demand was a "business-as-usual" scheme for the union, Walter jumped in to confront him with the high salaries and bonuses totaling more than six and a half million dollars a year that Mr. Wilson and three others at GM had made for the year. "Maybe these things ought to be brought up when Mr. Wilson talks of sacrifices and 'business as usual,' " he ended drily. Wilson and the local leaders got the point, and the meeting adjourned on an impasse. The UAW had been accusing industry of operating on a "business-as-usual" basis.

However, in late March, the government called for an end to all premium pay except time and a half for overtime. The CIO approved the proposal, so the UAW leadership had to go along with it. UAW advertisements appeared in the daily papers, needling Knudsen and the OPM for not adopting the Reuther plan right away, and repeating its gibes against big business. As Walter had predicted, the Executive Board decided on two definite steps—to ban strikes for the duration of the war, and to suspend premium pay for work on Saturdays, Sundays, and holidays as such. It never relinquished labor's revered doctrine of time-and-a-half pay for overtime. An emergency conference was called in April to take a vote of the membership on these patriotic proposals. The ranks, naturally, were less than enthusiastic, and while the leadership was unanimously agreed, delegates debated furiously for six hours over the advisability of such drastic measures. They hardly listened as the Reuthers, Frankensteen, Thomas, and Nat Ganley (the CP "whip" in the union) all spoke in favor of the wartime policies. It was not that the workers were unwilling or unprepared to make some sacrifices, but that they felt they would be doing more than their share while the big bosses gave up very little. John McGill, of the Flint Buick local, finally expressed the general feeling in no uncertain terms: "We are not convinced that giving up double time is vital to winning the war," he said, "Labor is making sacrifices everywhere. We gave up the right to strike. Our brothers and sons are dying in the trenches. Can anyone show any sign that the men who sign checks have made any sacrifices?" He glared defiantly at the faces around him.

Reuther, who had more or less expected this reaction, had drawn up an Equality of Sacrifice program, which began: "End all war profits; no luxuries in wartime and *no war millionaires*;

stop rising costs and halt inflation"; and other provisions that
would affect management as well as labor. The delegates, though
skeptical, were persuaded in the end to accept the ban on strikes
and suspend premium pay until the war was over. But discontent
remained. The union tried to mitigate the feeling by advertising
the Equality of Sacrific program in bold type: NO LUXURIES
IN WARTIME—NO WAR MILLIONAIRES—and Walter sug-
gested a maximum figure of $25,000 a year for individual incomes.
His idea was hailed by Eleanor Roosevelt in her column "My Day"
as "a constructive suggestion showing that someone is doing
some thinking." The President also took note of it in the wartime
economic program he sent Congress; but everybody else, including Congress, seemed to regard it as lip service to patriotism,
plus a little extra publicity for the redhead, brushing the idea off
as they would a pesky gnat.

Walter was in some respects the gadfly of the government, as
he had been ten years earlier at Detroit City College. A number
of his ideas were harebrained and came to naught; but these were
balanced by the contributions to faster and more efficient production, such as the use of "shaved" gears (replacing those that
were "ground," a much longer process) in standard planes. Taking
Ben Blackwood with him as technical adviser, he solved several
problems after visiting factories. He and Blackwood often went
back to their hotel room and concentrated until they came up
with a feasible solution. Walter might say, pounding the fist of one
hand into the palm of the other: "Damn it, Benny, there must be
a better way to do that! How do we do that kind of thing?" And
they proceeded from there. He never let up. Besides everything
else, he wrote two articles for *The New York Times Magazine*; one,
called "Labor's Place in the War Pattern," made a plea for better
grievance machinery. Responding to the unrest in the shops, he
declared that since labor had given up the strike weapon, it should
receive, in return, prompt settlement of grievances; and he proposed "a series of courts manned by impartial umpires." The War
Labor Board had finally arranged a settlement in the negotiations
Reuther had begun at General Motors in January, with a union
gain of a four-cents-an-hour wage rise, and a "maintenance of
membership" clause; but it had taken some time, and the day-to-

day grievance procedure, especially in newly organized plants, was dragging its feet. Walter thought complaints should be turned over to industrial arbiters who would have the obligation of rendering a decision within two or three weeks at the outside. There was scarcely a facet of the emergency economy he did not grapple with. If anyone close to him told him to take it easy, he would demand, "Is Hitler taking it easy?"

For once, the Communist faction of the union leadership voiced no dissent. But as the UAW convention in August drew near, there was more and more dissatisfaction in the ranks. Two elements for discontent came in July. First the UAW lost an NLRB election to the AFL Machinists' Union at the large Curtiss aviation plant of twenty thousand employees in Buffalo, because the machinists had not suspended premium pay; in the same month, the government War Labor Board put a tight ceiling on wages, limiting increases to 15 percent of the salary rates of January 1, 1941, regardless of the increase cost of living since that date, and it had been steadily soaring. War industries, however, collected a fat profit on all items produced under the "cost-plus" formula, which allowed industry to tack on its own wide margin of profit—supposedly the "cost" of production—which was paid by the government. Such a system lent itself to flagrant abuses, and the industrialists took full advantage of it.

The UAW convention held in Chicago was something of an anomaly in UAW history since its founding in 1936: for the first time, the leadership was strangely harmonious; and the delegates, left without sides to support, were generally but diffusely rebellious. Disgruntled to begin with, the respresentatives of the ranks felt bereft and rudderless at the sight of top officials all pulling together, and not in the direction the membership would have chosen to go. They did shout their approval at Walter Reuther's unbridled attack on "the chaos and confusion and nonsense going on in Washington," and backed his resolution demanding a supreme economic council with labor participation and a new method for allocation of strategic materials. But a series of events became too much to bear for the majority of delegates. Victor Reuther introduced a resolution for a second front in Europe, and Nat Ganley hurried to second it. George

Addes ran unopposed for secretary-treasurer, and Walter Reuther, in seconding the nomination, called for a unanimous vote with the stirring reminder: "There is one fight that we have got and that job is against Hitler, so, as I say, let's vote Brother Addes in unamimously. Let's support the officers of this union, back Philip Murray and President Roosevelt, and knock hell out of Hitler!" Finally, two vice-presidencies were created, one going to Frankensteen and one to Reuther. In the face of these developments, the delegates rejected recommendations right and left, refused to increase the dues by fifty cents, and cut down higher salaries for officers.

Their obstructiveness, however, had no focal point, and so did not bring definite results except on the question of sacrificing premium pay. There the officers realized they would have to take some fast action, or more NLRB elections might be lost to AFL unions. Walter appealed directly to the President, and on August 28—just three days after Linda was born—FDR met in the White House with Thomas, Reuther, Frankensteen, and Addes to hear their case for banning premium pay in *all* plants or run the risk of disrupting the war effort, since firms still offering premium pay could lure UAW workers away. On September 9, FDR signed an executive order forbidding all premiums except time-and-a-half pay for hours worked beyond forty. This helped to mollify the workers, and none too soon, as Walter told Wilson of General Motors: "We can't hold the men down much longer."

Walter hardly had a moment to realize he was the father of a baby girl, having seen only glimpses of her so far, at the hospital. He was dividing his time between Washington and Detroit; and by that fall, 1942, his brothers also were busy in some aspect of the war mobilization. Victor was assistant coordinator of the union's Defense Employment Division. Roy had been drafted in June, but his special ability to get along with people in his own quiet way brought a request for his release from the War Production Board for a post as field representative. While Walter was in Washington early in October, he turned down two different job offers on the War Production Board—that of Chief of Materials, and of War Production Chief. His refusal was based on the fact that he felt he was already making a meaningful contribution to production in the labor movement, one which he preferred. Soon afterward, he heard that Roosevelt, in meeting with his Victory Committee of labor chiefs from both the CIO and AFL, had proposed a new agency giving labor broad supervisory powers in production, and had suggested that Reuther head it. But William Green protested, "Why, Reuther's just a kid!" and the idea was dropped. FDR then considered Reuther for an Army commission as a special government aide on production problems; but this time the CIO objected, saying that Reuther was more needed in the labor movement. It is likely that Walter himself might have accepted either of these offers if the President had approached him directly; he had a real rapport with both the President and Mrs. Roosevelt, and he would have been sure of serious consideration for his ideas and suggestions. If Walter had taken a government post, even temporarily, it might have changed his whole career. On the other hand, his loyalty to the labor movement might have prevented him from ever becoming a bureaucrat or full-time government executive.

Yet he felt it important for labor to be in close touch with the federal government; and in January of 1943, at his urging, the UAW set up a permanent base in Washington, a twelve-man office to keep an eye on any legislation affecting labor, and to deal at first hand with federal agencies. Donald Montgomery, formerly head of the Agriculture Department's consumer council, was offered the post of supervisor, and he accepted. Both Walter and Victor worked out of the new office frequently, consulting with Montgomery. Walter helped to round up an "army" of UAW price watchers, to ensure observance of price ceilings and rationing regulations. In this way, violations of such measures as the program to roll back food prices were detected and investigated; and the same was true of labor-wage abuses that big companies tried to instigate in order to avoid time-and-a-half pay for the overtime hours in the seven-day workweek prevalent in wartime. Walter was quick to promote the establishment of a forty-hour guaranteed workweek in the auto industry, to be increased to forty-eight hours within sixty days, so that those who had been working forty hours would receive a 30 percent increase, in time-

and-a-half pay. The influx in labor caused by the sixty thousand or more Southern war workers who had migrated to Detroit between 1940 and 1942 allowed management to hire part-time (thirty-two hours a week) workers, and so avoid overtime pay.

The sudden increase in the work force brought other problems, namely racial tension and a severe housing shortage, which occupied both Walter and Victor in Detroit. The whites among newly hired auto workers had not had time to absorb the attitude of tolerance practiced by the UAW, and they objected to working alongside Negroes, let alone living beside them. Both Reuthers did what they could to preserve the measure of racial harmony developed by the UAW. At Walter's prompting, a racially integrated group of Army sergeants visited the auto plants early in 1943, their stay ending with a socially integrated dance given for them by the union at Detroit's old Book-Cadillac Hotel, the first of its kind ever held at this conservative, traditional gathering place of the city's elite. As tension grew into hysteria and several wildcats strikes in some plants because Negro workers had been promoted, Walter was instrumental in having a rally called by the UAW and the NAACP in Cadillac Square on April 11, where he spoke out strongly to a racially mixed crowd of about ten thousand workers. "The UAW-CIO will tell any white worker who refuses to work beside a Negro worker that he can leave the plant because he does not belong there. . . . No thinking American would discriminate against a fellow citizen," he declared. "It is against the Constitution of the United States, against the constitution of the UAW, and it is against the best interests of the country in winning the war." Though his was generally acknowledged to have been an excellent speech, Walter's audience, though they heard, did not *heed* his words to any great extent. Work stoppages continued here and there; in June, 25,000 workers in a Packard plant walked off the job because three Negroes had been promoted. It is interesting to note that in plants like Kelsey-Hayes, Briggs, and others, where the union was strong and alert, Negroes were upgraded without any serious trouble; most of the wildcat strikes occurred in newly organized plants.

The housing shortages added friction to the already combustible situation. Victor, along with George Romney, at that time head of the industry's trade association, had little success in the fight for desegregated housing, or even for some sort of housing projects for Negroes. And before the month was out, the bloody Detroit race riots of June, 1943, exploded with a roar of violence exceeding any of the sit-down strikes. Although blood flowed freely in the streets, however, there was little or none in the plants, a fact that Attorney General Biddle credited to "efficient union discipline." There, as Walter White of the NAACP wrote, "White union members fought against white mobbists to protect Negroes, and Negro unionists fought Negroes in protection of white fellow workers." Walter, in subsequent testimony on the riots before a Senate subcommittee, analyzed the situation accurately: "At the bench and on the assembly line where white and colored men have undergone the everyday experience of discovering each other's common humanity, there was no violence. The UAW-CIO, through the practice of democracy . . . had created an oasis of sanity in a city gone mad with frustration, bitterness, bigotry, and brutality." Ironically, at the height of the hysteria, Walter had addressed the 270 Negro graduates of Northwestern high school while eight military policemen guarded the auditorium and eighty local police patrolled outside. He was sorely distressed and did not try to cover up his feelings. "The most tragic thing I know," he told the seniors, "is that the same time you youths are graduating, soldiers in armored cars are patrolling the streets of Detroit with guns made here in the arsenal of democracy."

When the volcanic eruption of the race riots had simmered down to a smoldering residue, the intraunion issues that had been brewing in 1943—and before then among the rank and file— boiled up to a white heat at the UAW October convention in Buffalo. The main bone of contention concerned a maneuver by the Communist faction to exploit their beloved workers for the benefit of Stalin's forces in the war against Hitler. Stalingrad was then under seige, and Earl Browder, the CP leader in the United States, had proposed in the *Daily Worker* of February 25, 1943, that war production adopt the piecework system used in the Soviet Union to promote faster output of materials. "It is patriotic to demand increased earnings based on increased production," he wrote. George Addes got the message at once, and had proposed a variant, the incentive-pay system, at an Executive Board meeting, where it was voted down; but the Board commissioned Frankensteen to sit on a War Production Board committee set up to study the idea. In essence, the incentive-pay system was a combination of the old-time, long-abandoned piecework and the assembly-line speedup, prohibited in companies under contract with the UAW, which included all the major automobile and most of the airplane factories. Under the proposal, an especially fast worker would get more pay than the average. Management, conveniently ignoring the source, was *for* the plan; but the men on the assembly lines, all too familiar with the speedup, saw in it an opportunity for the bosses to pressure the average worker to keep up with those who could move at a faster pace; or, in the vernacular of the plant, it was "killing the job" for the average worker.

Walter Reuther knew that the very term "piecework" and its vicious corollary, "incentive pay"—by which the employer not only benefits from faster production, but receives as profit half the increase in pay*—were anathema to the average worker who had suffered under the resultant competitive speedup. He saw through the scheme to make the CP faction appear as a champion of both increased production for the war effort and higher wages for the worker when in reality it was the political tool of the Soviet Union. He had denounced the plan from the start as a shameful exploitation of the worker and a device that eventually could wreck all labor unions. Browder retaliated with a half-page ad in the Detroit *News*, attacking Reuther for "wrecking" the war effort and for the "most unprincipled demagoguery and lying propaganda." But Walter was sharp enough to realize that the plan would arouse bitter resentment on the assembly lines, and that those leaders connected with it might very well face political defeat in the union. And he no doubt saw that if he opposed the CP faction on these vital issues, he might be able to relieve the pressure on himself from members who had been

---

* For example, if a man received $8 a day for completing two engines, he would not receive $16 if he produced four engines, but only $12 a day, the difference going to the employer.

plaguing him about the "no-strike pledge" and the unequal "equality of sacrifice" program.

So far he had been correct in his estimate of the situation and the temper of the workers. Their resentment was heightened when Paul McNutt, of the War Manpower Commission, prodded by big business and the Communist tactic, tried to impose a wage freeze more restrictive than the Little Steel formula of early 1942 (limiting increase to 15 percent of the January, 1941, level). Angry himself, Reuther resigned from the War Manpower Commission, winning warm approval from the workers. They applauded John L. Lewis' independent flat demand for a $2-a-day increase for his miners, hoping that someone would break through the Little Steel formula. The most forceful indication of the restlessness in the ranks had come in May at a Michigan CIO convention. A group of lesser UAW leaders, headed by Emil Mazey, president of the powerful Briggs local, led a revolt against the no-strike pledge and passed resolutions calling for rescinding it, for opposition to the incentive pay, and for the formation of a labor party in America. After the May meeting, one labor observer wrote, "Reuther is the fair-haired boy of the UAW rank and file . . . principally for his stand against the introduction of the incentive pay system in the automobile industry."

The skirmishes launched in May over this burning issue mounted to a free-for-all battle at the UAW's own convention in October, 1943, in Buffalo. Sharp dissonance had replaced the harmony of the 1942 convention among the top leaders, of course, but the loudest voices heard were those of delegates representing the rank and file. It was "an exercise of democracy hardly matched in any other large organization," as Irving Howe and B. J. Widick wrote in their excellent analysis of the UAW and Walter Reuther, published in 1949. And raucous as those voices became at times, the remarkable fact is that they were permitted to rise to such a pitch, in the midst of war, when any opposition to the military effort might have been called treason. Such a convention could not have been held by any outher union in America during those years.

At the outset, it was obvious that George Addes and Richard Frankensteen, who had espoused the incentive-pay system, were

the targets of the strong Reuther delegations from Ohio, Indiana,
New York, and New Jersey. As a keynote, they concocted a
clever campaign ditty to the tune of an old ballad, "Reuben and
Rachel," that caught the carousing spirit of the rebel.

> Who are the boys who take their orders
>   Straight from the office of Joe Sta-leen?
> No one else but the gruesome twosome,
>   George F. Addes and Frankensteen.
>
> Who are the boys who fight for piecework,
>   To make the worker a machine?
> No one else but the gruesome twosome,
>   George F. Addes and Frankensteen.

Other verses, some unprintable, added spice to the doggerel.
In an effort to counteract it, the rival faction made up a set of
stanzas against Reuther, to the same tune; but they were not
as effective as the "Ballad of the Gruesome Twosome," which
blared out all over town, in bars and hotel corridors at night,
lines of delegates snake-dancing as they sang. This was only a
curtain raiser to the battle scene that held the stage at the convention hall for two days as soon as the issue of piecework came
on.

Richard Gosser, then a rising labor leader from Local 12 in
Toledo, led off the volley of dissent. "We fought nine years to
eliminate piecework and haven't been able to do it yet," he cried.
"You put it up now and, by God, our children's children won't
eliminate it!" Cheers and applause shook the rafters. Paul Krebs
from the Brewster airplane factory in New York testified: "I
think it might increase pay for a small majority when it is first
introduced. . . . Our own bitter experience with it taught us
that as we increase our earnings . . . management starts chopping
down the standards to get our pay down again." Speech after
speech in opposition forced the Addes group to resort to a tactical
presentation in the name of democracy, pointing out that some
locals had voted to try the piecework plan, and it would be
undemocratic to pass a resolution prohibiting their freedom to
do so.

Here Walter Reuther attacked him with fierce ridicule: "It

is fine to talk about democracy," he said scornfully. "Supposing a local union wanted to sign a wage agreement working twelve hours a day without overtime. Would you say that was interfering with local autonomy if it were stopped?" His logic put an end to that maneuver, but the debate continued. R. J. Thomas tried to straddle the fense, as usual, in a speech that could be taken either way. In the end, the delegates voted for Reuther's resolution opposing piecework and incentive pay in UAW plants. As a result, Addes barely managed to slip back into office as secretary-treasurer by a margin of 70 votes out of 7,422. And Reuther defeated Frankensteen to win the race for first vice-president.

On the second major issue, the no-strike pledge, the Addes and Reuther groups were not so sharply divided; both opposed resolutions by some of the locals calling for rescinding of the pledge, but Walter, more sensitive to the feelings of the men in the shops, tried to offer a compromise measure that would provide for the government take-over "in those plants where management is not bargaining in good faith and is taking advantage of the war situation and the union's no-strike pledge to destroy collective bargaining." Emil Mazey, usually his backer, scoffed at compromise, and declared that only the strike weapon could restore collective bargaining. "It is necessary to put that club back in our hands," he said. Thomas Burke, another member from Local 12 in Toledo—later elected to Congress by a PAC campaign in 1948—gave a graphic description of his feelings: "I believe that when we made our no-strike pledge, we held out our hands with palms out and set out our chins and said to the employers, 'Hit it,' and they did." But in the end, this issue also was resolved as Walter had hoped: the delegates voted by a large majority to adhere to the no-strike pledge.

Although he emerged from the Buffalo convention the winner on several counts, he still had not arrived at the point necessary to reach for his first big goal, the presidency of the UAW, and he was still too involved in the national war effort to devote the time needed to build his popularity with the union membership. He continued to be in Washington frequently, seeing both the President and Mrs. Roosevelt on official and friendly visits to the

White House. Whenever he got an idea for solving some wartime problem, "good or otherwise," he would present it to Eleanor Roosevelt first because she "had the President's ear." "I called her my secret weapon," he recalled smilingly. FDR also appeared to be fond of him. At one White House conference with labor chiefs, he took both of Reuther's hands in his, and exclaimed, "Here's my young redheaded engineer!" At that R. J. Thomas, who was standing nearby, protested: "Engineer? He's just a tool- and diemaker!"

In Detroit, however, and in shops all over the country, the rest of 1943 and 1944 brought increased snarls in the grievance procedure; increased hostility between management and labor; and, in their effort to get some action, increased militancy on the part of shop stewards. A fresh wave of wildcat strikes broke out as the workers lost patience with management's procrastinating method of referring even minor disputes to the War Labor Board, entailing yards of red tape to settle a grievance. Workers were caught in a squeeze between government restrictions on pay raises under the Little Steel formula and rising living costs estimated at 45 percent by the year's end, plus two federal-income-tax increases: first the normal tax went up from 4 to 6 percent, and in 1943, an additional 5 percent "victory tax" went into effect. The extra money they were earning due to overtime was eaten up by higher living costs and taxes. By the middle of 1944, feelings had mounted to such a pitch that when Chrysler workers walked off the job and Addes and Reuther tried to persuade them to return, both leaders were roundly booed.

By September of 1944, it was inevitable that another caucus should be added to the already over-caucused UAW convention. Indeed, caucusing had become the stamp of the auto workers' conventions to such an extent that even the children picked up the term. May Reuther used to tell the story of the little girl in the cooperative nursery school sponsored by her and other UAW wives, mostly war workers who needed a place to leave their children during the day. Since May had left her job to care for Linda, she decided to set up the center. When an instructor told the children to put their toys aside at the start of the day, one small girl, putting her doll to bed, admonished, "You stay here, honey; Mother has to go and caucus."

There was no make-believe in the caucusing at Grand Radips, where UAW delegates convened in a spirit of high dudgeon. Fighting in the hall and elsewhere, disorderly conduct and destructive use of hotel furniture in nightly brawls among various factions, including a grand slugfest in the headquarters hotel lobby, were among preconvention features.

The new caucus, formed as early as July, comprised principally the local presidents or shop committeemen who had raised their voices at the 1943 convention, now known as the Rank and File Caucus. Its platform had three planks: repeal the no-strike pledge, press for independent political action by labor; and elect UAW officers pledged to these views. The group, led by secondary leaders, conducted its debate largely from a union standpoint. They saw no conflict between their genuine support of the war and their opposition to the pledge against striking; in their eyes, part of the fight for democracy was the workers' right to strike. They were not going to have those rights taken away at home by tactics that resembled the totalitarianism the armed forces were supposed to be destroying abroad. A few of these men were from the Workers' party of Socialist origin, who hoped to further their own political views. But most of them were UAW members who otherwise would have supported Walter Reuther, and now posed a real threat to his ascending star.

The fierce floor debate on whether or not to repeal the pledge lasted five hours, with the delegates holding the floor most of that time, and proving that Reuther's premonition was justified. He chose a middle ground between the Rank and File stand for outright repeal and the Addes-Frankensteen (and conservative Norman Matthews) stand for complete retention of the pledge. Reuther's proposal was to retain the pledge only in plants engaged in war production, a plan that was assailed and soundly defeated. The proposal for unconditional retention of the pledge also failed to win a majority; and the rebellious Rank and File polled 37 percent of the vote, a "moral victory" in their eyes. One shrewd member of their delegation jumped to ask if the results meant that the UAW had *no* policy on wartime strikes, and if so, didn't that

signify that locals could decide their own—obviously the leadership had no unified course. Thrown unexpectedly into a dilemma,
the top leaders drew together in dismay. It was Walter and R. J.
Thomas, the most flexible ones, who devised a way out, calling
for a simple vote to retain the no-strike pledge until the entire
membership made the final decision in a referendum by mail.
The Communist faction tried to avoid the referendum, but Reuther saw to it that they did not. In the ballot-by-mail, the members voted to uphold the pledge; but at Grand Rapids, Reuther
was persona non grata except to his own loyal followers. His
stand cost him the first vice-presidency he had won the year
before: Frankensteen won his former post, and Reuther had to
return to second vice-presidency. Anyone less resilient than Walter Reuther would have been discouraged by the setback. But he
knew instinctively that once the war was over, the Rank and File
Caucus would disband for want of a valid plank and that most
of its members would come back to his camp, as they did.

In the meantime, he was not going to waste a moment brood-
ing over the outcome of the election. He was, in fact, already
embarked on a course of action designed for peace. Just as he
had conceived the conversion of auto plants in prewar months,
so he was ready with a reconversion blueprint for the postwar
era as early as May, 1943. He had announced then that since GM
had set aside $48 million for rehabilitation of machinery, he was
calling for a "security fund" just as large to provide for prewar
workers, especially those returning from military service. A year
later he was promoting his sixteen-point reconversion program,
which, he made clear, was capable of "infinite elaboration." It
outlined a postwar pool of men and machinery encircling all fields
of endeavor: a thirty-hour workweek—at that early date; government supervision of monopolistic industries and "continued operation of the thousands of government war facilities which can be
turned to the use of peace"; control of "normal" sales prices,
entailing "a wage-price policy capable of maintaining an effective
demand" for products; and, to begin with, civilian production
based on the most urgent social needs.

To this end, he urged the creation of a *Peace* Production Board,
an enlargement of the War Production Board, to take in agricul-

ture and consumers as well as representatives from labor, management, and government. Since business could not be relied on, judging from past performance, the Board would ensure a smooth conversion by allocating manpower, materials, and tools to meet the most pressing civilian priorities. Finally, realizing that the Rank and File Caucus would never have been formed if unionists generally had not felt cheated out of the role they were supposed to have played in wartime economy, Reuther stipulated that labor also would be given a voice in industry conferences to assist the Peace Production Board in setting up feasible conversion plans for every industry. Using *The New York Times* Forum as a springboard, he took off on a campaign to publicize his belief that the wartime advances in technology would make it possible to create as much wealth in a thirty-hour week as the forty-hour week had achieved in prewar days. "Work in itself is not an end," he declared. "It's the means to an end. The end is a more abundant life, to be able to conquer the job of feeding and clothing ourselves in as little time as possible, so that as civilized men we can enjoy the finer things—culture and education." It was a statement that was to run like a theme with endless variations, extended to the international scale, throughout the rest of his life.

He staged a public debate on the thirty-hour week with Eric Johnston, president of the U.S. Chamber of Commerce, and Henry J. Kaiser, one of the new generation of industrial geniuses. The latter's final remark, "Most of us will want to work more than thirty hours a week, anyway," should have given pause to Walter, who worked at least twice that number of hours every week. But Reuther did not consider the hours he put in as "work" in the sense that the man on the assembly line worked at a routine job such as putting six bolts on an engine as one after another went by, hour after hour. In the *Times* Forum, Reuther also put forth two more inventive ideas. The first was to turn government-owned airplane plants into factories for the mass production of low-cost housing, on which he placed top priority in postwar planning. Huge complexes like Willow Run—which was rife with so many production and social problems, particularly housing, that it was nicknamed "Willit Run?"—could be converted from making bombers to modern railroad equipment and low-cost housing. Further, he suggested setting up a "strategic job reserve" to furnish employment for idled war workers through public projects like hospitals, schools, recreation centers, flood control and power development, highways, airports, and waterways. Dick Frankensteen, UAW director of aviation, felt that bomber plants should be converted to the manufacture of civilian planes; but Walter insisted, probably with the 1943 race riots and the Willow Run workers' housing shortage in mind, that decent dwelling was the most urgent need. He remembered all too clearly that one of the principal causes of the 1943 race riots in Detroit was the wretched overcrowding of war workers in the Negro districts of the city.

In a later article, published in *The New York Times Magazine* under the title, "Our Fear of Abundance," he wrote eloquently of mobilizing for peace, just as for war, to "wipe out the slums and substandard housing, both rural and urban, which sap the health and dignity of millions of American families. We have spent billions to destroy cities. Let us be lavish in the equally challenging and more creative assignment of building homes and rebuilding cities in the United States. . . ." He went into detail on ways and means of doing so; and, in emphasizing that most war plants could "readily be converted to the production of civilian goods just as they were retooled for production of war materiel," he took good care to bring up his plan for "500 planes a day." In doing so, he anticipated management spokesmen, who would probably protest now that this could not be done, by reminding them that the "same cry was raised in the fall of 1940," and yet 89 percent of the auto plants had been converted successfully; a none-too-gentle jab at labor's perennial adversaries.

In whatever way the transition from war to peace was made in terms of social change and the economics of society, Walter was determined that labor would have a stronger voice than it had been allowed during the war. To gain recognition for labor as a constructive force in the overall architecture of society—and not merely as the bargainer for "a few cents an hour more"—had become a fixed principle with him. And Walter Reuther never abandoned a fixed principle.

XIX

"Open the Books!"

WHEN word was flashed around the world on the evening of August 14, 1945, that the Japanese had surrendered, the joy and relief of the workers in the war industries, after the tumultuous celebration had died down, was less than ecstatic. Besides the terrible impact of the atomic bomb, so much more destructive than any yet released, a source of mingled uneasiness and awe, the war workers, especially in the auto industry, were concerned about their jobs. They were more than ready to claim their share of the bulging war profits which had been filling industry's pockets. Although they had been making more money than ever before, many workers had not managed to save much for the inevitable employment slump that was predicted as soon as civilian needs were supplied. Already the government had reduced the number of contracts; overtime was drastically cut down; wage scales returned to the lower level of civilian production; yet prices remained as high as during the war. In many families, both husbands and wives had found work on wartime assembly lines; and the double pay check they had grown used to now stood to be cut in half.

Women as an emerging factor in the work force of the auto industry during the war years had wielded a definite influence in the changing picture. Though they had long been predominant in the needle trades, relatively few women had been employed in the auto and machine trades generally until the Second World War. And while many took a job out of patriotic motives to begin with, they soon found themselves enjoying the sudden freedom from the restrictions of child care and household chores, to say nothing of the added income they could contribute and which gave them a new feeling of independence. (Anyone interested in the genesis of the Women's Liberation movement might very well find it in the upsurge of women workers during World War Two, much greater than in World War One.)

Curiously enough, the subject of working women, particularly working mothers, was one cog in the whirling wheels of Walter Reuther's spinning brain that failed to move at the same pace as his ideas on social changes in other spheres. Probably because his own mother had always been at home, ready to serve, comfort, encourage, and participate in the lives of her children, Walter was downright old-fashioned in his views of "woman's place." He was ready to fight for equal pay for equal work, to protect the rights of working women, and to grant their effectiveness on the picket lines and at strike rallies, as he was soon to do in a titanic struggle with General Motors, when he urged that wives join the picket lines, adding boyishly, "Women can frequently make a swell contribution to the life of the party," an indicator of his general attitude toward the role of women in union affairs. But as late as 1955, he concluded the debate on the Women's Rights resolution with, among others, the revealing remark, "I come from a family that, thank God, had a mother who stayed home and took care of her children."

Some months before Linda's birth in 1942, May Reuther had not merely taken a leave of absence, but resigned from her job and never returned. Though she marched in picket lines with her husband, attended conventions, and spoke to the women's division, it was Walter's preference, and presumably hers, that she stay out of union activity by not resuming a definite post. She probably intended to get involved again at a later date. But as Walter's activities in the union and elsewhere increased over the years, she made her first job that of seeing to it that every second counted of the little time he could spend with his family. Between these two there was exceptional understanding and unity of spirit; and although some wives of UAW minor leaders criticized Walter for allowing "a brilliant woman like May Reuther to fade out of the picture," * it is likely that she agreed with his point of view. May Reuther was too strong a person in her own right not to have objected and made her point if she had wanted to do so.

In any case, with this one exception, Walter Reuther was definitely the most farsighted of the major leaders in the UAW. He responded to the postwar crisis of inflationary depression, combined with angry discontent among the workers, with the necessary insight and imagination to remedy the situation. He saw that labor could "no longer function effectively if it limited itself to mere dollars-and-hours issues." As usual, he studied Labor Bureau statistics and corporation reports to make sure of his facts and figures before constructing an economic brief which he filed with the War Labor Board, the Office of Price Administration, and the Reconversion Office as early as June 30, 1945, nearly a month before eighty-seven UAW local presidents met angrily in July to demand action. In his brief, Reuther contended speaking for labor, that "the economic facts of life prove that wages can be increased without increasing prices. Increased production must be supported by increased consumption, and increased consumption will be possible only through increased wages. The basic question . . . is: Where will American labor's improved wage status come from?" His answer was that "industry can pay higher wages out of the high profits it is making. It will not have to charge higher prices."

This basic premise seemed to him a perfectly clear, logical way of solving the insoluble problem of the wage-price spiral of wartime and postwar inflation; but the local union presidents shouting for action, and the business moguls, as well as the conservatives in government, considered Reuther's "GM strike program" another one of his "brainstorms," to be discussed from an academic standpoint, perhaps, but hardly a plan for immediate action. President Truman, in office less than six months follow-

* From an interview with the wife of Sam Sweet, education director of an East Side local, who left the union because he disagreed with Reuther's policy. His wife had helped to entertain workers in the sit-down strikes of the 1930's.

ing the death of Roosevelt, was under pressure from three sides: from labor, demanding higher wages; from business, demanding higher prices; and from cautious economists, who predicted that a rise in wages, which would inevitably result in higher prices, would start a new inflationary spiral. Finally, on August 16, 1945, he announced by executive order a new government policy of permitting wage increases on condition they do not result in price increases. His order was intended merely as an anti-inflation precaution, but Walter seized upon it as a golden opportunity. Two days later, on August 18, he submitted a preliminary brief to General Motors asking for a 30-percent wage increase *without any increase in the price of cars!* Now his "academic" theory suddenly became vital, dramatic.

This was revolution in management's eyes. "If Walter Reuther had maligned motherhood, he could not have produced a greater surge of outrage in the breast of GM," wrote Fred J. Cook*; and no doubt the executives of Ford and Chrysler, to whom the UAW made similar demands, felt the same way; but it was clear that the showdown would be with GM. At a UAW Executive Board meeting on September 22, Reuther received the support of his fellow officers to strike the Big Three one at a time, since the sharp competition for postwar (sales) profits would be an inducement for an early settlement of a strike; whichever corporation was struck would find it a severe blow to have to stand by while its competitors won the postwar markets. Reuther realized that a strike probably could not be avoided, but he was prepared to take the lead, in spite of the risk he ran of losing, in the postwar economic struggle; and he no doubt was aware that the one who took a bold initiative would be recognized as a leader of stature both within and without the labor movement.

On October 3, six weeks after Reuther's presentation of his brief, Charles E. Wilson replied to his proposal, rejecting the union's demands as "unreasonable," and, after listing his conventional corporate objection—that a 30-percent increase in wages would mean that automobiles would cost 30 percent more to produce—asked instead that Reuther join him in requesting Con-

* In *Building the House of Labor*. Chicago: Encyclopedia Britannica Press, 1963.

gress to establish a forty-five-hour week. Union men greeted that
idea with a dour grin; if the basic dispute had not been so serious,
they would have laughed outright.

Following the tactics he had used to publicize his "500 planes
a day" plan, Walter wrote, for a vote of confidence from consumers, in *The New York Times Magazine*: "This 'coming in on
a wing and a prayer' economics rests upon too many unwarranted
assumptions." He argued for strengthened buying power for the
mass of Americans to keep the economy strong. He also arranged
a debate with George Romney, general manager of the Automobile Manufacturers Association, on the still popular "Town
Meeting of the Air" program, hoping to duplicate his earlier
success in reaching a national audience by radio. Departing from
tradition in regard to negotiations, he had the UAW office send
a detailed document of GM demands to all the locals, urging them
to publicize it. "The success of a strike—if it becomes necessary to
strike—will, in large part, depend upon public opinion," he assured
local presidents across the nation. Perhaps the shrewdest move
he made was to suggest that negotiations between GM and the
UAW be open to the press and the public.

Although the corporation objected, when the opening negotiation session was scheduled on October 19, Frank Winn, the
publicity director, who saw eye to eye with Walter's theories and
the means of communicating them, invited reporters from the
national as well as local press to come into the conference room.
Obviously embarrassed and annoyed by the presence of the
correspondents, GM refused to negotiate unless the press were
barred. Reuther, pointedly apologizing for GM's "shyness," asked
the reporters to leave; but he saw to it that they were provided
with transcripts of the negotiations, along with the union's briefs,
thereby gaining the publicity he was seeking for his cause. Before the struggle was over, his proposal had become a *cause
célèbre*, if not an actual crusade, involving basic questions of
American social structure. This development was due to the
union's corollary demand, which came up during preliminary
talks, when Reuther conceded that the workers might accept
less than a 30-percent increase—without having to pay more for
cars—if GM could prove they couldn't afford a pay raise without

a rise in price; but *in order to prove it, the corporation must open all its books.*

Such a demand was nothing short of a bombshell hurled in high treason against the shibboleths of free enterprise, its target the *sanctum sanctorum* of the books. The debate that went on through eleven negotiating sessions from October 19 to November 19 was filled with acrimony, plentifully sprinkled with profanity; but the disparity in the viewpoints of capital and labor leaps from the lines of the transcript. A few exchanges with Harry Anderson and Harry Coen will show the difference:

ANDERSON: Walter, you must want a strike.

REUTHER: Harry, goddamn it, the way you are going about it you are forcing us to strike.

ANDERSON: You petitioned the NLRB for a strike vote before you were even in the room.

REUTHER: Harry, that is the damn law you had passed. (The Smith-Connally Act)

ANDERSON: That we had passed?

REUTHER: Sure.

ANDERSON: Horse manure. (Further argument about the Smith-Connally Act, with which the UAW had complied.)

COEN: There is nothing sincere in your approach. It's just another chance for you to get up on a soapbox before more people. . . . Is the UAW fighting the fight of the whole world?

REUTHER: We have been fighting to hold prices and increase purchasing power. We are making our little contribution in that respect.

COEN: Why don't you get down to size and do the job you're supposed to do as a trade-union leader and talk about money you'd like to have for your people and let the labor statesmanship go to hell for a while? [Further remarks about Reuther's "socialistic dreams," his "Alice-in-Wonderland" notions.] You say we can't raise prices, and if we say we have to raise prices you don't want thirty percent but you are going to have the thirty percent or else. . . .

CORBIN: (Elwin Corbin, UAW official, interjecting) Do you mean if we came in here with a thirty percent wage demand and

offered to join with you in going before the OPA for a thirty-per-
cent increase in the price of cars, you would talk business?

COEN: We don't ask you to join with us on the price of cars.
It is none of your damned business what OPA does about prices.

CORBIN: The hell it isn't! I intend to *buy* a car.

REUTHER (to Coen): But don't you think it is constructive for
us to relate our wage question to prices?

COEN: Nobody else is doing that but you. You're the fellow
who wants to get the publicity out of this whole thing. You want
to enhance your political position. That's what this whole show
is about. . . .

REUTHER (justifying his position): . . . when Reuther comes
and there is what you say is an attempt to be a statesman, you
think that is bad. I think if I didn't do it that way, it would be
bad. I think if we came in here on a selfish basis and said, "We
want ours and the world be damned," then you should take our
pants off.

COEN: I don't think the people out on the picket line care
anything about wage theories. What does the man carrying a
sign care about GM books?

REUTHER: He doesn't care anything about GM books, provided
you give him a satisfactory wage increase.

COEN: That is right.

REUTHER: But if you say, "No dice, we can't give you a wage
increase," he says, "Let's look at your books to see why you
can't."

As the negotiations dragged on, GM made its first offer—a
10 percent wage increase, provided OPA would permit a rise in
prices. On November 19 Reuther called a national convention
in Detroit of delegates representing GM's 200,000 workers to
consider the offer. It was unanimously rejected.

The delegates then proposed that the dispute be submitted to
a three-man arbitration board, to be made up of one representative each of management and labor, the third to be selected by the
other two. All books and papers of *both* sides were to be opened
for the board, and no wage increase should be used as an excuse
for raising prices. November 20 was set as the deadline. GM

announced that it would answer the proposal by November 23, the company's attitude increasing the irritation of its employees.

On November 21, 1945, GM's 200,000 workers in its ninety-six plants walked off their jobs and took their places in the picket lines. The longest strike in American labor history, up to that point, had begun, a strike that was to last 113 days. In addition to its length, it had another unique feature. It evoked no violence; GM did not attempt to use strike breakers. The heaviest concentration of pickets surrounded the GM office building in Detroit, where the fruitless negotiation dragged on and on.

Insisting that its ability to pay had nothing to do with the case, GM turned down the arbitration proposal, repeating over and over that the price it chose to charge for a car was "none of labor's damned business." As concern for the consumer had become a fixed principle with Walter Reuther, the right of business to set its own prices without interference from labor was a fixed principle with General Motors. On that issue there could be no compromise.

GM set in motion an extensive publicity program, reiterating its contention that the union's "open the books" demand was interference with the prerogatives of management.

A "look at the books," [the corporation stated in a pamphlet] is a clever catch phrase intended as an opening wedge whereby unions hope to pry their way into the whole field of management.

The fact is that the UAW-CIO is reaching for power. . . .

It leads surely towards the day when union bosses, under the threat of strikes, will seek to tell us what we can make, when we can make it, where we can make it and how much we can charge. . . .

Reuther's response was to invite to Detroit a group of economists, college professors, and clergymen to study the situation. Among them was Leon Henderson, who had been the original head of OPA. After studying all documents introduced by both sides, reading the transcript of the negotiations, and questioning Reuther and the other union men—GM's negotiators refused to appear—the committee recommended that President Truman appoint a fact-finding commission "to determine what increase can be given on the corporation's ability to pay without increase in prices."

"From the record," the report stated, "it is clear that the union in its refusal to accept a wage increase that involves a price increase has lifted the whole matter of collective bargaining to a new high level by insisting that the advancement of labor's interest shall not be made at the expense of the public. The union has shown a sense of social responsibility that indicates its growing maturity and is certainly to be commended."

General Motors retaliated by canceling its national agreement whereby UAW was its sole bargaining agent with its employees. The union made no reply, but negotiations at the bargaining table abruptly ended.

President Truman had earlier attempted to stop the strike by brusquely ordering the strikers to go back to work and the corporation to go into production. The union had rejected his order as "ill-advised and undeserved." GM had ignored it completely. When the negotiations in Detroit stopped, the President was under extremely heavy pressure to permit price increases. Strikes were breaking out all over the country—big strikes. By January 1, more than 1,650,000 workers would be out on the picket lines, including 640,000 steel workers. The strikers wanted more money and, with the exception of UAW, made no stipulation about rises in prices.

The UAW-GM strike attracted the most attention, however. In early December, President Truman appointed a fact-finding board to investigate the strike and make recommendations. Lloyd K. Garrison of the University of Wisconsin was chairman; the other members were Milton Eisenhower, then president of Kansas State College, and Justice Walter P. Stacy of the North Carolina Supreme Court.

Both sides appeared before the board at its first hearing, and both sides presented difficult questions. The union would accept any wage the board recommended, but only if it did not permit GM to raise prices. GM announced that it would not accept the board's jurisdiction if it considered the company's "ability to pay" a legitimate question. The board appealed to President Truman, and on December 28 he ruled that "ability to pay" *was* a legitimate question to be considered in the board's final decision. Whereupon GM withdrew from the hearings. Bowing to governmental authority, however, it had permitted the board to look at the books.

"We have made the fight," Reuther testified before the fact-finding board, "not because we want to indulge in the pleasure of going through the company's books. But the company wouldn't take up the challenge and wouldn't argue the facts, so the only way we can meet the problem is to say, 'Open the books,' because we know that if they did, the figures would confirm the union's economic conclusions."

The board found, in an announcement issued by President Truman on January 10, 1946, that General Motors could afford to pay an hourly wage increase of 19½ cents an hour *without* increasing the prices of its cars. Although it represented less than its original figure, the union accepted the board's finding, but warned that it would revert to its original demand if GM would not cooperate, which GM promptly refused to do.

The corporation's attitude brought immediate support to the UAW strikers and their families, who were beginning to feel the pinch with no wages coming in. Reuther gave advice to local officers on helping strikers to get on welfare rolls. From the beginning of the strike, Walter had turned back his own pay checks to the union. He was then earning $7,000 a year, and the Reuthers had nearly finished paying off the $3,700 mortgage on their house. Members of Reuther's staff, such as the GM director, followed his lead and received no salaries during the strike.

Among those who joined in supporting the strikers and their families were such influential liberals as Mrs. Franklin D. Roosevelt, Harold Ickes, Henry Morgenthau, Jr., Senator Wayne Morse of Oregon, and Helen Gahagan Douglas, then a member of Congress from California. One contributor was Henry Luce, publisher of *Time, Life,* and *Fortune.* Other top labor leaders, who privately disagreed with Reuther, got together to aid the strikers. A United Labor Committee was formed, with four AFL and four CIO national presidents. The Amalgamated Clothing Workers, the International Ladies' Garment Workers, and the steel workers— themselves on strike—contributed $100,000 each. Three hundred farmers in Montana sent in several carloads of wheat, a contribution that cheered the strikers considerably. It was then that Walter urged wives to join the picket lines and pep up the strikers. He also enlisted veterans, wearing their uniforms, to march in prominent positions.

All through December and into January the pressure on Harry Truman to drop the OPA and to permit prices to rise following wage increases continued, becoming more and more insistent until he finally announced that a rise in the price of steel would be permissible after the industry granted a raise in wages. Other unions all over the country were ready to join the steel workers in accepting an 18½-cents-an-hour pay raise. Even the UAW locals in the Ford and Chrysler plants agreed, ignoring both prices and ability to pay. The UAW workers in GM plants were now fighting alone. The strikers were bitter toward Phil Murray, president of CIO as well as of the steel workers, for giving in without more of a fight. "I wouldn't mind nearly so much losing to GM," one of the strikers said, "as I mind being slapped in the face by the president of CIO." Many of them described it as "Murray's stab in the back."

Walter Reuther was about to receive another stab in the back even more damaging than Murray's action. Among the GM employees were some thirty thousand electrical workers who belonged to a Communist-dominated union, which was also affiliated with the CIO, the United Radio, Electrical and Machine Workers of America, popularly known as the UE headed by John Matles, a "CP-liner." The electrical workers initially had joined with the UAW in its demands, including the insistence that any raise must not be followed by a rise in the price of cars. While the UAW was pressing Truman to insist that GM accept the 19½-cent raise recommended by his fact-finding board, the Communists in control of UE signed a secret agreement with GM, accepting the 18½-cent raise, with no mention of the company's ability to pay.

UE gave Reuther no warning of its intention, and he did not know about the agreement until it had been signed. Neither GM nor the Communists, mortal enemies though they were, apparently had any qualms about making a secret deal which they thought would serve the interests of both. GM was as determined as ever that its ability to pay should have no part in any agreement it signed with the union. The Communists quite frankly were out to "get Reuther." At first they thought they had succeeded, but in the end they only turned the majority of rank-and-file UAW members, who had tolerated their presence in the past, against them.

GM promptly reopened negotiations with Reuther and the auto workers, offering them the flat 18½-cent increase the other unions were getting, without any reference to prices. The GM auto workers, aware that the electrical workers among them were about to get a raise while they had nothing, loyally followed Reuther as he angrily turned down the offer. He strode out of the session exploding with typical firecracker blasts: "I won't be made a damn fool of forever! The President's offer of nineteen and a half cents was a compromise of our demand and I will be goddamned if I will compromise a compromise. We are not going to take less than this, and this is all horse shit about going back to work!"

Three days later, Murray led his steelworkers into signing a contract identical to that of the UE; this was to be expected after Truman issued his statement permitting the price of steel to go up, but the actual settlement by the steelworkers union dealt the death blow to the UAW's prospects of getting more from GM. Reuther, being *Reuther*, made a last-ditch try, through Chester Bowles, now director of economic stabilization, hoping to appeal to Truman to back up the recommendation his board had given for an hourly wage raise of 19½ cents at least. Talk of holding prices was now out of the question—the price of steel soon rose $5 a ton, and the wage-price spiral Walter had sought to break was off and spinning. But Truman refused to support the UAW now; and when the Rubber Workers CIO union also accepted an 18½-cent offer, GM claimed that only internal political differences prevented a settlement with the UAW. The needling and cursing at the bargaining table in Detroit went on and on into March. Finally, on March 10, after 113 days, the UAW accepted the 18½-cent wage increase through an agreement reached by Philip Murray and Charles E. Wilson; Reuther was not even there. The auto workers contended, probably to save face, that other benefits, including dues checkoff and improved seniority clauses, equaled the extra penny the Truman board had recommended. Prices were not mentioned; the long struggle to persuade the company to open the books and prove that it could not raise wages without raising the price of cars had been a lost cause, or so it seemed to most union men at the moment.

Yet it was never lost in Reuther's eyes. At one point, during a dark period of the strike, he had said to Frank Winn, with his usual resiliency, "Well, if this thing falls through, we'll just have to start all over again; but at least we've made a start." And twenty years later, he was still seeking pay raises without price increases. However, there were positive results from the historic struggle much before then. At its next convention, the CIO adopted his theory as a general scheme in future collective bargaining; and there was always a resolution approved at UAW and other CIO union conventions to work for the absorption of pay raises by the company. The Amalgamated Clothing Workers' education department issued pamphlets and newsletters hammering home the subject to its members. And there is little doubt that Reuther's goals in 1946, while ahead of their time, paved the way for such unprecedented agreements with GM as the cost-of-living escalator clause, annual pay raises based on production gains, higher pensions, and other benefits for retirees.

Although most capitalists looked upon Reuther as a threat to free enterprise, regarding his goals in the same light by which they viewed FDR's New Deal as "creeping socialism," Walter clarified his position early in the strike. "The grim fact is," he declared, "that if free enterprise in America is to survive, it has got to work; it must demonstrate more than an ability to create earnings for investment; It must master the technique for providing full employment at a high standard of living, rising year by year to keep pace with the annual increase in technological efficiency. . . . The fight of General Motors workers is a fight to save *truly* free enterprise from death at the hands of its self-appointed champions." He repeated the statement in essence till the end of his life.

President Without Portfolio

IF previous conventions had gained the UAW the "union label" of a freewheeling, uproarious, and constantly caucusing membership, the 1946 convention of the United Auto Workers in Atlantic City marked the all-time high in its reputation. When the convention opened on March 23, the top leadership, at sword's point for years, was sizzling with animosities. Walter Reuther was still steaming from the vicious undercutting of the Communist-led electrical workers that had ended the historic strike ten days before; he had ultimately signed the contract, on March 13, because he had no choice after Murray and GM officials came to an agreement. But Reuther and his supporters had determined that the time had come for Walter to make his bid for the presidency.

In fact, even before the strike ended, the presidents of seventeen large Detroit locals had issued a statement:

A large majority of the union's membership feels strongly the need for a change in the administration. . . . The membership feels the need for a chance to carry out a vigorous, intelligent, and progressive program in order to eliminate factionalism which has divided our forces for several years. . . . We know and respect Reuther's refusal to devote time to any activity other than fighting and winning the GM strike. It will not, however, be necessary for him to divert his attention from the strike to a political campaign. His acceptance of the candidacy will make his election certain, without further effort on his part.

And although he issued no formal statement of acceptance, acting
as if he were not aware of the infant campaign, Reuther had
made up his mind to run, to oust the Communists along with
the incumbent, and doubting, Thomas, if possible. The Communist faction, in turn, was equally set in its goal to "get Reuther"
before his influence grew any greater. As the Communist party
candidly declared in a resolution on its failures in the UAW two
years later: "Since 1939 our main line has been to weld a progressive coalition of Communist and non-Communist auto workers
to isolate and defeat the Reuther policy and leadership . . ." In
pursuing their "main line," the Communists had managed to
dominate the UAW Executive Board, principally by supporting
George Addes, who was willing to accept their support to further
his own advancement, and R. J. Thomas was his tool. It was no
secret among the rank and file that Addes intended to take
Thomas' place eventually. Thomas feared Reuther's drive and
unorthodox, innovative approach to labor problems more than
he did the Communists—who were actually small in number,
perhaps five hundred in a membership of a million—and he was
not perceptive enough to realize the scope of their influence.

So the battle lines were drawn, with the Addes-Thomas group
on one side and the Reuther group on the other. Never had so
many caucuses been held before (nor have there been since) in
the history of the UAW. As the delegates from all over the United
States and Canada streamed into Atlantic City, the Reuther forces
called caucus after caucus, in lunchrooms, taprooms, and hotel
rooms, sometimes until three o'clock in the morning. So prominent
was this feature that Philip Murray, the principal speaker, remarked in his address that the UAW "could give time and a half"
for attending caucuses. "You surely work overtime," he said
jokingly. "When an auto worker finishes his day's work in the
convention, he looks for a caucus at night—he doesn't care where
the caucus is or who is holding it; he wants to go to a caucus."
His words were something of a gibe at Walter, who was tireless,
his brain seething with ideas and suggestions as he spoke with
one delegation after another, sounding forth political indoctrination at many a midnight meeting.

As challenger for the presidential chair, he made a clear-cut case for a change in administration; and he was shrewd enough not to object to Communists on party lines, but instead he hammered home the point that they were the tools of a totalitarian regime in Moscow and would sell out labor anytime they received a directive from the Kremlin. To prove his thesis he had several telling instances to cite: the Communist-sponsored campaign for piecework and incentive pay; the Communist support of the proposed draft-labor law; and the UE's Communist-led undercover deal with GM in the recent strike. In his frequent public appearances during the war years, Reuther had developed his exceptional skill as a lucid, persuasive speaker, and his personal magnetism was at its height. As Hugh Alexander, a delegate from Leonard Woodcock's St. Clair, Michigan, region no. 1D, declared: "Walter was sheer fire!" By most of the membership, Reuther was referred to familiarly as "Walter," contrary to the image of him as aloof from the ranks. His spirit furnished extra flame for his lieutenants, and from the beginning until the day of the election of officers, Atlantic City was the scene of the most uproarious campaign ever witnessed by the convention resort. The icy ocean breezes that blew across the empty beaches in March must have been moderated by the fiery blasts that came from the heated struggle on the boardwalk, or from nearby bars and hotel rooms. Fisticuffs and scrimmages took place everywhere as the two rival factions sought to sway the uncommitted. One such bout occurred in the Chelsea Hotel lobby. Legend has it that some of Reuther's men, mistaking each other's identity, started a swinging clash at the Ambassador, until somebody yelled, "Hey, we're all for Walter, aren't we?" By then some furniture had been smashed, and the distraught manager of the Ambassador wrote the union, pleading for cooperation from the delegates in respecting the private property of the newly redecorated hotel. But the boisterous behavior continued in some quarters as delegates tossed firecrackers or dropped paper bags filled with water from hotel windows. Addes provided a hilarious note of unconscious humor with his serious warning that dropping bags of water from the upper floors of hotels "could be fatal to a delegate or a human being." After a few beers in the bars, impromptu troupes of Walter's boys frequently broke into a

buck-and-wing, chanting, "Reuther, Reuther, rah, rah, rah!"
On the floor of the convention, they heckled the Communist
delegates, when they rose to speak, with noisy sounds of "Quack!
Quack! Quack!" This was a reference to the trade-union maxim
regarding the best way to tell a Communist: "If he walks like a
duck and quacks like a duck, he must be a duck." Every time Nat
Ganley got up, the quacks were unmistakably loud, not only because he was the CP whip, but because his high-pitched nasal
twang mixed with a Brooklyn accent sounded amazingly like
Donald Duck.

For all their horseplay, however, the Reutherites meant business, and the Thomas-Addes forces knew it. They marshaled all
their strength to keep "R.J." in the presidency. Thomas himself
was relying on endorsement from Philip Murray, who was to
give the main convention address at the Monday morning session,
March 25. Thomas, in naming the escort committee to bring
the speaker from his hotel to convention hall, pointedly left out
Reuther, putting Frankensteen in charge. But Walter showed
up anyway, and he marched alongside the official group, manag-
ing somehow to get next to Murray as they went into the hall.
Murray was evidently not sure whether Reuther was a candidate
or not, but was trying to convince him not to run. However, Dick
Leonard heard Walter say, just as they went up the platform
steps, "Well, dammit, Phil, I'm going to run!"

Perhaps because Walter was so definite about his intentions,
Murray, the well-known neutralist, refrained from any clear-cut
endorsement of either candidate. He spoke briefly of the GM
strike and cleared up the fact that his steelworkers had backed
the struggle (without mentioning Reuther's revolutionary program) and had contributed to the strike fund. After joking about
the UAW's constant caucusing, he warned the auto workers
seriously not to tear down their little house with more factions
than it could contain. The delegates hung on every word, waiting
for him to indicate where his sympathies lay in regard to the
candidates, but it was not until the very end, as he expressed
his gratitude to all the officers—"to Secretary Addes, Vice-President Reuther, Vice-President Frankensteen, and to this great
big guy for whom I have a distinct fondness, the president of your

Union, R. J. Thomas . . ."—that he gave any inkling; and then no more than those few tender words for Thomas.

They were a meager endorsement, but more than enough for the Thomas backers. They used Murray's pat on the back to push their slogan "Support the CIO," the only one they could think of to match Reuther's bold "Against outside interference," which had been very effective in its implications: everyone knew he was referring to the Communist party and its Moscow-mandated moves. Thomas-Addes meetings lacked the zest and eloquent speeches of Reuther; neither Thomas nor Addes were skillful orators, and their talks were emotional, full of demagogy rather than hard-and-fast logic and the passionate belief in definite goals and principles which came through clearly at the Reuther caucuses, in spite of the high jinks, hoopla, and demagogy that went on in their sessions, too.

The convention was notably peculiar in that the main issue, the GM strike, was scarcely mentioned on the floor of the convention. Everything else received formal discussion and debate. As had been expected, the issue on women's rights was hotly argued as women delegates contested the resolution presented by Victor Reuther, head of the Resolutions Committee. The women wanted more "teeth" in the resolution to protect the seniority rights of women workers. They objected to giving up the four years of seniority they had gained since 1942, just because the war was over. Minnie Jones, a delegate from Local 600, in presenting the problem, said, "Some of our own union men— I hate to say it, but it is so—say, 'You should go back into your homes and cook on your stoves.' Some don't have a stove to cook on; our husbands have died overseas." War widows could not support orphaned children on jobs in other fields because they would have no seniority; department-store jobs, for example, paid only $15 a week to beginners. The women did not mind giving up their places in auto plants to returning veterans who had worked there before going into service; but many companies were hiring "men off the streets with no seniority," or laying off women and giving their jobs to men with less seniority. It was provisions like seniority rights, cherished by trade unions, that held many women war workers to their jobs long after peace had come. Several other women delegates echoed these objections and added a few of their own. Victor Reuther gallantly said the Resolutions Committee would be "especially delighted" to meet with a delegation of women; and the next day, when the revised version came up for a vote, Walter rose to speak in its favor. He stressed the union's commitment to protect and fight for the rights of working women, naming especially the newly added provision for maternity leaves and rest periods; but he made no mention of the return of working mothers to the home and cookstove, a burning issue. He was charged with having made promises before and not having carried them out universally; the whole question was debated hotly before the revised resolution passed.

Another important and far-reaching issue concerned the establishment of a Minorities Department. This had caused an open fight at the 1943 convention, when the Communists had introduced a resolution calling for such a department, the director of which must be a Negro, who would also serve as a member of the International Executive Board. It was obviously a bid for Negro support at the convention. It looked like a big step forward for Negroes in the union, but Reuther, supported by Thomas in this instance, had opposed it. Their contention was that a Negro should have the same right to any job as a white man, but to hand him a job simply because he was a Negro, without reference to his qualifications, was an insult to his dignity—"Jim Crowism in reverse," Reuther had pointed out then. The proposition was voted down in 1943, but now a new constitutional resolution was put forward to set up a Fair Practices and Anti-Discrimination Department. The UAW had always admitted Negroes, and since thousands had been hired during the war, there were many more Negro delegates at the 1946 convention than before. Again the question came up as to whether or not a Negro, heading the department, should also be a member of the Executive Board. This time even the committee was divided, there being a majority and minority report presented, the former having no provision for a Negro Executive Board member, while the latter proposed the election of such a member, who would head the new department, right then at the convention. An open fight ensued, carried over for three or four sessions, but Walter Reuther wisely did not enter the controversy. The majority report won, on the grounds that if a Negro member was elected to the Board, other minorities could claim rights to representation on that basis. (It was not until 1962 that a Negro was elected to the Executive Board, and then it was the director of the union's Independent Parts and Suppliers Department, Nelson Jack Edwards, who was not head of the Anti-Discrimination Department.)

Reuther kept challenging R. J. Thomas to a debate, and he was expecting the issue of the GM strike to come up on the floor of the convention right away; certainly it was debated everywhere else: in corridors, on the boardwalk, in bars, and at nightly caucuses. The CP, in the *Daily Worker*, had been attacking Reuther for weeks before the convention, and Thomas, at an early press conference, had parroted the CP line that the GM strike had started "too early, lasted too long, and accomplished too little." But on the matter of a public debate, the Thomas-Addes forces were significantly silent.

On the fourth day Leo Fenster, a delegate from Local 45 in Cleveland, rose to speak in favor of a resolution to support GM locals still on strike because of a piecework situation still in existence. In closing he said, "I think it is the problem of the entire convention to discuss the question of the GM strike, to discuss the question of how it was possible for us to go out first so far in advance and to stay out last so far in the future, getting no more than the other locals and the other unions." Walter quickly rose to speak in favor of passing the resolution at once to assist those locals still under the yoke of piecework; but the whole question was turned into a discussion of ways and means of supporting the remaining strikers; and Walter, knowing that Thomas was avoiding the real issue, again challenged him to a debate, this time at a night session excluding the press and public, "so we don't have to pull any punches." This must have been said tongue in cheek, since even a blind man could tell that nobody had been pulling any punches. Thomas, knowing full well that Reuther could win hands down in any contest requiring oratorical skill, refused rather foggily. He was rescued by the wily George Addes, who discovered a convention rule requiring such a proposal to receive a two-thirds vote of approval from the delegates. The motion lost by only a few votes, an encouraging sign for the Reuther forces.

So the electioneering continued offstage, both camps holding continuous meetings and midnight caucuses. Lacking talent, Reuther's adversaries tried every trick in the game to win votes, as one delegate said, including sex lure. Clay Fountain, one of Reuther's key staff members, gave a graphic description of "the importation of glamorous female comrades" from New York City, who "worked the swing shift in hotel rooms at night to convert delegates to the Thomas cause." The idea was that if the girls could not sway the delegates, they could at least keep them from voting by detaining them in hotel rooms. However, Fountain wrote, "Some of these babes got taken in by smarter and lustier delegates on our side who pretended they wanted to be converted—both for the joy of it, and for the practical purpose of wasting the time of the CP Mata Haris."

As election day, March 27, dawned, the emotion and agitation that surrounded the 1946 convention was echoed by messages R. J. Thomas received from Local 51 in Detroit. One spoke of the "three Axis partners, Lewis, Dubinski, and Reuther," whom they hoped he would defeat. Another read: "Reuther's actions at this convention place him in the ranks of Winston Churchill's spearhead of world reaction. Reuther has diligently memorized Hitler's *Mein Kampf's* phrases which caused the best sons to give their blood and lives. Your reelection as president will mean a victory for the American worker and a repudiation of Walter P. Reuther." A third sent a warning to its delegates that they should stick to the mandate given by the local and vote for Thomas, implying that there must have been a good deal of wavering. Reuther was nominated by a delegate from his own West Side Local 174, Edward J. Cote. He spoke concisely and to the point of "the man with whose intelligence, progressive, and aggressive leadership we can march side by side to our goal of a stronger, greater, and united UAW-CIO." The noisy hall was suddenly quiet as balloting began.

The first vote was cast by a delegate from Local 1, from Buchanan, Michigan, which was entitled to only one vote. In a loud voice he stood at the microphone and gave that vote to Walter Reuther. The ripple of laughter that ran through the hall was drowned out by cheers from Reuther supporters; it was a good omen. Just before the voting began, Walter had gone up to Thomas, offering to shake hands, but Thomas had huffily refused. The "redhead," not at all put out by the rebuff, checkmated the "great big guy" with one of his rapierlike retorts. "Tommy," he said, grinning, "if you're not big enough to lose, you're not big enough to win." With the first vote coming his way, he had a hunch he would be proved correct, but the race was neck and neck; cheers came from both Reuther and Thomas supporters whenever a big batch of votes was accorded either candidate.

The roll call was begun at 11:30 A.M., and at about 2:30 P.M., with the vote perhaps two thirds complete, a wild cheering went up from the platform, and several loyal Reuther supporters hoisted Walter to their shoulders, with their joyful campaign cry "Reuther, Reuther, rah, rah, rah!" sung out triumphantly. Taken by surprise, Walter waved and smiled, but because results had been so close he was not at all sure he had won. The demonstration had been the idea of Brendan Sexton of Local 50, staged without Walter's knowledge or approval as a ruse to create the impression that he already had a majority; it was hoped that delegates who were in doubt, or who had been planning to vote for Thomas, would get on the bandwagon. Later, observers from both camps agreed that the trick probably didn't change a single vote, but it no doubt set the tone of joyous victory in which the remaining Reuther votes were cast. R. J. Thomas conceded defeat just before the balloting ended. Tears stood in his eyes as he said to Walter, "It was a good race." Reuther nodded. "We'll work together, R.J.," was all he said.

At 4:00 P.M. Addes announced the new president, Walter P. Reuther. The tally, which came the next day, showed that he won by 4,444 to 4,320 votes, a narrow margin of 124 votes. But narrow or not, he received a tremendous ovation as he went up to the rostrum, accompanied by May. She had been sitting beside him on the platform, and he wanted her beside him at the podium. In his acceptance, he pledged to work for unity and "the kind of labor movement . . . *whose philosophy demands that it fight for the welfare of the public at large."* He went on, "There is much work to be done in the world. We won the war. The task now is to win the peace." This was a task he never shirked, no matter how frustrating it was at times. He also promised to uphold the principles of the CIO, concluding, "Let us go home motivated by the same spirit that motivated us back in 1936 and 1937, when all you could get for belonging to this union was a cracked head. Let's be guided by the sincere desire to place the union's welfare above any personal consideration or any personal differences."

That night he kept a campaign promise to his staff in celebration of his victory. He actually sipped a beer and sputtered over a few puffs of a cigar as his followers cheered and toasted his election. The rejoicing proved premature, however, for the next morning, when election of officers was resumed, the rest of the Reuther slate was for the most part defeated. The delegates returned a majority of the Thomas-Addes forces to office. Re-election of Addes by unanimous vote was no surprise because the Reuther forces had run no candidate against him. But the election of Thomas as first vice-president; of Leonard as second vice-president, and of the pro-Communist officers and Executive Board members was a keen disappointment, a puzzling surprise. One clue to the strange turnabout may have been found in the query of the delegate who asked if the union would protect those who voted contrary to the mandates of their locals. Addes curtly informed him that a delegate was bound only to his own conscience in voting and that no local could deal out any reprisals against him. It is possible that many delegates did not trust any leader completely, and hoped to provide a check on Reuther's dictatorial tendencies as well as mitigate the bitter reactions of the locals who had backed Thomas, so they sent most of the Executive Board members back into office.

One bright spot in the picture was the election of Emil Mazey, now regional director of Detroit's East Side and one of Reuther's most devoted followers, to the top-heavy board. Emil was still in service at Ie Shima, a tiny island in the Pacific, during the convention, and did not even know he was a candidate; but soon after his return he began to show the signs of the important figure

he would become. The resignation of Dick Frankensteen, who
bowed out of the UAW at this time, eliminated a potential challenger for Reuther's top leadership post. In the main, however,
the immediate future looked dark and stormy indeed, as Reuther
realized he was hedged in by hostile associates. He resolved
to fight them to the finish.

Back in Detroit, the first thing he discovered was that the
UAW's cupboard was bare; the treasury was in a much more
impoverished state than Addes' report, back-dated for the convention, had indicated. Walter's opening official act was to fly
to New York seeking funds from fellow CIO unions to tide the
UAW over its present financial crisis. He did not have to look
far, as Sidney Hillman, who had written a letter of sincere regret
in answer to the auto workers' invitation to speak at their recent
convention, granted a loan of $250,000 from the Amalgamated
Clothing Workers. It is interesting to note that Hillman, so ready
to extend his helping hand, was destined to make his final exit
from the labor scene just as Reuther was entering it in a position
of power. In a few months—on July 10, 1946—Hillman would die
of a heart attack; and it was almost as if he were handing the
torch now to the younger leader, with whom he did not always
agree, but for whom he surely felt an affinity. They were both
practical dreamers and idealists, were of the same Socialist background, and were both extremely, almost frighteningly, efficient,
more in the nature of high-powered businessmen than union
bosses.

Reuther's second unpleasant shock came on April 20, scarcely
a month after his election, when the Communist *Daily Worker*
zestfully reported that a statement on union policy, which had
not even been shown to him, had been approved by the "mechanical majority" vote of 14 to 7. The obviously CP-directed statement, among other insidious sections, denounced "Catholic-bait-
ing, Protestant-baiting, Jew-baiting, Negro-baiting, and Red-
baiting." The tactic was hardly subtle, trying to imply that when
Walter attacked Nat Ganley, for example, as the CP agent in the
union, he would thereby be in the same category with those who
dealt in antisemitism or Jim-Crowism, a practice condemned by
the UAW constitution. In this way, the Executive Board sup-

posedly would be limiting Walter's authority, as president, to
question or condemn CP influence within the UAW. Retaliating,
Reuther publicly announced that he would not appoint any
known Communist to union office. From then on, for the next
year and a half, the UAW went through a nightmare of factional
strife that made a mockery of the very word "union." Every issue
that came up in the locals, from the election of minor officers
to sending delegates to UAW summer school, brought on a
factional fight.

It was clearly apparent to Walter that a great deal of education
was needed by the membership before it would understand the
true nature of the motives and maneuvers of CP-led locals. In
a countermove, he made a deal with Thomas to support him for
directorship of the coveted Competitive Shops Department in
charge of organizing unorganized shops. This position entailed
a large staff who would owe their jobs, and hence political support, to the ex-president. In return, Thomas would support Victor
Reuther for the influential post of National Education Director.
Another key appointment was that of the genial, highly capable
Frank Winn, who, as Public Relations director, had been through
so many battles with Walter for their mutual goals. Frank's own
comment was typical: "There was a long and bitter controversy
over the appointment of Victor as director of Education," he
wrote, "and the resolution of it involved a great deal more than
appointing Thomas as director of the Competitive Shops Department. I'm afraid I can claim no such distinction as Victor. When
Walter named me public relations director, I was unanimously
approved by the Executive Board. They apparently didn't consider me much of a threat."

These two veterans of unionism went to work with a will.
Victor rejuvenated the UAW Education Department, taking the
campaign for his brother into outlying areas during the summer
of 1947, far in advance of convention elections. Speakers from
his department covered the country, addressing union locals to
expose the CP in America for what it was—not a small, relatively
harmless political party, but an international movement to dominate the world with Soviet doctrine, directed from Moscow.
Victor's staff did not indulge in name-calling, but encouraged

members to use their own judgment, thereby following one of Walter's favorite maxims: "Given all the facts, the average man can be depended upon to make a wise decision." Since his budget was small, Victor had recruited most of his staff from the leadership training base the UAW had set up in a CIO summer school near the resort area of Port Huron, Michigan, soon after his appointment in 1946. Here, public speaking, parliamentary law, and related subjects were taught to officers of key locals. Students were chosen for their potential ability to sway delegates at the next convention. With a youthful, intelligent staff, Victor's department supplied a new kind of aid to UAW locals, and they responded with a fresh, enthusiastic loyalty to Walter's program. Volunteers turned out radio and film scripts to be used as visual-aid materials, then new in education media.

Among Victor's most ardent assistants was Mrs. Mildred Jeffrey, whose exceptional ability later led to her appointment as head of the Women's Division of the UAW Education Department (and who in 1966 became national Democratic committeewoman from Michigan). In 1946–1947, Millie, as she was known in the union soon after her career began, concentrated, along with the rest of the crew, on lining up votes for Walter. In late 1946, the UAW held a huge educational conference which, with its undercover caucusing between discussions and speeches by such personalities as Eleanor Roosevelt and Walter White, took on the tenor of a junior convention as both sides tried to enlist converts.

All this time, of course, Reuther was busy in Detroit and nearby areas, trying to best the attacks of the Communists and assert his authority as president. At Executive Board meetings he was pushed around, sometimes literally. The "mechanical majority" acted with robotlike strength to put through Communist-oriented programs with or without his approval. The staff of the UAW headquarters took sides, and Walter had to bring in his own "shadow cabinet" before he could get his work done. Nat Weinberg, one of Roy's classmates at Brookwood Labor College, was hired to do research work, but his department head would never even give him an assignment. He had no stenographer, and if he wanted anything typed for Walter, he would have to hunt around the building for a girl who was on their side and would type it up in her spare time. Union meetings and CIO sectional conventions became a test of strength.

The first decisive show came a few months after Walter was in office, at the Michigan CIO convention. Heated contests for state or regional offices took place; and despite the fact that delegates from Murray's steelworkers backed the same candidates as the Thomas-Addes group, Reuther supporters won the convention. Murray could not help being impressed, and he continued to be favorably inclined by other Reuther triumphs in Ohio, Illinois, Indiana, and Wisconsin, all strongholds of the auto industry. Sensing his advantage, Reuther consciously consulted with Murray, seeking his advice and goodwill at once; before long they were Phil and Walter to each other, solidifying relations at the top. Walter was shrewd enough to invite Phil to an Executive Board meeting in October, so the CIO president, who by then was beginning to have his own fears about Communist influence, remarked that the factional fight had "sunk to a level of complete moral degeneracy." It was clear that he did not mean to criticize the Reuther forces. Walter himself made the rounds in Detroit, talking "to thousands of guys all over this town," he told an interviewer, convincing the ranks of the hidden evil of the Communist influence.

Searching for a more immediate way to stymie the high-handedness of the Executive Board, he studied the bylaws with a fine-comb thoroughness and discovered that checks had to be signed by the president personally as well as by the secretary-treasurer. Up to now, this had been regarded as a formality, and the president's signature was either printed or rubber-stamped on, while Addes was the actual financial power. Walter had suspected some payroll padding and swollen expense accounts; he seized the chance to demand control of the books, waving the bylaws in the hostile faces. The board members were not about to pay attention to the bylaws, but Walter, ignoring them, called the union's bank and announced that no draft on the UAW treasury was valid until he verified the number of the check by phone. He scanned every check and phoned the bank the numbers of those he approved. He further threatened the board to stop signing the paychecks of members unless they gave him access to the records. His opponents gave in. "Those fellows hated my guts," Walter chuckled. "But they loved their paychecks." That he was able to keep his sense of humor during the twenty months of harassment is a measure of Reuther's spirit.

Besides being beset by the hostile majority of the Executive Board, he was also besieged by a constant drumfire of abuse from the Communist party in the *Daily Worker*. Going farther, one of their masterpieces was a widely circulated comic book broadside entitled "The Bosses' Boy," which pictured Reuther as a traitor, the tool of auto industrialists—even as being actually on the management payroll! When Walter complained about this at a board meeting, and about Thomas' attacks on him in the reactionary antilabor press, Thomas, replying that Reuther often did the same, added revealingly, "Reuther wants unity of applause for Walter, Victor, and Roy Reuther, and, by God, anybody who doesn't go along with that program is a disrupter." Evidently one of the factors that entered into the tactics of the opposition was the fear of a long Reuther dynasty, indicated by the unity of feeling, action, and purpose among the three brothers. The CP "threw everything but their hammer and sickle" at them.

Walter of course received the heaviest barrage from the "Commies." They gleefully helped to spread a rumor, taken seriously by the late columnist Drew Pearson, who should have known better, that a group of Republicans had formed an organization to support a Taft-Reuther ticket in the 1948 presidential election—Senator Robert A. Taft for President, Walter Reuther for Vice-President. Since the very name "Taft" was poison to union men because of the detested Taft-Hartley Act, the story could have damaged Walter's standing badly; but the opposition on the UAW board became even more irresponsible and got out a petition to change the name of the labor-management bill to the Taft Hartley-*Reuther* Act, an absurdity too great for the men on the assembly lines to swallow.

The anti-Reuther forces persisted with their foul publicity to the last ditch, however. They did not draw the line at using the unsavory name of Gerald L. K. Smith, notorious American Nazi leader and general reactionary, in their attacks. A supposedly secret letter, attributed to Smith, appeared in a fiendish "yellow sheet" called FDR,* which was distributed to union halls all over the country. The letter implied that Reuther was actually an undercover Nazi agent and had warned the Nazis never to praise him publicly, since it might detract from the "sensational job" he was doing in fighting their common enemies. The letter continued: "Inside informers tell me that Mr. Reuther is thoroughly alert to the Jewish issue." This farfetched canard was bound to miss fire: Reuther forces were able to point out that Walter's wife was Jewish, her people having fled to the United States to escape the pogroms in Czarist Russia, in which thousands of Jews were persecuted and many were murdered during periodic outbreaks.

Besides the attacks on Reuther, his adversaries were constantly on the lookout for schemes to cause embarrassment and trouble to the UAW under his leadership. In the spring of 1947, for instance, they repeated a trick they had played on him the year before. Negotiations for a new contract were under way with GM, and again the Communist-led United Electrical Workers, with locals in many of the GM plants, negotiated a secret deal with management, accepting a wage increase about half as high as that which Reuther had proposed. Naturally their contract became the pattern, and Reuther, blazing with anger, was forced to accept it. Obviously the maneuver was supposed to damage Reuther's standing with his own automobile workers, but this time it missfired. The men in the shops and on the assembly lines were angry, too, but their resentment was directed this time toward the Electrical workers, who had double-crossed the UAW.

Following its final success in organizing the automobile industry, UAW had spread out. It was now called the United Automobile, Aircraft and Farm Implement Workers of America, having taken in thousands of members during the rapid World War Two expansion of the aircraft industry, as well as workers in other machinery industries, such as farm implements.

When Walter Reuther took office as president, a strike against Allis-Chalmers, one of the country's largest manufacturers of

* Reuther later filed suit for libel against the author and publisher of FDR.

farm machinery, had been dragging along for weeks. It had been
called by a UAW local believed to be under Communist leadership. When Reuther and CIO leader John Brophy went out to
Milwaukee to try to arrange a settlement, they discovered that
the men on the picket lines were brazenly distributing campaign
literature for the Communist candidate for governor of Wisconsin.
The outraged company executives refused even to see the UAW
president, and the strike was lost. (NO)

As the UAW convention drew near, the farm implement
workers were involved in one of the most devious, most cleverly
planned schemes of the Addes-Communist group. Within the
CIO there were two unions of farm implement workers. One
was part of UAW. The other, operating outside UAW, was called
the FE (Farm Equipment workers)—CIO. For the uninformed
it was difficult to distinguish one from the other. There was hot
rivalry between them, and both had had considerable success
in obtaining contracts with important companies. FE-CIO,
however, was generally believed to be Communist; it was consistently following the party line.

Addes began by secretly inviting FE-CIO to join the UAW
and merge with the union already operating there. The terms
were exactly to the liking of the FE-CIO comrades. The merger
meant that the newcomers would actually absorb the UAW
union and exist as an autonomous body, free to form its own
policies without regard to those set up by the national union.
It would take its own officers and staff along, and UAW would
assume its financial obligations, about which its leaders were
exceedingly vague. In return for these favors, the Addes-Thomas
group would have at its disposal an impressive solid Communist
bloc of 500 convention votes, enough to swing a close election.

In June the UAW Executive Board, stacked against President
Reuther, held a meeting in Chicago. Having waited until the
meeting was about to adjourn and Walter was leaving to catch a
plane to fulfill an important speaking engagement in the East,
Addes, smugly reasonable, brought up his proposal.

Stunned, the Reuther forces frantically tried to delay action
on the merger motion, but the mechanical majority adopted the
proposal. However, Jack Livingston managed to attach a proviso

calling for a referendum of the entire membership for approval
of the merger, to be conducted during the next month. The
Thomas-Addes group agreed, a trifle overconfident of the success
of its deal among the unsuspecting ranks. With less than a month
to go, Reuther and his group were faced with what looked like
an appallingly difficult job—to try to explain to the more than a
million auto workers the real meaning of that merger, with its
full implications. To Walter, the challenge was compelling, even
exhilarating. "Let's go out and beat the pants off of them!" he
counseled his staff cheerfully as they met in the basement workshop of his home on Appoline Street, though they all knew that
the risk was great: If they failed and the merger went through,
it would doubtlessly mean loss of the presidency for Walter, and
the downfall of the Reuther group.

But now the political training program began to pay off. Victor's recruits sped out across the country, from plant to plant,
calling meetings of the locals, prying the lid off the proposal,
exposing to workers exactly what was concealed by a lot of fine
print. And, as the Education Department had done its work well,
the rank and file, for the most part, understood. It was summer,
a time when the evening union meetings are apt to be poorly
attended; so before they could explain the issue, Victor's boys
had to beat the bushes to get their audiences. But when the people came they listened, and they got the message. Reuther himself raced all over Detroit, speaking in union halls, revealing the
fakery that was being maneuvered. On July 11, he and Addes
held a debate before 2,500 UAW members; here he carried out
his own directive and truly "licked the pants off" his adversary,
as even a pro-Addes man admitted. The outcome of the referendum was a defeat of the merger proposal by a two-to-one ratio,
a major victory for Walter and his devoted disciples.

Reuther withheld his most powerful attack until September,
when he published in the *United Automobile Worker* his report,
as president, to the UAW members. Since he was required by the
constitution to make the report, Addes could not have stopped it,
but he might have delayed official publication of it had he known
about it in advance. But Addes, Thomas, and their henchmen
were caught completely off guard, for Reuther had neither sub-

mitted it to them nor informed them it was coming out. An Executive Board session, with Reuther present, had just adjourned when someone brought in a copy of the *United Automobile Worker*, picked up in the headquarters lobby, where a bundle of the papers had been dumped and broken open. Duplicate bundles were on their way to the post office for mailing to the homes of every UAW member all over the country; as word got out about the report, the contents were eagerly read by the ranks.

Although he mentioned no names, Reuther's report was devastating in its detailed account of conditions in the UAW as he found them when he took office as president. His charges concerned financial mismanagement—waste, careless bookkeeping, padded payrolls and expense accounts, use of union funds to build up political machines for some of the leaders. It also gave many instances of Communist meddling, arousing factionalism, and dragging the union into situations that were seriously damaging to its reputation. Nothing was overlooked.

The Executive Board immediately went back into session, and, as one union man described it, "All hell broke loose." After heaping invective on Reuther, the Board then authorized Thomas and Addes to print and mail to every UAW member an equally devastating reply to the Reuther report. But by then it was too late.

As the opening of the convention (to be held in Atlantic City in November) drew near, the UAW held elections in every shop, to choose delegates. For the first time in its existence there were two slates of candidates for all seats, pro-Reuther and pro-Thomas-Addes. And for the first time, much campaign literature was distributed. Although Walter was not yet a candidate for reelection, his picture appeared on countless sample ballots. Right from the beginning, returns indicated an impressive ground swell in favor of Reuther. R. J. Thomas was defeated in his own local. Even in Local 155, long under Nat Ganley's CP domination, the Reuther group won a majority.

Alarmed, the opponents tried desperately to stop the tide. Leaders in Ford Local 600 limited the voting period to two hours on a hot summer Sunday, hoping that the Reuther followers would fail to show up. It was customary to hold elections during the week and to keep the polls open all day. Yet even in two hours, Reuther candidates won nine out of ten seats. Never averse to doing an about-face, if they thought it would suit their purposes, the Communists then scheduled a second election, on the ground that the allotted voting time had been too short! This time Reuther's men won all ten.

In late October the Reuther followers held a national caucus in Detroit, nominating Reuther for reelection—a mere formality; Emil Mazey for Addes' post as secretary-treasurer; and two "conservative" Reuther backers, John W. Livingston of St. Louis and Richard Gosser of Toledo, for the vice-presidential posts. This was a bold move, but Walter was determined to make a bid for total victory. As an added measure of ensuring it, he flew to Pittsburgh, not merely to tell Murray about his plan, but to warn the CIO chief against throwing support to the other side. "The Commies have got to go, Phil," he said. And Murray, though he tried to save Addes, as the UAW officer with the longest tenure, knew that Reuther was probably right, since he was beginning to have his own fears of CP influence on some top CIO officers.

The 1947 convention was the complete opposite of the one the year before. No real turmoil and not much suspense marked the proceedings; night caucuses altered few votes, because lines were already drawn hard and fast. From the hour the convention opened, Walter and the Reuther group were in control. The only debate took place when the Thomas-Addes faction proposed that the UAW leaders refuse to sign the anti-Communist affidavits required by the Taft-Hartley Act. Reuther advocated signing, with the proviso that UAW leaders comply under protest, challenge the oath in the courts, and strive for repeal. The proposal was rejected by a wide margin.

The Thomas-Addes forces conceded defeat before the election started by refusing to run any major candidate against Reuther. A couple of token challengers polled only 339 votes between them. Thomas and Addes instructed their followers to abstain from voting, and 1,219 did so. Reuther received 5,593 votes for reelection; had the abstainers cast their votes, he would have beaten them almost four to one. A contest was expected by Emil Mazey's bid to oust Addes as secretary-treasurer; the opponents did not abstain from *that* poll, but Mazey won by a comfortable majority. Livingston and Gosser also won easily. Finally, when the regional votes for Executive Board members were cast, 18 of the 22 seats were captured by the Reuther slate, an overwhelming victory.

Walter had invited his parents to come to this first convention he chaired as president, and now he proudly presented his father and mother, Valentine and Anna Reuther, to the delegates. In introducing them, he told the UAW about the time his mother made a shirt out of the big black umbrella that he and his brothers tried unsuccessfully to turn into a parachute. He was just as informal regarding Val. "My father has always been a good pal of mine," he said, "an old fighter in the ranks of labor, a trade unionist from way back, when the going was rough . . . who indoctrinated his boys when they were pretty young, and he told them the most important thing in the world to fight for was the other guy, the brotherhood of man, the Golden Rule. . . ."

Val Reuther, the veteran unionist, responding to the ovation he received, said to the delegates among other things, "I am extremely happy that the seed I have tried to sow in the minds of our children is bearing fruit . . . that they are engaged in the trade-union movement that has always been dear to my heart. . . ."

It was a happy moment for the whole family, as the three Reuther brothers, their wives and parents, celebrated the unprecedented victory, not only for official posts, but for diminishing the power of obstructionist "outside control" to a near zero. The delegates voted to raise the salaries of all UAW officers, the executive board members receiving a $1500 a year increase (from $5,000 to $6,500), and they wanted to give the president a $2,000 raise; but Walter insisted that $1,000 was plenty, bringing his salary up to $10,000; he could then retain his proud standing as the "lowest-paid head of any major union in the country." The keynote of his closing address was serious. "We are in the vanguard in America in that great crusade to build a better world," he said. "We are the architects of the future and we are going to fashion the weapons with which we will work and fight and build." He already had a slogan for the new administration: "Teamwork in the leadership and solidarity in the ranks."

Armed with full authority at last, Walter started to clean house at once. He fired Communist sympathizers in job lots—more than one hundred staff members were dismissed. George Addes left the labor movement to open a nightclub. R. J. Thomas, ever a unionist, took a staff post in the CIO. Dick Leonard went back into the shop, expecting to build a new political faction of his own; but he soon left for a pioneer post in the southwest offices of the CIO. The Reuther regime also started a campaign to drive lottery operators, particularly a ring of "numbers" racketeers, out of the factories.

One of the first to be ousted at the top was the union's general counsel, Maurice Sugar, who had been known for his pro-Communist stand. Donald Montgomery, who had been dismissed by the mechanical majority, regained his supervisory post of the Washington office; Nat Weinberg became UAW research director; Ken Bannon, who had directed the Reuther campaign, was made head of the Ford department; and other Reuther stalwarts replaced two Executive Board members of the Addes-Thomas faction, who stepped down voluntarily for lesser staff jobs rather than risk defeat at the next election—an illustration of the impact of the Reuther landslide. The clean-sweep helped to increase the union's bargaining power, since no time was wasted on internal struggling for power. It was a welcome respite from the endless factional fighting, and Reuther was already planning to make full use of the new unity in the next negotiations. That the auto magnates regarded him in a different light was evident when Henry Ford II was among the first post-convention callers. The namesake of his eccentric, tyrannical, genius grandfather, who had died a few months before (in April of 1947), may have been curious to meet the young labor leader who ten years earlier had been beaten up by thugs of Henry Ford the First. According to Walter, Ford "merely dropped by for a talk. Our chat was very satisfactory and very pleasant all around."

In any case, the weeks right after the convention were relatively calm. The Reuthers' second daughter, Elizabeth Ann, called Lisa, had been born in July during the heat of the summer and the convention campaign. Walter had little chance even to get a good look at his infant red-haired daughter, but now he became better acquainted with the baby, as five-year-old Linda referred to her younger sister. The holiday period, in which the family and the union—the "family" of workers—was toasted with Grandmother Reuther's traditional gift of homemade wine, was happy and peaceful. Of course there were rumblings of reprisals from various quarters of the losers' faction; but in regard to evil, Walter was a firm believer in the biblical viewpoint, "Sufficient unto the day . . ." As always, he made the most of the lull before the next storm.

In his closing convention speech he had refuted the editorial writers' assumption that the UAW leadership was becoming conservative. "This leadership is committed to the kind of militant, fighting trade-union program that will mobilize not only our union but all the *people in America in support of an aggressive overall economic, social, and political program.*" And he meant to carry out that commitment at any cost.

XXI

Violence Invades

JUST how high the price of power could be, Walter Reuther was soon to be violently, shockingly shown. As always, his life in the winter of 1947–1948 was crowded with activity. Besides purging the union of those he considered dangerous elements, he was involved in the political arena of the national election year as early as February, 1948, when he attended the ADA convention in Washington.* Like most liberals of a Socialist-Democratic background, Reuther had been deeply grieved by Roosevelt's death and felt that Truman, though he was a sincere man, was "inadequate for the job he inherited," as quoted by the Detroit News. Before he left for the nation's capital, a few of the UAW top executives met in Walter's basement on Appoline Street with Donald Montgomery, the union's Washington representative, to discuss presidential possibilities.

The cellar workshop was used more and more as a meeting-place, since discussions could go on till all hours and the children sleeping upstairs would not be disturbed. Several union leaders felt that Walter and May should move to a larger house now that he was in his second term as president of one of the nation's largest labor unions and was himself an important national figure

* Americans for Democratic Action, whose founding convention Reuther attended in 1947, appealed to him because of its independent approach to politics, its choice of candidates, and its aims for reform, a realignment of parties, sponsored by a group of liberals, including his good friend Mrs. Roosevelt.

258

in the political as well as labor field. But Reuther saw no reason to leave the modest house that was their first home, just as he saw no reason to increase his salary. The place was comfortable, and just the right size for his family, with Linda in the upstairs bedroom and the infant Lisa in the small spare bedroom downstairs; and it never occurred to him to move into a more substantial—or more secluded—house.

At this particular conclave, Montgomery informed them that the Democratic party leaders were seriously considering General Dwight D. Eisenhower as a likely candidate. Walter, although he saw Ike as a popular alternative to Truman, preferred Justice William O. Douglas, at that time an ardent New Dealer, who, he felt, would follow FDR's policies more than any other hopeful. The man who worried him was Henry Wallace, not because he had anything against Wallace's plan to get rid of poverty, but because the benighted former Vice-President and earlier Secretary of Commerce was already accepting support from the Communists in building up his idea for a third party, and the sentiment in the shops was favorable toward him. During the ADA convention, Reuther made an eloquent plea for Douglas, and succeeded in altering the ADA resolution on candidates to favor Eisenhower "and/or" Douglas for the Democratic ticket. When Eisenhower turned down the nomination and the Democratic party nominated Truman, the CIO, and consequently the UAW, endorsed him. But in the early part of the year, Wallace was gaining ground among the workers; and at the March meeting of the UAW Executive Board, Reuther, determined that he must be stopped, saw to it that a resolution was passed denouncing the Wallace candidacy as "a premature and ill-advised adventure" and "a Communist party maneuver." The Board also adopted a political goal of forming a *genuine* progressive party after the 1948 elections.

Such action only fostered the bitterness of feeling the Communists had for him since their ouster from all leadership posts, but Walter was not one to worry about personal reprisals. Early in April there was a two-day Education conference at the summer leadership training camp to coordinate the UAW's campaign material, its program, and plans for voter-registration drives with the CIO's Political Action Committee (PAC), which was started by Sidney Hillman in 1943 as a forceful political arm in the organization of industrial unions. Walter, always with a thousand details to attend to, was delayed in getting there. Finally he came, driving up in his seven-year-old Chevrolet sedan, arriving in a cloud of dust. Those who were watching for him, including his friend Dave Miller, one of the trade-union pioneers, burst out laughing when they saw his "beat-up" old car, hardly fit for a factory hand, let alone the president of the auto workers' union.

"That's our president!" somebody called out. "Why don't you get a car, Walter, instead of that ol' rattletrap?" called another.

He joined in the laughter with them as he got out, closing the door carefully; but he pretended to be offended. "What's wrong with it?" he demanded in mock indignation. "Listen, this old Chevy gives me twenty-eight miles to the gallon, and—" But they burst into another roar of laughter and waved him off; otherwise they would be in for a barrage of statistics.

The next day, after the workshop sessions were over, it was early enough and warm enough for a baseball game. Walter pitched, as in his Wheeling days, giving the ball a long windup and a tricky touch of English on the throw. As always, he played hard, for "keeps" as well as fun, and gave a triumphant shout when he struck out a batter.

Dave, who told this story, complained that no one ever showed this side of Walter Reuther in writing about him. "We always had so much fun," he said; "so many laughs. And he was like that till the end. I was on his doorstep at least twice a week, and he was always at my level."

Following the conference, Walter pushed a continuing effort of his, racial integration in sports; just then he was trying to promote participation of Negroes in the bowling leagues, to which he encountered stubborn opposition.* Soon afterward, he received two unsigned threatening letters—one on the interracial bowling-tournament issue; the other inveighing against his victorious ouster of the union's Communist bloc. Though both hinted

---

* Oddly, there was much less objection to integrated baseball teams than to the bowling leagues, probably as the latter were more social affairs, took place at night, with wives often present, and beer drinking usually.

at bodily harm coming to him, neither of them convinced him
to take steps to prevent any possible violence.

The April meeting of the Executive Board was held on the
twentieth, in the Book-Cadillac Hotel, and, as usual, it ran overtime while they argued the question of political alliance and the
future formation of a new, genuine farm-labor party, free of outside influence. Walter phoned May to hold dinner for him, as
she had come to expect; and after the session broke up at around
8:30 P.M., he and Jack Conway, his special assistant, drove to the
UAW offices to look after some routine business. Then he drove
home by himself in the Chevy "rattletrap." Their house was on a
corner lot, enclosed by a little white picket fence, and usually
Walter parked on the side street, opened the gate in the fence,
and came across the walk in the backyard, going into the house
by the kitchen door. But on this particular night, for some reason
he could not recall, he parked on Appoline Street and went in
through the front door. It was about 9:40 P.M.

Taking off his shoes—he usually walked around in his stocking
feet if he came home after the children had gone to bed—he sat
at the kitchen counter eating some stew May had kept hot for
him, between bites telling her how the meeting went. When he
had finished, he crossed to the refrigerator to get himself a bowl
of cooked, chilled fruit.* As he was standing there holding the
bowl, May asked some question in regard to his account, and he
turned to answer her. Simultaneously, there was the ear-splitting
roar of a rifle, and a torrent of buckshot smashed through the
window, tearing the storm sash and splintering the pane. The
blast of pellets from a 12-gauge shotgun caught Walter at such
an angle that at least four nearly ripped off his right arm and a
fifth pierced through his chest from right to left; the rest of the
barrage whizzed by him, perforating a cupboard, part of the wall,
and a ventilator. As May stared in horror, he fell forward on the
floor, crying out in agony and surprise: "They shot me, May!"

It looked as if he were all but murdered. He lay on his back,
halfway under the kitchen table, his right arm spurting blood
and sagging from his shoulder, immobile. May rushed to the

---

* First reports in the papers said Reuther had gone to get a soft drink, probably to point up the fact that he never touched hard liquor.

phone to call an ambulance, then Victor and Roy. The deafening roar had alarmed neighbors all around, and one of them, Richard Ruen, sprang out of bed and ran across the alley to the Reuthers'. Seeing Walter prostrate on the kitchen floor, he dashed down the block and brought the neighborhood physician, Dr. Angelo V. Lenzi, to the scene, who stanched the bleeding and gave Reuther a shot of morphine, for he was conscious and in terrible pain. Between moans, Walter gave vent to his anger, muttering, "Those bastards had to shoot me in the back. They couldn't come out in the open and fight." His first words at the sight of the doctor were a plea to save his arm, recalling his insistence years before, in the Wheeling factory accident, that his severed toe be sewn back on. Now he repeated several times: "Doc, don't let them cut off my arm." He was so insistent that the doctor put on an emergency splint, explaining later, "I decided Reuther would have a better chance to save his arm if we could get a splint on quickly, before he was transported to the hospital. The arm was hanging at such a crazy angle."

When the ambulance—and the police—came, Walter was taken to New Grace Hospital, where he had to undergo two and a half hours of surgery, during which he was given three pints of whole blood and one of plasma. The upper half of his body was placed in a cast, and his right arm put in traction; to prevent it from stiffening, electric shocks were administered at regular intervals. The pain persisted, so that, though he was under constant sedation, he hardly slept two hours out of twenty-four. Two detectives were put on guard, around the clock, outside the hospital room; and four more were on watch at Reuther's home, to protect his family, as well as to keep back the crowds of curiosity seekers that thronged to the site of the attempted assassination. Five-year-old Linda, who, like her nine-months-old baby sister Lisa, had slept through the entire turmoil, could not understand what was going on. May, who had spent the night at Walter's bedside in the hospital while relatives stayed in the house, told Linda that Daddy had fallen against the kitchen window and cut his arm.

Investigations on the morning after the shooting showed that Walter was lucky to be alive at all. The footprints found by police in the backyard grass under the window were so deeply impressed in the sod that it was plain the gunman had been standing in wait for Walter a long time, evidently knowing he usually came into the house that way. If he had followed his regular routine, he would have walked right into the muzzle of the gun—and into instant death, for the hail of buckshot would have struck him across the chest and certainly pierced his heart. But whatever power impelled him to alter his parking procedure that night—and it seemed as if Providence must have been guiding the old Chevy —forced the furtive assassin to stick to the spot and take a much more complicated aim through the closed window.

Several of the neighbors who had rushed out to see where the shooting came from reported seeing a man run out from the Reuthers' yard to a new Ford sedan, red or maroon, which was parked around the corner on Chippewa Avenue. The driver must have been waiting for him, because as soon as he jumped in, the car took off at top speed. One empty shotgun shell was picked up by police two blocks away along the route of escape, but by itself could hardly reveal the assailant's identity. A police inspector estimated that he must have been a short man or had fired from a stooping position, about two feet from the window. He seemed to be a professional killer with a deadly aim, since Reuther was standing seven feet away inside, and only his turning toward his wife in that split second had saved his life.

Police Commissioner Harry S. Toy sent out a search order of every garage in the city for a car resembling the getaway Ford sedan. In another sweeping show of efficiency, his staff issued a directive for "everybody who had any personal animosity" toward Reuther to be taken into custody and questioned. This covered an impossibly wide range of people including "Communists or anyone in industry or a union," hardly likely to lead to the criminal. Among the first to volunteer for court questioning was George Addes, who was acquitted at once. Gus Scholle, head of the Michigan CIO Council, was quite sure the Communists were behind the plot, and many agreed with him; others thought it was the underworld element in the union.

Meanwhile, Walter lay hovering near death at New Grace Hospital. His mother hurried up from Wheeling, and she and May took turns keeping a constant vigil by his bed. The sight of her son, whom she had last seen in such happy triumph at the 1947 convention, now struggling for his life, struck at the core of Anna Reuther's feeling for her family. She, who had always been so courageous and strong in the face of adversity, possessed by a deep faith in God and the union ideals of two generations of Reuthers, suddenly found this too great a test of her courage. Sitting at his bedside one day, she begged him to give up the life of a union leader. "Go into some other work," she said. "You could write books now, or go back to your trade. You would make just as much money. . . ."

Walter, in his drowsy state of sedation, opened one eye in surprise. "I'd make *more* money," he managed to tell her weakly.

"Then do it," she urged him.

He was silent for several minutes, then slowly shook his head. "No," he finally murmured. "I'm all tied up in this thing, all involved. I must do it. . . ." His voice wavered, as if he were trying to get across to her what was going through his mind. Anna caught a familiar phrase, one that Val Reuther had impressed on all his sons, "the brotherhood of man," just before Walter drifted back into semiconsciousness.

May, who had come to take her turn and was sitting at the other side of Walter's bed, pleaded for him. "Don't you see, he must do it," she said. "Surely you can understand." And Anna realized that she had understood all along: her Reuther brood did not give up. At night Victor and Roy came; Vic just took his brother's unharmed left hand and held it reassuringly. After a few days, when it was certain that Walter was not going to die, his mother told him frankly, "I feel worried about you, but I want you to know that, whatever happens to you, I want you to do what you think is right . . . even if you lose your life."

He smiled at her gratefully, and he never forgot this brave statement, so much more like her. "Mother was a tower of strength," he said afterward. And he needed that kind of support. Surgeons had pieced together the splintered bones in his arm, but they were not sure if the limb could be saved or, if it was, whether he would ever be able to use it again. The constant pain continued, and when they gave him the shock treatments to keep the tissues and nerves from decaying, it was agony.

The shooting had created a national sensation, and crowds of curious sightseers kept coming to the corner house on Appoline Street. Popcorn vendors set up stands on the sidewalk, while guards surrounded the house, and the UAW leaders, Conway in charge, set about taking security steps to protect the president and his family permanently. Walter at first was in too grave a danger to be told about all this, and he learned of it only when Linda was visiting him in the hospital one day. "Daddy," she asked, "why can't they leave us alone? Why can't I be like other kids?" Her question came as a shock to him, bringing the realization that, as he said much later, . . . "the greatest price that you pay for fighting for the things you believe in is that, in the process of acquiring a certain public prominence, you lose what I think is the most precious thing, and that's a sense of privacy."

Rewards totaling $117,800—the largest offered up to that date in a criminal case—brought in scores of tips supposed to be information leading to the arrest of the gunman; scores of witnesses were questioned, but they all led to a dead end. The assassin was still at large. The union took precautions against further attacks by providing Walter with bodyguards from the time he came out of the hospital and, to his distaste, a heavily armored, bulletproof twelve-thousand-dollar Packard sedan, which he used under protest. Bodyguards took Linda to and from school. Others were stationed around Victor's and Roy's homes.

Walter was not in condition to leave the hospital until the middle of May, and even then he was a long way from recovery. Aside from the pain and tedious knitting of his shoulder bones, the blood transfusions caused intermittent attacks of hepatitis and malaria. Most disturbing of all was the seemingly irreplaceable loss of response in the radial nerve controling his right hand. Dr. Barnes Woodhall, a neurological surgeon called in for consultation, told Reuther he had to decide on the position in which he preferred to have the hand permanently fixed. Without hesitation Walter replied that no decision was necessary: he had already made up his mind to regain the use of his hand; immobilization was out of the question. The doctor did not press it, but his comment was, "I admire your spirit, but your medical judgment is very bad."

Yet, in spite of physical trials, as soon as he came out of the semiconscious state, and while still in the hospital, he was preoccupied with union problems and imminent negotiations. The hundreds of telegrams, letters, and basketfuls of flowers that overflowed his room, most of them from locals and individual members, were a constant reminder that millions of people—they were "people" to him first, then workers—were relying on him and the other UAW officers to win a wage increase to compensate for the high prices that kept soaring even after the war. The shooting had come at a critical hour, no doubt by calculation. There had been strikes, some broken, some unresolved in court battles; some unions seemed uncertain about taking action. At the time Walter was gunned down, he was preparing to move against the Big Three in the auto industry.

With Reuther laid up, Emil Mazey took over as acting president. Mazey, vigorous and forceful on the picket line if not as colorful a speaker as Reuther, led the UAW in a strike against Chrysler on May 12, 1948. At the same time, according to plan, the UAW threatened to strike General Motors; and GM, seeing that the Chrysler picket lines were effective and not wishing to lose out on postwar sales, gave in. The terms included a wage increase of six cents an hour and the all-important escalator clause, which provided workers with automatic increases if the cost of living continued to rise. The provision, which was Charles E. Wilson's contribution to the settlement, was highly controversial then, though it later became a fixture in union contracts. Reuther, keeping his finger on the pulse of the negotiations during his convalescence, advising on various measures, had laid the groundwork for a cost-of-living adjustment in the 1946 strike, and held some reservations about this version of it; but since the clause included a "floor" and a "ceiling" on rates of rise and descent, he gave his consent. His initial response was, "The principle is right, but the arithmetic is wrong." He meant that the amounts must be raised.

He left the hospital near the end of May, his arm and hand in a half-cast with a steel brace at the wrist, and a fine steel wire running from the wristband to his middle finger. The middle finger caused him the most trouble, and was always slightly drawn inward. Later he carried his arm in a sling, but for months he wore the plaster-and-steel brace. By the time negotiations with Ford began, just three months after the shooting, he showed up alongside UAW Ford Department director Kenneth Bannon at the bargaining table. Except for the orthopedic apparatus on his right arm, one would never have known about his recent brush with death.

The Reuthers spent most of the summer at the Appoline Street home, but it was dangerous to stay there, and the place was still the object of curiosity seekers, a constant annoyance. When friends or some member of their families came from out of town, Walter and May didn't mind telling the story and showing the buckshot holes in the pellet-ridden cupboard, but now they wanted to move away from there. In the fall they found a two-story house on Longfellow Street, closer to UAW headquarters, and in the middle of the block. The union had bulletproof glass put in the ground-floor windows, erected a fence around the backyard, set up floodlights, and purchased two watchdogs to guard the premises.

Walter took part in an advisory capacity in the election campaigns he considered more important that year than the presidential contest, those for governor—G. Mennen Williams in Michigan and Adlai Stevenson in Illinois—and various liberals running for senator. But on election day itself, he was in the Medical Center at Duke University in Durham, where Dr. Woodhall spent five hours trying to piece together the shreds of the right radial nerve. At the end of the long operation, his verdict was that Reuther had one chance in a million of regaining the use of his hand. His redheaded patient was accustomed to taking long chances, and said so. The doctor could not help marveling at Reuther's endurance and resiliency. He had been under anesthesia when election returns began coming in, but early the next morning Jack Conway came over from Durham, where he had arranged to get the results from a local radio station, and found his boss sitting up in bed eating a light breakfast. "How did the election go?" he asked almost before Conway got into the room.

Reuther had taken a dim view of Truman's chances against Dewey, even with the famous last-minute "whistle-stop" campaign increasing the President's popularity, so Conway started with the victories (from labor's viewpoint) in the House; then he went on to the triumphs of Paul Douglas, Kefauver, Humphrey, and others in the Senate.

"God, that's great!" Walter beamed. "What about the governors?"

Conway told him of the stunning successes of Mennen Williams in Michigan and Stevenson in Illinois, adding almost casually, "Incidentally, Truman got elected, too."

Without batting an eyelash, Walter's reaction was: "That just goes to show you what happens when you take the issues to the people!"

He was still gloating when Dr. Woodhall came in to check on his condition. The neurosurgeon recommended whirlpool-bath treatments to stimulate circulation in the arm and relax the muscles. So as soon as Reuther returned to Detroit, he began making visits to the hospital's rehabilitation clinic twice a day. At first the treatments didn't seem to make much difference, but with typical patient persistence he kept on, determined not to have a withered hand or be forced to substitute a steel claw. And one day, about eighteen months after the surgery, while he was sitting beside the cylindrical tub with his arm immersed up to the shoulder in the churning, whirling water, he found he could move his right thumb about a sixteenth of an inch! His triumphant yell brought the attendant running.

"I knew I'd made it, right then," he said afterward. The next prescription was to exercise and stretch the fingers of his injured hand; and, like many patients trying to overcome a similar condition, he held a rubber ball or a square of foam rubber in his right hand, squeezing it for hours at a time, as he read at home or went over papers in the privacy of his office. In many respects, his recovery resembled Roosevelt's conquest of polio: the amazing tolerance for pain, the determination and experimentation of various methods to overcome the handicap, and keeping up with the mental demands of a challenging career while concentrating on physical therapy. Hoping to speed his cure as he gained freer movement, Reuther took up an early interest of his, woodworking, to develop his muscles further. But by the spring of 1949—

before he had discovered he could move his thumb—he was well enough to resume a major portion of union activity.

Then, on May 22, only thirteen months after the shooting, the enemies of the Reuther brothers struck a second time. That evening, Victor was in the living room of his home, reading *The New York Times Magazine*, while Sophie, across from him, was busy mending. It was especially quiet that night, because they had just given away their little cocker spaniel, who recently had been barking urgently for some unknown reason; and two anonymous complaints had brought visits from the police, warning the Reuthers that the barking was disturbing the peace, and they had better get rid of the dog. It seems odd that they would comply without further investigation; but evidently they had relaxed in regard to the possibility of another attack and were totally unprepared. When the bulb in the lamp by Sophie's chair went out, Victor got up, fetched another bulb, and started screwing it into the socket. As the new light came on—"illuminating the target," Victor later remarked with irony—a shotgun blast roared through the window, catching him in the face, throat, and right shoulder!

For a stunned second, he thought the light bulb must have exploded; then, as his mangled glasses and a dental bridge flew across the floor, he fell forward blindly into physical blackout. Sophie had the presence of mind to call the operator and shout for police, and then ran from the house, screaming, "Vic's been shot, oh my God, Vic's been shot!" As in Walter's case, neighbors who had rushed out of their houses reported seeing a man leap across the lawn and into a maroon car, which tore away down the street. But this time the assassin left more of a clue: the shotgun itself—a 12-gauge, perhaps the same one that had gunned down Walter—and two empty shells were lying in the shrubbery under the window.

Walter and May were at the hospital soon after they received word. At first unbelieving, the labor leader realized the terrible news was only too true when he saw Victor's dire condition. Two tiny leads had lodged in his brother's throat, one in his mouth; another had blown to bits his right eye, which had to be removed immediately. Who knew whether he would pull through? Taking his hand, Walter tried to reach him. "Remember, Vic, you held my hand a year ago," he said. "Now I'm holding yours. Keep fighting, Vic, keep fighting." Victor, bandaged, could not open his remaining eye, and his damaged throat would hardly let him speak, but he managed to murmur, "Look after the kids and Sophie. . . ." For several days it was touch and go, but Victor lived. The attack confirmed Walter's theory that, as he said in a formal statement to the press, "the same people who paid to have me shot paid to have my brother shot, and for the same reason. They could be diehard elements among employers, or they could be Communist or fascist agents." By "fascist" he was probably implying the Mafia, as he had been suspecting certain underworld elements in and out of the UAW.

For the second time, Anna Reuther rushed up from Wheeling; and, as soon as Victor was out of danger, the Reuthers held a family council at Walter and May's new house on Longfellow Street. They could not help fearing that Roy would be the next target, and talked about ways to prevent a third assault. But now their mother did not suggest that they leave the labor movement. "I've been thinking about this," she said to the circle around her, "and, you know, mothers in the whole history of the world have had to wrestle with this problem of losing their sons. Too many mothers have lost their sons in wars. I haven't lost any of my sons in wars. But you boys have made a decision—made a decision to give your time and your energy to the labor movement. That's what you believe in, and if you believe in it, as I know you do, you must be prepared to give your life for it."

Her spirit gave new strength to her sons, particularly Walter. "I came out of that meeting feeling like I could lift a mountain with one hand," he said buoyantly. Victor's response, when he heard of the family powwow, was one of valiant humor. "It's a good thing they didn't shoot out my tongue," he joked; "I couldn't make a living." Even Anna laughed.

Before the year ended, one more attempt was made to wipe out Reuther power. On a drizzly December 20, the Detroit *Times* received an anonymous phone call informing a reporter that dynamite had been planted in the building of the UAW headquarters (then on the corner of Milwaukee and Cass Avenues), "when the big guy was in the office," the voice said. Police were notified and made a thorough search of the building, but found nothing. Toward midnight, however, a watchman discovered a soggy red-and-green "Christmas package," tied with sleazy red ribbon, outside an unfrequented basement entrance. Under the flossy paper was a rain-soaked cardboard carton containing thirty-nine sticks of dynamite, enough to blow up the whole place if the crudely taped bomb had been more skillfully made and the rain hadn't doused the fuses. After this third narrow escape, the union added another $25,000 to the reward fund, now nearly $250,000; and the Reuthers, reluctant though they were to lead guarded lives, became convinced of the need for security measures.

It became more obvious than ever that thugs and underworld characters were gunning for them, or had been hired to do the job by diehard employers or sorehead Communists; perhaps there was a conspiracy of all three forces, though there was more evidence of alliance between the first two. It all tied in somehow— a leftover from the days of Harry Bennett's connections with hardened criminals. One company still harboring resentment toward the union was Briggs Manufacturing Company, the "sweatshop" of Walter's first working days in Detroit. Shortly before and right after Reuther and Emil Mazey took over as the top UAW officers, there had been a series of brutal beatings of Briggs union members who were followers of Mazey, president of the local, and strong Reuther supporters. Melvin Bishop, who was director of that region, who had his own Communist-led faction, had run for the post of secretary-treasurer at the 1946 convention. When he lost to Emil, these beatings were intensified; and one day Jack Conway discovered in Melvin Bishop's office the private phone number of one Santo, "Sam," Perrone, a Sicilian-born naturalized citizen, whose record of rumrunning, illegal importation of aliens, and "efficient" strikebreaking pointed to close ties with the Mafia. He and his brother had successfully broken a strike at the Detroit-Michigan Stove Works (where they had been coremakers), and immediately prospered. Sam was given a contract to haul scrap from the factory; he paid nothing for it, but made a huge profit in selling it.

There was a connection between the Briggs Manufacturing Co.

and the Stove Works: Dean Robinson, son-in-law of founder Walter O. Briggs, who became president of the company in 1945, and John A. Fry, president of the Stove Works, were old friends. In that same year, just before the brutal beatings began, the scrap-haulage contract of Briggs was awarded to Sam Perrone's son-in-law, twenty-eight-year-old Carl Renda, a graduate of Adrian College, who had no capital, no trucks, and no experience. He subcontracted the actual work to the firm that had always done it, but he still made a handsome profit, as high as a hundred thousand dollars in 1947. There had been a Wayne County grand jury investigation, plus a hearing by the Senate Crime Investigating Committee of these shady contract awards in an effort to find the thugs guilty of beating UAW members, but it had come to nothing. The same police inspector, Albert DeLamielleure, was the supervisor of investigations of the Reuther brothers shootings, but he was not very effective. (Melvin Bishop, whom Reuther had dismissed from the UAW staff in the 1947 purge, claimed he didn't know Perrone, although they had been arrested for deer-hunting without a license, and a 16-gauge shotgun was found in Bishop's possession. Bitter over his dismissal, he had joined the staff of the teamsters' union as organizer.)

Now, after the dynamite scare, the UAW officers, meeting at the Reuthers', tried to figure the answer to the puzzle. "It's all tied together somehow," Walter insisted. The others agreed with him, but how were they to prove it? The UAW finally hired Colonel Heber Blankenhorn, a nationally know figure who had been chief investigator for the LaFollette Civil Liberties hearings and had uncovered much of the scandal concerning the terrorism practiced by industry against union organizers. DeLamielleure sent him and Ralph Winstead, also hired by the UAW, searching with false clues for certain Communists in Europe and Mexico. It is strange that an expert like Blankenhorn would not have known this was a wild-goose chase, but at that time UAW officers had no proof that the police inspector was connected with the conspiracy.

In any case, the criminals were still at large. Walter and May decided to look for a place in the country where they could be sure of privacy. The summer before, they had tried to rent a cottage at a nearby lake, but resort landlords were afraid to risk possible gunfire on their property. The Reuthers located a four-acre tract of land on Paint Creek, a meandering stream about thirty-five miles northwest of Detroit. It had been owned by a landscape architect, who had put in some very good plantings and built a one-room redwood-and-glass cabin. But the shrubbery was shaggy and weedy, storms had turned young trees into deadwood, and the cabin was run down and neglected. The spot was idyllic, however, and the Reuthers bought it to provide a summertime and weekend retreat. When winter came, they were loath to return to the house on Longfellow Street, and Walter had already begun to consider making the cabin into a permanent home, with his own hands.

Late that fall (1949), the Detroit *News*, which had offered a "Secret Witness" plan to ferret out informants, received a letter containing the cryptic message, "Would you please Make Quiet Investigation of Clarence Jacobs Regarding the Walter Reuther Shooting." Another message, two days later, suggested that the inquiry should be made at a gas station on the corner of East Jefferson and Canton Street, right across from the Stove Works, since Jacobs and the owner of the station were "closely allied." The *News* turned both notes over to DeLamielleure, who very soon divulged that Perrone was the owner of the said station. At the same time, the U.S. Immigration office suddenly investigated the Stove Works, raiding the plant on January 9, 1950; they had been tipped off that sixty smuggled aliens were working there, and arrested about a third of that number as known illegal workers, all Sicilians. "The thread of suspicion of a smuggling ring has kept us busy," said the bureau chief. "We have no proof, but we made our biggest haul at the Stove Works."

Whether Clarence Jacobs could not be found or successfully evaded trial was not clear, but the mystery of the Reuther shootings remained unraveled for the time being. Early in the spring, Walter began to work on the cabin in the country. Painful as the hammering and sawing was, he realized soon after he began woodworking that this would strengthen his weakened arm and hand. The basic structure of the place was sound, so he left the beams and the shell, but slowly, room by room, he expanded and winterized it. He would saw and hammer till the pain became unbearable and he could not hold back the tears; then he would plunge his rigid hand in a bucket of hot water, wiggle his fingers for several minutes, and take up his tools again. Little by little, he was to get "a good house and a good hand—all for the same price," he declared, with typical Reuther satisfaction in a good bargain. At the end of the summer, he was well on the way; but not much progress had been made in solving the case.

The Senate Crime Investigating Committee under Estes Kefauver was called in and began hearings in Detroit on February 8, 1951. Governor Mennen Williams, who was the second witness, testified that the case of the Reuther shootings showed "ample reason to suspect that these crimes had their origin in a wide conspiracy"; and he appealed for a ruling that would allow a governor to seek assistance from the FBI "in the solution of crimes which appear to him to be beyond the scope of any single city or state police agency." The committee retraced much of the ground that had already been covered, but did little to establish any collusion between the company presidents and Perrone or between Perrone and Melvin Bishop. Asked to testify regarding his affluence, the Sicilian gangster (nicknamed "The Shark") apparently squirmed out of revealing the source. One benefit to the union from his trial and the unfavorable publicity of smuggling workers was that the UAW organizers were able to move in, mounting a drive at the Stove Works in June, 1951; and by fall they had won an NLRB election, after which a two-year contract was negotiated. In addition, Perrone was forced to relinquish his scrap-haulage contract with Fry.

That summer a report received by secret police revealed that the plans for the Reuther shootings had been hatched in a bar just two doors away from Santo Perrone's Esso station. Investigations showed that the "hidden owner" of the bar was none other than DeLamielleure! Although this explained why he had been in no hurry to solve the case, and he was put on trial, demoted, and ordered to sell the bar, those who did the shooting were still not to be found.

In the summer of 1952, Walter's hand-built house was sufficiently complete to become the family's permanent home. The property provided a continuing interest for him, an outlet for his creative ability, which, till now, had been sublimated by his tremendous organizational and leadership qualities. For present security measures, the UAW built a steel fence ten feet high around the acreage, fixed up a farmhouse near the road as barracks for the guards, and doubled the number of watch dogs: two for the house, whose picture windows and sliding doors were of bulletproof glass, and two prowling the pine woods and the edge of the grounds near the steel fence. Eventually Walter altered the course of the thirty-foot-wide trout stream so that it made three sharp turns, over which he constructed three small bridges, so that quick water surrounded the house. "I'm the only union leader who lives behind a moat," he used to joke. He might have added that his "moat" was a symbolic heritage from the Knights of Labor.

Just as the statute of limitations on the Walter Reuther shooting was about to expire, one of the union's privately hired detectives, Sam Henderson, received a tip in the summer of 1953, fully five years after the crime, that seemed to be "hot" at the time, and probably came closest to the correct trail leading to the criminal. Henderson learned that Clarence Jacobs, named in the "Secret Witness" notes, had fled to Canada in 1948; but his nephew, Donald Ritchie, an accomplice, at present a Canadian convict housed in a Windsor jail, was "in the know" about the whole plot. When contacted, Ritchie said he would inform, but demanded $25,000 for his common-law wife, plus $5,000 in $100 Canadian bills initial payment to her as soon as he had told his story. He claimed this provision was requested in case anything happened to him in reprisal for turning informer. The UAW agreed, with the consent of the Wayne County prosecutor. Emil Mazey marked the check "for the purchase of property in Canada," because he felt the underworld had contacts in his union; and the only way to protect Ritchie's life and solve the crime at long last was to make certain nobody outside of a few had any knowledge as to what the transaction was.

Ritchie in a signed statement before the county prosecutor confessed that he had been working for Santo Perrone for several years doing "odd jobs," at which he made $400 or $500 a week.

He was in the car the night Walter Reuther was shot. Clarence Jacobs, who approached him for this particular job, told him he would get five grand. The agreement took place in Perrone's gas station. Jacobs drove a red Mercury car that night, with Ritchie and one Peter Lombardo as passengers. Ritchie was to drive the car away in case there was trouble. Jacobs did the shooting; it was a long time till they heard the report of the gun, but when he came back, he said, "Well, I knocked the bastard down," and off they drove. They dropped Ritchie off at the bar near the gas station, and Carl Renda gave him a bundle of cash, amounting to "exactly five grand." (Renda was always the payoff man, Ritchie said.) The prosecutor confidently announced the "solution" of the Walter Reuther shooting, and issued warrants for the arrests of Santo Perrone, Carl Renda, Peter Lombardo, and Clarence Jacobs. Ritchie was held as a material witness under police guard, and he somehow convinced the court that he would be safer in a hotel than in the county jail, where the gangsters would expect him to be. At any rate, he was housed in a three-room suite in the Statler Hotel, with two guards. Here he pulled a bizarre stunt worthy of a James Bond story.

The three had been playing pinochle to pass the time, when Ritchie announced he was going to take a shower. His custodians nodded, and he went into the bath between the adjoining rooms. They heard the water come on a moment later, and so continued their game. The water kept running for nearly an hour before it dawned on the guards that their charge was taking quite a long shower. Investigating, they found an empty bathroom: Ritchie had simply turned on the spigots full speed and walked right through the door to the other room, out through another door to the hallway, and never stopped going till he was back in Canada. From there he telephoned the police reporter of the Detroit *Free Press*, said he was over the border, that his account of the Reuther shooting was all a lie, and that he would legally resist extradition. Authorities soon learned that a man of Ritchie's description had deposited $3,500 in a Chatham, Ontario, bank, and bought a 1952 Dodge sedan for $1400 cash. Over a year later, Ritchie revealed his identity to a reporter in a Hamilton, Ontario, bar, bragging and laughing about the way he had "conned" the union into giving him $25,000. An attempt to have him extradited to Detroit failed, and the case folded. The two guards who let him get away were docked a month's pay for neglect of duty.

As if this were not frustrating enough, Carl Renda had the colossal nerve to sue the UAW for $5,200,000 for "malicious prosecution." It was an obvious ploy to put a clean face on the whole operation; and at first the court awarded him $400,000. But the union appealed, and the suit dragged on. In December, 1957, at the crucial moment in the second court battle, Ralph Winstead, who had been working on the case since he and Blankenhorn had been hired eight years before, and who had uncovered important evidence, disappeared just before he was to testify. His body, clothed for ice-fishing, was found frozen in Lake St. Clair a few days later. The coroner's unquestioned verdict was "accidental death." Renda continued his claim, and in 1963, fully fifteen years after the shooting with intent to kill occurred, the UAW in an out-of-court settlement agreed to grant him $12,500. The statute of limitations ran out on April 20, 1968, exactly twenty years after the attempted assassination, and even if the assailants had been found, they couldn't have been prosecuted.

Walter Reuther wisely decided almost from the start not to try to be a Sherlock Holmes, as he said. True, in his private speculations, he felt quite sure that there was a triple alliance among disparate forces sharing the same common denominator: to get rid of him for their own various purposes in regard to the UAW before he completed the task of cleaning it up or became any more powerful. But if he turned detective, he would "get emotionally involved" and spend all his time on *that* instead of the things he felt came first, helping to achieve the good life for people working in mass production—those for whom he could and did speak out loud and clear.

XXII

Pioneer Boss
of the Bargaining Table

PERHAPS the most important step toward achieving his goal of the good life for everyone was to provide for union members who were "too old to work and too young to die," as Walter Reuther said in an inspired moment. With his right arm still in a sling, he was speaking at a mass meeting held in the fall of 1949 at Cass Technical High School to a cheering audience of some seven thousand Ford workers age sixty years or older.

All during his convalescence he had been preparing to move toward a towering gain for organized labor and, as it turned out, for all holders of Social Security cards—and that was a plan for company-financed pensions. Until then, corporations contended that any form of retirement pay was up to management and not subject to collective bargaining. Reuther contended that retirement pay should be no different from hourly-wage pay when it came to contracts, and therefore should be included in the terms. He had tackled the Ford Motor Company before the others in the Big Three because, for one reason, Henry Ford II, president of the company since his grandfather died in April of 1947, had shown both imagination and a willingness to cooperate with the union, perhaps to compensate for the long, bitter battle against unions the originator of the assembly line had waged. In fact, the company had even offered its employees a pension plan during negotiations that same year (1947), but it was turned down in favor of an across-the-board wage increase. Reuther was opposed to the terms of the company's pension proposal, but the very fact that they had offered to bargain about pensions made Ford the logical company in which to initiate new contract clauses dealing with social welfare.

Now, with the cheers and applause of UAW old-timers spurring him on, he made the irrevocable leap and pledged that he would refuse to sign a new contract unless it had a pension clause. He knew he was putting himself out on a limb and couldn't go back—as he admitted to a reporter, "I'm hanging on the last leaf on the last twig!"—but that was all the more reason to cling to his position. This was an old dream of his; he had seen too many retired workers who had to rely on Social Security payments averaging no more than $32 a *month*, struggling to get by on less than half the amount they might have earned in a *week*: unless they had purchased their own pension—and few did—it was impossible to survive on Social Security payments, which had not been raised since their inception, although the cost of living had tripled since then! But each time Congress had been on the verge of increasing the rates, big business had lobbied against the measure, and Congress had bowed to their dictates.

Walter, who had an uncanny sense of timing, felt that the hour had come for action that might have far-reaching results beyond the UAW-Ford negotiations—measures to improve the social welfare of the nation in general. In this frame of mind he returned from the rally to the bargaining table. And in October, 1949, under the threat of a strike, Ford agreed to pay the full cost of pensions covering all its workers, and for this purpose to put $20 million into a special fund. The plan was to provide every Ford retiree (one who had worked thirty years there) with an income of $100 a month, including Social Security, at age sixty-five. At first Reuther asked for $100 a month *on top of* Social Security payments, but that figure Ford would not "buy," and Reuther was flexible enough to realize that even with national welfare payments included, the $100 a month would more than triple previous retirement benefits. Douglas Fraser, now a UAW vice-president, who had worked closely with him for several years, commented, "I thought I was flexible, but Walter taught me real flexibility—adjustability."

The provision that made the agreement the first real breakthrough on pensions was Reuther's unprecedented demand that they be financed entirely by the corporation, which was required to put aside sufficient funds each year to guarantee the payment of pensions to those who had earned them. In a phrase that had to be explained even to the negotiating committee at the start, he wanted the plan to be "actuarially sound." Otherwise, UAW retirees would run the risk of having their pensions reduced if revenues from a "pay-as-workers-retire plan" (such as the United Mine Workers had just signed) were not sufficient to maintain the $100 figure. He proved to be 100 percent correct when, only ten years later, such a fate befell the UMW pension.

He stuck by his principle when the Chrysler Corporation, next to be tackled by the union, offered to match the $100-a-month figure that Ford had agreed to, but refused to stand the entire cost of the plan, objecting to the actuarial basis, which meant that the fund couldn't be used for anything else, no matter what happened to the company. Reuther's retort to Chrysler's rejection of his essential idea was a called strike that lasted 104 days. Before it was over, every rank-and-file member knew the meaning of "actuarially sound" funding, and questioned anything less, even when Chrysler offered to put $30 million into the bank as a guarantee and Walter explained that this was a step in the right direction, to be accepted.* When Chrysler finally capitulated, General Motors agreed without resistance, and subsequently raised the amount; at that, Ford and Chrysler increased their pensions. Reuther early realized that when one of the Big Three agrees to a certain formula, the others follow suit. In the years since the 1950 breakthrough, his funding principle has proved increasingly correct: most major pension plans have a similar provision to protect retired workers; and Congress has moved toward federal laws making it mandatory.

Walter himself was so positive he was right that he presented

---

* One of the secondary leaders he was talking to called out, "Yeah, but is it *actuarially sound,* Walter?" Even if he was joking, it showed that the principle involved was well understood.

his ideas to Congress soon after Ford had signed, his motive being to raise Social Security. In his own words, as he told the story in 1963 during an interview with a British newspaper woman: "In forty-eight hours in Washington we did what could not be done by Congress in twelve years. We took our collective-bargaining-process leverage to increase Social Security from thirty-two dollars to a hundred dollars a month for everyone." He laughed. "They say the pocketbook nerve is the most sensitive nerve. Congress hadn't been able to raise payments in all those years, but the industrialists suddenly gave the nod to regular increases. They prefer to do it in Washington rather than individually because in Washington they only have to pay half." He chuckled again.

Universal contract-negotiation history was also made in 1950, as preparations began for a new contract with GM. The 1948 agreement had worked out well for both labor and management, and the union planned to ask for a hundred twenty-five dollars monthly pension as well as wage increases. A series of private meetings took place between GM executives and UAW negotiators before Walter entered the scene, although he kept in close touch with his representatives and advised them on the next move even as he approved the initial tentative steps. General Motors agreed to the pension program; and, in an unprecedented move, proposed signing a five-year contract, including the cost-of-living clause and annual-improvement factor initiated in 1948. They also granted a union shop at GM, in which the employer hires the labor force, but after a probationary period of about ninety days, it is a condition of employment that the employee become a member of the union. (Ford had agreed to the union shop in 1941, but it was not until 1950 that GM and Chrysler came around.) The company made the historic proposal on May 15, 1950, which was Walter's cue to make his appearance at the bargaining table. A week later, he signed the contract for the UAW; there had been no talk of a strike. Then, when Ford and Chrysler reopened, they met the same demand for improvements.

If he had any doubts about signing a long-term contract, Reuther must have felt they were outweighed by this indication "that the whole relationship between the UAW and the automotive industry had been put on a new and permanent and more responsible basis. The industry at that point had made a decision that the UAW is here to stay." This was the kind of recognition he had sought ever since he entered the labor movement; further, the five-year contract deepened the confidence of the UAW membership in their president, added to his reputation in the labor movement, and won him the respect of the country in general as a labor leader with imagination, who could win far-reaching benefits without a battle.

The five-year contract, however, could not last its term because the Korean War, which started just two months after it was signed—in July, 1950, with the invasion of South Korea by North Korea—brought the usual inflation of wartime, and the workers were not protected against the increased cost of living. So in 1953, Walter asked the corporations to reopen negotiations. He held that a wage contract was a "living document" and must be adjustable; all UAW contracts say that workers have a right to strike during the life of a contract on matters of a speedup on work, and health and accident hazards. War inflation, while outside those categories, was in a sense a speedup and could be hazardous. He asked that the "annual improvement factor" be raised from four to five cents an hour for each year of the agreement, with higher rates for skilled workers, and larger pensions. The Big Three balked at reopening, so what happened was that key plants began to have strikes on production standards or local grievances that ordinarily might have been settled by Reuther's top assistants, but he made no move to dispatch them to trouble spots. The companies were forced to reopen, and the workers received wage and pension increases.

Reuther was criticized in some quarters for his "living document" theory, notably by David McDonald, who had become president of the steelworkers in 1952. And although "the redhead" sturdily defended his action by arguing that to deny a union the right to reopen a contract is "to say that labor is a commodity" instead of a community of human beings, whose needs command a moral obligation to alter the "relationship" set by the contract, he saw clearly now that the five-year contract was a mistake. Conditions could easily change in that length of time, and the union would have to go through the same sort of hassle they did to reopen in 1953. So new contract negotiations began again in 1955, after a two-year interval as formerly. However, it was not as feasible as Walter expected, because the expiration date occurred during an interval of retooling. The summer is not a good time to strike, because of the lull in production caused by retooling. Somehow, the union would have to find a way to ensure negotiations in the fall, when new models were about to be marketed.

The attitude among UAW negotiators was, "Leave it to Walter to find a way," and he did. When one considers that most of these years, from April, 1948, till 1953, at least, he was undergoing physical therapy for his arm and hand; building his house as part of that cure; dealing with national and international affairs in the labor movement; and was active in politics, Reuther's achievements are almost incredible. In 1955, a landmark for UAW gains, the union won what was sought, including the "check-off" of dues—by which the company withholds the workers' union dues from paychecks—with a three-year contract; but it still expired around June 1. In 1958, there was a tremendous inventory, and it appeared that the layoff period would be longer than usual. Management was extremely resistant because of a recession that year. The current contract could be extended on a day-to-day basis (usually either side can terminate on twenty-four hours' notice). In 1958, as the terminal date approached and no headway was made, it became apparent that the corporations were not going to extend by the terminal date: If negotiations were not settled, they would terminate no matter what. They figured the union would have to strike, or *accept a renewal*. GM was the most obstinate of the Big Three; they expected the UAW would undoubtedly strike. But Walter proposed a ninety-day extension, up to September, to which GM said, "No—either a three-year renewal or terminate." They assumed the union would be lost without the automatic check-off of dues. However, after a meeting of the Executive Board, the UAW retorted that they would "rock and roll all summer," in Leonard Woodcock's words; and they would collect the dues. They set up the administrative machinery for it, and the remittance was 98 or 99 percent, as large as that received under the check-off system. Walter said afterward that it was sheer nonsense to say, "No contract, no work," a favorite phrase in the labor movement, in his view "an asinine, unrealistic slogan." The union knew it would be a poor time to strike, and so did the company. Negotiations continued slowly, but in September Walter said, "O.K., now let's get down to business or strike."

A brief strike at General Motors lasted only a week. The union won substantial gains,* and the company's obstinate stand against extension boomeranged against them, because when settlement came, the contract was drawn up to terminate three years from *that* date—September—the one the union wanted originally. Such was Walter Reuther's strategy. As a result, the Big Three contracts all terminate in September since that time.

The 1955 contract negotiations, as previously mentioned, were of signal importance as the beginning of the guaranteed annual wage, or the initiation of it. This was another dream that the visionary in Walter Reuther had conceived in his earliest days in Detroit, when the fear of long layoffs during the retooling period, plus the deeper fear of not being rehired when the assembly line began to move again, was a dread condition of employment for every worker in the auto industry. At that time, the guaranteed annual wage was only a vague dream, as Walter said; but even before he was elected president of the UAW he had begun to plan for it, and with the 1950 agreement, he felt the union had enough strength and resources to begin the task of preparing for the contract provision that unquestionably provoked the monumental contest of his entire bargaining career.

Nat Weinberg, who had become one of the UAW's brain trusters working on the strategy for the extended campaign, wrote, "By 1951, the UAW was at last ready to begin its all-out drive for the guaranteed wage." That was the year the union completed its new home (months before Walter's private home

---

* One of these was an increase in pension pay. The company argued that they had given enough raises; but Walter, as in 1949, speaking at a retired workers' picnic, promised them the UAW would not sign without a raise for retirees. Fraser, who had left negotiations to go to Belle Isle to hear Walter speak, went back to the bargaining table and told the company that the issue was already out of the debate stage.

was ready for permanent occupancy). Called Solidarity House, the impressive structure represented yet another early dream of his, from the time in 1935, when the handful of UAW members could not afford to rent a ten-dollar room as their first head-quarters. The site for Solidarity House was purchased, by coincidence or deliberateness, from the family of Edsel Ford, the ill-fated son of the elder Henry Ford, who died before his father; his gray stone mansion, at 8000 East Jefferson Avenue, on the Detroit River, was symbolically still standing, facing the street in front of Solidarity House at the dedication, on June 9, 1951, and remained there for some years before it was demolished so the grounds could be landscaped. The new headquarters was designed by Oskar Stonorov, a Quaker friend of the Reuthers from the Brookwood College period, who had become an architect and talented sculptor. The building he planned and supervised for the union was modernistic and functional, providing abundant office space for the administrative, promotion, and research departments—the latter headed by Weinberg and his staff of experts.

As a preliminary to their campaign for the guaranteed annual wage, Nat and the UAW study committee Reuther had created combed through volumes of American and European statistical material on job security, state laws on unemployment insurance, social welfare studies, and so forth. They mounted a psychological program of speeches, articles, and radio-TV appearances, and staged debates before a wide variety of audiences in and outside the labor movement.

Walter himself wrote a number of articles. One of them, in the *Annals* of the American Academy of Political and Social Sciences, contained the heart of his approach toward the guaranteed annual wage: "It is more than a matter of economic justice to the wage earner. It is a matter of economic necessity to our nation," he pointed out, "for freedom and unemployment cannot live together in democracy's house." In the everyday parlance of the factory worker, he added, "Corporation executives get paid by the year—why not a worker?" As in the 1945–1946 GM strike, he set up a public advisory committee of leading economists, including two Harvard professors, to evaluate the union's proposal. The central idea of the UAW's final demand, paralleling the pension plan for retirees, linked the private-enterprise layoff payments with federal unemployment compensation, a controversial idea at the time. Inside the UAW, the guaranteed wage was explained, discussed, and debated at local union meetings, regional and national conferences, summer schools, weekend institutes, and night classes. Inadvertently, rank-and-filers helped to formulate the plan because they raised practical problems that had never been thought of by the economists studying the subject.

The union wanted the Big Three to "get the message" so "they could be aware of our thinking and begin to develop their own thinking," Weinberg said. Ford seemed to take it seriously, calling in outside consultants as well as having their top financial people work on it. They made it clear that they would have a plan in response to the union demand. General Motors, however, was completely negative in their reaction. They appeared to feel that yielding to the union's demand would weaken and destroy the company.

GM's contract that year, 1955, expired on May 29, and Ford's two days later. As finally presented, the UAW asked for a provision to ensure annual wages by company payments to increase unemployment compensation during layoffs to about 70 percent of a worker's regular salary. General Motors came up with a "matching money" plan: the company would put up dollar for dollar for the number of shares a worker could buy. The hitch was that the workers had to leave their money in until the stock matured to get the full benefit. They could withdraw sums if emergencies came up, and they needed money, but only the dollars *they* had put in—not the company's "matching" dollars. Further, the stockholding terminated if withdrawals were made! Workers would have to leave all their money in till it matured in order to realize the total benefit from their investment. The company claimed that this largesse would cost them more than the union's plan for a guaranteed annual wage. The UAW saw through the phony profit sharing, but Walter said they would think it over. In concrete terms he expressed his reaction: "Hell, that's for the provident! I'm interested in the folks who can't take care of themselves. That plan's a wheel-of-fortune deal!"

Reuther cannily extended the GM contract a week, so that Ford's would expire first, since top negotiators there had said the company was preparing a counteroffer, and, if it was acceptable, then perhaps GM would follow the pattern. But when he and UAW negotiators met at the Leland Hotel to hear John Bugas, vice-president in charge of personnel and chief spokesman for Ford, read the "counterproposal," they were stunned to find it was the identical plan that GM had presented. After one page of it, Walter recognized the "wheel of fortune" run around. Furious, he called the cards right away, and told John Bugas that Ford's trick was an insult to the integrity of both the union and the company. Among other objections he suggested that "it's very bad policy and it will get you nowhere. You guys have got rocks in your head," he finished.

There were further invectives from both sides; the hotheaded dialog came to be known as "Black Thursday" in union halls. Boldly, Reuther barked at Bugas: "You have just bought yourself a strike." He cleverly cited the decline of Willys-Overland Company through long walkouts, and the fact that strikes had prevented Chrysler from overtaking Ford as the second-largest auto producer. Finally, referring to Ford's apparent adoption of the GM plan, in a masterful turn of the screw, he asked the unanswerable question: "How will you produce Fords on the Chevrolet assembly line?"

Bugas, for the moment confounded, could only respond that Ford had taken a survey which showed that the workers in the plants favored the offer from management by a nine-to-one margin. It was an extravagant claim, but the union made no comment.

In view of the critical situation, Walter had called a meeting of the UAW National Council, and said the delegates would vote on the proposal. The company voiced the fear that their plan might not be fairly presented, so Walter sent a letter to Henry Ford II inviting him to present the plan in person. He of course sent a polite reply, declining the invitation but suggesting that all company workers should have a chance to express their opinions of the offer. Putting this aside until the National Council had voted—as expected, with a unanimous No!—the union considered what it should do next. Some Board members wanted

to strike immediately, but Walter said, "Not yet . . ." He was
mapping his own strategy, which was to approach John Bugas in
a more moderate tone. His opening remark, "Maybe we were a
bit hasty, John," disarmed Bugas at the outset. Then Walter said
he would like to sit down and talk over the company plan privately
with him, going over all the points again.

At an arranged meeting, he asked questions on each point,
taking it step by step, going into the provisions with great intensity—"That's very interesting," he interjected occasionally—
even showing enthusiasm. Bugas responded by warming to his
subject as they progressed, each outdoing the other in politeness
and zeal. (Afterward Walter chortled, "We really led him up
the garden path!") As they neared the end, Walter asked, "You
say a survey showed that the workers were in favor of this plan?"
Bugas thought victory was in the bag, and assured Walter that
the response was "overwhelmingly" in favor. Walter's rejoinder
was a proposition to put it to a vote by the UAW membership
in Ford plants. "If they vote for yours, we'll sign a contract containing your proposal. If they vote for ours, we'll sign a contract
with that. Since you say they want yours by nine to one, you're
not taking any chances." He could see Bugas wince at his words.
The company did not really want a referendum: the spot-check
made in the plants by foremen had been sketchy, to say the least;
and they knew full well the workers would turn thumbs down
on such a plan. Reuther, watching his adversary, said later, "Poor
John! I thought he'd die."

The upshot was that Ford then came forward with a prospectus
for a guaranteed semiannual layoff pay, which, as the union
suspected, they had in hand all along, but they were not going to
present it except as a last resort. The terms of Ford's offer were
not as much as the union had wanted—actually, it was a supple-
mental unemployment benefit, known as SUB—but it was a
toehold. The company agreed to put five cents an hour into a
fund that would be used to provide up to $25 a week to laid-off
workers for up to twenty-six weeks. With unemployment compensation included, the key to the whole concept, it would guarantee that a worker would receive 65 percent of his pay for the

first four weeks of layoff and 60 percent for the other twenty-two weeks. Since that time the amounts have been increased.

After Ford, the SUB settlement was presented to GM, who knew "the ball game had changed," as Louis Seaton, their chief negotiator, said. Reuther, who had emerged from the twenty-six-hour session at Ford looking as fresh and forceful as if he had had a night's sleep and a shower (while Bugas looked as if he had been dragged through a knothole), now plunged into five days of crash bargaining with GM. At the end, the company announced it would agree to Ford's SUB program. Seaton said, "We'll take a Chinese copy, even to the patch on the pants." For once, Walter was puzzled. He had never heard the story of the sea captain who "went to a Chinese tailor and said he wanted an exact duplicate of a pair of pants he was wearing, and got it— including the patch on the pants," the GM executive explained with a wry smile. Shortly after GM signed, Chrysler followed suit.

Although SUB was labeled by critics "rocking chair money," it proved of immense benefit during the 1957–1958 recession. Reuther, who was far from satisfied with the original SUB agreement, kept hammering for improvements in subsequent bargaining; and in the 1967 sessions he won increases which entitled a typical worker to receive 95 percent of his take-home pay for a maximum of fifty-two weeks—minus a $7.50 weekly deduction for the savings in transportation and lunch expenses of the unemployed—a figure he considered "the optimum level" the program could reach.

His energy during these endurance sessions was unflagging, a source of wonder to negotiators older than he on both sides of the bargaining table. When he entered the contest, usually during the final critical stages, carrying his briefcase packed with papers and toothbrush, everyone present knew they were in for a long haul. The toothbrush was not necessarily the sign of an all-night session, but a tool for keeping him awake and alert: During negotiation breaks he would brush his teeth briskly to refresh himself, a trick he had probably learned when he was working nights and going to school during the day and had to study until 3 or 4 A.M. (He would have scorned any stay-awake drugs; in

the hospital he once threw his pills out the window.) Louis
Seaton claimed he used bargaining recesses to take a "caucus
with a couch," but that is doubtful, as Walter was usually too
keyed up to take even a catnap during negotiations. Always on
the alert, he was able to shift gears on a second's notice if the
situation demanded. "He had a great sense of timing," Douglas
Fraser said.

In 1964, the union was facing a strike deadline at 11 A.M., and
it was then 4:00 A.M., the fag end of an all-night session; the
issue at stake again was the pension, the union asking $400 a
month, and the company offering $300 a month. Walter, sensitive
to the slightest change in mood, had suddenly stopped talking
after having hammered and pounded his point half the night.
A tense silence settled over the conference room; at the long,
brilliantly lighted tables, no one said a word, held by the power
of Reuther's silence. For two hours it lasted, until John Leary,
one of the company negotiators, burst out, "For God's sake, somebody say something! We've got to settle this thing by eleven
o'clock!" They knew they had him then. Reuther grinned. "OK,
let's get down to business."

Recognized as one of the most adroit, masterful negotiators,
Reuther was responsible for a good many "firsts" in historic,
highly praised labor gains achieved through collective bargaining. He brought into effect the first survivor benefit subsidized
by the company; the first transition and bridge benefit program to
assist surviving families of workers who die while in active employment; the first nationwide prescription-drug program; the
first nationwide short-workweek-benefit program; and the first
comprehensive hospital-medical-surgical health-care program covering the entire family, fully paid for by the company and including retired auto workers and their dependents. Yet, skillful
as he was at bargaining, Walter Reuther never confined his efforts
to union gains, but broadened them to include as wide a segment
of the world's needy population as his vision could encompass.

XXIII

Crusader for a Better World

THE matter of health care for workers, long standing among the many causes Reuther sponsored, he linked to public welfare, as he had the pension program. During his daily visits to the hospital in 1949, he had met and given encouragement to a young man also taking whirlpool treatments, who had been paralyzed for nine years. One morning when Walter came in to see him, the man was overcome with joy, announcing that he had just "been reborn": he could wiggle his big toe! A whole new world was opening up for him. Ten days later, when Walter looked in on the patient, he was crying, broken-hearted. When Walter asked the nurse if he wasn't doing so well, she said, "He hasn't any more money; he goes home tomorrow."

Reuther, outraged, told the story to a UAW conference in Milwaukee that year, emphasizing the injustice of a system that would allow a patient to suffer helplessly because he didn't have the money to pay for the treatment medical science could give. "I say it is morally wrong," he declared hotly. "No nation that has an ounce of self-respect or human decency, no nation that can spend four hundred billion dollars for war, can stand idly by and tolerate a continuation of that kind of double standard. . . ." He went on to recount in ironic tones the news story printed in the Detroit *Free Press* that same week, of the treatment, at enormous expense, given to GM executive Charles E. Wilson's bull, who had a bad back. "We are sorry about that," Walter slipped in with sly sarcasm. But when he told about the chartered plane that was flown in specially to transport a high-voltage X-ray machine, which was picked up by a GM truck and brought to Wilson's farm, where it was applied with a specially laid cable, Walter threw in a knife-edged dart: "That bull didn't even have to leave home to get medical care." Further, experts were flown in from all over the country to treat the bull with the best medical care that modern science could provide. He pointed out that in such instances "you begin to see what is wrong in America." And he summed up "the tale of C. E. Wilson's bull," as one of his researchers called it, by driving home the essential fact that if you ask why . . . "millions of these kids are not getting that kind of care? It is because C. E. Wilson's bull cost sixteen thousand dollars, and you get boys and workers for free. . . ." Or, as he said earlier, if you happen to be born on the wrong side of the railroad tracks, "your chances of getting good medical care were far less than those of a costly animal owned by a rich man." He was always able to translate his ideas into analogies his listeners could comprehend, and then to translate his words into action.

He considered having the UAW run its own hospital and health program; and, with his usual thoroughness, surveyed several plans. Dr. Edwin Daily, a public-health expert, and in 1955 a vice-president of the newly formed HIP—Health Insurance Plan —flew to Miami for a consultation with the UAW president, by then also president of the CIO, during Reuther's initial appearance at an AFL Executive Board meeting, just before the merger of the two labor bodies in 1955. As involved as he was with executive duties, projects, and plans, Reuther took time to investigate the possibilities of running a UAW hospital.

Daily, who was seeking financial support or its equivalent in UAW membership in his group medical plan, told of their meeting in the lobby of a Miami Hotel. "He had his bodyguards there," the doctor related. "At a nod from him, they stepped to one side, and for about half an hour Reuther and I sat on a sofa, talking. He listened closely while I was outlining the basic structure of our plan, and at the end he asked some very pointed questions. He had one of the sharpest minds in America. Within that half hour he had grasped all the important aspects, and I think he knew then that a union-run hospital and health plan wasn't feasible, certainly not for the limited membership of the UAW New York region. There was only one hospital available in the area, and it wasn't right for the purpose. He really wanted some plan that would benefit the general public. He had a great feeling for humanity."

The reason for his concerted action was the widespread dissatisfaction with Detroit's Blue Shield medical insurance, which proved to have serious deficiencies, covering only about half the average family's medical bill; and it often grossly overcharged patients for doctor's services. Patients were left with large bills for services they thought were covered. Hospitalization and surgery were overemphasized, while there was scarcely any provision for preventive medicine or early diagnosis of illness. Reuther was instrumental in establishing CHA—Community Health Association—in 1956 to provide "economically sound, socially responsible" prepaid health services to any group in the Detroit area. A fifteen-member board was set up, of which he became president, with the UAW in the minority of three out of the fifteen members. James Brindle and Martin Cohen,* who worked closely with him in setting up CHA, have related the history of the association, which became virtually a medical cooperative and is an indication of Walter's thoroughness in preparing any venture.

The UAW had set up a diagnostic clinic in 1947, right after acquiring the Edsel Ford property, utilizing the mansion for offices housing a staff of thirty-three medical specialists, principally internists. Walter, who had seen many workers suffering from occupational diseases, felt that if they were caught early enough, the patients could be cured, an operation avoided, and factory conditions improved to prevent workers from getting it in the future. The clinic had proved beneficial to UAW members suffering from any sort of illness, so when the Blue Shield plan became unsatisfactory to holders of medical insurance policies in and out of the UAW, he decided to see about the founding of a health-insurance plan to benefit all the people of Detroit who

* Now president and vice-president, respectively, of HIP in New York City.

needed coverage at a reasonably low cost and wished to join. He called in Jim Brindle, who had come to the UAW Social Security department in 1949, and had supplied Reuther with actuarial data for the pension fund and health and welfare benefits. After a conference, Walter told him to "go to work on it, especially the Kaiser plan." Henry J. Kaiser, a good friend of his, had been responsible for a successful health program out west; when Brindle presented the statistics on the Kaiser plan, Walter decided to look it over himself, so they flew to San Francisco. As usual, Reuther attracted news reporters, and a group was gathered in the receiving lobby when he and Brindle returned from a tour covering every office and department of the hospital and health clinic connected with it. When asked for details of the plan, Walter rattled off statistics, facts, and figures he had been given only a few hours before, and without an error. He spoke so authoritatively that Brindle, who had furnished the material, was himself impressed. "He made a much better impromptu speech than I could have made if I'd been *prepared!*" Brindle said. "He had a remarkable facility for assimilating facts, but that day I was especially proud of him."

Martin Cohen, who came to the UAW staff shortly after Brindle, has told of locating a run-down TB Hospital in Detroit which was up for sale. It was purchased, renamed "Metropolitan," renovated, and converted into a general hospital, with three floors devoted to handling out-patients. Funds for the project were loaned to the UAW by the Nationwide Insurance Company, whose president, Murray Lincoln, was also a friend of Reuther. Lincoln was prominent in the Co-operative movement in America, as well as being a highly successful businessman, and, like Henry Kaiser, he had been attracted by the labor leader's approach to social problems and his unceasing efforts to solve them within the democratic process and free-enterprise system. The CHA in Detroit borrowed some features of the Kaiser plan, but is not the same in many respects. The board is elected by the members, who are given "pre-choice" by rule. There were inevitable "bugs" during the first years, but CHA has worked very well, and today has some 75,000 members, who choose its services in preference to other existing medical insurance plans. Three more centers have been built in and around the city for handling out-patients.

Douglas Fraser also commented on Reuther's ability to grasp difficult situations and solve problems. "In the late fifties, the problem of leisure time for retirees came up, so Walter called in a couple of experts; and at the end of two days, you'd have thought *he* was the expert! They told him so, too; he got a kick out of that. . . . He had the ability to think through a problem quickly. He could go to six different meetings on six different problems, and usually find a solution for every one of them."

The solutions did not always work, but the point was that he almost invariably came forward with an idea, and if it proved unfeasible, he would change the details without altering the essentials until it was workable; he rarely discarded an idea completely. In the early 1950's he revived his formula for mass-produced housing, first conceived in his "reconversion plan" of 1943. He was concerned about the growing ghetto neighborhoods in Detroit, and felt that it was a national problem. In presenting the revised plan for "the mass production of complete homes" before the Senate Banking Committee, he exhorted, "We want the federal government to wipe out our slums because the tax structure of the local community is not adequate to take care of the decay in the cores of our big metropolitan cities." Even then he could see serious trouble ahead unless the government adopted a program to prevent it. Estimating that there was about twenty-one million square feet of unused space in aircraft plants and that federal stockpiles held enough tools to produce twenty million homes in ten years, he arrived at a figure of one hundred twenty billion dollars for the program, based on the calculation that a two-bedroom house could be manufactured for six thousand dollars through the savings mass production would bring.

He was working on the rough draft of the plan during the heat of negotiations with General Motors; and while they were waiting for a company decision that might have meant a strike, he was scribbling page after page on a pad of yellow legal-size paper. His UAW fellow negotiators, puzzled, wanted to know if he was preparing a press release on the bargaining. "Oh, no," Reuther smiled. "They're going to agree to what we want; don't worry about that. I'm writing a plan to rebuild the slums of America, using the people who live in them." That was Walter: While the others often played cards during a recess, he was busy with schematic concepts for the benefit of society as a whole. Eventually the government did establish a federal-housing authority, but it was totally inadequate to Reuther's way of thinking. He realized that the idea of mass-produced houses was not palatable to many people—himself included—but individual homes, even "prefabricated," were preferable to the huge, institutional high-rise housing projects set up for large cities. He was bitter about the burning in Negro neighborhoods during the 1967 riots, because he felt that much of the racial strife could have been prevented by providing decent housing at the time he proposed it, nearly two decades earlier. Yet he helped to form the New Detroit Committee in an effort to rectify the situation.

One of Reuther's continuing concerns was the maintenance of world peace, which he considered essential in the nuclear age. While he continued his drive against the Communists remaining in the UAW and convinced Philip Murray to oust them from top positions in the CIO during 1949–1950, he made it very clear in all his speeches—or "the speech," as it came to be known—that neither the Communist forces nor the United States and its allies could win a military victory with weapons like the H-bomb and nuclear missiles. There would be no one left to rule —no historians to record the victory; nothing but rubble and ruin. "The Only War That Man Can Win," the title of an address he made to the Electrical Workers—IUE-AFL-CIO—at their tenth convention in 1962, with a sizable contingent of delegates from the Japanese labor movement present, contained the kernel of his entire attitude toward war and social justice. It was a variation on a theme, or set of themes, which he made many times all over the world from 1949 on, with additions or deletions to meet the changing times.

"You can't have peace in America excepting as you have peace in the world," he told the IUE delegates in 1962. . . . "Our world is in severe trouble . . . because the genius of man has developed science and technology which have created the weapons of total self-destruction.

"And yet that same genius gives man the ability to forge the tools of peace, the promise of undreamed-of human progress and unimagined opportunities for human fulfillment. The great question in the world is: Will man use that genius to destroy himself in a nuclear war, or will he use that genius to wage *the only war that man can win today: the war against poverty, the war against hunger and ignorance and disease, the war against social injustice, and the war against tyranny that would enslave the human spirit?*" He answered the question: "This is the great decision, and what you and I do in the labor movement and what we do together as Americans on the world scene will have a tremendous impact upon the survival of freedom and democracy in the world." To drive home his point he gave some statistics that General John B. Medaris had cited "some time back: that the United States has a nuclear destructive capability equal to ten tons of TNT for every man, every woman, and every child in the world. The Soviet Union, it is estimated, has a comparable nuclear destructiveness. . . . So . . . the contest between our democratic system of freedom and the Communist system of tyranny cannot be won with nuclear weapons.

For all his strident message for peace, he was pragmatic enough to realize that a certain amount of preparedness was necessary. "We must be strong on the military front," he admitted. "Today's realities and the necessities of history dictate that, but we need to understand that the *real* contest is the contest between two competing social systems as to which system can solve the basic problems of a complex industrial world."

"*This* is the global contest—and the contest in which the world labor movement is involved. The overwhelming issue centers on taking technical progress and relating it to human progress."

He had said much the same thing earlier that fall at the World Congress of the ICFTU, the International Confederation of Free Trade Unions,* which the Reuthers and other CIO leaders had helped to establish along with AFL leaders in 1949–1950. The World Congress was held in Berlin in 1962 where he received

* This was originally the World Federation of Trade Unions, started by Sidney Hillman and other CIO leaders; it included Soviet unions, of which the AFL wanted no part. But when the Russian delegates began propanganda against the Marshall Plan, the CIO withdrew, to the Reuthers' approval. The CIO, *and* the AFL, then formed the ICFTU, with Walter as one of the CIO delegates.

a tremendous ovation from the West Berliners, at a rally staged strategically near the Berlin Wall. "The Wall of Shame," he called it; "an ugly symbol, and a colossal monument to the moral bankruptcy of communism." But he did not just talk about the wall: He drove home his thesis that "the real way to fight communism is to fight social injustice, and poverty and hunger." It is interesting to note that at almost the same moment Robert Frost, in Moscow and East Berlin—with sly intent, implied rather than overt criticism—read his "Mending Wall," with the lines:

> Something there is that doesn't love a wall
> That wants it down

and that Reuther ended his speech in West Berlin with the words, ". . . we can build that better world that the poets and the philosophers have dreamed about these many centuries, a world fashioned in the image of peace and freedom, in the image of social justice, and in the image of human brotherhood."

Three years earlier, in 1959, Reuther had tangled with Khrushchev when the then Premier of Soviet Russia visited the United States in a widely reported dinner meeting at Reuther's instigation, not only to challenge the Soviet leader but because he felt the meeting might lead to better understanding. Little was accomplished, probably because both were too antagonistic, but in regard to the issue of peace, Walter said, "Mr. Khrushchev was crude and cocky and confident because . . . he believes that a free society like ours is incapable, in the absence of the threat of war, of achieving a common purpose in the pursuit of the objectives of peace. . . . But we *can*, and this is the great need of America." He had sounded a more positive chord during the same year in West Berlin (where he appeared frequently from the end of World War Two on, and became a good friend of Mayor Willy Brandt) when he said, "The promise of a world at peace, dedicating its combined resources to the fulfillment of human needs everywhere, will kindle the same hopes and warm response in the hearts of the Russian people as among the people in the free world."

In 1956, during a highly successful eleven-day tour of India, whose Premier, Jawaharal Nehru, he considered "truly one of the great statesmen of the world," he voiced the important opinion that "freedom's struggle in Asia will be won primarily in the rice fields and not in the battlefields. Like many Americans, I have felt that U.S. foreign policy in Asia has placed undue emphasis upon military power, military pacts, and military alliances. This . . . has, in my opinion, tended to trade reliable democratic friends for doubtful military alliances." His attitude on the whole tour, "like a most welcome whiff of fresh air," said the Hindustan *Times*, helped to revive India's faith in the United States.

At home he was equally zealous in the cause of keeping some degree of world peace, in spite of the numerous "trouble spots." He spoke in countless cities, before varied audiences on a wide variety of subjects, always including peace and freedom, and altering the tone to be in tune with his audience. Speaking before a large group of lawyers of the Ohio and Toledo Bar Association in Toledo (April 25, 1957), he used more analytic language than before a labor audience. "*Freedom* is indivisible—*peace* is indivisible," he said: "we will never make freedom indivisible until we have made it *universal*." And, "The H-bomb has made *unconditional* and *lasting peace* a *condition* for *survival*." Employing a legalistic analogy, he asserted, "The mortgage on human freedom is never fully paid." In discussing the difference between a democracy and totalitarian government, he drew a definite distinction. "In America we achieve *unity* in *diversity*; Soviet Russia achieves it in *conformity*; we recognize *common* values while permitting *individual* values. The ideal we must strive for is a free world alliance, with a unity in which there is diversity." His delivery was marked by accenting about every third word, placing still greater emphasis on key words or phrases (those underlined).*

On a related subject, addressing the National Education Association—and using his academic approach—in Cleveland, Ohio, Reuther had proposed a plan that was probably the origin of the Peace Corps, a full four years before President Kennedy adopted

---

* Reuther had been introduced as a leader "committed to serve as counsel and champion of civil rights," by the President of the Toledo Bar Association, George Gould. "The field of constitutional rights and civil liberties is Reuther's field," he said—a rare recommendation to a conservative organization, in a traditionally conservative state.

it. "I happen to believe," he told them, ". . . that the more young
Americans we send throughout the world as technical missionaries
with slide rules, with medical kits, with textbooks, to fight communism on a technical basis, the fewer young Americans we will
need to send with guns and flamethrowers to fight communism
on the battlefields of the world. The kind of educational program
I am thinking about would make it possible to enlist thousands of
young Americans in the rewarding struggle to win the peace."
He had been a strong supporter of the Marshall Plan, and in a
highly significant gesture had invited Secretary of State Marshall
to address a CIO national convention. Reuther felt that "what we
need is more *Marshall plans* and *less military assistance* to the
emerging countries."

Other topics he included in "the speech" were the peaceful
uses of atomic energy; the sharing of United States abundance,
excerpts from an article called "Our Fear of Abundance," published in *The New York Times Magazine*, which contained a
simply stated epitaph "if we fail [to share]: We had the ingenuity
to unlock the secrets of the universe for the purposes of destruction, but we lacked the courage and imagination to work together
in the creative pursuits of peace."

Of course Walter Reuther had a lot to say about automation,
and the problems it posed, from the time big industry began to
employ the automatic process instead of men. In 1950, he was
shown through the first fully automated engine plant opened by
the Ford Motor Company near the Cleveland airport. As he went
through the factory with the UAW shop committee and top management, he recalled the long hours spent on one simple Model-T
engine when he started tooling at Ford's in 1927. Then, it took
almost three weeks for thousands of workers on individually operated machines to turn out one engine block; in this new process,
a V-8 complex engine block came out of the foundry, untouched
by any worker's hand, complete in 14.6 minutes! He was deeply
impressed, as he told the Ford executive who asked him. The man
from Ford smiled smugly. "Aren't you worried about how you're
going to collect union dues from those machines?" he asked.
Walter shook his head and flashed back: "That isn't what I'm
worried about. What worries me is how *you* are going to sell V-8's

to these machines!" Sometime later he said, "You can automate an automobile, and you can make a television set and a refrigerator and all these other things with automation, but thank God, you still make consumers the old-fashioned way, and that is where the shortage is."

Both of these quips were widely quoted by others and repeated by Reuther himself in speeches as late as the 1960's, when the Cleveland plant was already obsolete, though still operating. But in a more serious vein, he presented a long, detailed "Statement" on "The Impact of Automation" to the Joint Congressional Committee on the Economic Report, in Washington, October 17, 1955. He wanted to make it perfectly clear that he did not favor any curb on the use of advanced machinery. He felt that "nothing could be more wicked or foolish. You can't stop technological progress, and it would be silly to try it if you could." The catch was that it must be handled properly. "If there is no care and no foresight, if we subscribe to the laissez-faire belief that 'these things will work themselves out,' untold harm can be done to millions of innocent people and to the whole structure of our economy and our free society."

Using the historical data and current statistics of industry supplied by the UAW research department, he related the "second industrial revolution" of automation to the first, in the eighteenth century. He warned against the pitfalls of the latter, which allowed the greed of a few to misuse the tools of abundance. He gave staggering facts and figures to show the enormous changes automation had already wrought in factories, with the heightened speed of production and the radical dislocation of workers. At the same time, he asserted that labor leadership fully realized that "the potential benefits of automation are great . . . and should make possible a four-day workweek, longer vacation periods, opportunities for earlier retirement, as well as a vast increase in our material standards of living. . . . It can free workers from routine, repetitive tasks which the new machines can be taught to do, and can give to the workers who toil at those tasks the opportunity of developing higher skills."

In this connection he discussed the problems of retraining thousands of dislocated workers, skilled as well as unskilled labor.

It was all very well for management to talk about "the hand trucker of today becoming tomorrow's electronics engineer," but the means must be found to retrain him (and millions like him), and to support the families of these men while they are learning the new skills. Many more vocational schools must be set up, which would serve to retrain veteran workers as well as to train the young. Earlier retirement, and therefore earlier Social Security payments, would probably be necessary in the near future. The whole economic structure was going to require changes at every level, including "the businessman who lacks sufficient capital to automate his plant, yet has to face the competition of firms whose resources enable them to build whole new automatic factories." Although the industrialists (the National Association of Manufacturers, NAM) resented Reuther's concern, it was part of his shrewdness to bring up the problems facing business as well as labor, and indeed, every facet of society was included in addressing a congressional committee on the economic report. He warned against small businesses being "squeezed to the wall' by automation while "big firms grew even bigger. The danger must be minimized by government policies and actions to assist small business and prevent trends toward monopoly," he said. At such times the politician in him combined with the crusader; in private, or before a labor or liberal Democratic audience, he often spoke of the "economic ignorance" of Congress as "shocking" and "eighteenth century." But in this "Statement," he complimented the committee on the philosophy expressed, "however imperfectly," in the Employment Act of 1946; and went on, "We recognize today that it is not only possible, but necessary, for the government to analyze, to foresee, and to give direction to the economic forces that determine whether we shall have prosperity or depression."

Probably because Walter Reuther had experienced hardship and struggle in gaining his own education, interrupted and squeezed in between working hours for lack of funds, he was deeply concerned with all levels of education, which he tied in with the other social problems. In 1956, he outlined a plan for "The Future of Education," which was largely adopted within the next ten years. "I propose that we look at the educational problem within the framework of these new and challenging dimensions of war and peace, of freedom and communism in the atomic age," he said. "I propose a five-year federal-aid-to-education program in which the federal government would make available a sum equal to one and a half to two percent of our gross national product. I propose further that that amount of money would be used first to launch a comprehensive school construction program, to overcome at the earliest possible date the shortage of classrooms, to retire antiquated firetraps from use, and to take our children off the swing shifts." Perhaps the most important part of his plan was "a federal scholarship program on a competitive basis, so that we will not continue to lose about 60 percent of our top high school students, who cannot go to college. This is a tremendous waste of human resources. The only way we can stop it is by a federal program of scholarships. I propose that if a young person is willing to sign up in one of these federal scholarship programs after graduation, they would have the choice of enlisting in the teaching profession—or in some other fields where they are needed—*for a period of one year longer than, and in lieu of, their military service.*" Warming to one of his basic beliefs, he went on heatedly: "I think it is nothing short of *insanity* to train people and then to have tremendous shortages in the field of their specialized training because we dumped them in the army for two years of boot training!" For good measure, he added, "The Russians are not doing it, but we are."

It was then that he suggested sending "these young people around the world as technical missionaries to fight hunger, disease, . . ." an idea later developed to launch the Peace Corps abroad and VISTA at home. He closed this address to the National Council for Social Studies of the National Education Association with another creative idea that has been adopted by a number of schools in metropolitan areas. "Finally," he said, "we need to do more about the gifted child. We do more for the child who doesn't make the grade, and we do less for the gifted child. These are the students whom God has given that little extra spark of genius. . . . How many of these children do we have in America whose genius never had a chance to bloom? No one can know, but there must be many. How many Jonas

Salks did we lose? How many Thomas Edisons? How many other people who have this special gift of genius? We never shall know."

He summed up his ideas for the future of education by estimating that the annual cost of carrying them out would be between $6 billion and $8 billion a year, adding significantly that the figure "represents *one week* of the cost to the American taxpayers of World War Two." His voice took on the tone of a zealot as he spoke of tapping "the great spiritual reservoir, the great spiritual power that lies deep within the human breast, . . . to get people working, marching, building, and sacrificing because of positive peacetime motivations, and because they have common hopes, . . . and a common faith." His voice was not rich or resonant, but it had the ring of deep conviction and concern. It was this quality that made a clergyman say he should have been a minister; and as his brother Victor pointed out, Walter never seemed to be making a speech, "because he has such a deep sense of mission, he regards the chance to speak as a challenge to him to persuade his listener of the rightness of his views."

Frank Winn, who was his special assistant during Reuther's last years, tells of the day in 1964, when Walter had been wakened at 2:00 A.M. with a call from President Johnson to come to Washington for a conference on the seating of the delegates from Mississippi at the Democratic convention. Walter had to speak in Detroit that day to three different sets of press and TV representatives, explaining the issues of the contract negotiations then underway. Each time he presented his theories, it was with the same vigor, energy, and enthusiasm, although he said practically the same words every time. Then, in the afternoon, they flew down to Washington in a small chartered Lear; only four men were in the plane;* and Frank, who had marveled at Walter's ability, asked him how he could show the same enthusiasm each time he spoke to the various groups, even though his convictions were genuine. Walter smiled. "It *is* difficult," he admitted; "but I have to discipline myself the way an actor does, and throw myself into a subject anew each time. In this case, I wanted to be fresh in all of those press talks because I didn't know what TV or radio stations I would be on—probably at different times, on

---

* Winn, Reuther, the pilot, and one bodyguard went along.

different programs, before different audiences each time, and I didn't want to seem stale."

It was apparent that Walter "never missed a trick." That afternoon he threw himself into the committee meeting in Washington; the convention problem was that the "Freedom Democratic Party" members claimed they were the rightful delegates, because they had been duly elected, yet they were not allowed to vote in the Democratic party nominations. With Hubert Humphrey, Martin Luther King, Jr., and two others, Walter worked out a strategy of seating delegates from both factions. If Frank had not been with him ealier, he would never have suspected that Reuther had spent a strenuous morning speaking at three different press meetings in Detroit. He used to say it was a matter of educating the public to the issues and the social changes that had to take place if man, and the democratic system, were to survive. He believed that the union could not solve its particular problems in a vacuum, but must try to get the whole of society to find answers to the "big problems"; and that the future of human civilization "lies in America trying to provide leadership in the solution of the great issues." To that end, he was ready to expound his ideas before people in Lansing one night, Toledo the next, and Ann Arbor the third—he often spoke at universities and colleges; in Wilmington as well as in Washington, New York or San Francisco. And after 1950, his crusade for a better world virtually turned him into a globe-trotter.

XXIV

Spheres of Influence

THE UAW AND WALTER

As for the rank-and-file UAW members, the growing reputation of their dynamic president produced a variety of reactions, all the way from admiration and pride to vexation and resentment from those who thought he was going too far afield or was "power-hungry." But for the most part the membership stood solidly behind him. One of the more graphic expressions of loyalty and gratitude came from Bernice Keller, an inspector on second shift at Champion Spark Plug, Toledo, as she and others from her department relaxed at a neighborhood bar after work one night. They had been discussing some of the benefits Reuther had brought to the auto workers, as well as the pros and cons of his personality; and Sister Keller summed up her own feelings with, "Oh, Walter's a doll. He could put his shoes under my bed any night in the week; and what's more, I'd get up in the middle of the night and shine 'em for 'im!"

Her companions were convulsed with merriment, since it was well known that Reuther was straightlaced, to say the least; but they understood her sentiment exactly, accepting it as sheer esteem and devotion. Not all of them agreed with her, however. Not a few found it difficult to reconcile his visionary precepts for promoting the general welfare of all workers with his recondite views in regard to women, his stand against their ability to compete with men as organizers. At around this time, 1950, a group of women from Region 2-B in northwestern Ohio, workers who had been shop stewards or had served on the education committee and attended conferences or summer-school sessions as delegates, went up to Detroit for an interview with the UAW president in regard to appointing a woman to the organizing staff. Reuther received them with his usual reserved but friendly manner. There were only five or six of them, and he knew them all from their union activity, but he preserved the edge of formality that he had shown in the earliest days, when he stood up and formally thanked the gathering of seven people for electing him delegate to the 1936 convention. Much has been said about the distance Reuther put between himself and the membership, but it was never consciously done, and was probably due to this formality he had always assumed during official moments. He was never "a mere bureaucrat condescending to the workers, nor a demagogue pretending to be a regular guy." In this instance he may have been slightly more formal than usual because he knew in advance the subject of their mission, with which he was not in favor. He heard them out, in accordance with his principles of democratic procedure; but his reply came almost unhesitatingly: "I will *not* appoint a woman to the organizing staff *per se*," he said flatly. Several tried to tell him that they did not mean a woman as such—a token appointment—but one who had shown ability in the field. Women had worked in organizing drives, but none had ever been an official UAW organizer, which was considered a responsible post, with a salary and expenses paid by the union. But after listening to the arguments in favor, still adamant, he said, "As soon as I feel that a women has the ability to go out and organize auto workers, I will appoint one to the staff; but I will never do so until that day." And no entreaties could budge him beyond that point.

Just why he was so inflexible was hard to say. His reasons were rather abstruse: Women were not "geared" to organizing; there were too many risks connected with the job. And it was true, men organizing in the South were beaten up by management hirelings as late as 1957; but there were areas where women

might be able to do a better job than men in organizing small auto-
parts plants that employed a majority of women for light factory
work. The main reason for his objection may well have been that
Region 2-B was headed by Vice-President Richard Gosser, then
under fire from an investigation campaign conducted by the
Toledo *Blade*, which had exposed the labor chief's mishandling
of union funds in Toledo, charging him with lining his own
pockets with moneys collected from local union members for
various vague purposes. Particularly in question was one so-called
"Flower Fund," a misnomer of the first order. Ostensibly started
in the early days to pay for sending official UAW bouquets on
suitable occasions, it had long since lost its specific identity, and
had become a kind of miscellaneous expense account for which
no one was accountable, and no one knew even remotely how
the money was spent. Just how far the original fund had strayed
was revealed when a member of Local 12 called the UAW headquarters and innocently requested flowers for a brother who was
in the hospital. "Flowers!" exclaimed the secretary. "The Flower
Fund's not for *flowers!*" When the puzzled brother asked what
it was used for, she was hard put to tell him, and the poor fellow
finally hung up, bewildered.

Within hours the story spread throughout the union, and while
many thought it was hilarious, the secretary's artless answer was
a dead giveaway of Gosser's shady financial shenanigans. It may
have sparked the newspaper investigation; and Reuther's instant
response was to conduct some investigations of his own, interviewing small groups from various locals in Toledo before confronting the vice-president. He had suspected Gosser of crooked
dealings right from the start in 1946; but the man, for all his
carryings-on, was popular with the rank and file at that time
because he had secured good contracts from companies in his
region, like Auto-Lite, Champion Spark Plug, and Willys-Overland,* a logical reason for his popularity. He had not become
a UAW vice-president until 1947; since that time, there had been
occasional rumors of his infractions of the UAW's ethical code;
and perhaps, if Walter had not been laid up with his arm injuries
and the therapeutic treatments for so long, or, in late 1948 and

* See UAW Convention Proceedings, 1946, pp. 233, 234.

1949, had not been occupied with national and international matters, he might have taken steps to correct the situation before it reached the point of producing an attack from the outside. Reuther was always able to see the deeper implications of such assaults, and in this case he realized that the *Blade*'s editorial against Gosser could be harmful to the entire UAW, and that it indeed represented an attempt to lambaste the labor movement as a whole. Under the circumstances, he was reluctant to pursue any innovation, such as putting women on the staff, that might enhance Gosser's prestige with the rank and file.

He gleaned enough from those he interviewed—and from inquiries made by others—to convince him that action must be taken. In April, 1950, he called a special meeting of the Executive Board, which convened at the Secor Hotel in Toledo to consider whether or not Richard Gosser should be drummed out of the union. Reuther was fully expecting the verdict to be in the affirmative, as there was little doubt in his mind that Gosser was guilty of unethical practices, and the UAW top officers agreed with him. However, the surprise results of the meeting showed that "Dick Gosser had more clout with the majority of the board members than Walter did" in this instance, either because they were impressed by his past performance, or because they feared a large loss of membership if he were expelled: He was completely exonerated. Walter, who prided himself on the fact that the UAW Executive Board was the most democratic in the entire labor movement, accepted the decision, but he had grave doubts about the wisdom of it.

For the time being, everything "blew over." No more unfavorable publicity stories appeared; no rumors of further misuse of funds in Toledo reached top-level ears in Detroit. In 1951, Dorothy (Mann) Alexander,* one of the committee who had met with Reuther in regard to appointing women to the organizing staff, was placed on Gosser's staff of Region 2-B organizers—the first woman ever to hold that post in the UAW. Soon afterward, a number of others were appointed; and once the precedent was established, women organizers were accepted as part of the

---

* Inspector and shop steward at Champion Spark Plug, active in UAW Women's Education Conferences.

official setup in the auto workers union. Unfortunately, Gosser continued his undercover activity and became more and more of a martinet in his own region as his power grew from successful business, real estate, and sundry other deals. In a few years he would be exposed nationally during the McClellan hearings when, as will be shown, Reuther's estimate of him proved only too correct.

WALTER AND THE CIO

For the second time, Fate intervened in the career of Walter Reuther when, in November of 1952, Philip Murray suddenly died of a heart attack at the age of sixty-six; and, as if by some predestined agreement, twelve days later William Green, the venerable president of the AFL, bowed out of life at age eighty. Reuther, whose lightning mind raced ahead, saw two possible leaps to power for himself and the labor movement in this startling duo of deaths. As he stood on the "wind-swept hill" outside Pittsburgh where Murray, the Scottish-born miner, was buried with high honors, Reuther knew instinctively, even while mourning the loss of Murray, that he was going to be the next president of the CIO.

His feeling was confirmed when he received the unanimous support of the UAW Executive Board, whose members urged him to run for the CIO top office, even though Allan S. Haywood, executive vice-president of the CIO, seemed to be the logical successor to Murray. The sixty-four-year-old Haywood was a British-born coal miner from Yorkshire whose heavy Midland accent and genial personality had much the same appeal to the members as Murray's Scottish burr had had. The two men had been closely associated for years, and there was a good deal of sentiment connected with the loyal support of Murray's powerful steelworkers union, which stood solidly behind Haywood. He also had many friends among the smaller unions, who looked to top-level CIO officers for financial help and guidance, regarding them as parental figures in the organization.

Walter, on the other hand, appealed to the more progressive and independent unions like the auto workers, who backed him

100 percent, and the influential, "intellectual" Newspaper Guild, and many unions on the borderline, whose members really preferred the bright, energetic forty-five-year-old Reuther, but felt a compulsion to vote for Haywood as the next in line of succession. A single important ally was Arthur J. Goldberg, the astute general counsel for the steelworkers and the CIO, whom Murray, at Walter's prodding, had selected to replace Lee Pressman, the Communist-led former counsel. Goldberg, like Reuther, had been a poor boy of Socialist leanings who had pulled himself up by his own bootstraps in his native Chicago to reach the top rungs of the ladder in the field of labor law. He felt so strongly that Reuther, with his tremendous drive, would be the better leader for the CIO, that he broke with the steelworkers' Executive Board to campaign for Walter instead of Haywood.

The convention that was called in Atlantic City on December 4, 1952, to elect a new CIO president bore a striking resemblance to the 1946 UAW convention that had brought Reuther his first presidency. He was not the favorite, but his followers made up in enthusiasm what they lacked in numbers; and while caucusing was perhaps not quite as prevalent, much of it went on in the cocktail lounges and hotel rooms—as before. Walter confined his electioneering to the latter, but there were willing volunteers for the former, including Walter's old adversary Dick Leonard, now an officeholder in the CIO and an advocate of Walter's leadership, despite their differences in the past. As in 1946, the Reuther campaign gained momentum as it went along, and by election time many of the key delegates had swung their votes to him. Haywood had the backing of more unions, but most of them (outside the steelworkers) represented a small membership, and in the end he was defeated by nearly a million in favor of Reuther. In actual delegate votes, Haywood received 373 to Reuther's 180; but Haywood accepted the representational results with a tearful grace reminiscent of R. J. Thomas when he conceded in a given-name greeting, "May I be the first to say, President Walter. . . . We are going on from here." And he led the delegates in an emotion-fraught rendition of a rousing chorus of "We Will Roll Our Union On."

Taking his cue from the song, Walter's speech in accepting the

CIO presidency, "We Shall March Together," stressed unity in the labor movement as a whole as well as in the CIO. He emphasized the need to show management that labor was unified, attacking big industry for its attitude toward unions, and underlining the necessity for cooperation between the two if a free society were to be preserved. It was in this speech that he spoke of "the revolution going on in the world . . . of hungry men trying to get the wrinkles out of their empty bellies"; and, in an often-quoted remark, pointed out that "the Communists didn't start it. They are riding its back." From there, he took up the topic of foreign policy and the newly elected, not yet inaugurated Republican administration. Reuther had been bitterly disappointed by the defeat of Adlai Stevenson, whom he admired more than any man in public office since FDR; and he feared that the incoming regime would be antilabor, not so much because of Ike as because of reactionary Republican party control. In this connection, he told of an exchange he had had a few months earlier with Senator Nixon before the Republican Foreign Policy Committee. Nixon had asked him if there was anything in the foreign policy of the Truman administration that the CIO disagreed with. "He thought he had us over a barrel," Reuther said, grinning, "but I answered, 'Senator Nixon . . . in essence, on its basic positions we agree. We think in some places the emphasis is wrong: We believe we need to do more . . . in terms of Point Four, of helping people to help themselves. The essential difference between the CIO and the Republicans is that we criticize the Truman administration foreign policy for its *deficiencies*, and the Republican party criticizes it for its *virtues*. That is a fundamental distinction."

It was such rapid-fire retorts that brought Reuther *his* distinction as a remarkable public figure among labor leaders. There were other signs that he intended to be a different sort of labor leader from either of those lately deceased—or from George Meany who, with far less drama, was raised to the number-one position in the AFL by a simple vote of its Executive Board in Washington. Meany had long stood by Bill Green as the venerable craft-union chief's right-hand man; and it was no surprise that the fifty-eight-year-old, forceful lieutenant should step into the former president's shoes. He, too, was eager for labor unity, but the "common denominator" between him and Reuther did not extend much beyond the platform to merge.

Reuther announced that he expected no financial reward for the privilege of being president of an unwieldy body like the CIO, but would stay on the UAW payroll at his incredibly modest salary of $11,250. (Even the unassuming Phil Murray had received $40,000; and John L. Lewis at that time was drawing down $75,000 from his independent union.) Walter early indicated that he was no "spender," or "big shot" who felt he had to "pick up the tab; in fact, lunch with Walter was usually Dutch treat, even to splitting the tip," according to a labor newsman. His salary would have remained at that figure so far as he was concerned, but before the 1955 convention, the UAW Executive Board convinced him that he should receive a raise; it didn't look right for the president of a large labor union like the UAW and the federated CIO to earn such a meager amount. Walter said he was perfectly content with the salary he received. "So then they said, 'Well, if you don't want a raise, we *do*,'" Walter related in an interview, "'and *we* can't have one unless *you* do!'" He laughed. "So that's how my salary jumped to $18,500. They played on my sympathies. . . ." Later it went up to $20,920 a year, but never higher. At CIO headquarters in Washington he was equally stringent about expenses; but he did not hesitate to order a shielding panel for the receptionist's desk so the girl's shapely legs would not be subject to the stares of visiting males.

He also announced that he would advocate labor's participation in national politics to a greater degree in order to elect congressmen who were open-minded on questions of foreign policy, Social Security, labor legislation (in opposition to lobbying from industry). Dividing his time between the UAW headquarters in Detroit and his CIO office on Jackson Place, across from the White House in Washington, Walter was also making numerous plane trips abroad or to the West Coast to become better acquainted with the unions who had opposed his presidency. He managed to keep his finger on the pulse of matters at the heart of both offices, but it was difficult for CIO members to consult him. His secret in successfully conducting his many operations was to surround himself with efficient administrators; and now he called Victor home from a job as CIO representative in Europe to head up the CIO Washington office. Paul Sifton, Robert Oliver, and several other noted labor specialists served on the staff as Walter's spokesmen for a time.

His auto workers' membership was in the main proud of his many activities as president of the CIO, to them the choice position of the labor movement. In Saginaw, Michigan, the head of the UAW-CIO, Kenneth Forbes, a good friend and admirer of his, was a short, feisty redhead, who was often mistaken for Reuther, to his far-from-secret delight. Forbes was proud of looking like the nationally known leader and did his best to live up to the resemblance. He was proud that Walter came to his house to discuss local union affairs over a cup of coffee. Forbes's daughter recalled the first time she met the UAW president. At about the age of twelve, she came home one day to find her father drinking coffee at the kitchen table with two other men, one of whom was introduced to her as Walter Reuther. To her horror, she saw that the other man was wearing a gun in a holster. Not used to seeing armed men in the kitchen, she jumped to the conclusion he must be one of the gangsters in the union she had vaguely heard about. Without stopping to realize that Mr. Reuther and her father were calmly drinking their coffee, she ran out of the room and waited, trembling till she heard them leave. After they were gone, her father explained that the stranger was Walter Reuther's bodyguard and told her why he wore a gun.

However, there were dissident factions in the CIO, principally that led by David McDonald, now president of the steelworkers, who was still antagonistic toward Reuther for having struck out for the CIO presidency. McDonald felt that Allan Haywood, as a sort of interim figurehead, would keep that office where it belonged—in Philip Murray's union—and that at the next convention he, McDonald, would take over as president of the CIO. Reuther realized more than ever that if there was to be labor unity, the AFL and CIO must become one labor body.

WALTER AND THE MERGER

He had, in point of fact, begun almost immediately after election to work toward the achievement of this long-range goal shared by many leaders since the 1935 split in the labor movement. If one were asked to cite a Latin motto for Reuther's mode of procedure, it might well be *carpe diem,* for his ability to "seize the day," the moment for action, was amazing. Scarcely two days after the CIO convention, Walter met George Meany at a dinner of the International Confederation of Free Trade Unions, and as involved as he was with the workings of that organization, he nailed Meany to a private discussion and a pledge by both of them right then to move toward the merging of their respective organizations. Reuther was ready to set up a committee at once, but an unexpected delay was caused by an emergency operation for removal of his gall bladder. He was hospitalized during most of December but early in January, 1953, while he was still convalescing, he and Meany met over a light lunch in his hotel suite at the Statler. Both were committed to the cause of labor unity because they both realized that the sniping and raiding that went on was not only futile, but detrimental to the whole labor movement. As a first step they decided to revive a dying Joint AFL-CIO Unity Committee.

With enthusiasm from both leaders, who also formed and chaired a subcommittee, rapid progress was made toward a no-raiding agreement, which was announced on June 2, 1953, and the next year both AFL and CIO conventions ratified it. At a dinner celebrating its acceptance by 65 of 110 AFL unions and 29 of 32 CIO unions, Meany and Reuther made a joint statement: "This signing and ratification of the no-raiding agreement between our two organizations is a historic step. We are confident that the no-raiding agreement may function in a spirit of understanding and fraternal friendship." By fall of 1954, even David McDonald, who had threatened to leave the CIO and join with John L. Lewis and Dave Beck of the Teamsters to form a new labor alliance, issued a "surprising" call for immediate unity. Walter surmised that McDonald knew full well his membership would never let him pull the steelworkers out of the CIO. In the meantime, the Joint Unity Committee continued to explore ways to effect a merger. But its deliberations were kept secret, and outside official labor circles little was known what progress was being made. The aim of the merger was to facilitate "organizing the unorganized," of whom there were still many millions of workers, but the politics beneath the surface were complex and potentially explosive. Inside the UAW, Reuther conducted an educational campaign, including discussions and debates. One such debate, held during an organizers' weekend conference, brought out the mixed feelings of the membership. Sides were drawn by lot, and those who drew the negative had to defend it no matter what their private convictions. In this instance, the negative enumerated the following: A merger would take away the choice of the workers to vote for the union, for the top leaders. One vast labor organization would establish a labor hierarchy; the worker would have no voice. The AFL was a craft-union organization, as opposed to the industrial unions of the CIO, and was much larger than the CIO. Merging would mean running the risk of not getting the CIO social programs recognized or supported. The AFL was too strong; no matter how much Walter might want or deserve to be president of the merged body, Meany would probably get it, just because of the sheer size of the AFL; and once Meany was in, there would be little chance of ousting him. No chance of putting through the improvements in the free-enterprise society, as Walter envisioned the merger. All of these points were presented so clearly and cogently in the debate by organizer Hugh Alexander that the negative side won.

Reuther and the top-level officers probably wished the negative side had not been presented so clearly; Walter himself had these same reservations in regard to the merger, but he was willing to take all the risks in order to achieve the unity he felt was necessary if organized labor was to keep its strength, and expand to include all the unorganized. This was the point he kept hammering home in speaking to staff organizers, at meetings with the Joint Unity Committee, or with Arthur Goldberg, chief architect as well as advocate of the merger. Nevertheless, the debate decision may have had something to do with the inclusion of a clause in the merger agreement to the effect that "the identity of each affiliated national or international union would be preserved," and for the provision of a "little CIO," the Industrial Union Department, in the merged body. After many meetings and some peppery exchanges between Reuther and Meany, Goldberg, who later wrote a loving account of the marriage between the two labor bodies,* decided the time had come to present a written plan to Meany and his officers at the next AFL Executive Board meeting, in February, 1955, at Miami Beach, Florida, their regular winter meeting place.

The craft union thought nothing of reserving a large suite at the Monte Carlo Hotel for Reuther, who was of course invited to attend. He had always considered the glossy luxury of Miami Beach inappropriate for a labor gathering, aside from his personal distaste for it; but he felt he must be on hand when the merger plan was presented. However, he declined the hotel suite, which he let Jim Carey use, and took a single room, hardly big enough for two beds, for himself and his bodyguard. When newsmen came looking for him in the suite, Carey joked, "He's down the hall in the linen closet squeezing orange juice." It was not the first joshing Walter had received from his colleagues; and his detractors claimed that his parsimony was "just another form of exhibitionism" on his part: He was showing off in his thriftiness as much as those who displayed extravagance in showy cars or flashy diamonds. Even one of his admirers had to admit that the remark a wag once made of Aristotle might apply at times to Walter: "He carried moderation to extremes." Reuther was too much of an individualist to let comments on his personal habits bother him, or to alter his own set of values in any way.

Meany accepted Goldberg's plan in full, which was hardly a surprise, since the AFL, because of its larger membership, received the lion's share of authority. As labor-writer Foster Rhea Dulles commented: "The difficult problem of leadership in the new federation was resolved by the willingness of the CIO in the person of Walter Reuther to step aside in favor of the AFL. . . ." He was referring to the provision in the Goldberg plan that granted the AFL the right to fill both the presidency

* *AFL-CIO, Labor United*, by Arthur J. Goldberg. New York: McGraw-Hill Book Company, 1956.

and the office of secretary-treasurer, a much greater concession on Walter's part than most UAW members expected. They had assumed that the AFL—that is, Meany—would be president, but they never thought that the number two post would go to any but the CIO—that is, Reuther. Loyal UAW members thought Walter had been "screwed." As it was now proposed, the CIO would choose only the director of organizing. Whether or not Reuther knew of these arrangements in advance is hard to say, but it is likely that he did. He later pointed to them as proof that the CIO was more interested in organizing than in any prestige posts. He was to be in overall charge of the Industrial Union Department, although nominally merely one of the twenty-seven vice-presidents of the new body, but certainly the most prominent among them, more widely known than Meany, and his expectations were high. He undoubtedly felt that the sixty-year-old Meany would step down in a few years, and that he, Walter Reuther, would enlarge his sphere of influence not only in the labor movement but in the field of national affairs by being in line to step up as president of the AFL-CIO.

He reckoned without realizing Meany's tenacity, as stubborn as his own. A month after the Executive Board meeting, the AFL president spoke at the auto workers' convention in Cleveland, and the two leaders were photographed in a "candid" shot —Meany, big, stolid-looking, pugnacious, and Reuther, short, smiling, and confident—a study in contrasting personalities that seemed to presage the coming conflict between them. Yet at the founding convention of the AFL-CIO, which finally took place in December, 1955, all went smoothly. Reuther and Meany clasped hands around the handle of an enormous gavel, hoisting it together to call the meeting to order. In another joint statement they declared, "We feel confident that the merger of the two union groups which we represent will be a boon to our nation and its people in this tense period. We are happy that, in our way, we have been able to bring about unity of the labor movement at a time when the unity of all American people is most urgently needed in the face of the Communist threat to world peace. . . ." It was Reuther's concerted antiCommunism that led the AFL leaders to look upon him as the one man in the CIO who could bring about the merger in the first place, and the implications in their broad declaration of purpose revealed his attitude as much, if not more, than Meany's. The press almost universally hailed the promise held out by unity in encouraging labor responsibility for free and democratic unionism to the benefit of the entire nation.

The honeymoon did not last long. Although the first year saw a rise in the AFL-CIO membership to 15 million, it soon slackened, and, with the exception of the teamsters, began to fall off. Partly due to apathy among young workers, who took the gains of unionism for granted by 1955 and could not see the necessity of forming a union in new plants,* the principal cause of the decline was the racketeering and widespread corruption in the expanding unions, particularly the teamsters. The AFL-CIO set up an Ethical Practices Committee, which drew up "rules of conduct" in an effort to force offending union officials to cease their malfeasance or be expelled, as the Longshoremen's Union had been expelled by the AFL in 1953. Reuther, who foresaw a federal investigation, warned the unions to "clean house" with the "stiffest brush and broom" they could find, or the government would do it for them, using an *ax*, hoping to chop down the whole house of labor. His strong words fell on deaf ears, however, and by 1957 there had been so many examples of the grip that racketeers had on some unions that a Senate investigation was launched, headed by McClellan of Arkansas, whose chief counsel was the young, energetic Robert Kennedy. The stormy hearings revealed more corruption than Reuther had feared; in the teamsters' union, a score of witnesses testified to rigged elections, misuse of union funds, embezzlement and theft, extortion, and all kinds of corruption clear up to the top, Dave Beck as president receiving the most black marks. He took refuge in the Fifth Amendment, but was finally convicted on tax evasion and grand larceny. He was succeeded by James Hoffa, who had risen from warehouseman to vice-president as much by undercover deals as by his able, efficient organizing. "Jimmy" had tangled with "the redhead" in CIO politics more than once since the days when

* Or, as Walter said, workers, especially the young, were no longer "hungry" in the traditional sense.

their unions struggled together for recognition; and Walter knew that Hoffa (who referred to the UAW as "them squares on Milwaukee Avenue" before Solidarity House was built) would hardly reform the teamsters. George Meany was more than willing when Walter suggested expelling the teamsters' union from the AFL-CIO in December, 1957, so that all of labor would not have to suffer for the sins of the few. The entire labor movement was under suspicion and its leaders placed on the defensive by the malpractices of Beck and Hoffa, and several others of lesser note, including Gosser of the UAW.

Walter went so far as to offer to disclose his personal financial record before the committee. He commandeered the services of May Reuther, who managed the family finances, in submitting proof of his "dollar honesty," as Meany called it; and although she grumbled at hunting up old records, she did a thorough job of it. Reuther turned over to the Senate Committee a complete accounting of his modest salary range from $1,730 in 1936 to $20,920 in 1957; the earnings from his speeches and writings, totaling $11,290.96, which had been donated to the nonprofit Reuther Labor Foundation, as he was dedicated to the principle of living on the salary the union paid him, and felt that "these honoraria were the result of his position in the labor movement," the McClellan Committee report said. His expense account figures were so scrupulously spartan as to be ludicrous in the light of most such accounts, in and out of the labor movement. He would submit figures at the UAW rate of $7.50 to $12 per day; in case he was on business for the AFL-CIO, which had a per diem rate of $40 to $50, he would "elect to receive the lesser per diem rate from the UAW, and turn in to the union the $40 or $50 per diem from the AFL-CIO. His hotel bills were audited with the utmost care: On one bill, a valet charge of $1.50 was crossed off, when he had to have a suit cleaned, and paid for it himself instead of charging it to the union. May had included copies of his income-tax returns from 1942 through 1956, his savings account records and bank statements, canceled checks for the previous five years, from 1952 to 1957; their realestate transactions and United States Savings Bond investments; even his single sortie into the stock market, a $1,000 purchase of Nash-Kelvinator stock in 1948, which he sold for $1,001.26 in 1956. His net profit of $1.26 caused labor reporter John Herling to send a wisecrack up to the witness table: "Reuther—the fox of Wall Street." But men like Republican Senator Barry Goldwater, a member of the investigating committee and Reuther's political archenemy, whose vitriolic attacks in the press brought him the title of "my unpaid publicity agent" from Walter, knew well enough that the "redhead," in his own way, *was* "dumb like a fox" in revealing his miniscule Wall Street profit: He was slyly taking a poke at greedy profiteers, at the same time pointing out the honesty of at least one labor leader.

Goldwater felt that everything Reuther did—or said—had a political purpose, and Reuther returned the feeling twofold. As expected, these two opposing public figures tangled and practically took over the hearings during the three days of Reuther's voluntary testimony, beginning March 27, 1958. Walter had wanted to testify earlier, at the start of the hearings in February, because he felt that the Republican members of the committee (Carl Curtis, Karl Mundt, and Homer Capehart, besides the senator from Arkansas), particularly Goldwater, were using the investigation to carry on a political campaign against labor by means of a smear campaign against the UAW and its president. A month before the hearings began, Goldwater had lashed out against him at a dinner, "Walter Reuther and the UAW are a more dangerous menace than the Sputnik or anything Soviet Russia might do to America." Sputnik had just been launched (1957), and this was an updated echo of an old cant first sounded by George Romney in 1940, when he declared, "Walter Reuther is the most dangerous man in Detroit because no one is more skillful in bringing about the revolution without seeming to disturb the existing form of society." Both statements are an exaggeration, but they represent the fear of the Republican party that Reuther would advance the "creeping socialism" started by Roosevelt. Romney later changed his attitude somewhat, but Goldwater saw Reuther as a "menace" right up to the end.

Reuther's answer in 1958 was to suggest that each man choose three prominent clergymen to judge the truth of Goldwater's charge. If they found it correct, he vowed, "I will voluntarily resign from the presidency of the UAW, the vice-presidency of

the AFL-CIO, and from the labor movement entirely." But if the
verdict was in his favor, then Goldwater must search his soul to
decide whether or not to retire from the Senate. In a fiery flare-up,
he denounced the Senator as "the nation's number-one political
fanatic, its number-one antilabor baiter, its number-one peddler
of class hatred." Goldwater retaliated with a few invectives of
his own, including "liar." Walter's lightning reaction was to label
his assailant "a political hypocrite and a moral coward" at a news
conference. His printed thrust brought a fresh volley from Goldwater; and as a result, the committee chose to investigate the
UAW-Kohler strike as a lead-off.

This was the most glaring of the auto workers' few vulnerable
spots. The strike against Kohler, a family-owned, "closed corporation" manufacturing bathroom fixtures in Wisconsin, was fraught
with strife and emotional outbursts from its beginning in 1954,
after months of fruitless attempts to bargain. Two UAW organizers had been guilty of brutally beating two nonstrikers, at different times and in different situations, but both serious enough
to receive national attention and protest. Since both men were
from Emil Mazey's old Briggs local, the McClellan Committee
chose to hear his testimony instead of Reuther's; and Walter might
not have been called on at all if John Kennedy, then head of the
Senate Labor Committee, had not arranged for him to appear.
When his personal record proved beyond reproach, he was questioned about the Kohler strike cases and the general conduct of
the union. He termed the behavior of both men "reprehensible,"
but urged that one of them, Gunaca, whose trial was still pending
—the other, Vinson, had been sentenced to three years in jail, of
which he served thirteen months—should be tried at a different
site from Sheboygan Falls, where the beating took place and
where feeling was so high he could not get a fair trial. (The
contest was resolved according to Reuther's suggestion, and
Gunaca served eighteen months of a three-year sentence.)

The feud with Goldwater continued throughout Reuther's
three-day testimony. Ideologically they were poles apart: the
Senator contended that Kohler "had a right not to have a union"
if he could win the strike. But Reuther heatedly held that under
United States law "only the employees can make a decision

whether they want a union, and which union. An employer cannot make that decision without violating the law." Goldwater
had no answer except to say that someday he and Reuther would
"lock horns." His hedging turned the battle into bickering, until
McClellan finally interposed: "Can you folks not get off somewhere and talk this out?"

It soon became apparent that the Republicans on the committee
were trying to play up the political role of the UAW through its
leader. One of the less pertinent facts emphasized was that the
union supported the ADA (Americans for Democratic Action) by
supplying about 10 percent of the running costs. Senator Curtis,
finding this ineffective, tried to portray the UAW as a serious
offender in the use of violence, citing various news stories without regard to their veracity or reference to the auto workers.
Reuther finally struck out at him in a tirade concluding: "This is
part of a smear campaign. Our union has had *less* violence than
most unions. . . . This is the decision: Reuther has got to be
destroyed because his union is active in politics, and let's find
some way. We know Reuther didn't steal any money. We know
Reuther hasn't got gangsters running his union. We know they
kicked out the Communists. Now let's fabricate this theory of
violence. . . . The facts are that this union has done everything
to *avoid* violence. We have done everything in our power to
discourage it!" Senator Curtis responded with a mild, "All right."
But Reuther would not let it go at that, and continued to attack
the Republican technique of trying to discredit labor instead of
facing the real issues in coming election campaigns. The chairman
had to tell him to "shorten his speeches and let's get along."

Meany would probably not have gone on at such a rate or
volunteered to testify in the first place. Other unions to come
under the committee's fierce scrutiny were the Hotel and Restaurant Employees, the Bakery and Confectionery Workers, the
Laundry and Textile Workers unions. The AFL-CIO Ethical
Practices Committee commanded these unions to "clean house,"
but they did not, and so were suspended or expelled. Walter,
who had hoped that the merger would increase the welded body
of organized labor to thirty million in ten years, began to doubt

the wisdom of the move. He was also concerned about further investigation of the UAW in the case of Gosser.

Committee Republicans did not get around to detective work on Richard T. Gosser till 1959; but Reuther, learning that the UAW vice-president in Toledo was to be a target of the investigation, called a meeting of the Executive Board, and saw to it that Gosser was stripped of his authority by being "relegated to an inactive status under the guise of illness," as the Republican members complained in their report. Actually, Gosser was already suffering from the illness which took his life some years later, but that had not prevented him from enlarging his undercover dealings since 1950, still keeping them well disguised as union activity. Reuther, since he had abided by the majority decision of the board in 1950 despite his own misgivings, adhered to it publicly in 1959, and issued a statement defending the deposed vice-president before the Gosser hearings began. He spoke of Gosser's "great contribution" to the union, which was true enough, considering the large and loyal membership Gosser had brought into the UAW, although many of his staff had become disillusioned with him because of his arbitrary rules and his devious methods of enforcing them. Reuther also vouched for Gosser's honesty in a routine endorsement, but his heart was not in it, and his words had little effect on the committee Republicans conducting the inquiry.

From the testimony of the witnesses, the rank odor of the Flower Fund permeated Gosser's entire realm of irregular operations, including several conflict-of-interest situations. One of these was the Sand Lake and Farms project, run in connection with the UAW summer school, supposedly for the benefit and health of the members, who were given "the opportunity to work out in the open" during their stay, but which was actually for the financial benefit of the vice-president from Region 2-B. Part of the produce was marketed to the cafeteria and box-lunch caterering firm to whom, through his finagling, the contracts for factory eating facilities were granted, an arrangement in which graft no doubt figured. Another "project" involved owning a half-interest in a Toledo hardware store that did business with Local 12, to an affiliate of which he had once sold property he owned in partnership with others when he was president of the local. These various interests were loosely held together under the name Gosser Enterprises, the exact nature of which was never known. It was obvious, however, that the former vice-president enjoyed a greater affluence than most UAW officials, and the committee wanted to discover its source. They did not get very far, but the Republican members of the committee made the most of the evidence that came out at the hearings; Emil Mazey was called to testify again, but Reuther was not, and the Republican members charged that the committee as a whole did not investigate the case thoroughly enough. Their final report, issued separately in March, 1960, labeled the Gosser affair as being "of the same cloth from which the Hoffa pattern was cut." Listed as evidence from the hearings were "kickbacks, terrorism, collusion with gamblers, conflicts of interest, destruction of records, misappropriation of funds, falsification of records, and evasive tactics," which, if properly investigated, the report claimed, would have revealed "criminality" on a scale equal to Hoffa's.

The remarks were aimed at discrediting the committee's Democratic chairman and Walter Reuther's union, as well as trying to play up, and at the same time cut down, Reuther's political influence. Committee Republicans had earlier charged that Robert Kennedy, the committee counsel, had been remiss in pursuing charges against the UAW and Reuther because he did not want to endanger his brother's chances of getting the labor vote in the 1960 election. This was "politics," pure and simple, a smear tactic, since the one political appointee on Bob Kennedy's staff was Jack McGovern, a Republican backed by Goldwater, whom Kennedy had given a free hand in searching Reuther's private records. However, it was true that Gosser did engage in all sorts of machinations, finally attempting to alter his income-tax records, which proved his downfall. He was indicted for federal income-tax fraud, had a full-dress trial, was found guilty, and actually did serve two or three years in jail. Most of that time he was in ill health, which brought about his release, and he died a few years later.

The GOP report, aside from the Gosser findings, and the "violence and crime" exercised by organizers in the Kohler strike, which was used against Reuther rather than the organizers found guilty of breaking union rules, could discover little more with which to destroy the UAW president's power or political influence. Significantly, there was little or no mention of management's infringement of the fair-practices law, although the committee, as originally set up, was to investigate both. The committee Democrats' Report, also issued separately, took both management and labor to task for the strife in the Kohler strike. That struggle finally ended in September, 1960, when the NLRB found the company guilty of unfair labor practices and failure to bargain in good faith. Strikers regained their jobs, and the company agreed to pay them $4.5 million in back wages and pensions. Reuther made the most of the settlement, calling it a victory over antiunion forces. "How many unions have the faith to stay nine years in the struggle and spend twelve million dollars? Not many," he stated proudly.

He was increasingly disappointed, however, in the results of the merger, which was not working out. Instead of expanding, the membership had dropped every year since 1955, partly due to apathy among workers, many of whom felt they could "have a free ride," in the organizers' words, now that labor was established; and partly to the investigation, which was accompanied by corrective legislation against abuses. As early as 1958, Senator Kennedy had offered "a sweetheart-type bill," in the eyes of Barry Goldwater, who battled with the future President over his "Welfare and Pension Plans Disclosure Act," and won a stiffer bill, the Landrum-Griffin Act, which passed both Houses in 1959. Among other provisions, it imposed fines and prison sentences for misuse of funds, and put new curbs on picketing, as well as including a "no-man's land" clause, dealing with cases considered too unimportant for the NLRB, so the state could assume jurisdiction. Walter and other leaders were especially alarmed over the effect of the Landrum-Griffin Act on organizing in the South, where many small "run-away" shops were located, and the states were hostile toward unionism. The atmosphere at the 1959 AFL-CIO convention was gloomy; and in 1960, Walter declared bluntly to Meany and others on the Executive Council, "We are going backward!"

As it turned out, the Landrum-Griffin Act, while it did not entirely please anyone, was not as lethal as labor expected; there were fewer strikes, and less infractions of the AFL-CIO's own Ethical Practices Code, but the organization was not progressing as Walter felt it should. He was impatient with Meany's stolid, stand-pat, labor-businessman's methods; and Meany resented Reuther's rash, often arrogant assumption of authority to act without consulting him. The failure of the merger to succeed was probably due to the personality conflict between its two top leaders more than any other single factor. Walter, imaginative, articulate, dynamic, his whole career a fierce concentration on the goal of "promoting the general welfare" of working people on a worldwide scale by democratic means, was constantly bucking the more limited but steadfast goals of George Meany, a man who began his career as an apprentice plumber, then became business agent and then secretary of the New York Building Trades Council before taking on his post in the national AFL in 1939. A New York-born, Irish Catholic, Meany enjoyed a martini and a good cigar, was fond of dancing (despite his 228-pound bulk), and was the first AFL president to be an ardent golfer. This urbanity of tastes, in contrast to his looks and "blunt-as-a-plumber's wrench" speeches, belied his bulldog tenacity. Reuther's judgment of Meany, according to Frank Winn, was, "the only time Walter ever underestimated his adversary." Meany was as determined as he to wield control of labor.

The AFL-CIO president had bitterly opposed Reuther's "meddling in foreign policy," as he termed Reuther's proposed tour of India and talks with Prime Minister Nehru in 1956, especially since he—Meany—had just denounced Nehru and Marshal Tito of Rumania of doing more to promote Communism than any other leaders outside the Soviet Union proper, in spite of their "diplomatic verbiage." When Reuther argued with him (for two hours, at an Executive Council meeting), trying to convince him that Nehru was neutral and might be swayed in favor of democracy, Meany closed his mind. Seeing it was useless, Walter went directly to the President, received Eisenhower's blessing, and took off. The fact that his eleven-day tour was immensely

successful only proved to be a sharper thorn in Meany's side, and
made him distrust Reuther's motives all the more.

A year later, 1957, Walter's equal success in England, where he
spoke at the British Trade Union Congress and created a sensation by giving a full account to his mainly Socialist listeners of
the goals in wages and fringe benefits that American labor had
gained under the free-enterprise system, did not alter Meany's
attitude. If anything, he was probably irritated by the glowing
comment in the London *Daily Express*, which summed up Reuther's speech: "No overseas visitor in living memory has made
such an immense impact by his personality and tempestuous
oratory."

In 1959, Reuther twice overrode Meany's mandates in matters
of labor foreign policy. Early in the year, during Anastas I.
Mikoyan's visit to the United States, the Soviet Deputy Premier
expressed a wish to see the AFL-CIO headquarters, located a
block away from the White House; but George Meany refused
to allow him to enter since he represented a country that, in
Meany's view, stifled free trade unionism. Walter Reuther, however, jumped at the chance to show the Soviet official what American labor could do, and, with three other AFL-CIO vice-presidents, invited Mikoyan to have lunch at a union building close
by; then he could at least take a glance at the AFL-CIO headquarters through the lobby windows. The invitation was mixed
with a puckish mischief on Walter's part; the group even asked
Meany to join them, but he turned them down, indirectly re-
buking Reuther with an attack on "Americans who feel they can
meet the Soviet challenge at the conference table." This was
precisely Reuther's point in extending hospitality to the Russian
emissary, and he defended his position of telling Mikoyan "to his
face" that the free people of the United States would "resist
encroachment on their rights," in a statement that ended: "The
Soviet Union has made great industrial progress and the Soviet
workers have won more bread, but they have not won more
freedom. We in the free world want both bread and freedom."
The conversation over lunch was peppered with a biting exchange
between Reuther and Mikoyan; among other items, Reuther
flatly denounced Moscow's repression of the 1956 revolt in Hun-

gary. Yet the open debate somehow cleared the air, even winning the approval of Republican Senator John Cooper of Kentucky, who called Reuther's plain talk "a major service for peace." But George Meany continued to frown on such tactics.

In September, when Reuther planned a similar confrontation with Nikita S. Khrushchev during the latter's famous tour of the United States, Meany at once placed a resolution before the AFL-CIO Executive Council condemning the Soviet Union for its antiunion practices. Its passage put Reuther in an awkward position, as Meany intended; but the redhead defiantly went on with his plans, dramatically arranging a dinner with the Soviet Premier to coincide with the AFL-CIO convention in San Francisco, and he had the audacity to ask the AFL-CIO top command to endorse it. He was voted down, of course, but at least half a dozen Executive Council labor leaders accepted the invitation for the evening of September 20, 1959, a tempestuous dinner-meeting which lasted five hours.

The affair, which became a contest of verbal sword-play, punctuated by much table pounding on the part of the Soviet premier, was widely publicized in the papers; and while Reuther felt that he had bested Khruschev on many questions, Meany felt the whole dinner to be in bad taste. And indeed, it boomeranged against Walter, for the Soviet Trade Union paper *Trud* published a story obviously designed by Khrushchev to revenge himself on the American labor leader, whom he called a "lackey of the monopolists," by accusing him of having married and deserted a Russian girl during his stay in Gorki twenty-five years before. It was an absurd piece of yellow journalism, and even the Detroit *News* observed, "The UAW president has been assaulted with a variety of unkind nouns and adjectives in his own country, but it took Moscow to decide that he is a bigamist." Walter was away from home when the false account came out, and he immediately called May to allay any doubt in her mind that it was sheer propaganda. She must have laughed at his fears, since anyone who knew him as she had known him through the years would realize that the allegation was clearly meant to vilify Reuther's reputation, and had no basis in fact.

However, the unsavory publicity connected with the whole

affair of the dinner did not improve his already strained relations with George Meany. Over Walter's objections, the previous meeting of the AFL-CIO Executive Council had been held at San Juan, Puerto Rico, a winter resort even more fashionable than Miami Beach. Meany was battling a cold, so he could not make the opening session, and Reuther sought to occupy the president's chair, causing a flurry of alarm among the craft-union leaders, who saw it as a symbolic act. Futhermore, he pushed through, as chairman of the Economic Committee, temporary approval for a huge labor march on Washington, to protest the rapidly rising unemployment rate and demand some effective measures from the White House to combat it. Eisenhower, asked about the march at a news conference the next day, got a big laugh from reporters by merely remarking that the request came from the "sunny beaches" of Puerto Rico, far away from areas of serious unemployment. Walter, smarting from the derision of the President's quip, retaliated pointedly that he had opposed labor meetings in Florida or other luxury resorts but had been voted down by his fellow federation offiicers. "Mr. President," his statement ended, "I have spent no time on the sunny beaches of Puerto Rico, nor have I been with you and your many big-business friends on the golf course, the duck blinds, and the quail hunts."

But if he scored on Eisenhower, it was not so easy to win over Meany, who, hearing about the quasi-approved march on his arrival in San Juan, moved at once to thwart Reuther's plan, claiming that a mass demonstration in the streets could be invaded and taken over by Communists, "peaceniks," and other radical groups. He insisted angrily that the Economic Policy Committee reverse its position. Reuther just as hotly refused. "If you keep on, I'll resign as chairman!" he threatened. After further thrashing, a more moderate unemployment rally was finally authorized by the Executive Council, allowing Reuther a meager portion of victory over his adversary.

The clash of wills continued. Sometimes the issues were unbelievably petty; at others, the conflict between the two men revolved around their basic but separate concepts of unionism. Both of them had a strong need to satisfy the sense of power within them, and Meany was in the more favorable position to preserve it for himself. If Reuther had been more inclined to bow to protocol, he might have come into that position as expected after five years, when Meany turned sixty-five. However, at the 1960 AFL-CIO convention, when Walter observed gloomily that they were "going backward," Meany made no mention of any plans to retire. Like most union leaders, he regarded retirement as tantamount to death, and he was by no means ready to die.

By 1961, when Reuther made a speech before the Industrial Union Department of the AFL-CIO, just before the annual convention, he was sharply critical of Meany and the building-trades unions. In his opinion the long-drawn-out division over jurisdictional claims might very well destroy the federation after only five years. "We merged, but we did not unite," he declared grimly.

He urged formation of new machinery for settling disputes over job rights, and at the preconvention council meeting, Meany appointed a five-man committee headed by Machinists' Union Albert J. Hayes, and including Reuther, to devise a new means of dealing with intraunion disputes. After much hard work, the committee presented a plan for outside arbitration of disputes with court enforcement, if need be, to implement the decision. Meany knew this would never be acceptable to the building trades; so he called a special night session for the Hayes report, and, after it was read, motioned to put it aside and draw up a compromise plan. Furious, Reuther piled his papers back into his briefcase and stood up. "C'mon, let's get out of here," he said to his CIO colleagues. There was a moment of deadly silence while they all wondered if this was the breakup he had threatened. The other CIO members did not move. Then Joe Beirne, president of the Communications Workers, suddenly called out: "Wait a minute. We're not through. We've got work to do!" Since none of his allies had joined him, Reuther sat down.

Meany picked up the Hayes report, a sign that it would at least form a basis for compromise. All night long the council deliberated, argued, shouted, and tried to persuade one another until they came out with a modified plan for arbitration, including an appeals clause and less severe penalties. Walter was unsatisfied.

"It's no use—the building trade won't buy it anyway," he predicted. Meany merely said, "We'll see." He called the roll of craft-union presidents at the council table one by one, and each of them gave the nod to the new proposal. At four o'clock in the morning, Reuther found himself reversed and Meany emerged triumphant in the struggle for union strength and internal power between them. Later, at the convention itself, Meany failed to include Reuther on the AFL-CIO escort committee for President Kennedy, an "oversight" that must have been deliberate, although he denied it.

Reuther, who had worked very hard for Kennedy's election, and indeed, was closer to him than others on the escort committee, felt the snub keenly. As a result, he did not bother to consult Meany when a place in the United States delegation to the United Nations came up, and Walter was in line to serve under the friend he most admired, Adlai Stevenson, who, after a meeting with Mrs. Roosevelt (already seriously ill but still active), requested the Reuther appointment. Kennedy as a matter of course checked with Meany, who refused his approval, so the suggestion was dropped, a bitter disappointment to Walter. This was the one governmental post he really wanted, not only because he felt a labor leader should be in the delegation but because of his interest and active role in foreign affairs. And though Meany later said he would have agreed if Walter had proceeded through the AFL-CIO, his remark did not improve their sandpaper relations.

When a vacancy occurred in the post of Undersecretary of Labor, Reuther wrote directly to Kennedy recommending Jack Conway; and again Kennedy went to Meany, who told him the matter had not been cleared through AFL-CIO channels. Kennedy apparently felt it necessary to defer to the first-in-command of the merged labor organization, for he dropped Conway and appointed another union man to the Labor Department position. Meany tried to justify his action, claiming, "If Walter had spent five minutes on the telephone, Conway could have become undersecretary"; but Reuther felt the AFL-CIO president would have vetoed anyone connected with the UAW. Following a final 1962 blowup over naming a replacement for a seat on the Executive

Council, the two labor rivals entered into a long period of marking time, interrupted by only minor clashes through most of 1965. Meany would be seventy years old then, and everyone expected him to retire. Walter made an honest effort to modify his criticism of the administration, even to cease complaining about the "conspicuous consumption" during the yearly winter sessions at Miami Beach, though he never went so far as to join the gin rummy games around the swimming pool. The extent of Reuther's recreation was a movie and an ice cream sundae afterward, if he took any time at all. He liked to swim in the ocean, but he considered socializing in card games around a pool sheer waste of time and money.

Some of the union presidents found his constant speechifying on the issues, his insistence that the AFL-CIO broaden its horizons, irritating. (One morning during a room-service breakfast with two other council members, according to a staff writer, "in the middle of the scrambled eggs Walter jumps up, starts pacing, and makes a speech in his hotel room!") Not many could understand his all-consuming ardor, but when other labor leaders advised him to "lay off" his insistence on change "with a capital C," so Meany would give the nod to Reuther as his successor in the AFL-CIO, Walter answered, "That's all very fine, but I won't like myself. I have to live with me every day. I'm not interested in being president of the AFL-CIO under circumstances in which I cannot be true to the things I believe in." However, he did curb his carping about details like conspicuous consumption and minor matters of protocol.

As the 1965 convention drew near, a group of AFL-CIO Executive Council members, including Reuther, drew up a commendatory statement, paying tribute to "the courage and determined leadership" of George Meany, along with a generous pension plan to go into effect immediately on announcement of his retirement as AFL-CIO president, which they fully expected to come that year. But when the officers and delegates convened in San Francisco, the president of the AFL-CIO announced that he had no intention of retiring, though he was nearly six years beyond retirement age, and limping with arthritis in one hip. Walter, still young-looking and vigorous at fifty-eight in spite of

his many physical trials (the latest an operation for removal of
a lung tumor) began to wonder if Meany would ever retire or if
he (Walter) really wanted to be president of the AFL-CIO anymore. In 1964, he had negotiated a contract with GM including
unheard-of fringe benefits such as "short-term psychiatric therapy," tuition for job-related educational courses, severance pay,
and an incentive program for early retirees. He was exhilarated by
the achievement of new gains, and he realized that, as he said
earlier, "One of the tragedies of being president of the AFL-CIO
is that you're cut off from the main function of the labor movement and that's collective bargaining." If he were drafted—provided Meany ever retired—Reuther would certainly run for the
top office, but he was "not about to launch a campaign" for it.

As in 1960, the general atmosphere of the 1965 convention was
gloomy. In spite of the advances made by the Great Society
program, unemployment was rising; the new times brought new
problems, principally that of increasing automation, and there
was no precedent to follow in dealing with it. Walter felt that
Meany was allowing the AFL-CIO to drag its feet in organizing
the unorganized, especially in the grape workers' struggle for
recognition under the leadership of Cesar Chavez on the West
Coast. This proved to be one of the toughest bones of contention
between Meany and Reuther within the next year or two. Walter
also was privately concerned about the escalation of the war in
Vietnam, although labor in general supported it. He and (the
then) Vice-President Leonard Woodcock worked in a closed
caucus to revise the proposed resolution on the war so that it
would be less militaristic, placing more emphasis on economic
aid and governmental reform. At the same time, he had to go
along with Johnson's escalation of the war, a duo-policy that was
part of his inner conflict in connection with his secondary position
in the AFL-CIO. Late in the fall, after the convention, he went
out to Delano and marched in the picket lines with Chavez
leading the itinerant farm workers in their battle, an action that
George Meany would never have undertaken.

However, early in 1966, when Meany decided to risk serious
surgery on his arthritic hip in the hope of being able to walk
without pain, two of his first visitors after the operation were

Walter and May Reuther. They stayed for nearly two hours, diverting him with "delightful conversation" the whole time. "They were extremely friendly," Meany commented.

But before the year was half gone, the feuding had resummed —over foreign policy, over lack of progress on the domestic front, over protocol. At one point, Meany called an emergency meeting of the Executive Council to obtain a vote of confidence. He started off by demanding, "Walter, don't you know there's such a thing as a telephone?" And soon both were pounding the table and shouting invectives in a tumultuous confrontation that had to be interrupted several times by calls for order. It was the beginning of the fissure that was to widen the ideological gap between the two leaders and led to the irreparable split in the merger. Late in 1966, Reuther denounced the AFL-CIO in a stinging statement. "The AFL-CIO lacks the social vision, the dynamic thrust, the crusading spirit that should characterize the progressive, modern labor movement," he charged. "The AFL-CIO suffers from a sense of complacency and adherence to the status quo." And in February, 1967, he resigned from the Executive Council, followed by other UAW officers who left their posts on various committees.

Once the official ties were cut, it was only a matter of time until the UAW pulled out of the AFL-CIO entirely, in spite of efforts to keep it in the merged organization. Walter's proposal for a $90 million, six-year organizing drive, more unified collective bargaining, a $15 million national labor defense fund, and basic changes in the decision-making machinery of the AFL-CIO was granted a hearing at a special convention only if the UAW would be bound by decisions made at that meeting, a condition too arbitrary for Reuther to accept. The actual pullout came on July 1, 1968. He had been disappointed in the merger almost from the beginning, and now it was a relief not to be muzzled by Meany or suffer the consequences of criticism or frustration if he went counter to the AFL chief. Reuther, though flexible in negotiating, was used to "running the show" in his own union, and could not adjust to waiting in the wings until he was given the cue to act. As he said, he was "action-oriented."

As always, his resilience stood him in good stead; and soon

after he had made the break, he sought new strength in a merger of his own, the Alliance for Labor Action (ALA), with a seemingly strange bedfellow, the independent Teamsters' Union. But before signing a pact with the union that he had helped to expel from the AFL-CIO only ten years before, he made sure that its president, James Hoffa, who was serving a sentence in federal prison, would never resume office; and that Frank Fitzsimmons, Hoffa's administrative successor, whom Walter had known and trusted since the earliest days of Detroit unionism, would remain in charge. He and Fitzsimmons saw eye to eye on a number of progressive programs for social welfare in addition to traditional trade-union goals. Together their unions had a membership of nearly four million, and in the first year, two smaller unions, the International Chemical Workers and the National Council of Distributive Workers, joined the giant organizations to advance the "Declaration of Purpose" set forth by the ALA, including coordinated organizing drives, and new "community unions" for the poor and minority groups.

"We have not come together to divide the labor movement; we have come together to *revitalize* the labor movement!" Reuther emphasized in stating the Alliance's purpose. This organization would speak out on the issues as the AFL-CIO had never done. He and Fitzsimmons voiced strong opposition to the Vietnam war, in contrast to Meany's still moderate position, and the ALA officially opposed deployment of the anti-ballistic missile (ABM). In organizing, with Atlanta as its first objective, the Alliance won eleven bargaining rights elections in a row. One of the first community unions, organized in the Los Angeles-Watts area, received financial and technical aid, with Ted Watkins, UAW representative on leave, devoting full time to the project. The "left-wing labor movement" was not going at as fast a pace as its leaders would have liked, but Walter could say with a gleam of mischief, in 1969, "We have been accomplishing more reform in the AFL-CIO from outside than when we were in it."

XXV

Politics, Civil Rights, and the World Scene

WALTER REUTHER'S sphere of influence in politics, though considerable, never included plans for himself as the United States Chief Executive, although many people did not accept his disclaimer, and felt he was ready to take over as a "labor dictator." He did contemplate a third party briefly, but, as Victor pointed out, they agreed that "no third party has ever worked in the United States," not even a Roosevelt's—Teddy's "Bull Moose" party—so it was hardly likely that a Reuther-led third party would succeed. Walter was much interested in the British Labour party, and he had long talks about it with Harold Wilson, who became a good friend of May and Walter during their visits to England. Yet Reuther still felt it wiser for labor in the United States to function politically through Congress; the point was to elect responsible candidates. In September, 1962, he said, "You can't separate the bread box and the ballot box"; and as late as then he hoped to see a realignment of parties, so that, as he said in a television interview, "you can vote for the party that has the program and the policy that you believe in and you will get what you vote for." Yet, when there was a "Reuther for President" boom in the UAW New York and New Jersey regions, he emphatically vetoed the idea of his being a possible Democratic candidate with a letter to all union locals saying he was not interested in running for or holding any office. There were five in

337

competition already: Besides Adlai Stevenson, ready to make a third try, John F. Kennedy, Hubert Humphrey, Stuart Symington, and Lyndon B. Johnson had thrown their hats into the political arena. Humphrey was a "natural" labor candidate, and Stevenson might have been Reuther's private choice, except that he did not think his friend should run a third consecutive time; it was courting defeat. Kennedy seemed most likely to win, and Reuther had come to know him well during the McClellan investigations; he was young, vital, and he had vision. After he put Humphrey out of the running, Reuther knew that he—and labor— would support Kennedy. The crucial primary in West Virginia had turned the tide, and it was then that Walter had talked long and earnestly to Stevenson, trying to convince him not to run for nomination at the coming convention.

Although Reuther was not one of the forty-some UAW delegates to the Democratic convention, held in Los Angeles in 1960, the *Wall Street Journal* named him "the most influential labor leader present." Neither he nor anyone else, however, could persuade Humphrey to line up behind Kennedy for Vice President; or, after Humphrey refused, to dissuade Kennedy from choosing Johnson as his running mate. The small labor group, headed by Reuther, that met with him on the matter, was stunned when he announced that he felt obliged to offer "the second spot on the ticket to Lyndon." Reuther and the AFL-CIO had disapproved of Johnson's 1959 blocking a reform bill on Senate Rule No. 22, the "filibuster privilege," one of Walter's prime targets over the years; Johnson also had failed to back the first Medicare proposals, a lag the UAW and labor leaders in general found disturbing. Indeed, when the news of Johnson's tapping by Kennedy came to the UAW delegation, "you would have thought it was the end of the world," in Leonard Woodcock's words. He had been having a leisurely lunch with staff member Mildred Jeffrey, who was to do yeoman work in the UAW's voter-registration campaign, when Joseph Rauh told them about the unbelievable choice. Tears were rolling down Rauh's cheeks, and Millie looked stricken, Woodcock himself was shocked, and when they went up to the UAW suite, it was like a wake. May Reuther was weeping, and gloom filled the air; Walter was still with Kennedy. Woodcock, having second thoughts, finally said, "Well, goddamn it, I was a delegate in fifty-two, and I voted for John Sparkman. And Lyndon Johnson isn't John Sparkman, and Texas isn't Alabama. This is not he end of the world." Then David Dubinsky called to voice his opinion that "this is great . . . who's the genius who thought of this?" which helped to "pick them up off the floor," as Woodcock said.

Walter himself wasted no time in wailing once Kennedy's decision proved unshakable. There was work to be done—fast. Governor G. Mennen Williams, who had been repeatedly elected by the UAW's political and financial backing, was dead set aginst Johnson, ready to demand a roll call on the nomination. And George Meany, equally unwilling to accept it, called a meeting of the AFL-CIO Executive Council to draft a statement publicly endorsing his position. Delegating Woodcock to handle Williams, Reuther took on Meany at the meeting that night. When he and Arthur Goldberg were unsuccessful in counseling against the proposed action, Walter used all his powers of verbal persuassion in "two and a half hours of plain goddamn hard work to beat Meany down," Jack Conway said. "And once he'd beat Meany down, that council never does anything that Meany doesn't want to do." Woodcock, at he same time in a closed caucus of the Michigan delegation, was able to reverse the sentiment and throw the state's support to Johnson. An ugly floor fight was avoided, a raucus television image averted, and LBJ promised to support the entire Democratic program.

As soon as the convention was over, Kennedy invited Reuther to come to Hyannisport for a private conference of several days. Walter, carrying with him on the plane a seven-page memo on the rising unemployment rate, held a dozen different ideas in his head for the coming campaign. The first morning he and Kennedy had "a long bull session," during which both of them were on the phone with Johnson, who was down at his Texas ranch. "That afternoon Jack had some things to do," Walter related, "and he said, 'Why don't you go swimming with Jackie?' She was carrying their second child." After they had swum for a while, they lounged on the beach in the warm August sun and talked for a long time. Walter had met Jacqueline Kennedy as the Senator's wife, but had never had a chance for conversation with her. She wanted mostly to talk with him about "this whole business of security and privacy," which seemed to trouble her. Walter answered her questions honestly, and the picture he painted of the precautions necessary for life in high office revealed his own mixed feelings. He warned her that his would be the area in which she would have to pay the biggest price. She was making the decision as an adult, and so was Jack. "But your *kids* aren't making the decision," he told her. "You really have to work, and work hard, to have your children lead as nearly normal a life as possible. No matter where you go, you'll be a prisoner in the hands of security people. You may take over the White House, if Jack wins the election, but they will take over your lives. May and I try to get away by ourselves sometimes, but we don't succeed. It's a terrible thing to have somebody on your back all the time." He told her about the constant surveillance provided for Linda and Lisa everywhere they went in Michigan. "May and I wouldn't mind it so much except for the children," he said. "This is going to be the most difficult problem for you." (He later remarked sadly how true those things they talked about turned out to be.)

Still, he would never dream of giving up public service. A few days later, he and his brothers all plunged into the Kennedy-Johnson campaign, the three of them, with the UAW membership and staff, outranking any other labor group in the effort to win the election. Roy, as head of the UAW Citizenship Department, was summoned to a voter-registration meeting called by Robert Kennedy, who was much impressed by his ability and systematic approach to the project. Later, at Bobby's request, Roy took a leave from the UAW to be codirector of the Democrats' 1960 voter registration committee. Victor wrote reams of copy for consumption abroad, and Walter went "barnstorming" frequently with Kennedy as the campaign moved into high gear. Newsmen interviewed them together, and cameramen snapped photos of them. One, taken at a Labor Day picnic, indicates that these two public figures, of such different backgrounds, had the same inherent qualities that made for leadership: personal magnetism, sharp intellect, and tremendous drive, combined with a feeling for humanity; and, more significantly in Walter's eyes, the newsphoto proved that only in a democracy could the two stand side by side on equal footing. Wealthy Kennedy had used his money to help him attain his position; but Walter, without money, had to depend on his personal attributes alone to become a powerful labor leader. And although the Republican nominee, Richard M. Nixon, tried to distort the picture, calling Reuther "a labor leader turned radical politician," and predicted that, if Kennedy was elected, Reuther would "have a lot to do with calling the tune in the White House," Walter neither "called the tune" nor danced to Kennedy's after the former head of the Senate Labor Committee was in the White House.

Reuther was often there in an advisory capacity on problems of public welfare, particularly unemployment and ways of getting Congress to act to solve it. In 1962, the number of unemployed was still growing; it was almost 6 percent of the labor force. Talking it over with him, Kennedy asked, "How do you get people to understand the seriousness of that figure?" Walter's answer was that you "can't get anywhere by discussing the problem in terms of percentages. If you pose the issue in that framework, 6 percent unemployed . . . your opposition says instantly, 'But 94 percent *are* employed,' and you can't get anywhere . . . 94 percent is going to beat 6 percent any day. You must argue the case in terms of people." And he did just that, pointing out to congressmen that 6 percent is five million people; that of that number, well over one million were young people between sixteen and the early twenties, who were both out of work and out of school, and left with no place to go but on the streets. "You can see the enormous group pressures that are being built up . . . the tremendous potentialities for trouble."

Usually he spoke before committee hearings, but that year, in an effort to move the legislators, and to publicize the AFL-CIO Industrial Union Department, he invited all members of Congress to join him for a steak supper at the Mayflower Hotel, his single venture in large-scale entertaining. Two cabinet officers, 35 senators, and 167 representatives—of whom 55 were Republicans—attended the affair and they listened to his forty-three-minute speech on unemployment and other issues over dessert. One of his colleagues joked, "Reuther had a joint session of Congress there. I knew he couldn't resist a State of the Union Message." Whether the event accelerated action from Congress is doubtful; but at least they were prepared for his next assault.

Probably no other labor leader appeared before Congress as often as Walter Reuther. From 1946 on, he gave testimony on practically every social issue, making close to a hundred appearances before committees in both houses during his twenty-four years as president of the UAW. By 1951 he had addressed Congress on such perennial problems as price controls and a fair tax program, expanded Social Security, a national health program, repeal of the Taft-Hartley Act, the need for a Civil Rights Act, the Defense Production Act, federal aid to housing, and federal aid to education and creation of an expanded foreign policy program. One of his most moving appeals for change, which began in October of 1951 and continued until he died, was his strong, eloquent campaign to abolish Senate Rule 22, which he linked to the denial of civil rights to the minority groups in the South. He always emphasized that, legally, "Rule 22 is a very fundamental weakness in the democratic process"; that . . . "adequate debate should be ensured to permit a clash of ideas, but the filibuster is not a clash of ideas. The filibuster is a technique designed to impede the legislative processes, not to facilitate them." Further, he said, "There are millions in America who can make contributions in all kinds of fields, and they are being denied that opportunity because . . . under Rule 22, a minority in the Senate—wedded to bigotry and narrow, selfish special interests—has the tool with which to block the majority to act." Neither speech, nor anyone else's, moved the Senate to abolish the filibuster, but many congressmen praised his expertise in handling whatever subject he was discussing with full documentation. Senator William Benton, who presided over the hearings of the Rules Committee, remarked that his "thorough brief calling for the changing of Rule 22," was "a notable contribution to our hearings. . . . This is a more complete presentation by far than we have had brought to us before."

In an entirely different field, his usual testimony before the House Agriculture Committee in March, 1955, backing farm price support, led Representative Harold D. Cooley, committee chairman, to comment: "Mr. Walter Reuther . . . made the best farm speech that I have heard in our committee room during the entire twenty years that I have served on the Agriculture Committee." His speech on "The Impact of Automation" before a Joint Congressional Committee in 1955 made its own impact on the members of Congress, as did his ideas on "The Peaceful Uses of Atomic Energy," before a Joint Committee the next year. He was the first to propose a $1.25 hourly minimum wage to Congress in 1959, when he also spoke for aid to distressed areas and other welfare benefits for all. An almost annual event on Capitol Hill was Reuther's commentary to a Joint Economic Committee on the President's Economic Report.

After the perilous Bay of Pigs invasion in the Cuban crisis, Kennedy asked Reuther to set up a citizens' committee to seek release of the invaders captured and being held by the Castro regime. Cuba needed farm implements, and the President's idea was to ransom the men by furnishing farm machinery bought by public donations. Since the UAW included Agricultural Implement Workers, and Kennedy knew Walter's capacity for quick, organized action, he was the logical choice. Walter's bipartisan Tractors for Freedom Committee included Milton Eisenhower and Eleanor Roosevelt, the Reuthers' close friend and a willing ally, ill and aging as she was; this was the last committee on which she served. The funds were raised, but the rescue was delayed because Castro claimed he needed heavier implements than tractors. All donations were returned and the committee disbanded.

Walter, who had been involved in the off-year election campaigns to put in office congressmen who would implement the legislative program that Kennedy had sent to the Hill, did not go to Cuba himself; but late in September he and May made their annual visit to Mrs. Roosevelt at her Val-Kill Cottage in Hyde Park, New York. For years, ever since FDR had died, they had been going to see "Mrs. R.," as Walter called her, for a few days during the summer, and when Linda and Lisa were old enough, they sometimes went along. A cherished picture in the Reuther household was one of the four taken there the previous year with the former first lady. Her health had failed considerably since then, and, though she would not stay put, she was often confined to her bed on doctor's orders. Her physician and friend, Dr. David Gurewitsch, despaired of getting her to "cooperate anymore. Maybe you can convince her she must rest more," he said to Walter. And she did promise the Reuthers she would try to stay in bed, though they knew it would be difficult for her, since she "always had a strong sense of social obligation" to her house guests, whether they were family or friends.

During the week prior to their visit, Mrs. R. had been in the hospital for one of the many times she went in to have tests made, submitting to examinations and treatments she found distressing. The results were not encouraging, and she had been depressed and low-spirited when she came home. But in the course of the week-end and their conversations at Val-Kill Cottage, she suddenly revived and began to talk excitedly with Walter when he mentioned sending economic instead of military aid to stiffen the resistance of borderline countries against communism. She asked if she could "borrow" his idea for purposes of her own, perhaps presenting it to the United States delegation of the UN, and they launched into one of their regular animated discussions. To Joseph Lash, who was present and recorded it in his *Memoir* of Eleanor Roosevelt, written right after her death, Lorena Hickok, the Reuthers, and her daughter Anna, these moments of renewed vigor and enthusiasm in the former First Lady were a joy, although all were aware they could not last. And indeed, on Sunday, she was weak again.

This year, President Roosevelt's old "Uncle David" Delano, now in his nineties, was visiting there at the same time as the Reuthers. On Sunday morning Mrs. Roosevelt asked Walter to take them to church. "I think you're too ill," he told her. "You really ought to stay home, Mrs. R." She insisted: "But Uncle David has to go and I feel I should go with him." So he finally agreed to take them if she would promise to go back to bed as soon as they returned. She gave her word, and off they went. As always, they sat in the family pew way down in front, directly behind the chancel. There was no one sitting near them, Reuther realized to his dismay when, shortly after the "high" Episcopal service began, both Uncle David and Mrs. R. fell asleep. To a German Lutheran like Walter, the ritual here was "more Catholic than the Catholic Church," and he had always relied on his hostess to nudge him with her elbow when it was time to stand, kneel, or sit. Now he could hear "a lot of noise"—rustling, scraping of prayer hassocks—but he didn't know "when to get up and when to get down," so he just sat still until the service was finally over, and he managed to get Mrs. R. and Uncle David back home without mishap. She laughed at his discomfiture and apologized for falling asleep. "I must really be getting 'a little bit tired,'—Franklin's 'prayer' would be answered," she said with her old twinkle.

This was a reference to a standing joke between them over a quip by some malicious wag long before, when Eleanor Roosevelt's career as her husband's emissary was at its height. The saying went that FDR's nightly prayer was: "Dear God, please make Eleanor a little tired." They had laughed about it at the time and often since then; but that she should recall it now, in her weakened condition, recognizing its relevancy, was a measure of this remarkable woman's humor and objectivity. Walter and she made an annual ritual of exchanging bad press notices or any vicious verbal assaults that had been their lot during the year, a release for both of hem. This year Walter had most of the unfavorable clippings to display, since Mrs. R. had been too ill to arouse much antagonism. Walter told her of the invitation he had received to speak in Japan in December, where he was sure to arouse antagonism from Communists among the workers. She, of course, encouraged him to go; he had intended to do so anyway, but he welcomed her approval. She was of the opinion that he could help the Japanese Communists change their minds, as he had done so successfully in India. As Anna Roosevelt Halstead, who had been at her mother's on some of these occasions, commented, these two, though widely separated in background and age, "had mutual concerns about humanity throughout the world. When they met, no time was wasted . . . as they laid plans for future action."

A frequent caller at Mrs. R.'s, especially when she knew the Reuthers were there, was Lorena Hickok, former Associated Press reporter, and for years a member of FDR's staff. She and Mrs. Roosevelt had taken trips together after the President died, and "Hick" had written a book about their experience. "Hick," who lived nearby in Hyde Park, had met the Reuthers during one of their visits to Val-Kill Cottage, and had been so taken with Walter's conversant knowledge of world affairs that she never wanted to miss the talks between him and her close friend. It was Mrs. Roosevelt who encouraged "Hick" to write this biography of Reuther and persuaded him to cooperate with the idea.

Now they all discussed the coming election, and the possibility of "their" candidates' winning, providing greater opportunity for action in Congress to carry out Kennedy's program and lower the unemployment rate. As Fate would have it, Eleanor Roosevelt did not live to learn how the candidates came out; she died on election day, November 7, 1962, and the sad news of her death went out to the world at almost the same time the election results were broadcast. Walter and May Reuther were sorrow-stricken when they received word, even though they knew she had gone downhill rapidly since their visit. They learned from Lorena Hickok that they were the last house guests she had before she died. Walter, who had always admired her, considered her one of the great people of the world, and knew full well what a warm friend and ally he had lost.

Walter and May attended her funeral in the church at Hyde Park where she had fallen asleep just a few weeks before. She was buried in the family gravesite on the grounds at Hyde Park, next to her husband, the thirty-second President of the United States. Standing together were the three men who had followed him in office; Harry S. Truman, Dwight D. Eisenhower, and John F. Kennedy.

Reuther did not dream that a year later, almost to the day, Kennedy would be felled by an assassin's bullet, and that the man whom the labor leader had opposed for the number-two post on the Democratic ticket, Lyndon B. Johnson, would be the thirty-sixth President of the United States. Yet, during the year he had worked with the Vice President, and he had to admit that Johnson had kept his pledge as far as supporting the domestic program was concerned. Like the rest of the nation, the Reuthers were thunderstruck by the tragic news of the assassination, with its ominous implications. While the shock was still heavy upon him, the following day Walter received a phone call from the newly sworn-in President Johnson. "I need your help," he appealed. Walter, of course, promised all the assistance at his command, and within a few days was consulting with LBJ at the White House. Before many months were up, his was a familiar figure there, moving in and out even more frequently than he had during the Kennedy administration. He was the initiator of the War on Poverty—a phrase he had used for years—program, and early in 1964 presented his views before Congress. He testified many times in the years that followed.

As always, Walter was quick to "seize the day" to promote his own ideas for the general welfare of the nation. He had a hand in forming Johnson's Great Society proposals, which he hailed with high enthusiasm, and in fact was one of the main designers of the Model Cities program. He saw in all of this legislative charter a chance to realize his long-standing dream for a better world—as Vice President Humphrey said, it "was just what Walter Reuther had hoped and prayed for"—and he saw to it that labor, particularly his UAW staff, put forth concentrated effort in lobbying for it. Johnson also relied on him to some extent in matters of foreign policy and civil rights, and was apt to call him up at any hour of the day or night for consultation. He was more or less a behind-the-scenes operator in the Johnson theater of action. His White House visits were rarely announced by the press or publicized; sometimes he would be closeted with Johnson or Humphrey for two or three hours, and would be gone before any one on the outside knew about it. Besides his role in the convention strategy for Johnson's nomination in 1964, he was probably the most active labor leader in the election campaign. His only complaint was that the Great Society program did not move fast enough to suit him, and when he tried to urge a more rapid pace, the President cut him short. In the main, however, they proved to be a cooperative combination, much more so than Reuther himself would have thought possible in 1960.

In his enthusiasm, he conceived another Reuther plan for

preserving the prosperity of the auto industry, prompted by the growing competition from the importation of small cars, especially the Volkswagen, from abroad. He envisioned a joint venture by the large corporations for production of a "people's car,"—something he had long advocated—to compete in price and size with the foreign market. This would improve the economy, cut down on unemployment, and reinforce the nation's balance of payments. President Johnson was much interested in the ambitious idea, but it was dropped when a high-level study showed that centralized corporate resources would conflict with the Clayton antitrust law. In 1966, Reuther testified on federal safety standards for automobiles, besides his appearances in the same year on the problems of the cities and federal reinsurance of private pension plans. In 1967 he lobbied for improvements in Social Security benefits along with Medicare and Medicaid, as well as complete coverage for farm workers unions, which had never been included in the Social Security program. He also spoke up for the establishment of nonprofit corporation for public television.

In and out of Congress, Reuther championed the cause of civil rights for all races through his entire union career, as he had during his student days at Detroit City College. In one of his most inspired speeches to the National Association for the Advancement of Colored People at their 1957 convention in Detroit, he accused Congress of being "on the longest sit-down strike in the history of America—eighty long years. We think it's about time they terminate that sit-down strike and turn out some legislation." Those who heard him speak that day never forgot it. Dr. Samantha Adams, now president of an NAACP chapter in Ohio, attended that convention as a student and found it an exhilarating experience. "He made me feel I could really go out and be somebody," she said. "And I went out and got my education in my profession and started to practice."

In that year, 1957, Martin Luther King, Jr., began to emerge as a national figure, speaking before various labor groups; and Walter, moved by his eloquence, recognized his qualities as a leader and, as always, was in the vanguard in offering his support to King's cause. He spoke at rallies, saw to it that the UAW voted financial assistance to the Southern Leadership Council, and he himself became a leader of marching men and women. Along with King and other civil rights sponsors, Reuther helped to plan and carry out the immense March on Washington in 1963. Overcoming the objections of Meany, who wanted no involvement of the AFL-CIO, and Kennedy's fears of sit-ins, Walter, with his sense of showmanship and efficient organization, including help from Kennedy's staff, brought about a peaceful, impressive gathering of 200,000 people at Lincoln Memorial: a high point was reached with Marian Anderson's singing of Negro spirituals and Martin Luther King's long-remembered address, "I Have a Dream."

Both Walter and May Reuther marched alongside Coretta and Martin Luther King, Jr., at Selma, Alabama, where Walter made the most succinct speech he ever delivered. Climbing on a cane-bottom chair, he packed into three minutes the essence of his feelings about the civil rights movement: "The struggle will be carried on until every American can share in the blessings of human dignity," he said. ". . . Let us take heart; our cause is just, and human justice will prevail." The Reuthers joined the stalwarts who walked with James H. Meredith along the dangerous last five miles of his route to Jackson, Mississippi. Struggle and risk were two elements that fired Reuther's instinct for action, sending him headlong into the causes he held dear. When Cesar Chavez took the drastic means of fasting to draw attention to the grape pickers' plight, Reuther made the initial response among top labor leaders by appearing dramatically at Chavez's bedside, a canvas cot in strike headquarters at Delano, to give moral support and a check for $50,000 in UAW funds to the poverty-stricken, transient farm workers. To George Meany, this was another publicity stunt: and, though the AFL-CIO later voted $1 million in funds, Meany did not become personally involved in the California strike struggle.

Walter could not keep from it. His concern for minority rights and human welfare led him to form a Citizens' Crusade Against Poverty in 1964, enrolling many well-known professional and business leaders, corporation presidents included, to organize private support for the poor. They sponsored a Poor People's Convention in Washington in 1966, designed to evoke national concern. Reuther, who was critical of Johnson's small anti-poverty appropriations that year, issued a warning that "reason will yield to riots, and bitterness will yield to bloodshed" in a statement written for the opening. Oddly enough, he did not appear to deliver that statement. He was criticized sternly for his absence, especially as Sargent Shriver, then director of the Office of Economic Opportunity, tried to speak, but was drowned out by hoots and jeers, and left the hall. Many thought Walter was avoiding trouble he suspected in advance; but it is likely that he was trying to avoid criticism in his own city for his efforts to take care of the poor everywhere else. For, less than a year later, his dire prediction came true in Detroit, where the gunfire and rioting that erupted in 1967 was a worse disaster than the one in 1943. While the streets burned, Governor Romney debated with Washington about sending federal troops. Mayor Cavanaugh called on Reuther to intercede; and, though reluctant to do so, he felt that the city must be saved. He got in touch with the White House and spoke to Abe Fortas, the Supreme Court justice, who was helping LBJ cope with the crucial situation. Troops were dispatched, and the rioting quelled. As soon as quiet returned to the strife-torn city, the labor leader met with top-management executives in a common cause, forming the New Detroit Committee to rebuild the city on a basis of equality. Their aim was to get a fair-housing bill passed first; and during the fall Walter, along with Henry Ford II and GM Chairman of the Board James Roche, flew to Lansing to lobby personally for passage. But all the power in the world—"business power, labor power, money power"— could not move the state legislature, which voted down the bill, 55 to 47. It took only a few days for a small clique of Black Power leaders to declare the New Detroit Committee a failure, leveling unwarranted criticism at Walter Reuther.

UAW members sometimes referred to Reuther in affectionate amusement and often as "The Great White Father." The term had no racial overtones originally but was taken from American Indian background of the area. "Michigan" is the Indian name for "Land of the Sky-Blue Water" (Lake Michigan); the president is "The Great White Father"; and Reuther's desire to care for all workers led to the term. But the Black Power leaders now used it with scorn, to denounce him as "paternalistic," and as "trying to dictate to the black community ever since the UAW came to power." They spread a wisecrack around that there were "four generals in Detroit: Ford, Chrysler, General Motors, and General Reuther."

These and other vitriolic invectives as to this "Jekyll and Hyde" approach—"a liberal around the country and a despot in Detroit" —did not deter Walter from continuing to pursue his nationwide antipoverty program. At his insistence, the UAW financed a nine-month study by a Citizens' Board of Inquiry into Hunger and Malnutrition, made up of distinguished professionals, who discovered that at least ten million Americans were suffering from chronic hunger and malnutrition. The Food Stamp program was labeled "a nightmare for the hungry," deficient and unfair. The scandalous conditions reported led to a national television documentary, "Hunger in America," which stirred up so much controversy that a congressional investigation was held and certain reforms were made, all because of Reuther's ability to arouse action. He did not hesitate when the predominantly black sanitation workers began their famous strike in Memphis, but went at once to speak before fifty thousand workers, declaring, "I serve notice upon the mayor of Memphis and the people who have to make this decision that they will not starve these sanitation workers into submission." And he laid the sum of $50,000 "on the line," on behalf of the UAW, "to demonstrate we meant business," he said later. A few UAW members criticized him for going to the aid of sanitation workers, but he reminded the membership at the convention that the auto workers could never have organized at all if they had not had help from the coal miners and the clothing workers. The answers to today's problems, he told them, "will not be found in a contest between Black Power and white supremacy. . . . What we need is the power of human solidarity, the power built upon our common humanity, because the only differences there are, are only skin deep. We are all children of God."

That the strike, which was "finally worked out," should involve the tragic shooting of Martin Luther King, Jr., on April 4, 1968, was a source of deep sorrow to Reuther. Again troubled by the threatening portents of the cold-blooded killing, he marched in the funeral procession in Atlanta. Barely two months later, on June 5, before he—or the nation—had quite recovered, Robert Kennedy, who had sent a special plane for Coretta King at the time of her husband's murder, was cut down by an assassin also. It was a nightmarish period; Walter flew to Los Angeles, and back east to New York City to stand by the casket in St. Patrick's Cathedral as a member of the honor guard. In his sadness, he was profoundly disturbed by the trend toward renewed violence in America, with the vigilantes on one hand and the extreme radicals on the other. Moreover, it was all bound up with the endless costly war in Vietnam, which was dividing the country more and more.

If Bobby Kennedy had not been killed, Reuther would probably have supported him for President in 1968, since Kennedy's position on the war in Vietnam was closer to his own than Senator Eugene McCarthy's "peace now" platform of complete and immediate withdrawal, which to Reuther was rash and unsound, although for years he had been saying that the war in Asia must be won in the rice fields rather than on the battlefields. Even by 1967, he was already completely disillusioned with Johnson's policy of escalation in spite of his own strong anti-Communist feelings. He also joined a group of moderates who were seeking "negotiations now," which, perhaps because of his labor dealings, seemed much more feasible than complete withdrawal of forces, unaccompanied by plans for conversion to peace. He had in fact prepared a brief for postwar conversion, presented at his last appearance before a Congressional Committee in 1970.

At any rate, when LBJ withdrew from the race, Reuther and the UAW Executive Board felt that Humphrey was the only logical candidate that they could support; he had always been loyal to labor, in spite of his shortcomings in other areas. And at the ill-fated Democratic convention in Chicago, he did work with Walter and others in laying down a compromise plank for the party platform on the Vietnam question. It might have unified the various factions, but Johnson, still the Chief Executive, vetoed it. Nevertheless, labor supported Humphrey, and the UAW worked hard on his behalf. If it had not been for George Wallace's third party, Humphrey might have won the election, since he lost the popular national vote by only seven-tenths of one percent. He carried the state of Michigan by an ample majority.

The miserable, disruptive events of the Democratic convention, however, had repercussions in Detroit in another flare-up of the civil rights problem. Undoubtedly spurred on by the widespread publicity given the Black Panthers, a group of militants within the union began plaguing the UAW, and particularly its president. Even more distressing to Walter were the verbal assaults, the hissing opposition from the Students for a Democratic Society in universities. Inside the UAW, a group of "concerned Negro" UAW members, led by a vice-president from Local 600, formed a committee to seek more posts of authority in the union for their race. Stressing the fact that they did not doubt Reuther's integrity and commitment, but *because* of those qualities in him, they asked to resolve the matter with him at the conference table "rather than . . . take the issue to the streets and public press." Walter got the message, and did have meetings with leaders of the group, but progress was too slow for the militants, who threw their support to the small Detroit League of Revolutionary Black Workers.

The league was active in about twelve plants, and, like most extremists, relied on inflammatory language, proclaiming that "all-out war has been declared on Uncle Tomism in order for us to kill racism." Leaflets were handed to workers at the gate of the River Rouge plant, denouncing "that racist Walter Reuther" and "white racist pigs." This was a tactical error at the start, since Walter's reputation for pioneering in civil rights in the labor movement was so well known that the UAW headed all other unions; to use such stereotyped phrases as "white racist pigs" in this case was absurd, was so patently a "line" from outside sources, that the leafleting was ineffectual. The league then provoked acts of violence, and the UAW retaliated with a broadside against "this group of extremists and racial separatists, which has sought to spread terror among both white and black workers." By 1969, the league membership began to taper off for lack of proof in its claims, and because the workers realized that terrorist methods were, as Reuther said, "counterproductive" and only served to delay progress. At the 1970 convention, Nelson Jack Edwards, Negro member of the Executive Council, was elected vice-president when four new posts were created for that office. The others were Douglas Fraser, Kenneth Bannon, and Olga Madar, the first woman ever to be elected to the UAW Executive Board—four years later than the first Negro, signifying to some Women's Lib members that male supremacy takes precedence over white supremacy. The era of protest had finally had its effect on the union.

However, the problem of the SDS was more disturbing to Walter Reuther, because there was little reference point for the younger generation to which he could appeal, and the problems were not soluble within the framework of the union. He had several "confrontations" with the Students for a Democratic Society but found it difficult to reach them. Always in the past he had had great success in speaking to college students; at the University of California, hotbed of radicalism, his appearance had been hailed by huge attendance, surpassed only by Alfred C. Kinsey (discussing his famous *Report* on sex) and when Reuther spoke at sectarian Ohio Wesleyan University during obligatory chapel, when "a speaker had to be damn good or he'd soon be deafened by the rustle of textbooks," the labor leader was "electrifying," according to a graduate of the early 1950's, and "stirred up more talk and controversy than any other speaker. . . ." But the "SDS kids," as Walter called them, were simply negative or destructive. He tried to tell them he was called a "revolutionary" because he had led a successful fight at Wayne University (his old City College) against compulsory ROTC back in 1931–1932, and now they thought they had a "brand new idea." He tried to show them that violence couldn't solve problems by pointing out that the auto workers sat down in the plants because management wouldn't talk to them, and were blocking all efforts to meet, and that during the sit-downs the workers never wrecked any machinery (as the SDS had wrecked the libraries and administration buildings); moreover, when management finally did consent to meet, the workers had negotiable demands. The SDS groups were staging "sit-ins" because they didn't *want* to talk, and when they did, they had *non*negotiable demands, the first one that the president be fired. "That's crazy," he told them. "We knew what we were fighting for—and you only know what you're fighting against. . . . You have no moral right to destroy something unless you think you have something better to put in its place. . . . That's the difference between what we did when I was a young radical going to the university and what you're doing. And that's a fundamental difference."

His cogent arguments might have swayed some students, but when the UAW backed Humphrey, and after the events of the 1968 Democratic convention, the SDS antagonism intensified. At Ann Arbor, when he spoke to University of Michigan students on the subject of conservation, though the majority of those present wanted to hear him, the SDS group disrupted the meeting with boos, stompings, and obscenities. Walter did not give up on the extremists of the youth rebellion, however. In 1970, he planned to ask them to come, a few at a time, to the UAW Family Education Center then nearing completion at Black Lake, to give them a period of study and quiet discussion with young labor leaders. He crystallized his feelings of optimism in remarks to a young local union editor at the 1970 convention: "Age is a matter of the spirit," he said. "I know young people who are old in spirit, who don't *really* want to go out and change the world. I want to change the world. I feel it just as strongly now as I did when I was twenty-three. The people who feel as I do and the people who feel as you do—we have to bridge the generation gap and we have to join forces and do this job together."

Reuther was, of course, active in trying to "change the world" in person from the outset of his career. Probably no other union president was as well known abroad as in the United States. From the time he took office in 1946, he set forth (literally) to carry out the ideas he expressed in his initial speech: "We are building a labor movement . . . that will remake the world where the working people will get the benefits of their labor. . . . People of all nations and of all tongues want the same things we want— an opportunity to enjoy economic security and well-being, an opportunity to live with freedom and justice in human dignity, without fear of tomorrow." The 1949 convention authorized the first steps toward realization of his goal by adopting a proposal to enact an international fair-labor-standards treaty to eliminate the exploitation of workers, and it approved affiliation with the International Metalworkers Federation. It was that year that Walter headed the CIO delegation, including Victor and Roy, which, with delegates of the AFL and forty-seven free-world labor organizations, met in London and founded the International Confederation of Free Trade Unions to help workers in free countries build security through their own unions. To Walter and Victor, the ICFTU meant putting into practice the "social engineering" they had studied years before on their world trip.

The Reuthers and other UAW leaders worked closely with the ICFTU to establish schools for organizers during the 1950's, not only in the developed countries, but also in Asia and Africa, where "the inhuman exploitation of labor is a perpetual source of trouble. . . ." They built up "a cadre of leaders" in Africa and the Far East to help keep millions of workers from communism by giving them the democratic tool of militant trade unionism. To that end, the ICFTU and UAW, along with the Metalworkers Federation, raised funds for organizing drives on the plantations of Malaya, Ceylon, and the southern Cameroons.* Offices were set up in Bangkok, New Delhi, Bombay, Djakarta, Singapore, and Tokyo. Financial aid was given to union escapees from behind the Iron Curtain countries of Hungary, Poland, and East Berlin; Algerian and Spanish trade-union refugees were also aided, and those who escaped from Venezuelan dictatorship in the 1950's. The UAW on its own also provided legal aid for political prisoners in South Africa, the men and women struggling against apartheid; legal support for Nigerian trade-union leaders; and assistance in Cyprus that led to self-determination for trade-union members there.

In the 1960's, expanded production abroad of the Big Three, International Harvester, and many other firms posed a serious problem, since, as Reuther said, "Profits know no patriotism.

---

* Walter was an executive member of the American Committee on Africa; he and Victor were both active in the organization.

Twelve major auto manufacturers rule a worldwide industry employing two million workers," but the workers were divided by varying wage scales because of underdeveloped trade unions. There was nothing to prevent global corporations from producing cars at the lowest wage level and selling them at the highest profit market, thereby threatening American wages also. The UAW met this problem by establishing a Free World Labor Defense Fund at the Eighteenth Convention in 1962; and it was partly in this connection that Reuther went to Japan in December of that year. He spoke with both management and labor. The Communists, trying to make the most of the situation, led protest marches in Tokyo with signs reading, "Capitalist Spy," or "Yankee Imperialist"; in Kyoto they read, "Go Home, Walter Reuther." But he answered that he would go home only after he had helped them find a way to higher wages; and he told them what he had said to the Japanese manufacturers who complained that they had to export cars because there was but a small domestic market. He said, "Your own best market is your own back yard." Having noticed that Japanese factory parking lots were full of bicycles, he added, "Workers find it difficult to buy automobiles on bicycle wages." The remark stymied the Communists and delighted the Japanese trade unionists. Before he left, he met with officers of the four Japanese labor federations to plan an International Labor Wage Research Center, which the UAW helped to establish, where wage earners could get economic data connected with their collective-bargaining problems.

In telling May about the signs in Kyoto after he got back, Walter said, "I suppose you'd like to change it to "*Stay* Home"; but if she did, she knew it wouldn't do her any good. He had a compulsion to be at the scene of action, to go wherever he was called. As often as she could, May went with him, but it was not always possible, and when she did go they rarely had any time to themselves. There was one memorable occasion in Copenhagen when some kind Danish union officials scheduled a "free evening" for them. Walter said to May, "We've been liberated! Why don't we make the most of it?" Giving his bodyguards the slip, they strolled around the streets of the city, window-shopping and taking in the sights until long past midnight, all by themselves.

"It was the most wonderful evening," Walter said. "Nobody on our back." Most of the time they were not so lucky. In Venice one night, during a week-long ICFTU conference, they were relaxing in a gondola, blissfully quiet and listening to an open-air concert, when their serenity was broken by a brash yell from a passing water cab: "Hey, Mr. Reuther, can I see you at the hotel in the morning?" For a moment, Walter "felt like going over and upsetting his damned gondola"; but it soon passed. As a rule, his response to people was open and warm, ready to help. He used to say, "There are no values unrelated to people," and that perhaps was the secret of his ability to deal with them and to sway his listeners.

He had tremendous appeal to crowds, and he could not resist the opportunity of communicating with them whenever he was asked. His family never knew where he might go next. While May's brother, Leo Wolf, and his wife Eleanor, were traveling in Italy during the late 1960's, they happened to turn on the radio in Rapollo, and the first sound they heard was Walter's voice, broadcasting a labor speech from Turin. They listened, and when it was over, sent him a congratulatory telegram on the "wonderful speech." A couple of hours later they had a phone call from him. "I didn't know you were in Italy," he said, surprised and pleased to get their wire. They laughed. "We didn't know you were here, either," they told him, "till we turned on the radio."

One of the places where May usually accompanied Walter was to Sweden. It was natural for Reuther to be drawn to "the middle way" of that country's government and for Swedish officials to be impressed with the American labor leader's plans for social reforms on a worldwide scale. At the time the ICFTU was organized, Walter had become good friends with Arne Geijer, chairman of the trade unions in Sweden, as well as with Tage Erlander, Swedish Prime Minister from 1946 till 1969. Both entertained the Reuthers in their homes. The Geijers became close friends of May and Walter, and extended hospitality to members of their family, who came to Sweden at different times. When Vice President Humphrey and Reuther were there on a state visit during the Johnson administration, Erlander was their host;

another long-standing friend of Walter, Willy Brandt, then mayor of West Berlin, (now Chancellor, Federal Republic of Germany) was also a member of the party at Erlander's home in the country. Walter invited them all for a brisk row way around the lake and wouldn't let anyone else take the oars.

Another country May visited with Walter was Israel, an ancient land whose modern achievements in converting arid desert soil to fertile, productive ground could not fail to interest a man of Reuther's imagination and drive. The Israeli experiment in government, combining collective farming on the kibbutzim with a democratic legislative and executive system and free enterprise, with emphasis on labor organization and education in Histadrut,* fired his enthusiasm and support personally from the first time he and May toured Israel in 1955. In 1954, he had been named honorary co-chairman, with George Meany, of the American Trade Union Council for Histadrut, an organization of labor leaders who support the aims of that organization. Never content to hold office in name only, he and May enjoyed an extended stay in Israel, during which time, as usual, they won many friends, and Walter became involved in a number of projects. He was one of the founders of the Afro-Asia Institute in Tel-Aviv, to train African, Asian, and later, Latin-American labor leaders, where courses of study are given to aid labor groups in developing countries to solve the various problems that arise in their localities. In 1958, Walter was the recipient of the Humanitarian Award, one of Histadrut's most important honors, with a presentation dinner in New York, at which funds are raised to grant scholarships to needy children. Walter also helped to establish the Philip Murray Community Center in Tel-Aviv in honor of his old colleague, and in 1963, the Walter Reuther Youth Center in nearby Holon was so named as a mark of appreciation for his unswerving support. Always promoting the achievements of modern science for nonmilitary purposes, Walter was especially interested in the Weizmann Institute of Science of Rehoboth; and in 1968 a testimonial dinner in Detroit in his honor marked

---

* The literal translation is "Organization." Actually Histadrut is the central trade-union council of Israel which coordinate labor and education situations of the country.

the establishment of a Walter P. Reuther Chair in the Peaceful
Uses of Atomic Energy at the Institute. Seated next to him and
making the presentation was his friend, the Israeli foreign minis-
ter, Abba Eban, whom the Reuthers first had known at the
United Nations through Mrs. Roosevelt* and Adlai Stevenson.
A month after the Detroit dinner, May and Walter went to
Israel on what was to prove their last visit, to be feted in person
at the Weizmann Institute.

In an effort to equalize the wages of auto workers everywhere
as the American manufacturers kept adding to their sites of
production—by 1966 Chrysler alone had bought the French
Simca and a British auto firm—Reuther was instrumental in
forming the World Auto Council, made up of delegates from
the Big Three plants in fourteen different countries. Its aim
was to protect the right of workers in all countries to organize
and eventually to move toward uniformity of wages and working conditions. In 1967, he was the guiding spirit in the creation
of the World Agricultural Implement Council, for the same
purpose. As might be expected, he was president of both groups.

It is true that Walter Reuther inevitably made enemies in the
course of his long public career of pushing his plans for "changing the world." As Rabbi Morris Adler, one of the trustees on the
Community Health Association Board, who saw him in action,
observed, "Some people never forgive a man with a new idea."
But the remarkable fact about the labor leader is that, in working
to improve the lot of millions who could not speak for themselves,
he made enduring friendships with many heads of state, moving
among people in high places around the world.

* Mrs. Roosevelt was United States delegate to the UN from 1945 to 1953.

XXVI

Personal Profile

IN their perceptive analysis of Walter's personality, B. J. Widick and Irving Howe described it in 1949 as "*unfinished*," one that still retained the possibilities of drawing on the potential of his undeniable talent as a leader. Earlier they remarked that he had forgotten how to relax or play, but parenthetically suggested that his enforced rest after the assassination attempt might slow down his pace and bring personality changes. That he did realize his "potential" in large measure is clear from the tremendous scope of his activities—and achievements—recorded in the foregoing chapters. It hardly seems possible that he could have found time to relax, or "play," but he did, in his way. In fact, his whole life-style changed profoundly after the shooting, so that one could almost say he led two separate lives, albeit of unequal proportions.

For one thing, in the necessary seclusion of his private life, he perfected his woodworking until it became a fine art, and he had proved to be an expert cabinetmaker. He studied texts on the subject, learning about the best materials to use; and the low cabinets were finished with boiled linseed oil, as it made them easy to repair if they got scratched. He created an elaborate hi-fi set and built-in bookcases at arm's reach from deep, comfortable chairs. He designed and built the semicircular open staircase leading to the upper floor, with easy, shallow steps and a slim iron rail. Washrooms were fitted with accordian doors of hinged walnut. The chests he built had drawers that slid out smoothly at the slightest pull; they never stuck or needed tugging. The downstairs rooms were decorated with ceramics—bowls and vases—and wood carvings, mostly gifts to Walter from all over the world. May, of course, joined with Walter in all projects connected with the house, and as soon as the girls were old enough they had a share in it. Later, nephews from both sides of the family helped to build a small guest house with a sundeck roof, years after the Reuthers moved to the country. Roy and Victor (when he was in Detroit) and Leo Wolf pitched in also.

Both Walter and May became fascinated with landscaping and wildlife lore, especially with the wild flowers and birds of the region. As part of reclaiming the land they sent for the five hundred seedling trees offered by the state free of charge to those who would plant and nourish them. As a result, Reuther became an ardent conservationist, a facet of his life not generally known. He served on several conservation boards, and in so doing made friends with businessmen like C. Allen Harlan, president of the Edison Corporation. Learning that Walter and his family took great interest in wild flowers, he presented him with a huge two-volume set of *The WildFlowers of Western Pennsylvania and the Upper Ohio Basin*, illustrated with fine watercolor plates, which contained a long, admiring inscription "To Walter Reuther" in Harlan's hand, invoking the "dreams and dreamers" of Washington, Jefferson, Madison, and Lincoln, and linked Reuther's dreams to theirs. It ended: "The fullness of our democratic ideals have not been attained. Perhaps more than any other force in America, Walter, you have set into motion a positive force for that kind of Progress. . . ." This was a remarkable tribute to a labor leader from the head of a corporation. The Reuthers and their relatives made good use of the volumes whenever they discovered a "new" wild flower.

Fishing, of course, continued to be Walter's favorite recreation, angling for black bass, pike ("wall-eyes"), pickerel, and big "muskies" (muskellunge) in the lakes of northern Michigan, as well as casting for trout whenever he had the chance. "Walter was a real fanatic about fishing!" his sister-in-law said. He carried a collapsible rod in his luggage when traveling a territory known for freshwater fish. He could stay quiet for a long time, if necessary, but he usually did not have to wait long, and rarely came back empty-handed with stories of "the one that got away." Once he was so proud of his prize in the Mississippi that he took it to a taxidermist to have it mounted and then flown to Detroit by air freight. Back at Solidarity House, he bragged about his triumph, silencing all doubters by promising that they could soon see it for themselves. After several days had passed without a sign of the shipment, smug smiles greeted him in the offices, so he started calling the airlines. The package was finally located, to his relief; when the airlines man who phoned the good news was curious to know what could be in the box to rate such urgent calls, Walter told him, "My reputation is in that box."

Inevitably he was challenged by other anglers to test his skill in other waters. Salmon fishing was a real sport, they suggested; he might not find it such a cinch. That was all Walter needed. The next time he had to attend a convention in San Francisco he arranged for an expedition to the northwest Pacific coast to try his luck. He promised his nephews, who loved to go fishing with him, that if he had any luck at all, he would let them know. And before he got back to Detroit, they received an enlarged snapshot, inscribed to "Peter and Tommy" (Wolf), holding up "a real beauty" in each hand, a huge, happy grin on his face.

He would have been fully content with his personal life in the country except that it never could be truly private for him or his family because of the constant security measures that always had to be taken. He felt especially concerned about his daughters. He never quite recovered from Linda's query while he was in the hospital after the shooting: "Why can't I be like other kids?" During their primary-school years, Linda and Lisa were driven to and from school in the armored car, with the guards on hand to watch over them, as they watched over Walter wherever he went. But when Linda was nearing high school age in 1956, Walter and May decided it would be much better to send her to a good boarding school. As usual, Walter made a thorough study of the situation, and of all those he, May, and the girls considered, the Putney School in Vermont seemed most appealing, offering the sort of education he wanted his children to have. He had heard of the coeducational secondary school, located on a farm, which its founder Carmelita Chase Hinton, had had the temerity to start in 1935, the middle of the Depression. Its values were those of what he would have liked all schools to have: students "would study because they were really interested in intellectual ideas; . . . they would have work jobs; . . . they would not stop creative activities for college preparation but would carry on with music, art, handcrafts; . . . they would try to share with the community what they were doing; . . . they would live a really vigorous outdoor life."

Of course the tuition was high—this was one area in which Walter departed from his usual frugality. But because his own education had been so sketchy, he wanted his children to have the best. Such schools could hardly be carried out on a "mass production" scale, except in some far, distant Utopia; but if he could have brought it about, this was the kind of education Walter Reuther would have liked to see every child enjoy. Linda entered the Putney School that fall, taking part in its various programs, and she discovered a distinct talent for ceramics, spending much time at the potter's wheel in the handcraft workshop. In Linda's junior year, May and Walter invited her and five other Putney students to attend the UAW's Seventeenth Constitutional Convention held in Atlantic City in October of 1959. It was probably the first and perhaps the only time high school students from a private institution had the opportunity of witnessing a labor convention in action. No amount of instruction in a classroom course on social studies could give them as accurate a picture as this experience. With a young teacher, Bob Treat, the six went down to Atlantic City, where the Reuthers were on hand to greet them. Before the convention, Walter met with the group at breakfast and gave them a "briefing on issues," so they would be prepared for the problems to be dealt with in the resolutions that year. His talk was listed among the highlights in the report the students gave to their classmates on their return to Putney. Some of the others were: observing the convention from the speakers' platform; a private dinner party with Marian Anderson, whose singing opened the convention; a press conference with

Senator Kennedy, soon to be nominated for President, with whom Walter and the group had their picture snapped by a news photographer one day; and a regional dinner.

The following year, since Linda was to graduate, the Putney School faculty asked Walter Reuther to be the speaker at the graduation exercises, which marked the twenty-fifth anniversary of the school's existence. He was glad to accept and not a little moved at the idea of giving a talk at his elder daughter's high school graduation. He and May, with Lisa, who already planned to attend Putney, went to Vermont for the day-long events, which took place on June 10, 1960. When they arrived, the faculty was rather amazed by the big, armored Packard that came driving up with the bodyguards in front; several people wondered if the labor leader thought he needed protection* from a handful of teachers and not many more students. Walter hated the security measures and had hoped to elude them on this occasion, but the union would not hear of it.

Although he gave little outward sign, he was embarrassed for Linda's sake, and Lisa's.

He probably felt much less "like a prisoner" when his nephew, Billy Wolfman, son of May's older brother Earl, became his bodyguard in the late 1960's. Billy, a strong, athletic boy, two years older than Linda, had the same love of the outdoors and interest in conservation that Walter had; and the two could sometimes be by themselves, carpentering outdoors without breaking the rule of security protection. The Reuthers bought a small vacation cottage near Fort Myers, Florida, not far from a colony called "Florida Sun Coast Council of Retired UAW Members," and here Walter found seculsion without the need for strict security measures. A labor reporter from Detroit strolled onto the premises one day and saw Billy and Walter up on the roof, repairing some weather damage. Walter was saying, "Let me have the hammer, Billy. . . . Now move that over there. . . . Hit her here, Billy." Both were so intent on the job that they never noticed the newsman, who stood below, watching them for at least three minutes before he called to them. He said he "could have set a match

* A decade later, at some universities, the precautions did not seem out of place.

to the place in that time and burned them out," but Walter only laughed at him.

In Michigan, the Reuthers spent as much time as possible outdoors, taking family hikes on spring and fall weekends. When Lisa, who followed her sister at the Putney School, was a senior, she took as an elective a field-study course in wild flowers of the region; and at her graduation in 1965, the first thing she did on her parents' arrival was to take Walter down to the brook to show him a species of water plants the class had found. To those who knew Walter Reuther only through news stories as a tough-minded labor leader and keen collective bargainer, the sight of him as a nature-lover hiking across the meadow with his redheaded daughter seemed an amusing anomaly; but this was merely another part of his many-faceted personality.

He would have liked to spend more time with his daughters, but in the face of his ambitious program he had to sacrifice a close relationship with his children. Linda graduated from the University of Michigan at Ann Arbor and went out to the West Coast to teach,* by the time Lisa enrolled at Oakland University, a branch of Michigan State College near the Reuthers' home in Rochester. Five years younger than Linda, Lisa was part of the sudden overwhelming "youth rebellion" that began in late 1967 and early 1968, with the first campus sit-ins and protest marches. She was part of the scene that revolted in a complete reversal of all the values Reuther's generation had cherished.

At first he was astonished at some of the things his younger daughter said and did. But he came to realize that she was part of a different generation, living in a different world than he was; and he didn't expect her to behave as he used to behave. And once he made up his mind to that, Lisa didn't surprise him anymore. In view of his moral rectitude, she still shocked him, but she didn't surprise him. Shocked or not, however, both Walter and May were "devoted, loyal, and proud parents," as Dr. Durward B. Varner, then Chancellor of Oakland University and a neighbor of the Reuthers, was to say of them. The Varners and Reuthers became friends as well as good neighbors and were

---

* At present, she is teaching disadvantaged children in a preschool program in San Francisco.

instrumental in starting the drive for the Meadowbrook Music Festival, on the order of the Berkshire Festival at Tanglewood, Massachusetts, and within price range of working people's incomes. Located between Detroit and Rochester, it was easily reached by bus from the city. In conjunction with the Music Festival, the Meadowbrook Theater was also established by dint of hard work on the part of a handful of people like the Reuthers and the Varners, who were unwavering in their effort to fulfill the idea of making the arts available to many more people than the privileged few who "subscribed" to the Detroit Symphony or Bonstelle Repertory Theater, year after year. And though there were those, especially students at Wayne University, who complained that they didn't have bus fare to get out to the grounds, let alone money to buy a ticket, there is no doubt that Meadowbrook became an asset to the environs of an industrial city like Detroit.

At Christmas time, the Reuthers' home was always glowing with gay decorations and warm hospitality; the girls were back for vacation, and the house was open to relatives of all ages and to neighbors and friends dropping in. When the Varners came over they brought a simple gift like Texas pecans from their family in the Southwest in exchange for Grandmother Reuther's homemade wine from Wheeling. The Reuther family ties remained strong throughout the years, aside from the bond between the three brothers connected with the UAW. Walter's parents, of course, took great pride in his triumphs, and gave unswerving support to his venturesome ideas for "a better world," no matter how farfetched they might seem to others. His mother was always ready with some consoling thought in her letters if those dreams were frustrated, or to defend him sturdily when she read an attack on the labor leader in the papers. His father was on hand at conventions whenever he could make it, ready to enjoy a private joke with Walter over some incident that might have taken place behind the podium or in a caucus room. One of the happiest family occasions was the sixtieth wedding anniversary of Valentine and Anna Reuther, when all the children gathered in Wheeling to help them celebrate the event in the spring of 1963. The four brothers and their sister Christine stood in a semicircle around their parents, who were seated in the old-fashioned wooden porch swing, to have their picture snapped by a relative. Neither Val nor Anna looked their years, though both were past eighty and had worked hard most of their lives. Nor for that matter, did their sons look their ages, who were all in their fifties. Walter, who led the most strenuous life, looked the most vigorous and youngest of the four. Christine was much younger than her brothers.

Perhaps the secret of Walter's buoyant youthfulness was that very element of unceasing activity, plus the ability to relax when he chose to do so, even if only for a short time. He and Victor attended a World Conference of Auto Workers in Rome, given under the auspices of the International Metalworkers at around this period,* and afterward they went up to Florence at the invitation of Mayor Georgio LaPira. They had an appointment with him at five o'clock, and spent most of the day touring the city of art treasures on their own. Late in the afternoon they were tired, and, having about half an hour to wait, went to an outdoor café on the Piazza della Signoria, graced by Michelangelo's *David*, among other statues by Italian masters, and a fountain. Everything was peaceful, beautiful and quiet, the beginning of a soft spring sunset. Completely relaxed, the two brothers were enjoying a cool drink, hardly saying a word. And then, "About twenty minutes later, all hell broke loose!" Offices had just closed, and a noisy melange of midget cars, mixed with motorbikes and buses, roared past them, seemingly from every direction—buzzing, honking, letting out noxious exhaust, and completely shattering the peace.

Walter was furious. "C'mon!" he said to Victor. And although it was not quite time, he strode to the mayor's office and went in without waiting to be announced. "Mr. Mayor," he burst out, "you ought to ban autos from the city!"

Mayor LaPira was both astonished and perplexed. "But Mr. Reuther," he protested. "You're president of the auto workers!"

"Automobiles are made to meet man's needs, not to destroy

* Victor set the date first as April, 1963, then as 1961; at any rate, it was in the early 1960's.

his environment!" Walter was still angry. "They're befouling your beautiful city."

The mayor couldn't believe his ears, and Walter was well aware that it must seem incongruous for someone in his position to suggest a move that might destroy a billion-dollar industry. It was a dilemma, no doubt of that, but a problem that he felt could be solved somehow.* His interest in conservation had soon led him to see the danger of overproduction from an ecological and aesthetic, as well as an economic, standpoint; he had been concerned about the whole question for some time, and in the coming years was to advocate various improvements in fuel, size, safety and silence devices, and the number of cars permitted on highways. At this date, the early 1960's, he had already told newsmen during an interview that "we are now approaching the point where man becomes less an economic being and more a cultural being. In the future, it's possible that the average worker will spend less time making Fords, and more time working on a concerto or a painting. . . ." The statement was no doubt the result of his pursuits during the small segment of his life not connected with the public figure of a labor leader.

Occasionally he played a set or two of tennis, but ever since the shooting his backhand was weak because of his injured fingers, and although his opponents volleyed to his forehand, he tired easily at a game requiring a fast pace. He hated to admit it, however, and would play until his opponent was ready to quit. His game was still energetic, but when his assistant, Irving Bluestone, who challenged him one weekend afternoon, confessed after a couple of sets, "I've had enough," Walter admitted, "I was waiting for you to say that." Sports, except for fishing, occupied very little of his limited recreation time after the shotgun injuries cut down the strength of his right arm.

One of the places he discovered in his search for good freshwater fishing, Black Lake in northern Michigan, led to a fusion of Reuther's "two lives," in the concept and realization of a Family Education Center for the UAW members and their coming generation. An idyllic spot, set in a thousand-acre site of

---

* Some years later, in 1971, autos *were* banned from this and other parts of Florence—Walter's protest may have initiated the traffic control.

virgin forest, Black Lake gave him the inspiration to build on its shores a retreat from the pressures of the city, where auto workers could both relax and learn, and where, more importantly, new leadership could be trained for the future. He was deeply concerned about the quality of leadership that was to follow him, because he did intend to retire at age sixty-five, according to the resolution passed at the 1959 convention, no matter what his critics in and out of the union said about his single-handedness in running the UAW, implying that he would never relinquish his power by stepping down when he reached retirement age.

Outwardly he gave little sign of his intentions. B. J. Widick, whose estimate of Reuther in 1949, referred to at the beginning of this chapter, was fairly favorable, criticized Reuther severely in 1964* for operating the UAW "with the iron grip of an infallible man." Widick asserted that AFL-CIO leaders knew that the UAW Executive Board had been reduced to a "rubber-stamp body," so Reuther's moralizing in the labor movement had an air of hypocrisy to them." Inside the union, comments were apt to be more succinct and just as sharp. Two telling quips that went the rounds were: "Oh, sure, Walter's for a democratic union, as long as he gets his own way!" and again; "The Great White Father commands everything done 'the Reuther way.'" Of course, this censure of union leadership was by no means limited to Reuther. One well-known intraunion story was that Walter was bragging about the democratic UAW conventions to another AFL-CIO union president, who countered, "We have democratic conventions, too; but we let those s.o.b.'s know who's boss." Certainly Reuther must have been aware of this sentiment, as well as the hostility of the league activists, and the apathy of young workers prone to absenteeism who took the union for granted. One of the things he hoped to make them see was that the price of labor gains, like that of freedom, was "eternal vigilance," and that the future held a great deal of challenge in the face of advanced technology.

At any rate, he and May talked over the idea of the Black Lake center at some length—he usually discussed his "brain waves"

---

* Labor Today by B. J. Widick. Boston: Houghton Mifflin Company, 1964, p. 186.

with her first of all—before he presented the plan to his aides; and it was 1966 before the Twentieth Constitutional Convention authorized construction of the $18 million project, which became his Camelot.* Indeed, it served as much as a retreat for him in the last stormy years of his affiliation with the AFL-CIO as he meant it to be for the families who would share its beauty and benefits. Getting in touch with his friend Oskar Stonorov, who had designed Solidarity House, he outlined the kind of structure he had in mind, and after the designs were laid out for the simple, long two-story buildings that blended in with the wooded land-scape, the two worked closely together in making the center a reality. Walter devoted all the spare time he had away from his union work (negotiations in 1968 and plans for those in 1970) and public commitments to this latest—and last—dream. In-creasingly, he made on-the-spot inspections to be sure that the natural setting of pine and birch on the southern shore of the lake, the location of the site, was preserved as much as possible. Hardly a tree was touched without his, or Stonorov's, permission. Walter gave as much care and concern to the center as he had to his own home, except that he had to refrain from doing the job himself. He was impatient at the inevitable delays, of which there were several, including labor trouble, when the construc-tion workers balked over jurisdictional rights and wage settle-ments.

In the main, however, those buildings rising among the trees and reflected in the shining waters of the lake were a refuge and source of consolation to him. He especially needed a place of peace and solitude in 1968, a year of personal sorrow for the Reuther family. Right after the first of the year, Roy suffered a serious heart attack, and he died in the hospital in Detroit on January 10. He had had a previous attack a few years before, but had recovered and, though on a limited schedule, had seemed quite well when the second and fatal one occurred, a shock to all of them.

Walter was deeply grieved by the loss of his brother, two years younger than he, the one closest to him during their school days

---

* Rabbi Jacob Weinstein, a member of the Union's Public Review Board, gave this symbolic name to the Center.

in Wheeling. As the two "middle boys,"—Ted was the oldest and Victor the youngest in the family until Christine came along—they were the brothers closest to each other during those years, sharing the same pursuits, nearly equal in athletic skills, able to understand each other's boyhood ambitions, with Roy usually following Walter's lead. The most genial of the four, Roy had been highly successful in public relations for the union, though he was not a speech-maker and he preferred personal contact rather than public appearances before crowds. He took everybody's troubles to heart, and as a result was one of the best-loved men in the union. A labor official remarked that Roy was "the only one of the Reuther brothers George Meany really liked"; and a UAW staff member called him "one of the sweetest guys you'd ever want to know."

Walter missed him sorely, and before he or any of them had adjusted to his being gone, Valentine Reuther died in Wheeling. Whether Roy's death hastened his own, or whether it was simply his age—he was in his eighty-seventh year and had led a full life—the family circle was sadly diminished by this double blow. Walter knew he would miss Val, the *Vater* who had given his children a heritage of unionism and the religious concept of the brotherhood of man as a philosophy to live by, instead of a routine Sunday school liturgy; who had always been there with advice and encouragement if needed. Their mother, as always, showed great courage in her grief, but it would not have been so difficult for any of them if Roy, only fifty-eight when he died, had been spared.

One event that gave Walter some feeling of consolation, because he knew it would have pleased his brother, was that the United Farm Workers Building in Delano, California, where Roy had done his usual quiet job in helping to solve knotty administrative organizing problems, was named for him. A commemorative plaque was presented to his son, Alan, and to Walter, who flew to Delano for the cornerstone ceremonies. They both accepted the plaque which read, "In Memory of Our Brother, Roy L. Reuther, Who Understood Our Struggle." Cesar Chavez handed it to them while hundreds of transient farm workers, with sorrowful faces, pressed in around them to get a closer look.

Walter was deeply moved by the simple inscription, so appropriate for Roy's memorial.

The family's grief, plus that he felt at the fatal shootings of his friends, Martin Luther King and Bobby Kennedy—the latter had been the only person outside the family to sit with Walter at Roy's funeral—combined to make 1968 a year of "trial by existence" for the labor leader. Yet he somehow kept up with the demands of his public career, even to taking the decisive step of breaking away from the AFL-CIO and forming his own Alliance for Labor Action with the Teamsters. Small wonder that he sought and found refuge in the sylvan surroundings of the northern lake shore on which his latest dream was slowly being realized. The buildings were completed at last in the early months of 1970, and even before the education program was authorized by the convention delegates, Walter began holding UAW councils there, mostly to give people a personally conducted tour of the entire center. Since the wooded hills were heavy with snow, though viewed from indoors through the wide windows of the buildings, he wore the "Tyrolean guide" hat he had once bought in Switzerland, and no amount of teasing from May, who usually accompanied him in leading the groups around, could deter him from wearing it. Visitors were taken from the meeting rooms and dining halls through the huge gymnasium (Walter's pride and joy) and Olympic swimming pool, through the classrooms and bright playrooms for children to the restful lounges and living quarters. He could have conducted the tour blindfolded; he knew every detail by heart. As he and May led the way down the elevated corridors connecting the center's buildings, he explained the purpose of this "Round Table" retreat. "The center is about the most crucial issue of our times: The quality of leadership. . . . The great changes taking place around us are straining the fabric of the human community, and we must find the leadership at all levels, to solve the problems ahead—leaders who combine technical competence with social vision, idealism, and commitment."

As for the near future, it was no secret that Reuther was grooming two possible successors when he retired—Leonard Woodcock and Douglas Fraser. Both were highly capable and personable, and of the same progressive union persuasion as he.

Woodcock was more academic in his approach, less zealous than Walter. Instead of the term "bright young businessman" so often applied to Reuther's appearance, Woodcock might be described more as a university professor, and since becoming president of the UAW, he has been called "scholarly" in dealing with problems. Fraser, endowed with more of Walter's ebullience, seemed to him to combine the qualities of both himself and Woodcock. At any rate, he felt the union would be in good hands with either of them. It was of a more distant future he was thinking when he spoke of finding and training new leaders, the younger—and youngest—generation, who had to learn the values that would save mankind from destroying itself and its environment. It is likely that he meant to do much of this indoctrination himself, and felt that the center would inspire renewed faith in the power of mankind to prevail. To one group he said, after showing them around, "We made it this beautiful to bring the best out of everyone who comes here. I believe no one can leave here without being enriched spiritually." He could scarcely wait for the education program to get started officially.

But first he had to oversee preparation of the collective bargaining program for 1970, to be voted on at the convention in Atlantic City, April 20–27. A few days before it opened, he appeared on an NET television program of The New York Times, "Detroit Report," with Times reporters Jerry Flint of the Detroit Bureau and Edwin L. Daley of the Washington Bureau as a team of questioners, and Clifton Daniel, associate editor as chairman. Reuther answered their inquiries vigorously, outlining the aims of the convention, which, besides an across-the-board pay increase and an all-time-high pension figure of $500 a month, was going to articulate workers' needs with a strong accent on youth. His most recent labor concept was for a "juniority system," or "inversed seniority," because he felt that the most serious problem was the high percentage of hard-core unemployed among the young. So far the manufacturers had refused to lay off older men and keep younger men, but he hoped the convention would pass a resolution to work for the plan. As a corollary, the UAW had been promoting a "30 years and out" idea, whereby a worker would retire after 30 years of work no matter what his age. When asked about overproduction, the crowding of highways and the safety of cars, he said the reason for trouble in America was the failure to work out a balance between the overloading of roads with cars and the mass transportation of people. "The individual vehicle will be tied in with mass transportation somehow; individuals can't drag two thousand pounds of metal every time they want to go some place!" As for safety in cars, he pointed out that "the speed of production and inspection is too fast: a hundred cars per hour, the required production figure, is too fast for safety and quality. The relation of the human being to the production process is forgotten, the man on the assembly line hasn't got enough time to put on six nuts or bolts before the next block is in front of him!" And that led him to absenteeism, an increasing problem because the job was so mechanical. "The young worker feels that things are in the saddle, and he is being shunted off today." He also answered questions on air pollution, the reduction of carbon-monoxide emission, and on sources of power—all the aspects of the auto industry that had come under attack. For most of them, the union had offered solutions, but management was as yet unwilling to accept them.

He was strong in his defense of labor, but when Clifton Daniel later was asked by an interviewer if he thought Reuther was "on the defensive," he replied, "No, I don't think so. He just wanted the most for his union members"—somewhat missing the point of Reuther's remarks, which had to do with a lot more than wage increases and benefits, by way of social reforms through changes in the automotive and other big industries. "When the economy sneezes, the auto industry gets pneumonia," he sallied in assailing the Big Three.

The convention gave practically 100 percent approval to the new contract proposals as put forward in the resolutions. A curious detail of the April 20 opening-day events came at the end of Reuther's keynote address, which he completed by observing that "violence can never provide an equitable solution to social problems." Emil Mazey, who followed him, then reminded the delegates of this "Twenty-Second Constitutional Convention" that it was exactly twenty-two years ago, on the night of April 20, 1948, that the attempted assassination of Walter Reuther had taken place; the delegates paused during their deliberations to note that tragic anniversary, to reflect with gratitude on the fact that he was saved because he had moved an instant before the blast. He was, of course, reelected by an overwhelming majority for what would be his thirteenth term in office.

The signs of the times stood out plainly at this convention. May Reuther, speaking to the women, praised the all-out "Women in Society" resolution, the most comprehensive ever adopted by any group for women's rights. It called for the repeal of abortion laws, paid maternity leaves, a national program of child-care centers, and enactment of an equal-rights amendment to the United States Constitution. Walter spoke informally with a large group of local union editors, many under thirty—the UAW had its share of bearded young men in jeans and mod shirts, girls in mini skirts or pants suits—in a plea to get young militants to work within the union if they really wanted to change the world. "Here's this tremendous organization called the UAW," he said. "And here's an opportunity for a young fellow to get in there and help us do these things he's so impatient about." He listed ending the tragic war in Vietnam; getting on with the black revolution (legitimately, without violence) to make *one* America; cleaning out ghettos, and building decent cities. "We have to say to a young fellow: Look, don't try to do it outside of here, as though we were part of the Establishment and that we're hopeless. Come in here and get your teeth into it and get with us because here is a chance."

As if to underline his plea, the Twenty-second Convention on April 24 took up the resolution closest to his hopes for the future, empowering the Executive Board to implement the education program at the Family Education Center "with all possible speed." The basic program was to be of two weeks' duration for those who receive a UAW scholarship to attend the center, to include the spouse and, in the summer months, the children as well as the worker. Longer periods of residence were to be given to those awarded UAW fellowships, so they would have the advantage of more intensive training. A third catergory was to be a UAW "internship," of extended duration "for comprehensive, intensive educational instruction." A companion resolution calling for the center to be named for him, the formal designation bearing the Reuther name to be "deferred until the conclusion of his service as president of the UAW," did not interest Walter. He had been waiting for the mandate to begin the educational program, and it was given by unanimous approval of the resolution. The center was to be opened officially, "with appropriate dedication ceremonies," in the summer. Walter was determined to spend every weekend at Black Lake before then, to be sure all was in readiness.

A few days after the convention closed, alarming events occurred. President Nixon ordered the invasion of Cambodia by American troops without consulting Congress, and in the upheaval of college protests that his reckless action aroused, four students were killed at Kent State University in Ohio by National Guard troops. To Walter and May, it was sickening. A course of action was called for, and the UAW president did not hesitate to draft a statement of protest, seeking the aid of clergymen, educators, industrialists, and prominent Americans in other fields to form a new coalition against international and domestic violence. He sent a strongly worded telegram to the White House, deploring the President's move. The text said in part,

Your decision to invade the territory of Cambodia can only increase the enormity of the tragedy in which our nation is already deeply and unfortunately involved in that region. . . . Widening the war at this point in time once again merely reinforces the bankruptcy of our policy of force and violence in Vietnam. Your action taken without consultation or authorization by the Congress has created a serious Constitutional crisis at a time when there is growing division in our nation . . . by your action you have driven the wedge of division deeper and you have dangerously alienated millions of young Americans. The bitter fruits of this growing alienation and frustration among America's youth have been harvested on the campus of Kent State University, where the lives of four students . . . were ended by the needless and inexcusable use of military force. . . . With the exception of a small minority, the American people, including our young people, reject violence in all its forms as morally repugnant and counterproductive. The problem, Mr. President, is that we cannot successfully preach nonviolence at home while we escalate mass violence abroad.

It is your responsibility to lead us out of the Southeast Asian War—
to peace at home and abroad. We must mobilize for peace rather than
wider theaters of war in order to turn our resources and the hearts,
hands, and minds of our people to the fulfillment of America's unfinished agenda at home.

The telegram sent, he made arrangements to go up to Black
Lake for the weekend; Oskar Stonorov was coming to Detroit,
and they planned to fly up together for inspection of the final
construction. Walter had to take along some statistics he had requested for the coming contract negotiations, but he would be
glad to get to the quiet beauty of his beloved center. "You're
coming along, aren't you?" he said to May.

She was not sure. She had ordered evergreens and shrubs for
some planting they had wanted to do on a little "island" chunk
of ground rising out of Paint Creek in front of the house in the
country, intending to rid it of straggly weeds; and she wanted to
see that everything was in before the weather got too warm.
She debated whether to go or not, speaking several times about
the matter on the phone with her brother and sister-in-law, Leo
and Eleanor Wolf, who had built a house not far from theirs on
Paint Creek. As far as they knew, she still had not made up her
mind on Friday, but that night she called again. "I've decided to
go to Black Lake tomorrow after all," she told them. "Walter's
going to be starting negotiations pretty soon, and I know I won't
be seeing much of him for about six weeks once they begin, so
I want to be with him now. . . ."

As usual, the UAW office hired a Lear jet plane to fly the four
passengers—Walter and May, their friend Oskar, and nephew-
bodyguard Billy Wolfman—from the Metropolitan Airport in
Detroit to the little airfield at Pellston, Michigan. There a union
car and driver would be waiting to take them to Black Lake,
about forty miles from Pellston. And, as usual, Walter had so
much to do that they could not leave until evening on Saturday, May 9. It was 8:44 P.M. before they finally took off, with
George Evans and Joseph Karaffa, two seasoned pilots who had
flown them before, at the controls. A steady spring rain was falling, doubtful flying weather, with scattered clouds as low as

four hundred feet, and an eight-hundred-foot ceiling; but they had all made this flight under far worse weather conditions. Oskar usually had so much to tell them they never paid any attention to the weather or the flight. The neat little Lear rose smoothly and headed north. Evans, an experienced navigator, used instruments to head them on course through the foggy drizzle. Twenty-six minutes later, he contacted the radio tower at the Emmet County airfield near Pellston, and the plane was cleared for landing: "Cloud ceiling at 800 feet, easterly winds at ten miles an hour, light rain with a visibility of seven miles," the report said. Evans radioed back the calm words, "I've got the airport in sight. . . ." It was 9:28 P.M. when he turned on the wing-tip landing lights, prior to the descent.

The pilot began slowing his speed, bringing the plane earthward through an inky darkness. The landing strip was only one and a half miles away when the little craft, much lower than it should have been, suddenly sheared off the top of a fifty-foot elm tree. Branches blew into both engines with such force that they burst into flame and Evans could not control the plane's course; it crashed crazily to the ground, skidding through a small pine grove, toppling trees with foot-thick trunks, and flared to a flaming mass. All six lives were lost in the burning wreckage by the time the airfield attendants reached the spot a few minutes later. At about 9:33 P.M.—by eerie coincidence, it was approximately the same hour the assassin's shotgun bullets had struck him twenty-two years before—Walter Reuther died at age sixty-two. No move he might have made could have saved him this time; or his wife, May, or any of them. There was not time enough for them to escape. May Reuther was fifty-nine years old; Stonorov, their kind and gifted Quaker friend, sixty-four; May's nephew Billy, only twenty-nine. The pilots, both of Columbus, Ohio, were in their forties: George Evans was forty-eight, and Joseph Karaffa, forty-one. The bodies were charred beyond recognition in the smoking ruins; only dental records could supply positive identification.

The news of Walter and May Reuther's sudden, unforeseen death was a nightmare to their immediate families, a tragedy that left Walter's "family" of United Auto Workers shaken and overcome with grief, an unbelievable shock felt around the world. If Walter Reuther had known that his telegram to the United States President was to be his last public pronouncement, he could not have left a more cogent argument for his whole philosophic and pragmatic approach to the social problems of his lifetime, particularly in the last half of the twentieth century; and if May Reuther had known she was uttering her last words to her relatives in that Friday night phone call, she could not have given a more eloquent testimony to the serene marriage between these two like-minded people, so devoted to each other and to the causes they embraced. Not long before the accident, she had observed, "I guess if Walter and I had to do it over, we would lead our lives in much the same way."

Lisa, who had almost accompanied her parents, but had at the last minute decided to stay at home, had invited some friends to spend the weekend. When the terrible word came, her first thought was to call Linda, who took the next plane from California. The Reuther home and the guest house, at Walter's suggestion occupied by a retired auto worker and his wife, who had wanted to live in the country and who kept an eye on the place when the Reuthers were away, was the scene of crisis activity half the night. Unexplainably, there was no answer to one of the many calls to relatives, and that was at the home of May's brother Leo. The reason was that he and his wife Eleanor had been planting trees all day, Walter having suggested that they apply for the five hundred free seedlings from the state, as he and May had done years before. They had gone to bed at 8:30 P.M. and were so exhausted they did not hear the phone. At about 5:00 A.M., Leo woke up, and from force of habit turned on a transistor radio to get the news, completely unprepared for what he heard as the sound came on: "Walter Reuther . . . wife May . . . killed in a plane crash . . ." Stunned, he hardly knew what to do. He didn't want to wake Eleanor, but he couldn't stand it, and finally did. It was still half dark; they got dressed and went outdoors, walking around in a trance, counting the trees they had planted until it was light enough to call Lisa. They learned that she had just gone to sleep, having been up most of the night; among other calls, she had been trying to get them since 10:00 P.M., right after word came.

At Solidarity House, UAW officers Leonard Woodcock, Douglas Fraser, Emil Mazey, and all the rest, hardly less numbed by the tragic news, gathered to proclaim a week of mourning for the nearly two million members of the union. All hope that the report might have been a mistake was gone when investigators from the National Transportation Safety Board examined and reconstructed the wreckage. It would be months before they determined the cause of the crash—a faulty altimeter*—but there was no doubt that this was the Lear jet the UAW president had chartered. Somehow the necessary arrangements were made, stricken though everyone was; and on Wednesday morning, May 13, at Veterans' Memorial Building on the Detroit River, thousands of mourners began coming as early as 8:00 A.M. to file past the oak caskets in which Walter and May Reuther lay in state, a single bouquet of daisies, placed there by their daughters, between them.

For two days, from the time the doors opened until the 10:00 P.M. closing, people came streaming in to pay their last respects to the man who had "made the union strong," and to his lovely wife. Workers on their way to or from their shifts at the plants, executives and government officials, pensioners reaping the benefits he had bargained for during his twenty-four years as president of the UAW; from all walks of life and from distant points they came, but mostly the workers. Sam Smith, a "broom pusher" at Dodge, was followed by a contingent from Chrysler and a group of Highland Park welders. Among the first was former Governor G. Mennen Williams, his face grave and reflective, recalling the staunch support he had received from Reuther in his several terms in office. One of the many delegations paying final homage early on the second day was the Executive Board of the Spicer unit of Local 12 from Toledo, Ohio. Headed by the chairman, the thirteen-member board, all wearing their light-

---

* The report regarding the cause of the crash was published on February 17, 1971. Due to the faulty altimeter, part of which was installed upside down, the reading was incorrect, reinforcing the pilot's belief that he was higher than he was as they approached the airport, especially since no lights were visible on the runway, which was blanketed by fog.

blue union jackets, filed past the biers at 8:15 A.M., having left Toledo seventy-five minutes before. George Bouhana, from St. Clair Shores, Michigan, a businessman who still bore scars of wounds he suffered at the hands of strikebreakers in the thirties at Briggs', where Walter had his first job, said he just had to come down to pay his respects to "so great a man. He was able to *do* the things we were fighting for!" Some wept openly; all were sad.

The funeral services took place, significantly, on the stage of the Ford Auditorium in downtown Detroit, decorated simply with the flags of the United States, Canada, the United Nations, and the flag of Peace. The coffins stood at the front of the stage, Walter's covered with the blue-and-white emblem of the UAW. Three clusters of red roses had been placed on white pedestals, at either end and in the middle of the stage; and again a small bouquet of white daisies stood between the two caskets. That was all. The family had requested that no flowers be sent from outside.

As the funeral service began, assembly lines in auto plants across the country stopped for three minutes while workers paid silent tribute to their president. On the roads, thousands of truck drivers who belonged to the Teamsters Union pulled over to the side for a three-minute halt. At least thirty thousand UAW members stayed away from work on the day of the funeral, giving up a day's wages out of respect to "Walter."

The service was simple. A recording by Marian Anderson, singing "He's Got the Whole World in His Hands," was followed by eulogies from eleven speakers, from different walks of life, each signifying a separate area of the Reuthers' concerns. They spoke of Walter's giant ambitions and achievements in the past, of his ideals and hopes for the future, of his fervent faith in people; and of May's loyalty and understanding, of her search for truth, of her service to children—from preschoolers to those about to become "of age." And those listening in the auditorium, 3,400 "big and little" people, present by invitation because the space was limited—shop stewards and United States senators, educators and captains of industry—relived the events that had made Walter Reuther a controversial and great labor leader. Linda and Lisa, sitting together in the front row, held hands tightly and listened with serious, tender faces to the praises accorded their parents.

Victor, the only remaining member of the "triumvirate," or "the brothers Reuther," as some called them, in the labor movement, showed that he had learned to accept sorrow. He had spoken with the staff members at Solidarity House earlier, his voice husky with emotion. "We must learn to dry our eyes and go on," he had said. Perhaps the saddest person in the auditorium was Anna Reuther. The mother who had always borne her troubles so bravely—wavering only once, when Walter was shot—now seemed bereft, bowed down by grief, and she made little effort to hide it. As the service ended, with the singing of an old labor ballad, a favorite of Walter, "I Dreamed I Saw Joe Hill Last Night," the audience softly joining in at the third stanza, "Where working men are out on strike, Joe Hill is at their side," and at the final " 'I never died,' says he," Anna Reuther's shoulders shook visibly.

Out on the sidewalk, the crowds, listening over loudspeakers, sang, and voices broke with sobs. Flags on city buildings and at the headquarters of General Motors, Ford, Chrysler, and American Motors were flown at half-mast. The millions who watched the proceedings on television were moved as well. "I don't know when I was so shook up," a former UAW shop steward commented afterward.

Among those who gave the eulogies were Senator Philip A. Hart of Michigan; Whitney Young, executive director of the National Urban League in Washington, whose own accidental death (by drowning during a trip to North Africa) was soon to occur; former cabinet member John W. Gardner, chairman of the National Urban Coalition and a close friend of the Reuthers; Ivar Noren of the International Metalworkers; Mrs. Martin Luther King, Jr., and Sam Brown, National Youth leader. Dave Miller, head of the UAW Retiree Center and close to eighty, was deeply moved to find himself the first speaker, and he reminisced about the early days of the union; Irving Bluestone, Walter's administrative assistant for the past several years, represented the present-day union. Chancellor Varner spoke as friend and neighbor of the Reuthers, and Dr. William J. Rioux, of the Merril Palmer Institute, delivered a eulogy for May. He was followed by Rabbi Jacob J. Weinstein of Chicago.

Senator Hart used the language of his office in saying of Reuther, "We are here not so much to discuss his life, but to read his will, to examine his legacy." By "will," Hart meant "that unwritten document that he spent a lifetime composing. And everyone here today is an heir. . . . You were part of Walter Reuther's constituency if you were poor, powerless . . . if you were old, if you were sick, if you were weak, and if you are just."

Both Whitney Young and Coretta King stressed the fact that Walter was "there" when and wherever he was needed. "Whenever the going was tough," Young said, "Walter Reuther was there. . . . He was one leader who never had to be convinced of the claims black people were making on society, and he was one leader who never needed detailed interpretation of what was happening in the ghetto. He knew. He was there. . . ." And Mrs. King emphasized the point eloquently: "For blacks, he was preeminently the most widely known and respected white labor leader in the nation. The secret of his success with blacks is that he was there in person when the storm clouds were thick. We remember him in Montgomery. He was in Birmingham. He marched with us in Selma and Jackson and Washington. And he was in Memphis. . . ."

Perhaps the finest and most personal tribute to the Reuthers came from John Gardner. "None of us can speak of May and Walter without emotion and without the deepest gratitude," he began. "A friend of mine once said that the purpose of a free society is to produce great individuals, and in producing May and Walter Reuther this society justified itself many times over. When we speak of them as typical Americans, we flatter ourselves. They were the kind of Americans we would all like to be. They were the good, vital, generous, loving people that many of us strive to be and never quite are . . . ; they renewed our faith, they thought better of us than we thought of ourselves, and by thinking so, made us better people."

In his own country and all over the world, Walter Reuther was saluted by those in high office. President Nixon, whom Walter had criticized so sharply two days before he died, valued his qualities as "a man devoted to his cause, spoke for it with eloquence and worked for it tirelessly. Mr. Reuther's death is a deep loss not only for organized labor, but also for the cause of collective bargaining and the entire American process. . . . Even those who disagreed with him had great respect for his ability, integrity, and persistence." At the United Nations, Secretary U Thant said, "The world has lost a wise, courageous, and statesmanlike humanitarian." And Ralph Bunche wrote: "I admired him for his courage, his forthrightness, and wisdom, but above all for his ability to interpret the aspirations of and to keep in tune with the common man." Secretary of Labor George P. Shultz said, "He believed passionately in the democratic system and the rights of man. . . . His death is a bruising loss, not only to American labor, but to all of us. . . ." Senator Edward Kennedy commented on Reuther's contribution to health care: "For more than three decades, he was one of the most powerful advocates of health care as a matter of right. Walter Reuther made the wave of the health revolution that is cresting now in America." And Republican Senator Jacob Javits paid him high tribute: "Posterity will be grateful to him for his great contribution to world peace and world development."

So the messages read. His colleagues in the Alliance for Labor Action, especially William Schnitzler of the teamsters, felt Reuther's death deeply; and even George Meany granted him his "unique and lasting contribution to the auto workers." Former Michigan Governor G. Mennen Williams offered the interesting comment: "Walter Reuther affected the life-style of the United States like few in his generation. . . ." Cables by the hundreds came from government and trade-union leaders around the world. Tage Erlander, who attended the funeral services, sent a message beforehand from Sweden: "The world has lost a great leader, we have lost a friend who has always been a model for all of us." Harm Buiter, general secretary of the International Confederation of Free Trade Unions, which the Reuthers had helped to form, wired from Brussels: "For all who prize freedom, the death of Walter Reuther is an irreparable loss. As founder and Executive Board member of ICFTU, his was a magnificent contribution to our international cause." Willy Brandt, Chancellor of the Federal Republic of Germany, mourned Walter's passing as "a man who was among the first to offer the hand of reconciliation to a former adversary and to help smooth the path to a democratic and peaceful partnership with the peoples of the world. . . . His good relations with the leaders of European social democracy helped decidedly with the improvement and solidification of relations between America and Europe." Golda Meir, prime minister of Israel, sent a moving message: "The people of Israel will sorely miss a true and devoted friend of our people whose memory is enshrined in the hearts of all of us who knew the warmth of his friendship and the immenseness of his contribution to so many causes of mankind." And Y. Benaharon, secretary general, Histadrut, from Tel Aviv, wired: "America and Free Labor have lost an outstanding leader and workers of Israel a dedicated friend." The Philippine Labor Secretary, the president of the Ghana Trade Union Congress, T. C. Douglas, leader of the New Democratic party of Canada, even the Presidium, Central Committee, Engineering Workers Union of USSR in Moscow, expressed "deep sorrow of Walter Reuther's passing."

The press, which over the years had attacked Reuther as often as it had praised him, was lavish in its accolades. *The Christian Science Monitor*, noted for its objectivity, led off with: "When Walter Reuther was on hand, organized labor never seemed to merit the accusation that its leadership was elderly and stuffed shirt. . . . Mr. Reuther sought to identify his union with the younger workers, the blacks, the peace campaigners. This loss affects the entire American labor movement."

The *Wall Street Journal*, in the same vein, observed, "At a time when many liberals were disenchanted with the labor movement, Walter Reuther was a symbol of enlightened unionism and social activism." And *The New York Times*: ". . . The death of Walter P. Reuther is an even more substantial loss for the nation than it is for the labor movement . . . the void of his death will be greater still in the realms of idealism and social inventiveness." *The St. Louis Post Dispatch* gave a thumbnail portrait in its assessment: "Mr. Reuther was the liveliest, most far-sighted and most significant labor leader of his generation. What set him apart was his ability to translate his ideas into practical action. . . . He was a product of the machine age who understood the machine and tried to find a way for men to live with it. Industrial workers—

and management, too—have much to thank him for." One of the leading Negro publications, the *Michigan Chronicle*, wrote: "The impact of his loss on those of us in the national black community could not be equaled by the death of any other American leader who is not black." The San Francisco *Examiner* commented: "Walter Philip Reuther, a fighting liberal who hated communism, was one of a rare breed." And *Newsweek*, the bible of many businessmen, concluded: "During his 24 years as president of the UAW, the dynamic Reuther exerted an influence on American life far beyond his role as a fighter for fatter paychecks for his 1.6 million members. At the time of his death . . . he was working on a plan for mass-produced housing, and was deeply involved in the civil rights struggle, the fight for cleaner air, and a legislative campaign for low-cost health insurance."

Finally, Reuther's adversaries across the bargaining table, the executives of the auto industry, acknowledged his stature unhesitatingly. James M. Roche, his special sparring opponent, who had often assailed him for his "socialism" in the early days, was among the first to say, "We are shocked by this tragedy. Mr. Reuther was an able and dedicated leader. Our industry and our country will miss him." Henry Ford II, who, from the time he became head of Ford Motor Corporation, had tried to compensate for his grandfather's eccentric absolutism in dealing with labor, assessed Walter's ability: "Walter Reuther was an extraordinarily effective advocate of labor's interest. His tough-minded dedication, his sense of social concern, his selflessness and his eloquence all mark him as a central figure in the development of modern industrial history"; Karl E. Scott, president of Ford in Canada, said much the same thing. The third of the Big Three, Lynn Townsend, Chrysler's chairman of the board, pointed out, "His devotion to the ideals and principles in which he believed were evident not only at the bargaining table but also in his untiring efforts to improve the condition of his less fortunate fellow men." And Roy D. Chapin, of American Motors Corporation, added, "Industry, the labor movement, and the nation will long remember him as a great and dedicated leader.

It is significant that all of these estimates emphasize Walter Reuther's ability as a leader, not solely of labor, but of the world-at-large. If he erred on the side of overenthusiasm and an inevitable appetite for personal power, he nevertheless achieved more of the goals for which he strove than any other labor figure in modern times. And, although about to retire when his untimely death occurred, he was at the zenith of his powers, which undoubtedly would have been channeled to other fields, trying, even as he was struck down, to reach the one he felt would be the most fertile.

Thirteen months after the fatal accident, on June 9, 1971, in a private ceremony attended by members of their families and top UAW officials, the ashes of May and Walter Reuther were scattered on a hillside overlooking the "Round Table" he had planned as his final contribution. It was named in their honor after their deaths, The Walter and May Reuther Family Education Center, a fitting memorial to both of them.

Bibliography

A primary source of material in regard to Walter Reuther's leadership of the United Auto Workers union is to be found in the Convention *Proceedings*, bound volumes beginning in 1936, which are available to researchers upon application to the Labor Archives at Wayne State University in Detroit. For purposes of this biography, the most informative were, besides the first, those of 1943 (war-time convention); 1946, the year Reuther was elected President; 1949, containing the adoption of his initial pension plan as the bargaining goal; 1955, for his innovative "guaranteed annual wage," and official announcement of the coming AFL-CIO merger; 1963, for unusual fringe and health benefits sought by Reuther; and 1970, as a record of the last convention at which he presided, the 22nd, and largest to date, "Constitutional Convention" of the UAW.

Unfortunately, the record of books consulted by Lorena Hickok is incomplete. Those I know about are included in my selected Bibliography below. I also consulted many labor pamphlets, UAW publications, and magazine articles, too numerous to list here.

Bennett, Harry H., *We Never Called Him Henry*. New York: Gold Medal Books, 1951.

Burns, James MacGregor, *Roosevelt: The Lion and the Fox*. New York: Harcourt, Brace and Co., 1956.

Campaigne, Jameson G., *Check-Off: Labor Bosses and Working Men*. Chicago: Henry Regnery Co., 1961.

Cook, Fred J., *Walter Reuther: Building the House of Labor*. Chicago, New York, and London: Encyclopedia Britannica Press, 1963.

Cormier, Frank, and Eaton, William J., *Reuther*. Englewood Cliffs: Prentice-Hall, Inc., 1970.

Dayton, Eldorous L., *Walter Reuther: The Autocrat of the Bargaining Table*. New York: Devin Adair Company, 1958.

Dulles, Foster Rhea, *Labor in America*. New York: Thomas Y. Crowell, 1966 (New edition; 1st ed., 1949).

Ervin, Charles W., *Homegrown Liberal*. (Autobiography of; ed. by Jean Gould) New York: Dodd, Mead & Company, 1954.

Ford, Henry, *My Life and Work* (in collaboration with Samuel Crowther). New York: Doubleday and Co., 1922.

Fountain, Clayton W., *Union Guy*. New York: The Viking Press, 1949.

Galenson, Walter, *The CIO Challenge to the AFL*. Cambridge: Harvard University Press, 1960.

Goldberg, Arthur J., *AFL-CIO Labor United*. New York: McGraw-Hill Book Co., 1956.

Gould, Jean, *A Good Fight: FDR's Conquest of Polio*. New York: Dodd, Mead & Company, 1960.

———, *Sidney Hillman: Great American*. Boston: Houghton Mifflin Co., 1952.

Hardman, J. B. S., and Neufeld, Maurice F., *House of Labor*. Englewood Cliffs: Prentice-Hall, Inc., 1951.

Howe, Irving, and Widick, B. J., *The UAW and Walter Reuther*. New York: Random House, 1949.

Josephson, Matthew, *Sidney Hillman: Statesman of American Labor*. Garden City: Doubleday & Co., 1952.

Kempton, Murray, *Part of Our Time*. New York: Simon and Schuster, 1955.

Kennedy, Robert F., *The Enemy Within*. New York: Random House, 1959.

Lash, Joseph P., *Eleanor Roosevelt: A Friend's Memoir*. New York: Doubleday & Co., 1964.

———, *Eleanor and Franklin*. New York: W. W. Norton, 1971.

Levinson, Edward, *Labor on the March*. New York: University Books, 1956. (A re-issue, with Introduction by Walter Reuther, of 1938 pub., Harper.)

McDonald, David J., *Union Man*. New York: E. P. Dutton & Co., 1969.

Madison, Charles A., *American Labor Leaders*. New York: Harper, 1950.

Myrdal, Gunnar, *An American Dilemma*. New York: Harper and Bros., 1944.

Perkins, Frances, *The Roosevelt I Knew*. New York: The Viking Press, 1946.

Reuther, Walter P., *Selected Papers*, ed. by Henry M. Christman. New York: The Macmillan Company, 1961.

Roosevelt, Elliott, ed., *FDR, His Personal Letters, 1928–1945*, Vol. I. New York: Duell, Sloan and Pearce, 1950.

Roosevelt, Franklin D., *The Public Papers and Addresses of*, Vols. 3 & 5. New York: Random House, 1938.

Salinger, Pierre, *With Kennedy*. Garden City: Doubleday & Co., 1966.

Schlesinger, Arthur M. Jr., *The Coming of the New Deal*. Boston: Houghton Mifflin Co., 1960.

Sorenson, Theodore, *Kennedy*. New York: Harper & Row, 1965.

Stegner, Wallace, *The Preacher and the Slave*. Boston: Houghton Mifflin Co., 1950.

Stieber, Jack, *Governing the UAW*. New York: John Wiley and Sons, 1962.

Sward, Keith, *The Legend of Henry Ford*. New York: Rinehart & Co., 1948.

Taft, Philip, *Organized Labor in American History*. New York: Harper & Row, 1964.

White, Walter, *A Man Called White*. New York: The Viking Press, 1948.

Widick, B. J., *Labor Today*. Boston: Houghton Mifflin Co., 1964.

Wilson, Edmund, *The American Jitters*. Chas. Scribner's Sons, 1932.

Index